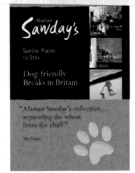

Published Nov 2011

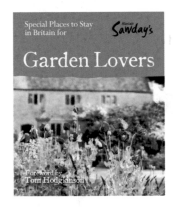

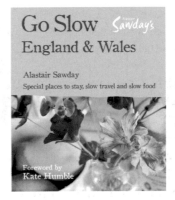

Alastair
Sawday's

Special Places to Stay

Thirteenth edition
Copyright © 2011
Alastair Sawday Publishing Co. Ltd
Published in October 2011
ISBN-13: 978-1-906136-54-3

Alastair Sawday Publishing Co. Ltd,
The Old Farmyard, Yanley Lane,
Long Ashton, Bristol BS41 9LR, UK
Tel: +44 (0)1275 395430
Email: info@sawdays.co.uk
Web: www.sawdays.co.uk

The Globe Pequot Press,
P. O. Box 480, Guilford,
Connecticut 06437, USA
Tel: +1 203 458 4500
Email: info@globepequot.com
Web: www.globepequot.com

Series Editor Alastair Sawday
Editor Tom Bell
Assistant to Editor Claire Wilson
Editorial Director Annie Shillito
Content & Publishing Manager
Jackie King
Writing Tom Bell, Jo Boissevain,
Carmen Cox, Claire Wilson
Inspections Tom Bell, Carmen Cox
Sales & Marketing & PR 01275 395433
And thanks to those who did an inspection
or write-up or two.

*We have made every effort to ensure the accuracy
of the information in this book at the time of
going to press. However, we cannot accept
any responsibility for any loss, injury or
inconvenience resulting from the use of
information contained therein.*

Alastair Sawday has asserted his right to be
identified as the author of this work

Maps: Maidenhead Cartographic Services
Printing: Butler, Tanner & Dennis, Frome
UK distribution: Penguin UK, London
Production: The Content Works

Cover photo credits: 1. The Montpellier Chapter, entry 117 2. Lucy Pope 3. Lucy Pope

Alastair Sawday's

Special Places
to Stay

British
Hotels & Inns

4   Contents

Have you ever thought of lifting sagging spirits with a quick flit to a hotel?

A grey pall hung over Britain's hotels from autumn to spring. Petrol prices and food prices rose relentlessly and everyone has felt the pinch. So, we wondered, would the travellers of the UK lift their spirits by escaping to a good hotel, or would they sink more deeply into their sofas and gaze at the telly?

It is hard to get a clear picture, but it seems that our hotels have cheered many of you. Those that charge over the odds have seen a drop in bookings; those that remain good value (whether simple or plush) are holding firm. The extra bank holiday (bless the Windsors) has helped. The general picture seems to be that those hotels that are terrific have lost no friends. The others have had to work hard. Luckily, ours are nearly all terrific.

Photo: Tom Germain

We've held on to many long term favourites, and have over forty new hotels, including some great new city places and a couple on the Channel Islands and the Western Isles. The awful era of standardisation is largely over, though I worry a little about the constant repetition of decorative themes. When will hotels stop draping a useless swathe of material across the bottom third of the bed? And what is the purpose of the piles of cushions by the pillows?

We continue to celebrate the small and the rustic, and inns with rooms are growing in popularity. Serviced apartments are becoming popular with those who need a bit of privacy; one even has a cordon bleu chef and a chauffeur.

The generosity shown to our inspectors, often spontaneous rather than calculated, has been as heart-warming as ever. Tom Bell, who many of our owners know, has always been treated with special warmth. This has rubbed off on Carmen, who did a little inspecting and was treated to homemade wine and a gorgeous room with a claw-foot bath on her trip to Sark. Only a few harsh weeks back at HQ will wean her off such treatment.

So, please, dear reader, promise yourself a lifetime of avoiding chain hotels and using only those run with love. We have enough of them here for any lifetime.

Alastair Sawday

It's simple. There are no rules, no boxes to tick. We choose places that we like and are fiercely subjective in our choices. We also recognise that one person's idea of special is not necessarily someone else's so there is a huge variety of places, and prices, in this book.

Those who are familiar with our Special Places series know that we look for comfort, originality, authenticity, and reject the anonymous and the banal. The way guests are treated comes as high on our list as the setting, the architecture, the atmosphere and the food.

Inspections

We visit every place in the guide to get a feel for how both house and owner tick. We don't take a clipboard and we don't have a list of what is acceptable and what is not. Instead, we chat for an hour or so with the owner or manager and look round. It's all very informal, but it gives us an excellent idea of who would enjoy staying there. If the visit happens to be the last of the day, we sometimes stay the night. Once in the book, properties are re-inspected regularly, so that we can keep things fresh and accurate.

Feedback

In between inspections we rely on feedback from our army of readers, as well as from staff members who are encouraged to visit properties across the series. This feedback is invaluable to us and we always follow up on comments. So do tell us whether your stay has been

a joy or not, if the atmosphere was great or stuffy, the owners and staff cheery or bored. The accuracy of the book depends on what you, and our inspectors, tell us. A lot of the new entries in each edition are recommended by our readers, so keep telling us about new places you've discovered too. Please use the forms on our website at www.sawdays.co.uk, or later in this book.

However, please do not tell us if your starter was cold, or the bedside light broken. Tell the owner, immediately, and get them to do something about it. Most owners, or staff, are more than happy to

Photo: Howard's House, entry 239

correct problems and will bend over backwards to help. Far better than bottling it up and then writing to us a week later!

Subscriptions

Owners pay to appear in this guide. Their fee goes towards the high costs of inspecting, of producing an illustrated book and of maintaining our website. We only include places that we find special: it is not possible for anyone to buy their way onto these pages. Nor is it possible for the owner to write their own description. We will say if the bedrooms are small, or if a main road is near. We do our best to avoid misleading people.

Disclaimer

We make no claims to pure objectivity in choosing these places. They are here simply because we like them. Our opinions and tastes are ours alone and this book is a statement of them; we hope you will share them. We have done our utmost to get our facts right but apologise unreservedly for any mistakes that may have crept in.

You should know that we don't check such things as fire alarms, swimming pool security or any other regulation with which owners of properties receiving paying guests should comply. This is the responsibility of the owners.

Photo: Stocks Hotel, entry 274

Finding the right place for you

All these places are special in one way or another. All have been visited and then written about honestly so that you can take what you want and leave the rest. Those of you who swear by Sawday's trust our write-ups precisely because we don't have a blanket standard; we include places simply because we like them. But we all have different priorities, so do read the descriptions carefully and pick out the places where you will be comfortable.

Maps

Each property is flagged with its entry number on the maps at the front. These maps are a great starting point for planning your trip, but please don't use them as anything other than a general guide – use a decent road map for real navigation. Most places will send you detailed instructions once you have booked your stay.

Ethical Collection

We're always keen to draw attention to owners who are striving to have a positive impact on the world, so you'll notice that some entries are flagged as being part of our 'Ethical Collection'. These places are working hard to reduce their environmental footprint, making significant contributions to their local community, or are passionate about serving local or organic food.

Sawday's Travel Club

We've recently launched a Travel Club, based around the Special Places to Stay series; you'll see a 💼 symbol on those places offering something extra to Club members, so to find out how to join see page 388.

Symbols

These are explained at the very back of the book. They are based on the information given to us by the owners. However, things do change: bikes may be under repair or a new pool may have been put in. Please use the symbols as a guide rather than an absolute statement of fact and double-check anything that is important to you – owners occasionally bend their own rules, so it's worth asking if you may take your child or dog even if they don't have the symbol.

Wheelchair access ♿ – Some hotels are keen to accept wheelchair users into their hotels and have made provision for them. However, this does not mean that wheelchair users will always be met with a perfect landscape. You may encounter ramps, a shallow step, gravelled paths, alternative routes into some rooms, a bathroom (not a wet room), perhaps even a lift. In short, there may be the odd hindrance and we urge you to call and make sure you will get what you need.

Limited mobility – The limited mobility symbol ⬤ shows those places where at least one bedroom and bathroom is accessible without using stairs. The symbol is designed to satisfy those who walk slowly, with difficulty, or with the aid of a stick. A wheelchair may be able to navigate some areas, but in our opinion these places are not fully wheelchair friendly. If you use a chair for longer distances, but are not too bad over shorter distances, you'll probably be OK; again, please ring and ask. There may be a step or two, a bath or a shower with a tray in a cubicle, a good distance between the car park and your room, slippery flagstones or a tight turn.

Children – The ♀ symbol shows places which are happy to accept children of all ages. This does not mean that they will necessarily have cots, high chairs, etc. If an owner welcomes children but only those above a certain age, we have put these details at the end of their write-up. These houses do not have the child symbol, but even these folk may accept your younger child at quiet times. If you want to get out and about in the evenings, check when you book whether there are any babysitting services. Even very small places can sometimes organise this for you.

Pets – Our 🐕 symbol shows places which are happy to accept pets. It means they can sleep in the bedroom with you, but not on the bed. It's really important to get this one right before you arrive, as many places make you keep dogs in the car. Check carefully: Prince's emotional wellbeing may depend on it.

Owners' pets – The 🐈 symbol is given when the owners have their own pet on the premises. It may not be a cat! But it is there to warn you that you may be greeted by a dog, serenaded by a parrot, or indeed sat upon by a cat.

Photo left: Prawles Court, entry 235
Photo right: Stocks Hotel, entry 274

Types of places

Hotels can vary from huge, humming and slick to those with only a few rooms that are run by owners at their own pace. In some you may not get room service or have your bags carried in and out. In smaller hotels there may be a fixed menu for dinner with very little choice, so if you have dishes that leave you cold, it's important to say so when you book your meal. If you decide to stay at an inn remember that they can be noisy, especially at weekends. If these things are important to you, then do check when you book.

Rooms

Bedrooms – these are described as double, twin, single, family or suite. A double may contain a bed which is anything from 135cm wide to 180cm wide. A twin will contain two single beds (usually 90cm wide). A suite will have a separate sitting area, but it may not be in a different room. Family rooms can vary in size, as can the number of beds they hold, so do ask. And do not assume that every bedroom has a TV.

Bathrooms – all bedrooms have their own bathrooms unless we say that they don't. If you have your own bathroom but you have to leave the room to get to it we describe it as 'separate'. There are very few places in the book that have shared bathrooms and they are usually reserved for members of the same party. Again, we state this clearly.

Meals

Breakfast is included in the room price unless otherwise stated. If only a continental breakfast is offered, we let you know.

Some places serve lunch, most do Sunday lunch (often very well-priced), the vast majority offer dinner. In some places you can content yourself with bar meals, in others you can feast on five courses. Most offer three courses for £25-£35, either table d'hôte or à la carte. Some have tasting menus, very occasionally you eat communally. Some large hotels (and some posh private houses) will bring dinner to your room if you prefer, or let you eat in the garden by candlelight. Always ask for what you want and sometimes, magically, it happens.

Prices and minimum stays

We quote the lowest price per night for two people in low season to the highest price in high season. Only a few places have designated single rooms; if no single rooms are listed, the price we quote refers to single occupancy of a double room. In many places prices rise even higher when local events bring people flooding to the area, a point worth remembering when heading to Cheltenham for the racing or Glyndebourne for the opera.

The half-board price quoted is per person per night and includes dinner, usually three courses. Mostly you're offered a table d'hôte menu. Occasionally you eat

à la carte and may find some dishes carry a small supplement. There are often great deals to be had, mostly mid-week in low season.

Most hotels do not accept one-night bookings at weekends. Small country hotels are rarely full during the week and the weekend trade keeps them going. If you ring in March for a Saturday night in July, you won't get it. If you ring at the last moment you may. Some places insist on three-night stays on bank holidays.

Booking and cancellation

Most places ask for a deposit at the time of booking, either by cheque or credit/debit card. If you cancel – depending on how much notice you give – you can lose all or part of this deposit unless your room is re-let.

It is reasonable for hotels to take a deposit to secure a booking; they have learnt that if they don't, the commitment of the guest wanes and they may fail to turn up.

Some cancellation policies are more stringent than others. It is also worth noting that some owners will take the money directly from your credit/debit card without contacting you to discuss it. So ask them to explain their cancellation policy clearly before booking so you understand exactly where you stand; it may well avoid a nasty surprise. And consider taking out travel insurance (with a cancellation clause) if you're concerned.

Arrivals and departures

Housekeeping is usually done by 2pm, and your room will usually be available by mid-afternoon. Normally you will have to wave goodbye to it between 10am and 11am. Sometimes one can pay to linger. Some inns are closed between 3pm and 6pm, so do try and agree an arrival time in advance or you may find nobody there.

Closed

When given in months this means for the whole of the month stated. So, 'Closed: November–March' means closed from 1 November to 31 March.

Photo: The Plough at Clanfield, entry 191

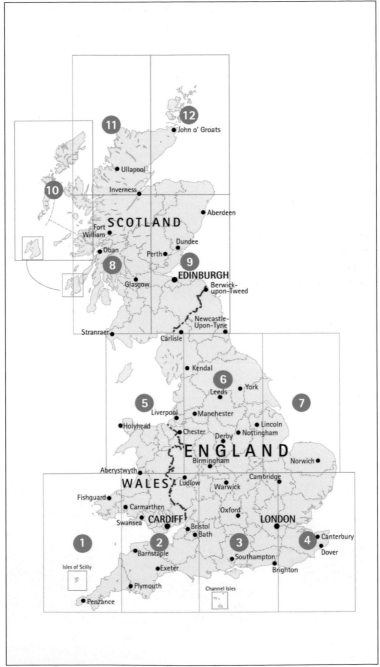

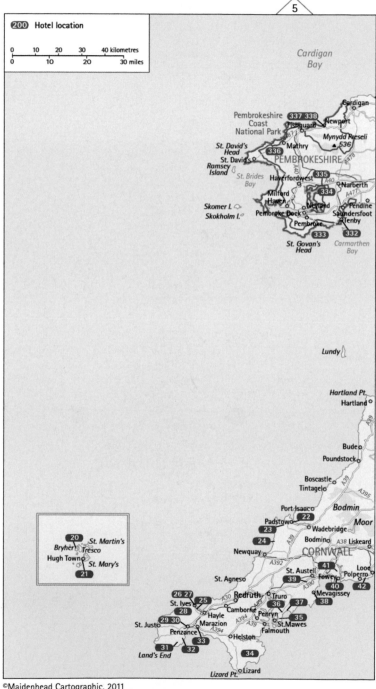

5

200 Hotel location

| 0 | 10 | 20 | 30 | 40 kilometres |
| 0 | 10 | 20 | 30 miles |

Cardigan Bay

Cardigan

Pembrokeshire Coast National Park   **337 338**
Fishguard   Newport
Mynydd Preseli
St. David's Head   Mathry   ▲ 536
336
St. David's   PEMBROKESHIRE   *A478*
Ramsey Island
St. Brides Bay   Haverfordwest   **335**
334   Narberth
Milford Haven   *A477*
Skomer I.   Neyland   Pendine
Skokholm I.   Pembroke Dock   Saundersfoot
Pembroke   Tenby
333   **332**
St. Govan's Head   *Carmarthen Bay*

Lundy

Hartland Pt.
Hartland

Bude
Poundstock

Boscastle
Tintagel
Port Isaac   *Bodmin*
22
Padstow   *Moor*
23   Wadebridge
24   Bodmin   Liskeard
Newquay   CORNWALL
A392
St. Austell   **41**
39   Fowey   Polperro   Looe
St. Agnes   **40**   **42**
26 27   Redruth   Truro   **38** Mevagissey
25   **36**   **37**
St. Ives   **28**   Camborne   Penryn   **35**
St. Just   **29 30**   Hayle   St.Mawes
Marazion   Falmouth
Penzance   Helston
31   **33**
32
Land's End   **34**
Lizard Pt.   Lizard

20   St. Martin's
Bryher   Tresco
Hugh Town   St. Mary's
21

©Maidenhead Cartographic, 2011

Map 2

17

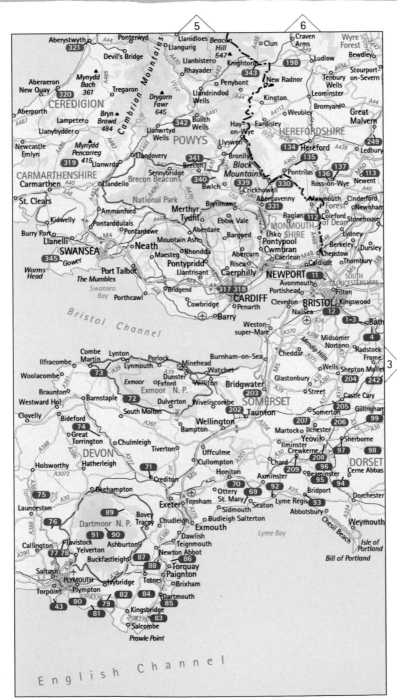

Map 4

19

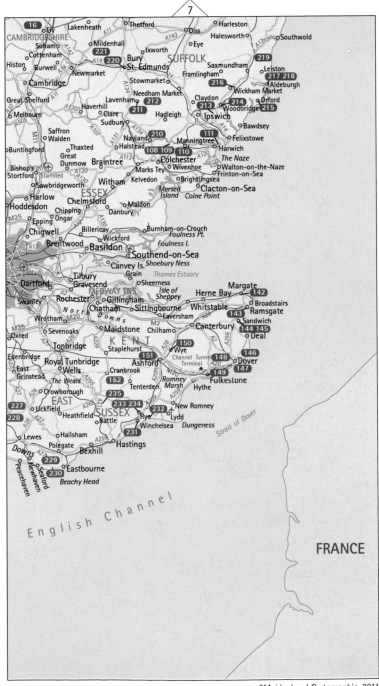

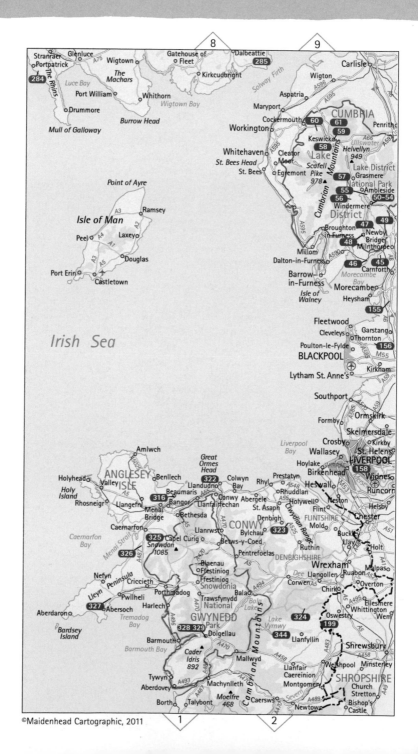

8   9

Stranraer   Glenluce   Wigtown   Gatehouse of   Dalbeattie
Portpatrick   A75   Fleet   285   Carlisle
The Rhins   The   Kirkcudbright   Solway Firth
284   Luce Bay   Machars   Wigton   A596
Port William   Whithorn   Aspatria   A595
       Wigtown Bay   Maryport   CUMBRIA
Drummore   Cockermouth   60   61   59   Penrith
    Burrow Head   Workington   Keswick   58   A66
Mull of Galloway   Helvellyn   Ullswater
                Whitehaven   Cleator   Lake   949
                St. Bees Head   Moor   Scafell   Lake District
                St. Bees   Egremont   Pike   57   Grasmere   National Park
Point of Ayre   978   55   Ambleside
            Ramsey   56   50-54
A3   Windermere
Isle of Man   A2   District   49
Peel   A4   Laxey   A1   Broughton   47
      A5   in Furness   Newby   45
     A3   Douglas   48   Bridge   Milnthorpe
Port Erin   A5   Millom   46   Carnforth
     Castletown   Dalton-in-Furness   Morecambe
                Barrow-   Bay
                in-Furness   Morecambe
                Isle of   Heysham
                Walney   155

Irish Sea   Fleetwood
                  Cleveleys   Garstang
                    Thornton   156
                 Poulton-le-Fylde   M55
                BLACKPOOL
                        Kirkham
            Lytham St. Anne's
                 Southport   Ormskirk
                 Formby   Skelmersdale
                  Crosby   Kirkby
              Liverpool   Wallasey   St. Helens
              Bay   LIVERPOOL
Amlwch   Hoylake   Birkenhead   158
      Great   Heswall   Widnes
      Ormes   Prestatyn   Runcorn
Holyhead   ANGLESEY   Benllech   Head   Colwyn   Rhyl   Neston
Holy   ISLE   322   Llandudno   Bay   Rhuddlan   Helsby
Island   Valley   A5   Beaumaris   Conwy   Abergele   Holywell   Chester
Rhosneigr   Llangefni   316   Bangor   Llanfairfechan   St. Asaph   Flint   FLINTSHIRE
             Menai   Bethesda   Denbigh   Mold
Caernarfon   Bridge   CONWY   Buckley
Caernarfon   Llanrwst   Bylchau   323   Llay   Holt
Bay   325   Capel Curig   DENBIGHSHIRE
326   Snowdon   Betws-y-Coed   Ruthin   Wrexham   Malpas
     1085   Pentrefoelas   A5   Llangollen   Ruabon
         Blaenau   Dee   Corwen   Chirk   Overton
Nefyn   Ffestiniog   A495
Lleyn   Peninsula   Criccieth   Ffestiniog   Ellesmere   Whittington   Wem
      Pwllheli   Porthmadog   Snowdonia   Balaa   324   Oswestry   199
327   Abersoch   Harlech   National   Bala   A5
Aberdaron   Tremadog   Park   GWYNEDD   Lake   344   Llanfyllin   Shrewsbury
     Bardsey   Bay   328   329   Dolgellau   Vyrnwy
     Island   Barmouth   SHROPSHIRE
         Barmouth Bay   Cader   Welshpool   Minsterley
                Idris   Mallwyd   Llanfair
                892   Caereinion   Church
Tywyn   A470   Montgomery   Stretton
Aberdovey   A493   Machynlleth   A49
              Moelfre   Bishop's
Borth   Talybont   468   Caersws   A489   Newtown   Castle

1   2

Map 6
21

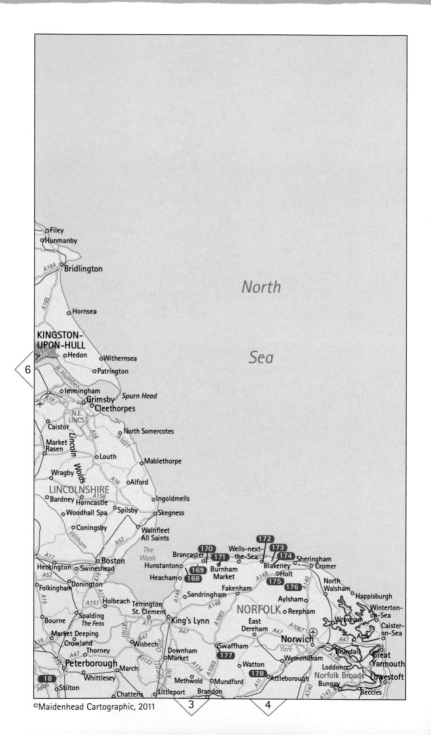

Map 8

23

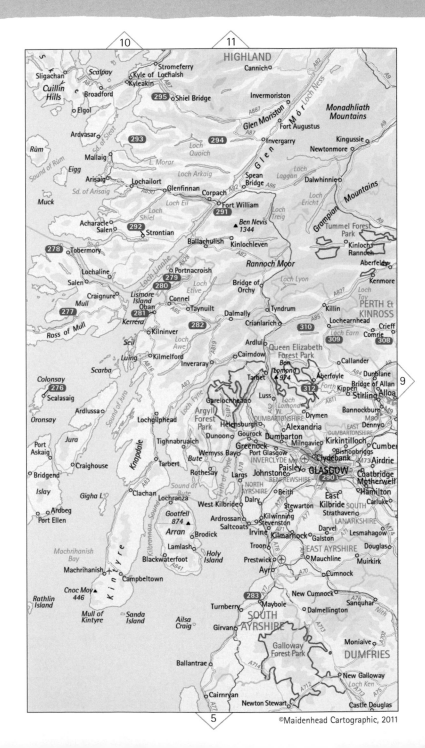

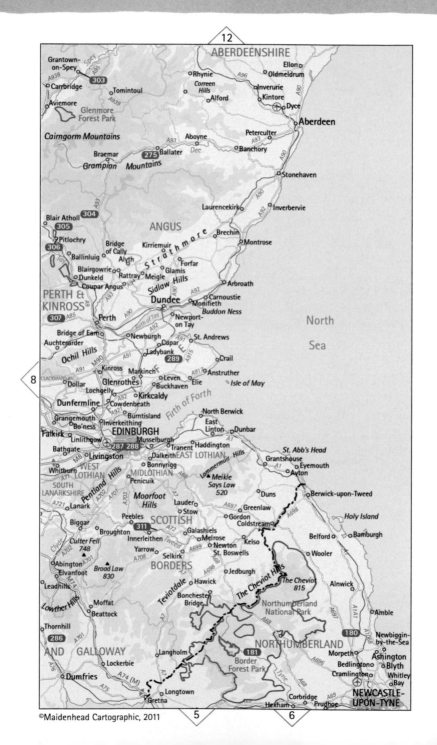

Map 10

25

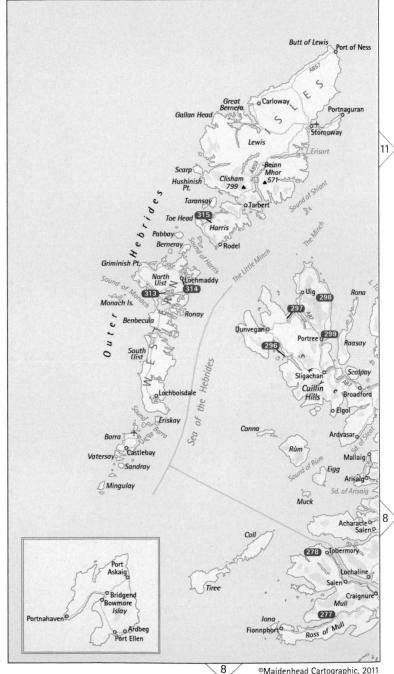

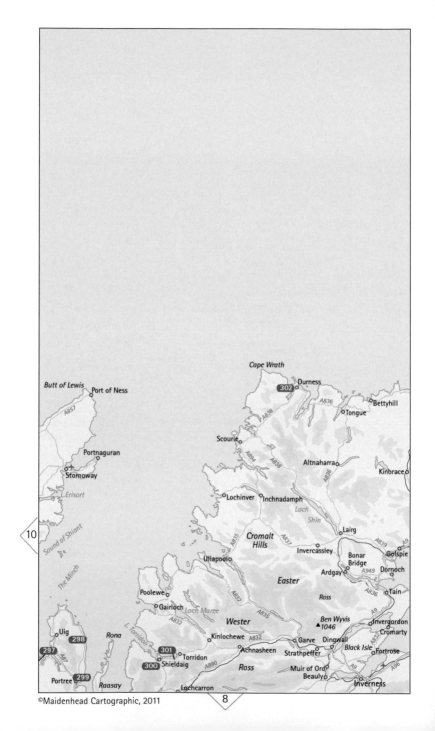

Cape Wrath

Butt of Lewis   Port of Ness

302 Durness

A836

Bettyhill

A838

Tongue

A857

Scourie

Portnaguran

A894

A838

Altnaharra

A836

Kinbrace

Stornoway

L Erisort

Lochinver Inchnadamph

Loch
Shin

Sound of Shiant

Cromalt
Hills

A837

Lairg

A839

A9

10

Invercassley

Bonar
Bridge

Golspie

A835

The Minch

Ullapool

Ardgay

A949

Dornoch

Easter

Poolewe

A832

Ross

A836

Tain

Gairloch Loch Maree

A9

Uig

298

Rona

A832

Wester

A835

Ben Wyvis
▲1046

Invergordon

Cromarty

297

L Torridon

Kinlochewe A832

Garve   Dingwall

Black Isle

Fortrose

301

Torridon

Achnasheen

Strathpeffer

A96

Portree

299

300 Shieldaig

A890

Ross

Muir of Ord

A9

Raasay

Lochcarron

Beauly

Inverness

8

Map 12

27

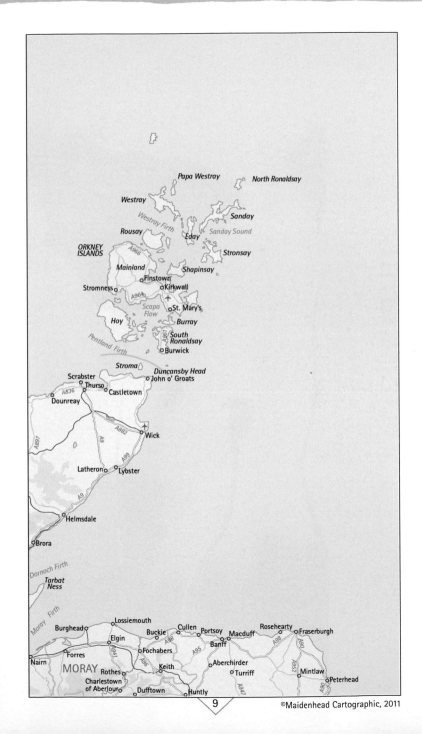

England

SACO Bath Serviced Apartments

Fabulous Bath is England's loveliest city, Georgian to its bone. It's built of mellow golden stone, so wander its streets for elegant squares, beautiful gardens, pavement cafés, delicious delis and the imperious Roman Baths (there's a spa if you want to take a dip). Close to the river, bang in the middle of town, these serviced apartments bask behind a beautifully restored Regency façade – look out for the pillared entrances. Inside you find a collection of airy studios and apartments, all of which come with sparkling kitchens fully stocked with ovens, dishwashers, washer/dryers, microwaves, fridges, and freezers if there's room. Some are small, some are big. If you need a bolthole for a night, a base for a fun-filled weekend or a cool pad for a week, you'll find one here. You get white walls, Italian designer furniture, flat-screen TVs, CD players and good-sized bathrooms. There's a lift to whisk you up and away, 24-hour reception, and high-speed broadband connection throughout. Supermarkets are close, but there are masses of great restaurants on your doorstep, too. *Minimum stay two nights at weekends.*

Price	Studios £78–£144. Apt for 2 £148–£189. Apt for 4 £251–£304.
Rooms	9 studios, 29 apartments for 2, 5 apartments for 4.
Meals	Self-catered. Restaurants within 0.5 miles.
Closed	Never.
Directions	In centre of town, 5-minute walk from station. Full directions on booking.

Karen Sheppard
37 St James's Parade, Bath BA1 1UH

Tel	+44 (0)1225 486540
Email	bath@sacoapartments.co.uk
Web	bath.sacoapartments.co.uk

Bath Paradise House Hotel

You'll be hard pressed to find a better view in Bath. They draw you out as soon as you enter the cosy intimate Georgian interiors, and the 180-degree panorama from the garden is a dazzling advertisement for this World Heritage city. The Royal Crescent and the Abbey are floodlit at night and, in summer, hot-air balloons float by low enough for you to hear the roar of the burners. Nearly all the rooms make full use of the view; the best have bay windows but all have a soft, luxurious country feel with contemporary fabrics and robes in fabulous bathrooms. There are also two garden rooms in an extension that planners took years to approve; it's a remarkable achievement, in keeping with the original Bath stone house, and David is justly proud. The whole place has glass in all the right places, and the sitting room has lovely stone-arched French windows that pull in the light. In summer, don't miss afternoon tea in a half-acre walled garden, a perfect place to lose yourself in the vista. The occasional peal of bells comes for a nearby church. The Thermae Spa with its rooftop pool is a must. *Seven-minute walk down to centre.*

Price	£75–£175. Singles £65–£115.
Rooms	11: 4 doubles, 3 twins, 1 family room, 3 four-posters.
Meals	Restaurants in Bath 0.5 miles.
Closed	24 & 25 December.
Directions	From train station one-way system to Churchill Bridge. A367 exit from r'bout up hill; 0.75 miles, left at Andrews estate agents. Left down hill into cul-de-sac; on left.

David & Annie Lanz
86-88 Holloway, Bath BA2 4PX

Tel	+44 (0)1225 317723
Email	info@paradise-house.co.uk
Web	www.paradise-house.co.uk

Brooks Guesthouse Bath

Owners and staff go out of their way to make your stay here special. Add to this comfy rooms, excellent breakfasts and a central position and you have a great base from which to explore Bath. The house is close to Victoria Park (hot-air balloon rides, children's playground, botanical gardens) and just below the stupendous Royal Crescent, a three-minute walk. Inside, an easy style flows. There's a sitting room in vibrant yellow, an honesty bar if you fancy a drink and a breakfast room for smoked salmon and scrambled eggs or the full cooked works; there are daily specials, free-range eggs, while the meat is reared in Somerset. Bedrooms are split between two Victorian townhouses. A couple are small, a couple are big, most are somewhere in between. All have a similar style: big colours, good beds, crisp white linen, excellent shower rooms; two have baths. A map of town, compiled by guests, shows the top ten sights: don't miss the Roman Baths or the Thermae Spa. One of the best pubs in Bath is around the corner and serves great food. Expect a little noise from the road.

Price	£75–£150. Family rooms £120–£160. Singles from £70.
Rooms	21: 10 twins/doubles, 7 doubles, 2 singles, 2 family rooms.
Meals	Restaurants close by.
Closed	Christmas Day.
Directions	Head west on A4 from centre of town. On right before Victoria Park, below Royal Avenue.

Carla & Andrew Brooks
1 Crescent Gardens, Bath BA1 2NA

Tel	+44 (0)1225 425543
Email	info@brooksguesthouse.com
Web	www.brooksguesthouse.com

Bottle of champagne for bookings of 2 nights or more.

Wheelwrights Arms

In winter grab the table in front of the ancient fire where the wheelwright worked his magic; in summer, skip outside for a pint on the terrace. You're in the country, three miles south of Bath, so drop down to the nearby Kennet & Avon canal and cycle or walk through glorious country into the city. The Wheelwrights dates to 1750. Inside, contemporary colours mix with soft stone walls and exposed timber frames. Logs are piled high in the alcoves, the daily papers are left on the bar and the food is delicious, perhaps seafood tempura, grilled lemon sole, warm treacle tart with stem ginger ice cream; in summer you can eat in the garden illuminated by lights in the trees. Airy bedrooms in the wheelwright's erstwhile annexe come in fresh, original style. Expect dark wood floors, shuttered windows, old-style radiators, flat-screen TVs. Wooden beds are covered in immaculate linen, white bathrooms come with robes and L'Occitane potions. The inn holds two season tickets for Bath Rugby Club. Guests can take them at cost price, so book early. Dogs and walkers are very welcome. *Minimum stay two nights at weekends.*

Price	£100–£150. Singles from £80.
Rooms	7: 5 doubles, 1 twin, 1 single.
Meals	Lunch, 2 courses, £11. Sunday lunch £11.50. Dinner, 3 courses, about £25.
Closed	Never.
Directions	A36 south from Bath for 3 miles, then right, signed Monkton Combe. Over x-roads, into village, on left.

 10% off room rate Mon-Thurs.

David Munn
Church Lane, Monkton Combe,
Bath BA2 7HB

Tel	+44 (0)1225 722287
Email	bookings@wheelwrightsarms.co.uk
Web	www.wheelwrightsarms.co.uk

The Christopher Hotel

The Christopher, an old coaching inn, sits quietly on Eton High Street, with the school running away to the north and Windsor Castle a short walk across the river. Many years ago the hotel stood opposite the school, but was politely asked to move as too many boys were popping in for refreshments; remarkably, it obliged. Recently a new broom has swept through, bringing with it colour and comfort in equal measure. A brasserie-style restaurant and a half-panelled bar stand either side of the coach arch and both come in similar vein with warm colours, stripped floors and big windows that look onto the street. In the restaurant you can stop for a bite, perhaps whitebait, wild boar sausages, lemon meringue pie; in the bar you'll find sofas, armchairs and champagne by the glass. Bedrooms – some in the main house, others stretching out at the back in motel-style – have comfy beds, padded heads, crisp white linen, a sofa if there's room. Those in the main house have the character, three are in the old magistrate's court, all have internet access and adequate bathrooms.

Price	£145-£186. Singles from £105.
Rooms	34: 25 twins/doubles, 9 singles.
Meals	Breakfast £10-£12.50. Lunch & dinner from £8.
Closed	Never.
Directions	M4 junc. 5, into Datchet, through to Eton & left onto High Street. On right.

Janet Tregurtha
110 High Street, Eton,
Windsor SL4 6AN

Tel	+44 (0)1753 852359
Email	reservations@thechristopher.co.uk
Web	www.thechristopher.co.uk

20% off room rate on Sunday nights.

The Elephant at Pangbourne

There are elephants everywhere – all benign, including those in the Ba-bar. This is a super hotel on the edge of town, renovated in unremitting style, with huge sofas in front of the fire, a tongue-and-groove bar for Sunday brunch and a cocktail lounge where candles flicker. It's a big hit with the locals but hotel guests are treated equally well. Eclectic bedrooms come fully loaded and spin you round the world in style: an Indian four-poster in 'Viceroy'; collage wallpaper in 'Charlestown'; colonial chic in 'Rangoon'. Beds are dressed in crisp white cotton, there are flat-screen TVs, perhaps leather sofas, regal colours and rugs on stripped floors; bathrooms come mostly in charcoal grey. Back downstairs eat informally in the bar (locally sourced steak frites, smoked ham with free-range eggs) or in the restaurant for something fancier, perhaps chicken liver parfait with onion marmalade, braised blade of beef with champ mash, forced pink rhubarb and custard tart. There's an enclosed garden for a summer pint and a well-priced wine list, too.

Price	£140–£160. Singles from £100.
Rooms	22: 18 doubles, 2 twins, 2 singles.
Meals	Lunch from £9.95. Bar meals £5.50–£15.50. Dinner £11.95–£25.
Closed	Never.
Directions	M4 junc. 12, A4 south, then A340 north. In village on left at roundabout.

One dinner with 2-night stays Friday-Sunday. Terms apply.

Dominic Bishop
Church Road, Pangbourne,
Reading RG8 7AR

Tel	+44 (0)118 984 2244
Email	reception@elephanthotel.co.uk
Web	www.elephanthotel.co.uk

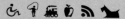

Crown & Garter

An unreformed country local. On the night we stayed Gill was serving at the bar and her son was running through questions for the pub quiz. Gamekeepers and village footballers come for a pint and hearty food. In summer life spills onto a stone terrace and into the pretty garden, and cockerels crow in the fields. Inside you get wooden floors, red curtains and a huge settle by the fire. There's a small restaurant, so dig into smoked mackerel with horseradish cream, venison sausages with red onion gravy, then burnt cream with Drambuie and shortbread. Bedrooms are in a single-storey building that looks prettier in summer when the vine is out. Rooms, however, are big. Four have painted floorboards, all surround a pretty private garden and its fish pond. Beds are brass or wooden, linen is crisp and white, there are quilted bedspreads, coloured rugs and floral curtains; two rooms interconnect. Piping hot water flows in super little bathrooms. You can walk from the front door, try your luck at Newbury Races or watch the early morning gallops at Lambourne. James II is said to have visited.

Price	£99. Singles £79.50.
Rooms	9: 6 doubles, 2 twins, 1 single.
Meals	Bar meals from £6.95. Lunch & dinner from £9.95. Sunday lunch £22. Not Sun eve or Mon/Tues lunch.
Closed	Rarely.
Directions	A4 from Hungerford to Newbury. After 2 miles left for Kintbury & Inkpen. In Kintbury left at corner shop onto Inkpen Road; inn on left after 2 miles.

	Gill Hern
	Great Common, Inkpen,
	Hungerford RG17 9QR
Tel	+44 (0)1488 668325
Email	gill.hern@btopenworld.com
Web	www.crownandgarter.co.uk

Half price on Friday nights if eating in the restaurant and staying Saturday night. Late checkout (12pm).

Drakes

Drakes has the lot: cool rooms, a funky bar, big sea views, the best food in town. It's stands across the road from Brighton beach with the famous pier a three-minute stroll. Inside, you find one of the chicest boutique hotels in the land. Bedrooms are exemplary. Eleven have free-standing baths in the room, while the list of must-haves is as long as your arm, from waffle bathrobes to White Company lotions. Yet what impresses most is the detail and workmanship. Handmade beds rest on carpets that are changed every year, contemporary plaster mouldings curl around ceilings like mountain terraces, Vi-Spring mattresses, wrapped in the crispest linen, are piled high with pillows. Don't worry if you can't afford the best rooms; others may be smaller and those at the back have city views, but all are fantastic and the attic rooms are as cute as could be; Kylie loved hers. As for the food, expect the best, perhaps half a dozen oysters, roast lamb with grilled kidney and pommes Anna, banana parfait with bitter chocolate sauce. The Lanes are close and packed with hip shops. *Minimum stay two nights at weekends.*

Price	£115–£275. Suite £295–£345.
Rooms	20: 16 doubles, 1 twin/double, 2 singles, 1 suite.
Meals	Breakfast £5–£12.50. Lunch from £29.95. Dinner from £39.95.
Closed	Never.
Directions	M23 & A23 into Brighton. At seafront, with pier in front, turn left up the hill. Drakes on left after 300 yds.

 Bottle of wine with dinner on first night.

Richard Hayes
43-44 Marine Parade,
Brighton BN2 1PE

Tel	+44 (0)1273 696934
Email	info@drakesofbrighton.com
Web	www.drakesofbrighton.com

Kemp Townhouse

The sea rolls in at the end of the road, the pier is a pleasant five-minute stroll and the restaurants and bars of St James Street are on your doorstep. Russell and Claas renovated this Regency townhouse from top to toe; only the walls survived and now they shine in period colours. Elegant, uncluttered interiors are the order of the day; charcoal carpet running throughout, ceiling roses, plaster moulding, a fine Art Deco-style chandelier in the fabulous first-floor dining room/bar – and umbrellas at the front door. Bedrooms come in different shapes and sizes but all have the same graceful restraint: cool little wet rooms, gorgeous linen, incredibly comfortable beds, padded headboards, waffle bathrobes, the odd antique. One has a free-standing bath in the room and you can glimpse the sea from those at the front. Spin down to the dining room for an excellent breakfast (real orange juice, baskets of patisserie, pancakes with lemon and sugar, the full cooked works) or drop in for a drink before heading out for the evening. The service is impeccable, too. *Minimum stay two nights at weekends.*

Price	£95-£185. Four-poster £195-£215. Singles from £75.
Rooms	9: 5 doubles, 1 twin/double, 2 four-posters, 1 single.
Meals	Pubs/restaurants nearby.
Closed	Occasionally.
Directions	South to seafront, then left at r'bout in front of pier. Uphill, past New Steine, then left at lights into Lower Rock Gardens. Right at lights; 1st right into Atlingworth. On left.

Russell Braterman & Claas Wulff
21 Atlingworth Street,
Brighton BN2 1PL

Tel	+44 (0)1273 681400
Email	reservations@kemptownhouse.com
Web	www.kemptownhousebrighton.com

Bottle of wine in your room.
Late checkout (12pm).

brightonwave

A small, friendly, boutique B&B hotel in the epicentre of trendy Brighton. The beach and the pier are a two-minute walk, the bars and restaurants of St James Street are around the corner. An open-plan sitting room/dining room comes in cool colours with big suede sofas, fairy lights in the fireplace and ever-changing art on the walls. Bedrooms at the front are big and fancy, with huge padded headboards that fill the wall and deluge showers in sandstone bathrooms. Those at the back have been renovated in style this year. They're smaller, but so is the price, and they come with spotless compact showers; if you're out more than in, why worry? All rooms have fat duvets, lush linen, flat-screen TVs and DVD/CD players and the lower-ground king-size has a private garden. Richard and Simon are easy-going and happy for guests to chill drinks in the kitchen (there are corkscrews in all the rooms). Breakfast, served late at weekends, offers pancakes, the full English or sautéed tarragon mushrooms on toast. *Minimum stay two nights at weekends.*

Price	£90–£175. Four-poster £130–£175. Singles from £60.
Rooms	8: 2 twins/doubles, 3 doubles, 2 singles, 1 four-poster.
Meals	Restaurants nearby.
Closed	Rarely.
Directions	A23 to Brighton Pier roundabout at seafront; left towards Marina; 5th street on left. On-street parking vouchers £7 for 24 hours.

10% off room rate Sunday-Thursday (excluding bank holidays).

	Richard Adams & Simon Throp
	10 Madeira Place, Brighton BN2 1TN
Tel	+44 (0)1273 676794
Email	info@brightonwave.co.uk
Web	www.brightonwave.co.uk

Berwick Lodge

Berwick Lodge – an 1880s wedding present from a general to his daughter – is quite some feat. It stands in 15 acres at the top of a hill with long views west to the Bristol Channel; at night the lights of Avonmouth flicker in the distance. Inside, a small fortune has been lavished on a recent refurbishment. There's a fire in the hall, a piano on the landing, a sitting room/bar with enormous sofas. Best of all is the airy restaurant, a contemporary take on the classical original; expect mullioned windows, ceiling roses, stripped floors, the odd Doric column. Upstairs, vast suites are staggering: sleigh beds, slipper baths, marble fireplaces, stupendous bathrooms. Rooms on the second floor are simpler, but still spoiling. Outside, the gardens are a work in progress: fountains, a tennis court and a small lake are on the way in. Best of all is Chris Wicks's fabulous food… scallops with Périgord truffles, Anjou pigeon with dates and hazelnuts, rhubarb with pink champagne. The house stands between the M5 and M49; you can't see one and can barely hear the other, so don't be put off. *Cookery courses available.*

Price	£125. Suites £159. Singles £85.
Rooms	10: 3 doubles, 2 singles, 5 suites.
Meals	Lunch, 3 courses, £31.50. Dinner, 3 courses, £41.50.
Closed	Never.
Directions	M5 junc.17, then A4018 for Bristol. At 3rd r'about double back over bridge, 1st left for rugby club. Right, then immediately left. Follow track up over M5 to hotel.

Fevzi & Sarah Arikan
Berwick Drive, Bristol BS10 7TD

Tel	+44 (0)117 958 1590
Email	info@berwicklodge.co.uk
Web	www.berwicklodge.co.uk

Bottle of champagne for bookings of 2 nights or more. Late checkout (12pm).

Brooks Guesthouse Bristol

Super rooms, irresistible prices and a great position in the middle of the old town make this funky hotel a great launch pad for England's loveliest city. You're close to the floating harbour, St Nicholas market stands directly outside, and there's a fabulous sun-trapping courtyard for inner city peace. Inside: airy interiors, leather sofas, and walls of glass that open onto the courtyard. Free WiFi runs throughout, a computer is on hand for guests to use, and you can help yourself to drinks at the honesty bar. Breakfast is served leisurely — though if you're in a hurry you can take it with you — and you eat at pretty tables while watching the chef whisk up your scrambled eggs. Stylish bedrooms aren't huge, but nor is their price. You get super comfy beds, crisp white linen, Cole & Son wallpaper and iPod docks. Excellent travertine shower rooms have underfloor heating and White Company oils. Rooms at the back get noise from nearby bars, so ask for a room at the front if that matters. Bristol waits: the water, the Downs, Clifton's 'camera obscura', Brunel's spectacular suspension bridge.

Price	£79–£99. Triples £99–£149. Singles from £69.
Rooms	23: 17 doubles, 4 twins, 2 triples.
Meals	Restaurants on your doorstep.
Closed	Christmas Day.
Directions	Hotel entrance on St Nicholas Court, an alleyway marking the western flank of the covered market; it runs between St Nicholas St & Corn St.

 Bottle of wine in your room.

Carla & Andrew Brooks
St Nicholas Court, Exchange Avenue,
Bristol BS1 1UB

Tel	+44 (0) 0117 930 0066
Email	info@brooksguesthousebristol.com
Web	www.brooksguesthousebristol.com

Three Horseshoes Inn

London may be only an hour's drive, but you'll think you've washed up in the 1960s. Red kites circle a bowl of deep countryside, smoke curls from cottages that hug the hill. As for the Three Horseshoes, you find flagstones and an open fire in the tiny locals' bar, exposed timbers and country views in the airy restaurant. Simon, chef/patron, has cooked in The Connaught, Chez Nico, Le Gavroche – all the best places – and dinner is a treat, the homemade piccalilli worth the trip alone. Come for lunch and dig into baked camembert with garlic and rosemary, stay for dinner and try tiger prawns, boeuf bourguignon, then poached pear with chocolate mousse. Guests have a private entrance, stairs lead up to super-smart rooms with silky quilts, goose down pillows, funky furniture, Farrow & Ball paints. Also: views of the Chilterns and two garden rooms (nice and quiet). Breakfast indulgently, hike in the hills, walk by the Thames, hop over to Windsor. In summer you can eat on the terrace while ducks circle a sunken phone box in the pond. Only in England.

Price	£90–£150.
Rooms	6: 2 doubles, 2 garden rooms, 2 suites.
Meals	Lunch from £6.50. Bar meals from £7.50. Dinner from £15. Sunday lunch £27.50. Not Sunday night or Monday lunch.
Closed	Rarely.
Directions	M40 junc. 5, A40 south thro' Stokenchurch, left for Radnage. After 2 miles left to Bennett End. Sharp right, up hill, on left.

	Simon Crawshaw Horseshoe Road, Radnage, High Wycombe HP14 4EB
Tel	+44 (0)1494 483273
Email	threehorseshoe@btconnect.com
Web	www.thethreehorseshoes.net

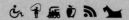

The Mole & Chicken

The Mole & Chicken started life in 1831 as a workers' cottage, became the village store, turned into a pub and is now a restaurant with rooms. It's gorgeous inside and out, an epitome of Englishness that has drawn admirers; *Midsomer Murders* came to film. Inside, Steve and Suzanne have brought huge warmth and style to their new pad. Airy timber-framed interiors dominate, a log fire crackles under original beams, a carved owl juts out from the red-brick bar; the staff are rather lovely, too. A couple of leather sofas wait in one corner and three hand pumps are on tap at the bar, but most people come to eat and with good reason: the food is delicious, from the devilled kidneys and grilled lemon sole to the caramelised tarte tatin. Sunday roast is exceptional, you get live jazz once a month, Thursday night is steak night and there's a garden for summer barbecues. Uncluttered bedrooms in cottages next door are perfect for a couple of nights. Two are small but all have beautiful beds, excellent bathrooms and lots of colour; the family room has a neat terrace.

Price	£95. Singles £70. Family room £125.
Rooms	5: 4 doubles, 1 family room.
Meals	Lunch & dinner £5–£30.
Closed	Rarely.
Directions	North from Thame on B4011 to Long Crendon. Right on main street opp. the Gurkha, signed Chilton. Left at T-junction; pub on left after 0.5 miles.

Steve Bush
Easington Terrace, Long Crendon,
Aylesbury HP18 9EY

Tel	+44 (0)1844 208387
Email	enquiries@themoleandchicken.co.uk
Web	www.themoleandchicken.co.uk

Five Arrows Hotel

Baron Ferdinand de Rothschild began building Waddesdon Manor in 1874. Modelled on the grand châteaux of the Dordogne, it was built in Renaissance style, then filled with the baron's enormous art collection. As for the Five Arrows (the Rothschild coat of arms), it stands by the main gate and was built to accommodate the architects and artisans who built the house. It's not as vast as you might expect, but few inns have mullioned windows and gilded ironwork, or a lawned garden tended by the gardeners from the manor. You enter through a cobbled courtyard to the rear, where wicker chairs flourish in summer, then step into the house for high ceilings, green leather armchairs by reception, pictures from the big house, warm reds and yellows. Bedrooms upstairs have period colours, one has a half tester, others are simpler with padded headboards, perhaps a chandelier; ask for one away from the road. The bridal suite, in the old stables, has high ceilings and a four-poster bed. Delicious dinner is an English affair: tea-smoked salmon, venison pie, treacle tart with clotted cream. The inn is owned by the National Trust.

Price	£99–£129. Suites £175. Singles from £69.
Rooms	11: 8 twins/doubles, 2 suites, 1 single.
Meals	Lunch & dinner £5–£30.
Closed	Never.
Directions	In village on A41, 6 miles west of Aylesbury.

Alex McEwen
High Street, Waddesdon,
Aylesbury HP18 0JE
Tel   +44 (0)1296 651727
Email   five.arrows@nationaltrust.org.uk
Web   www.thefivearrows.co.uk

 10% off room rate Mon-Thurs. Bottle of champagne for bookings of 2 nights or more. Late checkout (12pm).

The Anchor Inn

A real find, a 1650 ale house on Chatteris Fen. The New Bedford river streams past outside. It was cut from the soil by the pub's first residents, Scottish prisoners of war brought in by Cromwell to dig the dykes that drain the fens. These days cosy luxury infuses every corner. Inside, you find low beamed ceilings, timber-framed walls, raw dark panelling and terracotta-tiled floors. A wood-burner warms the bar, so stop for a pint of cask ale, then feast on fresh local produce served by charming staff, perhaps deep fried whitebait, local venison, pear tarte tatin; breakfast is equally indulgent. Four rooms above the shop fit the mood exactly (not posh, supremely comfy). Expect trim carpets, wicker chairs, crisp white duvets and Indian cotton throws. The suites each have a sofabed and three rooms have fen and river views. Footpaths flank the water; stroll down and you might see mallards or Hooper swans, even a seal (the river is tidal to the Wash). Don't miss Ely (the bishop comes to eat), Cambridge, or the nesting swans at Welney. Brilliant.

10% off room rate Sunday-Thursday.

Price	£79.50-£99. Suites £115-£155. Singles from £59.50. Extra bed £20.
Rooms	4: 1 double, 1 twin/double, 2 suites.
Meals	Lunch, 2 courses, £13.95. Dinner, 3 courses, £25-£30. Sunday lunch from £11.50.
Closed	Never.
Directions	From Ely A142 west. In Sutton left on B1381 for Earith. Right in southern Sutton, signed Sutton Gault. 1 mile north on left at bridge.

Adam Pickup & Carlene Bunten
Bury Lane, Sutton Gault, Ely CB6 2BD
Tel   +44 (0)1353 778537
Email   anchorinn@popmail.bta.com
Web   www.anchorsuttongault.co.uk

The Old Bridge Hotel

A smart hotel, the best in town, one which inspired the founders of Hotel du Vin. A battalion of devoted locals come for the food (delicious), the wines (exceptional) and the hugely comfortable interiors. Ladies lunch, business men chatter, kind staff weave through the throng. You can eat wherever you want: in the muralled restaurant; from a sofa in the lounge; or sitting in a winged armchair in front of the fire in the bar. You feast on anything from homemade soups to rack of lamb (starters are available all day), while breakfast is served in a panelled morning room with Buddha in the fireplace. Beautiful bedrooms are scattered about. Expect warm colours, fine fabrics, padded bedheads, crisp linen. One has a mirrored four-poster, several have vast bathrooms, others overlook the river Ouse, all have spoiling extras: Bose iPod docks, Bang & Olufsen TVs, power showers and bathrobes. Finally, John, a Master of Wine, has an irresistible wine shop opposite reception, so expect to take something home with you. The A14 may pass to the back, but it doesn't matter a jot.

Price	£150-£199. Singles from £99. Half-board £95-£125 p.p.
Rooms	24: 13 doubles, 1 twin, 7 singles, 3 four-posters.
Meals	Lunch & dinner £5-£35.
Closed	Never.
Directions	A1, then A14 into Huntingdon. Hotel on southwest flank of one-way system that circles town.

	Nina Beamond
	1 High Street, Huntingdon PE29 3TQ
Tel	+44 (0)1480 424300
Email	oldbridge@huntsbridge.co.uk
Web	www.huntsbridge.com

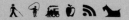

The Crown Inn

A dreamy inn built of mellow stone that stands on the green in this gorgeous village. Paths lead out into open country, so follow the river up to Fotheringhay, where Mary Queen of Scots lost her head. Back at the pub, warm interiors mix style and tradition to great effect. You can eat wherever you want – in the bar, where a fire roars, in the airy snug with views of the green, or in the orangery, which opens onto a terrace. Wherever you end up, you'll eat well, perhaps langoustines with garlic and dill, saddle of venison with poached pear, Bramley apple and cinnamon crumble. In summer life spills onto the gravelled front, on May Day there's a hog roast for the village fête. Six hand pumps bring in the locals, as do quiz nights, live music and the odd game of rugby on the telly. Bedrooms are excellent. The two courtyard rooms are nice and quiet and come with padded bedheads, pretty art, lovely fabrics and flat-screen TVs; one has a magnificent bathroom. Those in the main house overlook the green. The small room has a four-poster, the big room is perfect for families.

Price	£95. Singles from £65.
Rooms	5 doubles.
Meals	Lunch & dinner £7–£25. Restaurant closed first week in January.
Closed	Rarely.
Directions	A1(M), junc. 17, then A605 west for 3 miles. Right on B671 for Elton. In village left, signed Nassington.

10% off room rate for 2- or 3-night stays.

Marcus Lamb
8 Duck Street, Elton,
Peterborough PE8 6RQ

Tel   +44 (0)1832 280232
Email   inncrown@googlemail.com
Web   www.thecrowninn.org

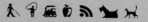

Judges Country House Hotel

This fine old country house is English to its core. It stands in 26 acres of attractive gardens with lawns that sweep down to a small river and paths that weave through private woods. Inside, wonderful interiors sweep you back to grander days. There's an elegant entrance hall that floods with light, a sitting room bar in racing green, and a golden drawing room where doors open to a pretty terrace for lunch in summer. Wander about and find fires primed for combustion, the daily papers laid out in reception, a elegant staircase that rises towards a glass dome. Country-house bedrooms are full of colour. You get bowls of fruit, beautiful beds, gorgeous linen, garden flowers. Bigger rooms have sofas, all have robes in super bathrooms. Back downstairs, there's serious food in the restaurant, perhaps Whitby crab with mango and lemongrass, local venison with chicory and orange, macadamia nut parfait with pears and Earl Grey jelly. If that's not enough, then bring a party and dine in style in the Dom Perignon room surrounded by an irresistible supply of champagne. The Moors are close.

Price	£130-£220. Suites & four-posters £160-£220. Singles from £110. Half-board from £97.50 p.p.
Rooms	21: 14 twins/doubles, 2 singles, 3 four-posters, 2 suites.
Meals	Lunch from £14.95. Dinner, 3 courses, £49.
Closed	Never.
Directions	A1(M), then A19 for Middlesbrough. Left onto A67, through Kirklevington, hotel signed left.

Tim Howard
Kirklevington Hall, Kirklevington,
Yarm TS15 9LW

Tel	+44 (0)1642 789000
Email	enquiries@judgeshotel.co.uk
Web	www.judgeshotel.co.uk

 25% off room rate.

Hell Bay

Magical Bryher. In winter, giant rollers crash against high cliffs; in summer, sapphire waters sparkle in the sun. There are sandy beaches, passing sail boats, waders and wild swans, absolute peace. The hotel lazes on the west coast with sublime watery views – there's nothing between you and America – so grab a drink from the bar and wander onto the terrace to watch a vast sky blush at sunset. Inside, you get stripped floors, coastal colours, excellent art and airy interiors that look out to sea. Step outside and find a heated pool in the garden and a courtyard stocked with rosemary and lavender; castaways would refuse rescue. Bedrooms offer beach-house heaven, most with terraces or balconies, most with views of sand and sea. You get tongue-and-groove panelling, walls of windows, crisp fabrics, super bathrooms. In summer dig into crab and lobster straight from the ocean, fresh asparagus from Tresco, succulent strawberries from the island. There's a sauna, a Nintendo Wii for kids, golf for the hopeful. Low-season deals are exceptional. *Surcharge for dogs £12 a night.*

Price	Half-board £130-£300 p.p. Child in parent's room £50 (incl. high tea). Under 2s free.
Rooms	25 suites.
Meals	Lunch £5-£15. Dinner included.
Closed	November to mid-March.
Directions	Ship/helicopter from Penzance, or fly to St Mary's from Bristol, Southampton, Exeter, Newquay or Land's End; boat to Bryher.

Bottle of champagne for bookings of 2 nights or more.

Philip Callan
Bryher,
Isles of Scilly TR23 0PR
Tel   +44 (0)1720 422947
Email   contactus@hellbay.co.uk
Web   www.hellbay.co.uk

Star Castle

This Grade I listed castle is shaped like a star, dates back to 1593 and was built to defend St Mary's from Spanish attack. It has hosted English royalty – Charles I and Queen Victoria both stayed – and it stands in four acres of peaceful gardens; spectacular views from the ramparts roll downhill to the sea. Inside are low beamed ceilings, stone walls, a fine oak staircase, a first-floor sitting room and a bar in the old dungeon. Outside, three guardhouses have morphed into wonderful single rooms (children adore them). Bedrooms in the main house aren't huge, but have the atmosphere; those in the garden have a more contemporary feel and come with terraces; half have sea views. Elsewhere, a swimming pool, a tennis court and a small kitchen garden. You eat extremely well in the castle dining room – perhaps Cornish scallops, cauliflower soup, a sublime hunk of fillet beef, a hot chocolate fondant. In summer, the conservatory restaurant also opens; expect the freshest seafood in town. Elsewhere, boats and beaches, gardens and golf. A very English adventure.

Price	Half-board £83-£189 p.p.
Rooms	38: 7 twins/doubles, 1 single. Guard houses: 3 singles. Garden rooms: 18 doubles, 9 suites.
Meals	Lunch & picnics from £8. Dinner, 3 courses, included; non-residents, £32.50.
Closed	1-22 December; 2 January-12 February.
Directions	Ship/helicopter from Penzance or fly from Bristol, Southampton, Exeter, Newquay or Land's End.

Robert, James & Ella Francis
The Garrison, St Mary's,
Isles of Scilly TR21 0JA

Tel	+44 (0)1720 422317
Email	info@star-castle.co.uk
Web	www.star-castle.co.uk

Bottle of wine with dinner on first night.

The Seafood Restaurant

In 1975 a young chef called Rick Stein opened a restaurant in Padstow. Thirty-five years on and he has three more, a deli and a pâtisserie, a seafood cookery school and 40 beautiful bedrooms. Despite this success his homespun philosophy has never wavered: buy the freshest seafood on the quay from the fisherman, cook it simply and eat it with friends. It is a viewpoint half the country seems to share and The Seafood Restaurant is now a place of pilgrimage, so come to discover this glorious stretch of Cornish coast, walk on the cliffs, paddle in the estuary, then drop into the lively restaurant for a delicious meal, perhaps razor clams with garlic and parsley, chargrilled Dover sole with sea salt and lime, apple and quince tartlet with vanilla ice cream. Book in for the night and a table in the restaurant is yours – though beautiful bedrooms are so seductive you may find them hard to leave. They are scattered about town, some above the restaurant, others over at the bistro or just around the corner. All are immaculate. Expect the best fabrics, gorgeous bathrooms, and the odd terrace with estuary views.

Price	£97–£280.
Rooms	40: 6 doubles, 8 twins/doubles, 16 four-posters, 10 doubles with sofabeds.
Meals	Lunch, 3 courses, from £29.95. Dinner, 3 courses, about £55. Tasting menu £67.
Closed	24-26 Dec (rooms); 24-27 Dec & 1 May (restaurant).
Directions	A39, then A389 to Padstow. Follow signs to centre; restaurant on left opposite Harbour car park.

Pre-dinner drink.

Rick & Jill Stein
Riverside, Padstow PL28 8BY

Tel	+44 (0)1841 532700
Email	reservations@rickstein.com
Web	www.rickstein.com

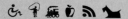

Woodlands Country House

A big house in the country, half a mile west of Padstow, with long views across the fields down to the sea. Pippa and Hugo came west to renovate and have done a fine job. You get an honesty bar in the sitting room, a croquet lawn by the fountain and stripped floors in the airy breakfast room, where a legendary feast is served each morning. Spotless bedrooms are smart and homely, some big, some smaller, all with a price to match, but it's worth splashing out on the bigger ones, which are away from the road and have watery views. Expect lots of colour, pretty beds, floral curtains, Frette linen. One room has a four-poster, another comes with a claw-foot bath, there are robes in adequate bathrooms. All have flat-screen TVs and DVD players, with a library of films downstairs. WiFi runs throughout, there's a computer guests can use, taxis can be ordered – but make sure you book restaurants in advance, especially Rick Stein's or Jamie Oliver's Fifteen. Hire bikes in town and follow the Camel trail, take the ferry over to Rock, head down to the beach, walk on the cliffs. Dogs are very welcome.

Price	£98–£138. Singles from £74.
Rooms	8: 4 doubles, 3 twins/doubles, 1 four-poster.
Meals	Picnic £18. Restaurants in Padstow, 0.5 miles.
Closed	20 December–1 February.
Directions	On A389, just before Padstow, left for Newquay, then west on B3276. House signed on right in village.
🎁	Use your Sawday's Gift Card here.

Hugo & Pippa Woolley
Treator, Padstow PL28 8RU
Tel   +44 (0)1841 532426
Email   info@woodlands-padstow.co.uk
Web   www.woodlands-padstow.co.uk

10% off room rate Mon-Thurs.

The Scarlet

A super-cool design hotel which overlooks the sea; a vast wall of glass in reception frames the view perfectly. The Scarlet does nothing by halves — this is a serious contender for Britain's funkiest bolthole — but it also offers a guilt-free destination as it's green to its core. Cutting-edge technology here includes a biomass boiler, solar panels and state-of-the-art insulation. You'll find a couple of swimming pools to insure against the weather, then log-fired hot tubs in a garden from which you can stargaze at night. There's a cool bar, a pool table in the library, then a restaurant that opens onto a decked terrace, where you eat fabulous Cornish food while gazing out to sea. Exceptional bedrooms come with huge views and all have balconies or terraces, private gardens or viewing pods. Expect oak floors from sustainable forests, organic cotton, perhaps a free-standing bath in your room. Some are enormous, one has a dual-aspect balcony, another comes with a rooftop lounge. If that's not enough, there's an ayurvedic-inspired spa, where tented treatment rooms are lit by lanterns. Amazing. *Minimum stay two nights at weekends.*

Price	£180–£285. Suites £255–£360.
Rooms	37: 14 doubles, 11 twins/doubles, 12 suites.
Meals	Lunch, 3 courses, £19.50. Dinner, 3 courses, about £40.
Closed	4 January–12 February.
Directions	North from Newquay on B3276 to Mawgan Porth. Signed left in village halfway up hill.

30-minute hot tub.

Emma Stratton
Tredragon Road,
Mawgan Porth TR8 4DQ
Tel   +44 (0)1637 861800
Email   stay@scarlethotel.co.uk
Web   www.scarlethotel.co.uk

Boskerris Hotel

A gorgeous little hotel with glass everywhere framing huge views of ocean and headland. In summer, sofas are strategically placed on the decked terrace so you can gaze out in comfort. Godrevy lighthouse twinkles to the right, St Ives slips into the sea on the left, the wide sands of Carbis Bay and Lelant shimmer between. Back inside, white walls and big mirrors soak up the light. You get bleached boards and smart sofas in the sitting room, fresh flowers and blond wood in the dining room. Airy bedrooms in various sizes are delightfully uncluttered, with silky throws, padded headboards, crisp linen. Eleven rooms have the view, all have fancy bathrooms, some have deep baths and deluge showers. You'll find White Company lotions, Designers Guild fabrics; in one room you can soak in the bath whilst gazing out to sea. Staff are kind, nothing is too much trouble, breakfasts are exceptional. A steep coastal path leads down to St Ives (20 mins), mazy streets snake up to the Tate; and there's a branch line. Sustenance, too: don't miss the Porthminster Beach Café for the fanciest nosh in town.

Price	£115–£240. Singles from £80.
Rooms	15: 10 doubles, 3 twins, 1 family room, 1 triple.
Meals	Dinner, 3 courses, about £30.
Closed	Mid-November to mid-February.
Directions	A30 past Hayle, then A3074 for St Ives. After 3 miles pass sign for Carbis Bay, then third right into Boskerris Road. Down hill, on left.

	Jonathan & Marianne Bassett
	Boskerris Road, Carbis Bay,
	St Ives TR26 2NQ
Tel	+44 (0)1736 795295
Email	reservations@boskerrishotel.co.uk
Web	www.boskerrishotel.co.uk

Upgrade subject to availability.
Late checkout (12pm).

Blue Hayes Private Hotel

The view from the terrace is hard to beat, a clean sweep across the bay to St Ives. You breakfast here in good weather in the shade of a Monterey pine, as if transported back to the fifties' French Riviera. As for the rest of the hotel, it's an unadulterated treat, mostly due to Malcolm, whose infectious generosity is stamped over every square inch. Few hoteliers close for four months to redecorate over winter, but that's the way things are done here and the house shines as a result. It comes in ivory white, with the occasional dash of colour from carpet and curtain. The bar has a vaulted ceiling and a wall of glass that runs along the front to weatherproof the view. Big bedrooms are gorgeous, two with balconies, one with a terrace, all with sparkling bathrooms. If you want to eat, light suppers are on hand, but Porthminster beach is a short stroll, so book a table at its eponymous café and treat yourself to the best food in town; torches are provided for the journey back up. Penzance, Zennor and the New Tate are close – but no one will blame you if you hole up in luxurious isolation for a day or two.

Price	£160–£190. Singles from £130. Suite £210–£230.
Rooms	6: 4 doubles, 1 suite, 1 triple.
Meals	Packed lunch by arrangement. Light supper from £12.
Closed	November–March.
Directions	A30, then A3074 to St Ives. Through Lelant & Carbis Bay, over mini-r'bout (Tesco on left) and down hill. On right immed. after garage on right.
🎁	Use your Sawday's Gift Card here.

Bottle of champagne for bookings of 2 nights or more.

Malcolm Herring
Trelyon Avenue, St Ives TR26 2AD
Tel   +44 (0)1736 797129
Email   info@bluehayes.co.uk
Web   www.bluehayes.co.uk

Primrose Valley Hotel

Roll out of bed, drop down for breakfast, spin off to the beach, stroll into town. If you want St Ives bang on your doorstep, this is the hotel for you; the sands are a 30-second stroll. Half the rooms have views across the bay, two have balconies for lazy afternoons. Inside, open-plan interiors revel in an earthy contemporary chic, with leather sofas, varnished floors, fresh flowers and glossy magazines. Bedrooms tend not to be huge, but you can't fault the price or style, so come for Hypnos beds, bespoke furniture and good bathrooms; the suite comes with a red leather sofa, hi-tech gadgetry and a fancy bathroom. Andrew and Sue are environmentally aware, committed to sustainable tourism and community projects. Their hugely popular breakfast is mostly sourced within the county; food provenance is listed on the menu. There's a cool little bar that's stocked with potions from far and wide and treatment and therapy rooms that use the best natural products. The Tate and Barbara Hepworth's garden both wait, as does the Porthminster Beach Café for the best food in town. *Min. stay two nights at weekends.*

Ethical Collection: Environment; Food. See page 386 for details

Price	£105–£170. Suite £199–£240.
Rooms	9: 6 doubles, 2 twins, 1 suite.
Meals	Platters £8. Restaurant 200m.
Closed	Christmas; 3 weeks in January. Open for New Year.
Directions	From A3074 Trelyon Avenue; before hospital sign slow down, indicate right & turn down Primrose Valley; under bridge, left, then back under bridge; signs for hotel parking.

Bottle of prosecco on arrival for stays of 2 nights or more.

Andrew & Sue Biss
Primrose Valley, St Ives TR26 2ED

Tel	+44 (0)1736 794939
Email	info@primroseonline.co.uk
Web	www.primroseonline.co.uk

The Gurnard's Head

The coastline here is utterly magical and the walk up to St Ives is hard to beat. Secret beaches appear at low tide, cliffs tumble down to the water and wild flowers streak the land pink in summer. As for the hotel, you couldn't hope for a better base. It's earthy, warm, stylish and friendly, with airy interiors, colour-washed walls, stripped wooden floors and fires at both ends of the bar. Logs are piled up in an alcove, maps and art hang on the walls, books fill every shelf; if you pick one up and don't finish it, take it home and post it back. Rooms are warm and cosy, simple and spotless, with Vi-Spring mattresses, crisp white linen, throws over armchairs, Roberts radios. Downstairs, super food, all homemade, can be eaten wherever you want: in the bar, in the restaurant or out in the garden in good weather. Snack on rustic delights – pork pies, crab claws, half a pint of Atlantic prawns – or tuck into more substantial treats, maybe mussels with white wine, pork loin with grain mustard, then lemon posset and rhubarb. Picnics are easily arranged and there's bluegrass folk music in the bar most weeks.

Price	£95-£165. Singles from £75. Half-board from £70 p.p.
Rooms	7: 4 doubles, 3 twins/doubles.
Meals	Lunch from £4.50. Dinner, 3 courses, about £27.50.
Closed	24 & 25 December & 4 days in mid-January.
Directions	On B3306 between St Ives & St Just, 2 miles west of Zennor, at head of village of Treen.

25% off midweek stays of 2 or more nights, November-March.

Charles & Edmund Inkin
Zennor, St Ives TR26 3DE

Tel	+44 (0)1736 796928
Email	enquiries@gurnardshead.co.uk
Web	www.gurnardshead.co.uk

The Summer House

A glittering find, a small enclave of Mediterranean goodness a hundred yards up from the sea. It's stylish and informal, colourful and welcoming; what's more, it's super value for money. Linda and Ciro, English and Italian respectively, run the place with great affection. During the week it runs as a B&B, at weekends Ciro whisks up culinary delights for dinner. Linda, bubbling away out front, is the designer, her breezy interiors warm and elegant with stripped floors, beautiful art, panelled windows and murals in the dining room (the breakfast chef is a sculptress). Ciro worked in some of London's best restaurants before heading west to go it alone, and in good weather you can eat his ambrosial food in a small, lush courtyard garden, perhaps langoustine with mango and chives, rack of lamb with herbes de Provence, warm apple tart with crème Chantilly. Breakfast – also served in the courtyard when the sun shines – is a feast. Stylish rooms are the final delight: seaside colours, well-dressed beds, freshly cut flowers, flat-screen TVs, super little bathrooms.

Price	£120-£150. Singles from £100.
Rooms	5: 4 doubles, 1 twin/double.
Meals	Simple suppers, £25, by arrangement. Dinner £38.50 (Saturday & Sunday only).
Closed	November-March.
Directions	With sea on left, along harbourside, past open-air pool, then immediate right after Queens Hotel. House 30 yds up on left. Private car park.

Linda & Ciro Zaino
Cornwall Terrace, Penzance TR18 4HL

Tel +44 (0)1736 363744
Email reception@summerhouse-cornwall.com
Web www.summerhouse-cornwall.com

The Abbey Hotel

The Abbey is a rare gem, a hotel that refuses to enter the modern world, choosing instead to linger in its serenely elegant past. The feel is of a smart country house, and the drawing room — roaring fire, huge gilt mirror, walls of books, rugs on stripped floors — is hard to beat. Drinks are brought to you, there's a bust of Lafayette, exquisite art and huge arched windows that rise to the ceiling and open onto the loveliest walled garden; step out in summer for afternoon tea or a breakfast to remember. The house dates from 1660 and has views to the front of Penzance harbour and St Michael's Mount. Country-house bedrooms are grandly quirky; in one you pull open a cupboard to find an en suite shower. Sink into big comfy beds wrapped up in crisp linen. There are chandeliers, quilted bedspreads, French armoires, plump-cushioned armchairs. You breakfast indulgently in a panelled dining room with a fire crackling and assorted busts and statues for company. Kind staff go the extra mile and point you in the right direction; St Ives, Zennor, Mousehole and the Minack all wait.

Price	£105–£200. Suite £150–£210. Singles from £75. Flat £115–£170.
Rooms	7 + 1: 4 doubles, 1 twin, 1 family room, 1 suite. Self-catering flat for 4.
Meals	Restaurants nearby.
Closed	Rarely.
Directions	Follow signs to town centre. Up hill (Market Jew St). Left at top, then fork left & 3rd on the left.

3 nights for the price of 2, Sunday-Wednesday (not July or August).

Thaddeus Cox
Abbey Street, Penzance TR18 4AR

Tel   +44 (0)1736 366906
Email   hotel@theabbeyonline.co.uk
Web   www.theabbeyonline.co.uk

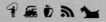

The Cove

You're lost in the lanes west of Penzance with a pirate's cove at the end of the garden. The position here is fabulous, with views from the terrace that shoot out to sea. As for the Cove, well, it's not your average hotel. The trick here is that every apartment comes with a cool little kitchen, so you can look after yourself if you want. Not that you have to – the hotel has a fabulous restaurant that will cater to your every need, from Easter to November. Most people tend to do a bit of both and it works particularly well for young families, so much so there's a kids' club in summer. An airy seaside elegance runs throughout (white walls, coastal art, lots of glass to bring in the light), but the hub of the hotel is the terrace, where loungers circle the pool. Rooms – some huge, others smaller – all have a similar style: sisal matting, aqua blue fabrics, comfy beds, super little bathrooms As for the restaurant, you can nip down for breakfast, lunch or a rather good dinner, perhaps Serrano ham with black figs, poached lobster with a rocket salad, a plate of West Country cheeses.

Price	Studios: £115–£195. Apartments: £115–£375. One-week minimum mid-July to August.
Rooms	15: 2 studios, 13 apartments.
Meals	Continental breakfast to your door; full English £9.95. Lunch from £5. Dinner £22–£25; à la carte £35–£40.
Closed	Self-catering open all year; hotel open Easter to October.
Directions	West from Penzance on B3315 (left in Newlyn). Clearly signed after 3 miles for Lamorna Cove and the hotel.

Lee Magner
Lamorna, Penzance TR19 6XH

Tel   +44 (0)1736 731411
Email   contact@thecovecornwall.com
Web   www.thecovecornwall.com

Old Coastguard Hotel

Not much happens in Mousehole. The Spanish sacked the place in 1595 and since then it's been pretty quiet. As for the Old Coastguard, it sits bang on the water with lush lawns running down to the sea. There are decks on two levels to make the most of it all, while eight bedrooms have balconies with views across jostling boats to an ancient harbour. Follow the coastal path down and you'll find fishermen mending their nets before heading out to catch lobster, scallops and crab, much of which will land on your plate. Expect to eat well, perhaps deep fried crispy squid, crab linguine with chilli and garlic, treacle tart with vanilla ice cream. Airy interiors mix seaside colours to great effect. You'll find stripped boards, tongue-and-groove panelling, walls of glass to frame the view. Bedrooms come in uncluttered style: most look out to sea, you get white walls to soak up the light, flat-screen TVs, DVD players, robes in sparkling bathrooms. There's a small reading room and free internet access, then 20 palm trees in the garden. Head west for the Minack, then north to Zennor and St Ives. Wonderful.

Price	£120-£180. Suite £190-£210.
Rooms	14: 11 doubles, 2 twins/doubles, 1 suite.
Meals	Lunch from £4.95. Dinner, 3 courses, about £25.
Closed	9 January-10 February.
Directions	Follow A30 to Penzance & signs to Mousehole. Hotel on left as you enter the village. Limited parking on first come first served basis or public car park next door, £2 on departure.

10% off room rate
Sunday-Thursday.

Charles & Edmund Inkin
The Parade, Mousehole,
Penzance TR19 6PR

Tel	+44 (0)1736 731222
Email	bookings@oldcoastguardhotel.co.uk
Web	www.oldcoastguardhotel.co.uk

Mount Haven Hotel & Restaurant

A magical hotel with sublime views of St Michael's Mount, an ancient Cornish totem that's been pulling in the crowds for millennia. Most rooms look the right way and have a balcony to boot, but there's a decked terrace in case yours doesn't and the causeway leads over at low tide, so make sure you discover the ancient castle and church. Back at the hotel, sink in to comfy sofas in the bar where huge windows frame the view, making sunsets rather special. Elsewhere, Eastern deities jostle for space, local art hugs the walls, and there's a treatment room for a soothing massage, the profits of which fund an orphanage and medical camp in India. The restaurant comes with big mirrors and doors that open onto a terrace where you eat in good weather; try Newlyn crab cakes, duck breast with a ginger marmalade, then chocolate pave with blood-orange sorbet. Bedrooms are lovely. Most aren't huge, but nearly all have balconies or terraces and those on the top floor have unblemished views. They come with fresh flowers, crisp linen, flat-screen TVs. Bathrooms tend to be small but sweet.

Price	£110–£170. Four-posters & suite £150–£210. Singles from £90.
Rooms	18: 10 doubles, 4 twins/doubles, 1 family room, 2 four-posters, 1 suite.
Meals	Lunch from £5. Dinner, 3 courses, about £30.
Closed	Mid-December to mid-February.
Directions	Leave A30 for Marazion 1 mile east of Penzance at middle roundabout on dual carriageway. Left at T-junction by sea, then through village and signed on right.

Orange & Mike Trevillion
Turnpike Road,
Marazion TR17 0DQ

Tel	+44 (0)1736 710249
Email	reception@mounthaven.co.uk
Web	www.mounthaven.co.uk

Bottle of house wine with dinner on first night.

Bay Hotel

The Bay Hotel sits beneath a vast sky with views to the front of nothing but sea – unless you count the beach at low tide, where buckets and spades are mandatory. Outside, the lawn rolls down to the water, sprinkled with deckchairs and loungers, so grab a book, snooze in the sun or listen to the sounds of the English seaside. Stylish interiors are just the ticket, but you can't escape the view: dining room, conservatory and sitting room look the right way, with big windows to keep your eyes glued to the horizon. Warm colours fit the mood perfectly, there are flowers everywhere, cavernous sofas, a telescope to scan the high seas, a small bar for pre-dinner drinks. Airy bedrooms vary in size. Suites are big – one has it's own balcony – and all have sea views (some from the side). Expect smart whites, leather armchairs, tongue-and-groove bathrooms. As for Ric's delicious food, fish comes straight from the sea, perhaps deep-fried calamari with chilli dip and Cornish sole with anchovy butter, followed by chilled Grand Marnier crème brûlée. The coastal path passes directly outside. Don't miss afternoon tea.

Price	Half-board £70–£120 p.p; suite £115–£140 p.p.
Rooms	13: 5 doubles, 6 twins/doubles, 2 suites.
Meals	Dinner, 3 courses, included; non-residents, £29.95.
Closed	December–March (open Christmas & New Year).
Directions	A3083 south from Helston, then left onto B3293 for St Keverne. Right for Coverack after 8 miles. Down hill, right at sea, second on right.

Bottle of house wine for stays of 2 or more nights.

Ric, Gina & Zoe House
North Corner, Coverack,
Helston TR12 6TF

Tel	+44 (0)1326 280464
Email	enquiries@thebayhotel.co.uk
Web	www.thebayhotel.co.uk

The Rosevine

A super-smart family bolthole on the Roseland peninsular with views that tumble across trim lawns and splash down to the sea. Tim and Hazel welcome children with open arms and have created a small oasis where guests of all ages can have great fun. There's a playroom for kids (Xbox, plasma screen, DVDs, toys), an indoor pool, and a beach at the bottom of the hill. High teas are on hand, there are cots and highchairs, babysitters can be arranged. Parents don't fare badly either: an elegant sitting room with sofas in front of the wood-burner; sea views and Lloyd Loom furniture in an airy restaurant; sun loungers scattered about a semi-tropical garden. Suites and apartments come with small kitchens (fridge, sink, dishwasher, microwave/oven); you can self-cater, eat in the restaurant or mix and match (there's deli menu for posh takeaways). Suites are open-plan with sofabeds, apartments have separate bedrooms. Expect airy, uncluttered interiors, flat-screen TVs, Egyptian cotton and robes in good bathrooms. Eight have a balcony or terrace. St Mawes is close.

Price	Studios £145-£225. Family suites & apartments £185-£385.
Rooms	12: 4 studios, 4 family suites for 2-4, 4 apartments for 2-5. All with kitchenettes.
Meals	Breakfast £3-£8. Lunch from £5. Dinner, 3 courses, about £30.
Closed	January.
Directions	From A390 south for St Mawes on A3078. Signed left after 8 miles. Right at bottom of road; just above beach.

Local food/produce in your room.

Hazel & Tim Brocklebank
Rosevine, Portscatho,
Truro TR2 5EW

Tel	+44 (0)1872 580206
Email	info@rosevine.co.uk
Web	www.rosevine.co.uk

Driftwood Hotel

A faultless position, one of the best, with six acres of garden that drop down to a private beach and coastal paths that lead to cliff-top walks. At the Driftwood, Cape Cod meets Cape Cornwall and airy interiors shine in white and blue. The sitting room is stuffed with beautiful things – fat armchairs, deep sofas, driftwood lamps, a smouldering fire – and there's a telescope in the bar with which to scan the high seas. Best of all are the walls of glass that pull in the spectacular watery views; in summer, doors open onto a decked terrace for breakfast and lunch in the sun. Bedrooms are gorgeous (all but one has a sea view), some big, others smaller, one in a cabin halfway down the cliff with a private terrace. All have the same clipped elegance: big beds, white linen, wicker chairs and white walls to soak up the light. There are Roberts radios on bedside tables, cotton robes in excellent bathrooms. Drop down to the dining room for seriously good food that makes the most of the sea. High teas for children, hampers for beach picnics and rucksacks for walkers, too. *Minimum stay two nights at weekends.*

 Bottle of wine with dinner on first night.

Price	£165–£275.
Rooms	15: 11 doubles, 3 twins, 1 cabin.
Meals	Dinner £44.
Closed	Early December to early February.
Directions	From St Austell, A390 west. Left on B3287 for St Mawes; left at Tregony on A3078 for approx. 7 miles. Signed left down lane.

Paul & Fiona Robinson
Rosevine, Portscatho,
Truro TR2 5EW

Tel	+44 (0)1872 580644
Email	info@driftwoodhotel.co.uk
Web	www.driftwoodhotel.co.uk

The Nare Hotel

The Nare is matchless, English to its core. It sits above Gerrans Bay with sublime views of sand and sea, and wherever you go, inside or out, something beautiful catches the eye. There are two swimming pools, croquet and tennis, mature gardens that sparkle in summer, a hot tub overlooking an enormous beach. Interiors are equally wonderful – the art in the gallery is worth the trip alone. You'll find crackling fires, a cocktail bar, even a billiard room that doubles as a library. Afternoon tea 'on the house' is served every day by smartly dressed waiters, so sip your Earl Grey out on the terrace and watch the waves roll in. Recently refurbished country-house bedrooms are nothing short of gorgeous. Expect beautiful fabrics, fresh flowers, antique furniture, fabulous bathrooms. Most have watery views (you can lie in bed and gaze out to sea), balconies or terraces. As for the food, the dining room is formal, the Quarterdeck restaurant is less so; expect fabulous fish, lobster every day, game in season or delicious Cornish beef. We haven't even scratched the surface. Out of this world.

Price	£262-£488. Singles £136-£260. Suites £324-£746.
Rooms	37: 21 twins/doubles, 6 singles, 10 suites.
Meals	Lunch from £6. Dinner in brasserie, 3 courses, about £30; in restaurant, 5 courses, £49.50.
Closed	Never.
Directions	A390 west from St Austell, then B3287 to Tregony. Pick up A3078 for St Mawes and hotel signed left after two miles.

Toby Ashworth
Carne Beach, Veryan-in-Roseland,
Truro TR2 5PF

Tel	+44 (0)1872 501111
Email	stay@narehotel.co.uk
Web	www.narehotel.co.uk

Trevalsa Court Country House Hotel

This Arts and Crafts house has a fine position at the top of the cliffs with sprawling lawns that run down to Cornwall's coastal path; either turn right and amble along to Mevagissey or drop down to the beach with your bucket and spade. Don't dally too long: Trevalsa is a seaside treat – friendly, stylish, seriously spoiling. In summer, you can decamp onto the terrace and lawns and fall asleep in a deckchair, but the view here is weatherproofed by an enormous mullioned window seat in the sitting room, a great place to watch the weather spin by. Elsewhere, you'll find a small bar packed with art, then a panelled dining room where you dig into bistro-style food – homemade fishcakes, coq au vin, chocolate fondant with basil ice cream. Bedrooms are lovely, all recently refurbished. They come in seaside colours with designer fabrics, the odd wall of paper, padded headboards and super new wet rooms. There are TVs and DVD players and most have sea views, while bigger rooms have sofas and spoil you all the way. The Lost Gardens of Heligan are on your doorstep.
Minimum stay two nights at weekends & in high season.

Price	£105–£185. Singles £75–£95. Suites £195–£235. Half-board £75–£140 p.p.
Rooms	14: 7 doubles, 2 twins, 2 singles, 3 suites.
Meals	Dinner £26.50–£30.
Closed	December & January.
Directions	B3273 from St Austell signed Mevagissey, through Pentewan to top of the hill, left at the x-roads, over mini r'bout. Hotel on left, signed.

Susan & John Gladwin
School Hill, Mevagissey,
St Austell PL26 6TH

Tel	+44 (0)1726 842468
Email	stay@trevalsa-hotel.co.uk
Web	www.trevalsa-hotel.co.uk

The Cornwall Hotel, Spa & Estate

The Cornwall started life as an Edwardian retreat for the landed gentry, but a recent development of this 43-acre estate has moved the hotel firmly into the 21st century. At its heart is the White House, now a contemporary pleasure dome with fantastic art, seriously good food and warmly stylish design. Here you find a cool little brasserie with the kitchen on display, an attractive drawing room with sofas in front of the fire, then a super-smart restaurant which overlooks the manicured grounds; doors open onto a terrace in summer. Bedrooms in the main house are seriously fancy, those out back come with balconies overlooking the Pentewan valley. All are lovely, with smart colours, cool bathrooms and technological excess. Elsewhere, a groovy spa, where an indoor infinity pool overlooks a walled garden strewn with sun loungers. You can hire bikes, spin off to the Eden Project or simply take to the coastal path. Whatever you do, come back for some great food, perhaps St Austell Bay mussels, local rib-eye, sticky toffee pudding. There are 22 woodland homes if you want to stay longer and self-cater.

Price	£99–£220. Self-catering £600–£1500 per week.
Rooms	65 + 22: 62 twins/doubles, 2 four-posters, 1 suite. 22 self-catering woodland homes for 4–6.
Meals	Lunch from £5.95. Dinner, £11–£35.
Closed	Never.
Directions	South from St Austell on B3273 for Megavissey. Hotel on right after 1 mile.

Ivan Curtis
Pentewan Road, Tregorrick,
St Austell PL26 7AB
Tel   +44 (0)1726 874050
Email   enquiries@thecornwall.com
Web   www.thecornwall.com

10% off room rate Mon-Thurs. Bottle of Cornish Sparkling wine for bookings of 2 nights or more.

The Old Quay House Hotel

You drop down the hill, navigate the narrow lanes, then pull up at this boutique hotel which started life as a seaman's mission. It's a perfect spot, with the estuary lapping directly outside and a sun-trapping terrace for summer dining, as good a place as any from which to watch the boats zip past. Inside, stylish bedrooms spoil you all the way with goose down duvets, beautiful fabrics and seriously spoiling bathrooms (replete with bathrobes, the odd claw-foot tub and maybe a separate shower). Most rooms look the right way, eight have balconies and the view from the penthouse suite is unbeatable. Downstairs great food waits, so trip down to the bar for a cocktail, then dig into excellent brasserie-style food, perhaps crab and crayfish tian, roast chicken with purple broccoli, pecan pie with pumpkin ice cream. Fowey is enchanting, bustles with life and fills with sailors for the August regatta. If you want to escape, take the ferry across to Polruan where Daphne du Maurier lived and wrote. You can potter over to spectacular Lantic Bay for a picnic lunch on the beach. *Minimum two nights at weekends in high season.*

Price	£180–£320 Singles from £130.
Rooms	11: 5 doubles, 5 twins/doubles, 1 suite.
Meals	Lunch (April–Sept) about £15.
	Dinner £27.50–£35.
Closed	Rarely.
Directions	Entering Fowey, follow one-way system past church. Hotel on right where road at narrowest point, next to Lloyds Bank. Nearest car park 800 yds.

 Bottle of wine with dinner on first night. Late checkout (12pm).

Anthony Chapman
28 Fore Street, Fowey PL23 1AQ

Tel   +44 (0)1726 833302
Email   info@theoldquayhouse.com
Web   www.theoldquayhouse.com

The Cormorant Hotel

A sublime position on the side of a wooded hill with the magical Fowey river curling past below. Oyster catchers swoop low across the water, sheep bleat in the fields, sail boats tug on their moorings. The hotel is one room deep and every window looks the right way, but a recent renovation has added small balconies to most of the bedrooms, so doze in the sun and listen to the sounds of the river. As for the hotel, it couldn't have fallen into better hands. Mary rescued it from neglect, poured in love and money, and now it shines: new windows, new bathrooms, new swimming pool, new everything. A terrace sweeps along the front, a finger of lawn runs below, and, inside, the river follows wherever you go. You get fresh flowers in the bar, an open fire in the gorgeous sitting room, wooden floors in the airy dining room. Super bedrooms come without clutter: light colours, trim carpets, walls of glass, white linen. One has a claw-foot bath from which you can gaze down on the water. Swim in the pool, tan on its terrace, jump in the hot tub, then dine on fabulous Cornish food. Boat trips can be arranged.

Price	£95-£250.
Rooms	14: 11 doubles, 3 twins.
Meals	Lunch from £12. Dinner, à la carte, from £30.
Closed	Rarely.
Directions	A390 west towards St Austell, then B3269 to Fowey. After 4 miles, left to Golant. Into village, along quay, hotel signed right up very steep hill.

Mary Tozer
Golant, Fowey PL23 1LL

Tel +44 (0)1726 833426
Email relax@cormoranthotel.co.uk
Web www.cormoranthotel.co.uk

Talland Bay Hotel

The position here is magical. First you plunge down rollercoaster lanes, then you arrive at this delicious hotel. Directly in front, the sea sparkles through pine trees, an old church crowns the hill and two acres of lawns end in a ha-ha, where the land drops down to the bay. Vanessa came to renovate and has done so magnificently, breathing new life into this venerable old hotel. There's a sitting room bar in blue and white, a roaring fire in the half-panelled dining room, refurbished bedrooms that take your breath away. Masses of art hangs on the walls, there are vast sofas, polished flagstones, a gravelled terrace for afternoon tea. Follow the coastal path over the hill, then return for an excellent dinner, perhaps chicken liver pâté with pistachio brioche, fillet of sea bream with olives and lemon, hot chocolate fondant with white chocolate sorbet. And so to bed. All rooms have been refurbished and are ready to pamper you rotten. Expect rich colours, vast beds, beautiful linen, the odd panelled wall. One has a balcony, a couple open onto terraces, all have seriously swanky bathrooms.

Price	£100–£200. Suites £155–£225. Half-board from £80 p.p.
Rooms	22: 17 twins/doubles, 3 suites, 2 singles.
Meals	Lunch from £4.95. Dinner £32–£38.
Closed	Never.
Directions	From Looe A387 for Polperro. Ignore 1st sign to Talland. After 2 miles, left at x-roads; follow signs.

Vanessa Rees
Porthallow, Looe PL13 2JB

Tel	+44 (0)1503 272667
Email	info@tallandbayhotel.co.uk
Web	www.tallandbayhotel.co.uk

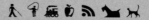

Westcroft Gallery with Rooms

This idyllic bolthole down by the sea was one of Tatler's 'Best Hotels on the Planet' for 2011. Lost in Kingsand's mazy lanes, it stands twenty paces up from the water. You can arrive by boat, just take the train to Plymouth, then decant onto a small ferry that zips across the estuary. 'Shipwreck chic' waits for those who make the journey. You slip through an ancient courtyard decked out with designer clutter, then step into this old coaching inn that feels like a fisherman's cottage. Inside, Sarah and Dylan have covered every square inch with something beautiful, be it a brass bed, a muralled breakfast table or framed photos of Iggy Pop. The room in the eaves has a French bed from which you can stargaze, another comes complete with a magnificent sitting room (sea views, walls of books, fantastic art, your own computer). Then there's the gallery; if you like a piece and are tempted to buy, they'll hang it in your room overnight. Don't come looking for hotel service, do come looking for style, comfort, informality. Whitsand Bay is close for miles of sandy beach. Matchless. *Minimum stay two nights at weekends.*

Price	£95–£140.
Rooms	3: 2 doubles, 1 twin/double.
Meals	Restaurants in village.
Closed	Never.
Directions	A38 west into Cornwall, then A374 for Torpoint. Right before Sheviock, signed Kingsand. Use car park by Halfway Inn. House on left just past clock tower.

Sarah & Dylan McLees Taylor
Market Street, Kingsand PL10 1NE

Tel	+44 (0)1752 823216
Email	info@westcroftguesthouse.co.uk
Web	www.westcroftguesthouse.co.uk

10% off stays of 2 or more nights.

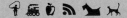

The Sun Inn

Extreme pleasure awaits those who book into The Sun. Not only is this ancient inn a delight to behold – thick stone walls, wood-burners, windows onto a cobbled passageway, beer pumps ready for action – but the town itself is dreamy, another jewel of the north. The inn backs onto St Mary's churchyard, where wild flowers prosper and bumble bees ply their trade. Potter across and find 'one of the loveliest views in England, and therefore the world' to quote Ruskin. Herons fish the river, lambs graze the fields, hills soar into a vast sky. Turner painted it in 1825. Back at The Sun, all manner of good things. Warm interiors, recently refurbished, come in elegant country style, keeping the feel of the past while dressing it up in smart clothes. You'll find old stone walls, boarded floors, cosy window seats, newspapers in a rack. Airy, uncluttered bedrooms upstairs are just as good; expect trim carpets, comfy beds, crisp white linen, super bathrooms. Finally, the food – homemade soups, mussels in white wine, loin of local lamb, apple and chocolate pudding. Don't miss it. *Minimum stay two nights at weekends.*

Price	£100–£150. Singles from £70.
Rooms	11: 8 doubles, 1 twin/double, 2 family rooms.
Meals	Lunch from £8.95. Dinner from £14.95. Not Monday lunch.
Closed	Never.
Directions	M6 junc. 36 then A65 for 5 miles following signs for Kirkby Lonsdale. In town centre.

Mark & Lucy Fuller
6 Market Street, Kirkby Lonsdale,
Carnforth LA6 2AU

Tel	+44 (0)15242 71965
Email	email@sun-inn.info
Web	www.sun-inn.info

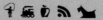

Number 43

The position here is fabulous: a vast sky, a pretty village, the Kent estuary spilling into Morcambe Bay. Huge views shoot off to the Lake District, where distant peaks take to the skies. You're at the end of the road, more likely to be disturbed by commuting birds than a car, so sit on the terrace and watch the train puff across the viaduct or follow a flock of geese as they sweep through the valley. As for Lesley's super-smart B&B, interiors shine after a total renovation. You get glossy books and great views in the sitting room, then an honesty bar in the dining room, where delicious communal breakfasts set you up for the day: freshly squeezed orange juice, baskets of patisserie, porridge with honey and sugar, the full Cumbrian works. Bedrooms vary in size, but all are elegant with warm colours, fabulous linen, excellent beds, sparkling bathrooms. Two have the view, one has a free-standing bath by the window. Platters of meat and cheese can be ordered at night, but there's a good pub in the village and a legendary fish and chip restaurant (BYO). The Lakes are close.

Price	£120–£135. Suites £175–£185.
Rooms	6: 1 twin/double, 3 doubles, 2 suites.
Meals	Lunch & dinner platters £14.95. Dinner £22.50, by arrangement, October–March. Pub in village.
Closed	Never.
Directions	A6 south from Kendal. Right at Milnthorpe, 4 miles to Arnside. Hotel on promenade.

Lesley Hornsby
43 The Promenade,
Arnside LA5 0AA
Tel +44 (0)1524 762761
Email lesley@no43.org.uk
Web www.no43.org.uk

Complimentary upgrade subject to availability. 10% off room rate Mon-Thurs, October-March.

Aynsome Manor Hotel

A small country house with a big heart. It may not be the grandest place in the book but the welcome is genuine, the peace is intoxicating and the value is unmistakable. Stand at the front and a long sweep across open meadows leads south to Cartmel and its priory, a view that has changed little in 800 years. The house, a mere pup by comparison, dates to 1512. Step in to find red armchairs, a grandfather clock and a coal fire in the hall. There's a small bar at the front and a cantilever staircase with cupola dome that sweeps you up to a first-floor drawing room where panelled windows frame the view. Downstairs you eat under an ornate tongue-and-groove ceiling with Georgian colours and old portraits on the walls. You get good country cooking, too, perhaps French onion soup, roast leg of Cumbrian lamb, rich chocolate mousse served with white chocolate sauce. Bedrooms are warm, cosy, simple, spotless, colourful. Some have views over the fields, one may be haunted, another has an avocado bathroom suite. Windermere and Coniston are close. The kippers with lemon at breakfast are a treat. *Minimum two nights at weekends.*

Price	£80–£126. Singles from £80. Half-board £75–£90 p.p.
Rooms	12: 5 doubles, 4 twins, 1 four-poster, 2 family rooms.
Meals	Packed lunches by arrangement £8.95. Dinner, 4 courses, £30.
Closed	25 & 26 December; January.
Directions	From M6 junc. 36 take A590 for Barrow. At top of Lindale Hill follow signs left to Cartmel. Hotel on right 3 miles from A590.
	Use your Sawday's Gift Card here.

Bottle of wine with dinner on first night.

Christopher & Andrea Varley
Aynsome Lane, Cartmel,
Grange-over-Sands LA11 6HH
Tel   +44 (0)15395 36653
Email   aynsomemanor@btconnect.com
Web   www.aynsomemanorhotel.co.uk

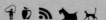

Masons Arms

A perfect Lakeland inn tucked away two miles inland from Windermere. You're on the side of a hill with huge views across lush fields to Scout Scar in the distance. In summer, all pub life decants onto a spectacular terrace – a sitting room in the sun – where window boxes and flowerbeds tumble with colour. The inn dates from the 16th century and is impossibly pretty. The bar is wonderfully traditional with roaring fires, flagged floors, wavy beams, a cosy snug... and a menu of 40 bottled beers to quench your thirst. Rustic elegance upstairs comes courtesy of stripped floors, country rugs and red walls in the first-floor dining room – so grab a window seat for fabulous views and order delicious food, anything from a sandwich to Cumbrian duck. Apartments (in the pub) and cottages (with bunk beds and sofabeds for children) are a steal; all come with fancy kitchens and breakfast hampers can be arranged. You get cool colours, comfy beds and Bang & Olufsen TVs. Best of all, most have a private terrace; order a meal in the restaurant and they'll bring it to you here. Brilliant. *Min. two nights at weekends.*

Price	£75–£140. Cottages £110–£165.
Rooms	5 + 2: 5 apartments. 2 cottages: 1 for 2-4, 1 for 2-6.
Meals	Self-catering. Breakfast hampers £15–£25. Lunch & dinner £5–£30.
Closed	Never.
Directions	M6 junc. 36; A590 west, then A592 north. 1st right after Fell Foot Park. Straight ahead for 2.5 miles. On left after sharp right-hand turn.

John & Diane Taylor
Cartmel Fell,
Grange-over-Sands LA11 6NW

Tel   +44 (0)15395 68486
Email   info@masonsarmsstrawberrybank.co.uk
Web   www.strawberrybank.com

 10% off standard room rate.

The Swan Hotel & Spa

This rather pretty hotel stands on the river Leven, a wide sweep of water that pours out of Windermere on its way south to Morecambe Bay. It's a fabulous spot and the Swan makes the most of it: a stone terrace runs along to an ancient packhorse bridge. The Swan was flooded in the great storm of 2009 and a recent refurbishment has breathed new life into old bones (this is a 17th-century monastic farmhouse). Inside, airy interiors have taken root. There are a couple of sitting rooms, open fires, the daily papers, a lively bar and a good restaurant to keep you going. There's also a spa: hard to miss as the swimming pool shimmers behind a wall of glass in reception. Treatment rooms, a sauna, a steam room and a gym all wait. Pretty bedrooms have the same crisp style: comfy beds, smart white linen, a wall of paper, a sofa if there's room. Those at the front have watery views, the family suite has a dolls house and a PlayStation. Back downstairs, dig into tasty food in the bar or brasserie, perhaps tiger prawn and chickpea broth, Chateaubriand steak with chunky chips, honeycomb cheesecake.

Price	£119-£270. Suites £209-£340.
Rooms	52: 30 doubles, 15 twins/doubles, 7 suites.
Meals	Lunch & dinner £5-£30.
Closed	Never.
Directions	M6 junc. 36, then A590 west. Into Newby Bridge. Over roundabout, then 1st right for hotel.

	Sarah Gibbs
	Newby Bridge LA12 8NB
Tel	+44 (0)15395 31681
Email	reservations@swanhotel.com
Web	www.swanhotel.com

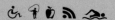

The Punch Bowl Inn

You're away from Windermere in a pretty village encircled by a tangle of lanes that defeat most tourists. This is a great spot, with views sweeping across a quilt of lush fields and a church that stands next door; bell ringers practise on Friday mornings, the odd bride ambles out in summer. Yet while the Punch Bowl sits in a sleepy village lost to the world, it is actually a seriously funky inn. Rescued from neglect and renovated in great style, it now sparkles with a brilliant mix of old and new. Outside, honeysuckle and roses ramble on stone walls; inside open fires keep you warm in winter. A clipped elegance runs throughout – Farrow & Ball colours, sofas in front of a wood-burner – while Chris Meredith's fabulous food waits in the airy restaurant, perhaps Lancashire cheese soufflé, pan-fried sea bass, bread and butter pudding. Super bedrooms come with beautiful linen, lovely fabrics, Roberts radios, gorgeous bathrooms. Four rooms have big valley views; the vast suite, with double baths, is matchless. There's a sun-trapping terrace, too, but don't miss the lakes and the hills.

Price	£95–£235. Suite £225–£305. Singles from £75.
Rooms	9: 5 doubles, 1 twin/double, 2 four-posters, 1 suite.
Meals	Lunch from £5. Dinner, 3 courses, £30–£35.
Closed	Never.
Directions	M6 junc. 36, then A590 for Newby Bridge. Right onto A5074, then right for Crosthwaite after 3 miles. Pub on southern flank of village.

Len van Limburg
Crosthwaite, Kendal LA8 8HR

Tel	+44 (0)15395 68237
Email	info@the-punchbowl.co.uk
Web	www.the-punchbowl.co.uk

Gilpin Hotel & Lake House

One of the loveliest places to stay in the country, simple as that. Staff are delightful, the house is a treasure trove, the food is heavenly. Run by two generations of the same family, Gilpin delivers at every turn. Clipped country-house elegance flows throughout: smouldering coals, Zoffany wallpaper, gilded mirrors, flowers everywhere. Afternoon tea, served wherever you want it, comes on silver trays, while the cellar is on display in an exceedingly groovy bar. You're in 20 acres of silence, so throw open doors and sit on the terrace surrounded by pots of colour or stroll through the garden for magnolias, cherry blossom and a fine copper beech as well as the odd pond. Bedrooms are divine with crisp white linen, exquisite fabrics, delicious art; nothing is left to chance. Over half the rooms open onto the garden and a mile away is the new Lake House with six stunning suites by a private lake. As for the food, expect the best, perhaps terrine of rabbit with toasted brioche, Cumbrian veal with a Parmesan crust, passion fruit soufflé with dark chocolate jelly. Unbeatable. *Minimum stay two nights at weekends.*

Price	Half-board £155–£290 p.p. Singles from £210.
Rooms	26: 8 doubles, 12 twins/doubles, 6 suites.
Meals	Lunch £10–£35. Dinner included; non-residents £58.
Closed	Never.
Directions	M6 junc 36, A591 north, then B5284 west for Bowness. On right after 5 miles.

Champagne afternoon tea on day of arrival.

John, Christine, Barnaby & Zoe Cunliffe
Crook Road, Windermere LA23 3NE
Tel   +44 (0)15394 88818
Email   hotel@gilpinlodge.co.uk
Web   www.gilpinlodge.co.uk

Miller Howe Hotel & Restaurant

The view is breathtaking, one of the best in the Lakes, a clean sweep over Windermere to the majestic Langdale Pikes. As for Miller Howe, it's just as good, an Edwardian country-house hotel made famous by TV chef John Tovey. These days a fine new look is emerging, all the result of a super refurbishment by passionate owners Helen and Martin Ainscough. Inside, new and old combine with ease. Contemporary art and beautiful fabrics blend seamlessly with period features, and the atmosphere is refreshingly relaxed. You can sink into a deep armchair by an open fire and soak up huge views of lake and mountain, then spin into the dining room where walls of glass open onto a dining terrace. Menus bristle with local food, perhaps Lancashire cheese soufflé, Cumbrian lamb, Yorkshire rhubarb crumble. Handsome bedrooms vary in size and style. All are individually designed with handmade fabrics, period furniture and posh TVs, while some have balconies for fabulous views. Cottage suites in the glorious garden offer sublime peace. Perfect whatever the weather. *Minimum stay two nights at weekends.*

Price	Half-board £105–£155 p.p.
Rooms	15: 7 twins/doubles, 5 doubles, 3 garden suites.
Meals	Lunch from £6.50. Sunday lunch £27.50. Dinner included; non-residents, £45.
Closed	Rarely.
Directions	From Kendal A591 to Windermere. Left at mini-r'bout onto A592 for Bowness; 0.25 miles on right.

Helen & Martin Ainscough
Rayrigg Road, Windermere LA23 1EY

Tel	+44 (0)15394 42536
Email	info@millerhowe.com
Web	www.millerhowe.com

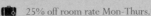 25% off room rate Mon-Thurs.

Linthwaite House Hotel & Restaurant

The view is magnificent – Windermere sparkling half a mile below, a chain of peaks rising beyond – so it's no great surprise to discover that the terrace acts as a *de facto* sitting room in summer. Linthwaite is a grand Lakeland country house run in informal style. Everything is a treat: wonderful bedrooms, gorgeous interiors, glorious food, attentive staff. The house dates from 1900 and is soundproofed by 15 acres of trim lawns, formal gardens and wild rhododendrons. Totter up through a bluebell wood to find a small lake surrounded by fields where you can fish, swim or retreat to a summer house and fall asleep in the sun. The house is no less alluring with logs piled high by the front door, fires smouldering, sofas waiting and a clipped colonial elegance in the conservatory sitting room. Sublime food is served in elegant dining rooms (one is decorated with nothing but mirrors), while gorgeous country-house bedrooms come in a contemporary uncluttered style. Those at the front have lake views, you can stargaze from the suite. Mountains wait, but you might just decide to stay put. *Minimum two nights at weekends.*

Champagne & afternoon tea.

Price	Half-board £126–£204 p.p. Suites £197–£308 p.p. Singles from £155.
Rooms	30: 22 doubles, 5 twins/doubles, 3 suites.
Meals	Lunch from £6.95. Dinner included; non-residents £52.
Closed	Rarely.
Directions	M6 junc. 36. Take A590 north, then A591 for Windermere. Left at roundabout onto B5284. Past golf course and hotel signed left after 1 mile.

Mike Bevans
Crook Road, Bowness-on-Windermere,
Windermere LA23 3JA

Tel	+44 (0)15394 88600
Email	stay@linthwaite.com
Web	www.linthwaite.com

Cedar Manor Hotel

A small country house on the edge of Windermere with good prices, pretty interiors and a footpath that leads down to the water, so potter off before breakfast and glimpse England's most famous lake before the crowds descend. The house, originally a 17th-century cottage, has grown over the years and was once home to a retired vicar, hence the gargoyle and ecclesiastic windows. Outside, an ancient cedar of Lebanon shades the lawn. Inside, warm colours and a cheery style are the order of the day. You'll find clumps of sofas, local art and the daily papers in the sitting room, then sparkling glass, cool colours and a big window overlooking the garden in the dining room. Bedrooms upstairs are halfway through an attractive refurbishment. Zoffany fabrics, Lloyd Loom wicker and flat-screen TVs are on the way in, as are DVD players, handmade furniture and excellent bathrooms. Good food downstairs is sensibly priced, perhaps crab cakes with beetroot purée, fillet of pork with wild mushrooms, then lavender panna cotta. All things Windermere are on your doorstep. *Minimum stay two nights at weekends.*

Price	£110-£140. Suite £160. Singles £80.
Rooms	10: 7 doubles, 1 twin, 2 suites.
Meals	Dinner, 3 courses, £30-£40.
Closed	12 December-23 January, but open for New Year.
Directions	From Windermere A591 east out of town for Kendal; hotel on right, next to church, before railway station.

Jonathan & Caroline Kaye
Ambleside Road,
Windermere LA23 1AX

Tel	+44 (0)15394 43192
Email	info@cedarmanor.co.uk
Web	www.cedarmanor.co.uk

 10% off room rate Mon-Thurs.

Jerichos

You'll be hard-pressed to find better value in Windermere. This is an attractive restaurant with rooms one street away from the middle of town. Chris and Jo had a small restaurant here, wanted something bigger, found this hotel, then spent a king's ransom doing it up. The results are excellent, but it's the way things are done that make it so special: this is a friendly, very personal place. Step inside to find airy interiors with stripped wooden floors, Victorian windows and a splash of colour on the walls. There's a residents' sitting room with a couple of baby chesterfields, then a super restaurant where candles flicker at night. So come for a good meal, perhaps English asparagus, local lamb, milk chocolate panna cotta with rum and raisin ice cream. Spotless bedrooms are very well priced. Those on the first floor have high ceilings, there are leather bedheads, comfy armchairs, fat white duvets and excellent bathrooms, most with fancy showers. Also: iPod docks, cool wallpapers, Lakeland art. The lake is a short stroll: a good way to round off breakfast. *Minimum stay two nights at weekends.*

Price	£70–£125. Singles from £40.
Rooms	10: 9 doubles, 1 single.
Meals	Dinner, 3 courses, £30–£40. Not Thursdays.
Closed	Last 2 weeks of Nov; 1st week of Dec; last 3 weeks of Jan.
Directions	A591 from Kendal to Windermere. Pass train station, don't turn left into town, rather next left 200 yards on. First right and on right after 500m.

Chris & Jo Blaydes
College Road, Windermere LA23 1BX
Tel   +44 (0)15394 42522
Email   info@jerichos.co.uk
Web   www.jerichos.co.uk

Holbeck Ghyll Country House Hotel

Holbeck's majestic setting is hard to beat, a sublime position on the side of the hill with huge views tumbling down to Lake Windermere. Acres of gardens abound, there are sweeping lawns, a tennis court and colour in abundance. The house was bought by Lord Lonsdale in 1888. Inside, super-smart country-house interiors reveal grand sitting rooms, golden panelling, roaring fires, rugs on wood floors. Wellington boots stand to attention at the front door, there are mullioned windows, fresh flowers everywhere and a sun terrace for al fresco meals in summer. Best of all is the restaurant – Michelin-starred for 11 years – serving ambrosial food, perhaps roasted scallops with spiced cauliflower, lion of venison with pumpkin purée, nougat glace with a passion fruit sorbet. Bedrooms come with an overdose of elegance. Most in the main house have lake views, while the Potter Suite has a hot tub on its terrace; Madison House and The Sheiling, a couple of cottages, are perfect for families. Wonderful staff know every guest by name. Sunsets are amazing. *Minimum stay two nights at weekends.*

Price	£189–£370. Suites & cottages £231–£490. Half-board £122.50–£285 p.p.
Rooms	23: 15 twins/doubles, 2 four-posters, 2 cottages, 4 suites.
Meals	Lunch from £24. Dinner £60. Tasting menu £78.
Closed	Rarely.
Directions	M6 junc. 36, A591 to Windermere. Continue towards Ambleside, past Brockhole Visitor Centre, then right towards Troutbeck (Holbeck Lane). Half a mile on left.

A glass of champagne and afternoon tea on arrival.

Andrew McPherson
Holbeck Lane, Windermere LA23 1LU

Tel	+44 (0)15394 32375
Email	stay@holbeckghyll.com
Web	www.holbeckghyll.com

Drunken Duck Inn

The Duck is a Lakeland institution, blissfully hidden away from the crowds. Afternoon tea can be taken in the garden, where lawns roll down to Black Tarn and Greek gods gaze upon jumping fish. You're up on the hill, cradled by woods and highland fell, with huge views from the terrace that shoot across to towering peaks. Roses ramble on the veranda, stone walls double as flowerbeds. As for the Duck, she may be old, but she sure is pretty, so step into a world of airy interiors: stripped floors in the beamed bar, where home-brewed ales are on tap; timber-framed walls in the popular restaurant for super food. Wander at will and find open fires, grandfather clocks, rugs on the floor, exquisite art. Bedrooms come in different shapes and sizes with colours courtesy of Farrow & Ball and peaty water straight off the fell. Rooms in the main house are snug in the eaves; those across the courtyard are seriously indulging. Some have private terraces, one comes with a balcony, several have walls of glass to frame the mighty mountains. Don't miss Duck Tarn for blue heron and brown trout.

Price	£95–£285. Singles from £71.25.
Rooms	17: 15 doubles, 2 twins.
Meals	Lunch from £5. Dinner, 3 courses, £30–£35.
Closed	Christmas Day.
Directions	West from Ambleside on A593, then left at Clappersgate for Hawkshead on B5286. After 2 miles turn right, signed. Up hill to inn.

Stephanie Barton
Barngates, Ambleside LA22 0NG

Tel	+44 (0)1539 436347
Email	info@drunkenduckinn.co.uk
Web	www.drunkenduckinn.co.uk

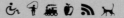

Lancrigg Vegetarian Country House Hotel

Lancrigg sits in 15 lush acres with fine views west to Silver Howe; only birdsong will disturb you. It was bought on behalf of Elizabeth Fletcher by her old friend William Wordsworth, costing £1,000 in 1840. Connections with a long list of eminent Victorians ensued; Walter Scott, Robbie Burns, Tennyson and Dickens all knew the house. Rob, a zoologist turned pioneering green hotelier, has been at the helm for 25 years. You sweep up the drive, pass trespassing sheep eating ancient rhododendrons, then find croquet on the lawn and Wellington boots at the front door. Inside, the style is homely rather than grand: squashy sofas in the yellow sitting room, original stripped floors in the panelled restaurant, Lakeland art on the walls. Colourful bedrooms are fairly simple and it's a little like staying with friends, though one has a four-poster with a claw-foot bath in the room and another opens to a small balcony. Back downstairs the vegetarian food is so good it'll please the most resolute carnivore: goat's cheese tart, Thai green curry, espresso mousse with coconut sorbet. The Lakes wait, dogs are welcome. *Min. two nights at weekends.*

Price	£130–£190. Singles from £65. Half-board from £95 p.p.
Rooms	11: 6 doubles, 2 twins/doubles, 3 four-posters.
Meals	Lunch from £4.95. Dinner, 3 courses, £25–£28
Closed	Never.
Directions	A591 north to Grasmere. In village left into Easedale opposite small green. Signed right after half a mile.

Rob Whittington
Easedale, Grasmere LA22 9QN

Tel	+44 (0)15394 35317
Email	info@lancrigg.co.uk
Web	www.lancrigg.co.uk

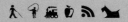

The Cottage in the Wood

Small is beautiful at the Cottage in the Wood, where delicious food, attractive prices and a winning position on the side of Whinlatter Pass have won a devoted band of happy guests. This 17th-century white-washed building sits on the side of a forested hill, with three-mile views from dining-room windows across the valley to Skiddaw; a terrace for summer meals looks the right way. Inside, chic simplicity is the virtue: an airy sitting room, a fire that burns on both sides, books and games to keep you amused, windows galore in the restaurant. Excellent food hits the spot, perhaps grilled langoustine with saffron aioli, local venison with beetroot risotto, chocolate tart with ginger ice cream. Airy bedrooms vary in size; some are big, some are small, all are spotless with honest prices. Expect crisp linen, trim carpets, flat-screen TVs and big white towels in super bathrooms (and a wet room in the garden room). Also, a drying room for walkers, secure storage for bicycles, a burn that tumbles down the hill and starry skies on clear nights. *Minimum stay two nights at weekends.*

Price	£110-£180. Singles from £88.
Rooms	10: 7 doubles, 2 twins/doubles, 1 suite.
Meals	Lunch from £6.50. Sunday lunch £25. Dinner £32-£44. Not Sunday night or Monday.
Closed	January.
Directions	M6 junc. 40, A66 west to Braithwaite, then B5292 for Lorton. On right after 2.5 miles (before visitor centre).

10% off room rate Mon-Thurs.

Kath & Liam Berney
Braithwaite, Keswick CA12 5TW
Tel   +44 (0)17687 78409
Email relax@thecottageinthewood.co.uk
Web   www.thecottageinthewood.co.uk

Swinside Lodge Hotel

Swinside is a dream – a small, intimate country house that sits in silence at the foot of Cat Bells. Fells rise, spirits soar, and Derwent Water, Queen of the Lakes, is a short stroll through the woods. Kath and Mike came back from France to take up the reigns of this ever-popular hotel and they haven't stopped; sash windows have been replaced, bedrooms have been given a makeover, fancy bathrooms are now de rigueur. Downstairs, you'll find fresh flowers and comfy sofas in the yellow drawing room, shelves of books and a jukebox in the sitting room, red walls and gilt-framed mirrors in the airy dining room, where windows frame views of Skiddaw. Super food waits in the restaurant, exactly what you want after a day on the fells – tasty fishcakes, local lamb, chocolate mousse. Upstairs, a new regime is taking shape in the bedrooms with warm colours, golden throws and padded window seats spreading a cool country elegance wherever they go. Outside, a host of characters visit the garden: a woodpecker, red squirrels, roe deer. Wonderful. *Children over 12 welcome. Minimum stay two nights at weekends in high season.*

Price	Half-board £94–£144 p.p.
Rooms	7: 5 doubles, 2 twins.
Meals	Dinner included; non-residents £45. Packed lunches £8.50.
Closed	Christmas.
Directions	M6 junc. 40. A66 west past Keswick, over r'bout, then 2nd left for Portinscale & Grange. Follow signs to Grange for 2 miles. House signed on right.

	Mike & Kathy Bilton
	Newlands, Keswick CA12 5UE
Tel	+44 (0)17687 72948
Email	info@swinsidelodge-hotel.co.uk
Web	www.swinsidelodge-hotel.co.uk

10% off room rate Mon-Thurs for stays of 3 nights or more.

The Pheasant

A 15th-century coaching inn with Sale Fell and Wythop Woods rising behind. A glorious English garden looks the right way, so grab a deckchair and settle in for an early evening drink; heaven on a good day. Interiors are no less beautiful. This is an extremely comfortable country-house inn with open fires in elegant sitting rooms and a fabulous bar, a treasured relic of times past; a couple of Thompson sketches hang on the wall (he exchanged them for drink). Cosseting bedrooms, warm in yellow, come with pretty pine beds, crisp linen, Roberts radios and robes in spotless bathrooms. Most are in the main house; two in a nearby garden lodge are dog-friendly. There's lots to do: Skiddaw to be scaled, and Bassenthwaite, the only lake in the Lake District, close. So explore by day, then return for an excellent dinner. You eat either in the elegant bistro at the front (period colours, oak flooring) or the airy dining room at the back (fresh flowers, big art). Wherever you go, the food is delicious, perhaps peat-smoked salmon, saddle of Lakeland lamb, Irish whiskey crème brûlée. A treat. *Min. stay two nights at weekends.*

Price	£150–£210. Singles from £90.
Rooms	15: 8 twins/doubles, 6 doubles, 1 single.
Meals	Bistro lunch & dinner £5–£30. Restaurant: dinner, 3 courses, £35; à la carte £40–£50.
Closed	Christmas Day.
Directions	From Keswick A66 north-west for 6 miles. Hotel on left, signed.

Matthew Wylie
Bassenthwaite Lake,
Cockermouth CA13 9YE

Tel	+44 (0)17687 76234
Email	info@the-pheasant.co.uk
Web	www.the-pheasant.co.uk

Overwater Hall

If you want to escape the tourist trail, this is the place to do it. Overwater Hall sits in blistering country, lost in the hills above Bassenthwaite Lake. You drop down a tiny lane only to find this crenellated house wrapped up in 18 acres of woodland and pasture. Banks of daffodils erupt in spring, deer and red squirrel visit frequently, views to the front shoot up Latrigg Hill (a 40-minute walk to the top). Inside, a warmly traditional country house waits. The daily papers lie on a grand piano, there's vintage wallpaper, a snug bar, a double-aspect drawing room in yellow. Fires burn, a grandfather clock chimes, French windows open onto a balustraded terrace, good views come as standard. Bedrooms are full of comfort and colour. One on the ground floor opens onto a terrace, two upstairs have beautiful bay windows. All come with bowls of fruit, crisp white linen and super bathrooms. As for the food, expect a four-course feast for dinner, perhaps pan-roasted quail with thyme and orange, grilled king prawns with lime and ginger, Cumbrian lamb with garlic mash, raspberry crème brûlée. Skiddaw is close.

Ethical Collection: Environment; Community; Food. See page 386 for details

Price	Half-board £100–£115 p.p.
Rooms	11: 7 doubles, 3 twin doubles, 1 four-poster.
Meals	Light lunches from £5. Dinner included; non-residents, 4 courses, £45.
Closed	First two weeks in January.
Directions	A591 north from Keswick for 7 miles, then right at the Castle Inn, signed Uldale and Ireby. Hotel signed right after 2 miles at sharp left-hand bend.

Adrian & Angela Hyde & Stephen Bore
Ireby, Wigton CA7 1HH
Tel   +44 (0)17687 76566
Email   welcome@overwaterhall.co.uk
Web   www.overwaterhall.co.uk

Bottle of wine with dinner on first night.

Lovelady Shield

Not much happens in the High Pennines, which is a very good reason to come. As for Lovelady, it sits in the middle of nowhere, sheltered by Alston Moor, with sheep bleating in the fields and the river rushing past. Inside, you find a smart, friendly hotel that comes in warm country colours. Much has been refurbished in the last few years. There are fine sofas in the sitting room, a cosy bar that opens onto the terrace, an airy restaurant for super food, a garden for croquet in summer. Bedrooms have an uncluttered style: crisp linen, Vi-Spring beds, excellent bathrooms (some compact), beautiful views. Bigger rooms have sofas, one has a four-poster, a couple are snug in the eaves. The longer you stay, the less you pay, while Sunday nights are a steal. By day, you spin through pristine country – up to Hadrian's Wall, down to the Dales, east to Durham, west to the Lakes. Whatever you do, come back for some fabulous food, perhaps white crab with lime mayonnaise, chickpea, chilli and coriander soup, Gressingham duck glazed with ginger, dark chocolate soufflé with piña colada sorbet. The walking is divine, so bring your boots.

Price	£100–£170. Cottages £380–£900 per week.
Rooms	12 + 3: 12 twins/doubles. 3 cottages for 4–6.
Meals	Lunch from £4.50. Sunday lunch £24.50. Dinner, 4 courses, £46.50.
Closed	Never.
Directions	From Alston A689 east for 2 miles. House on left at junction of B6294.

10% off room rate.

Peter & Marie Haynes
Nenthead Road,
Alston CA9 3LF

Tel	+44 (0)1434 381203
Email	enquiries@lovelady.co.uk
Web	www.lovelady.co.uk

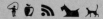

The Tufton Arms

Appleby is an ancient market town, one of the loveliest in the north. It has a fine Norman castle, a Grade II listed high street and a cricket pitch that overlooks the river. This Victorian coaching inn stands in the middle of it all, a hub for the local community. It's a mildly eccentric place, one that mixes traditional décor (almost extinct) with contemporary elegance (a beautiful conquest). Downstairs, you find a smart drawing room, a bar at the front and an attractive dining room for good country fare, while outside a small café in the courtyard/car park comes with a stone terrace. Back inside, bedrooms are the big surprise. All but two rooms have been recently refurbished. Some are hugely grand with half-testers and chandeliers; some are smaller with padded headboards and warm colours; others fall between the two. All have beds dressed in crisp white linen and fluffy white robes in excellent bathrooms. As for Appleby, follow your nose and you won't find a single high street name. Further afield you can play golf, fish the Eden or potter through glorious country.

Price	£130–£205. Singles from £77. Half-board from £87.50 p.p.
Rooms	22: 14 twins/doubles, 3 suites, 5 singles.
Meals	Bar meals from £3.95. Sunday lunch from £16.95. Dinner, 3 courses, £28–£35.
Closed	25 & 26 December.
Directions	M6 junc. 38, then north to Appleby on B6260. On high street.

Nigel Milsom
Market Square,
Appleby-in-Westmorland CA16 6XA

Tel	+44 (0)17683 51593
Email	info@tuftonarmshotel.co.uk
Web	www.tuftonarmshotel.co.uk

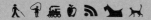 25% off room rate Mon-Thurs.

The Black Swan

This fabulous small hotel is hard to fault. Bang in the middle of a pretty village surrounded by blistering country it's all things to all men: a smart restaurant, a lively bar, a village shop; they even hold a music festival here in September. A stream runs through an enormous garden, where you can eat in good weather; free-range hens live in one corner. Inside, warm country interiors fit the mood perfectly. You get fresh flowers, tartan carpets, games on the piano, books galore. There's a locals' bar for local ales and a sitting-room bar with an open fire, but the hub of the hotel is the bar in the middle, where village life gathers. You can eat wherever you want, including the airy restaurant at the front where you dig into delicious country food (the meat is from the fields around you), perhaps smoked trout terrine, steak and venison casserole, lemon and ginger syllabub. Excellent bedrooms are fantastic for the money. Expect pretty colours, beautiful linen, smart furniture, super bathrooms. The Lakes and Dales are close, children and dogs are welcome. A very happy place.

Ethical Collection: Community; Food. See page 386 for details

10% off room rate Mon-Thurs.
Free pick-up from local bus/train
station. Late checkout (12pm).

Price	£75-£100. Suites £115-£125. Singles £50.
Rooms	14: 11 twins/doubles, 2 suites, 1 single.
Meals	Lunch from £3.95. Dinner, 3 courses, £20-£30.
Closed	Christmas Day.
Directions	Off A685 between M6 junc. 38 & A66 at Brough.

Alan & Louise Dinnes
Ravenstonedale,
Kirkby Stephen CA17 4NG
Tel   +44 (0)15396 23204
Email   enquiries@blackswanhotel.com
Web   www.blackswanhotel.com

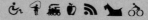

Augill Castle

A folly castle built in 1841. Outside, five acres of lush gardens are patrolled by a family of free-range hens, whose eggs are served at breakfast each morning. Inside, grand interiors come properly furnished: chesterfield sofas in a vast hall, a grand piano in the music room, an honesty bar in the drawing room, ribbed ceilings, open fires, fine arched windows. The house is run informally: no uniforms, no rules, just Wendy, Simon and their staff to ply you with delicious food, big pillows, massive tubs. A stained-glass window on the staircase shines under a vaulted ceiling, then come wonderful country-house bedrooms. One is enormous, another has a wardrobe in the turret. You'll find beautiful beds, cavernous bathrooms, lattice windows and vintage luggage. All rooms have the view, there are sofas if there's room, interesting art, antique wood, one huge dining table. Perfect for house parties and small weddings. The aptly named Eden Valley waits outside, while the Dales, the Lakes and the High Pennines are all close, making this a great base from which to explore the North.

Ethical Collection: Environment; Community; Food. See page 386 for details

Price	£160–£180. Family suites £240. Singles from £80.
Rooms	14: 6 doubles, 4 twins/doubles, 4 family suites.
Meals	Dinner, 4 courses, £40 (Fri & Sat). Midweek supper, 2 courses, £20. Afternoon tea £18. Booking essential.
Closed	Never.
Directions	M6 junc. 38; A685 through Kirkby Stephen. Just before Brough right for South Stainmore; signed on left after 1 mile. Kirkby Stephen railway station 3 miles.

	Simon & Wendy Bennett South Stainmore, Kirkby Stephen CA17 4DE
Tel	+44 (0)17683 41937
Email	enquiries@stayinacastle.com
Web	www.stayinacastle.com

 Late checkout (12pm).

The George

Charlotte Brontë set part of *Jane Eyre* here. She called the village Morton, referred to this hotel as The Feathers and stole the name of an old landlord for her heroine. These days a copy of her famous novel sits on the shelves of 'the smallest library in the world'; it occupies a turret in the sitting room. The big turret, equally well employed, is now the bar. The George, a 500-year-old ale house, has grown in stature over time and a smart refurbishment has recently propelled it into the 21st century. As a result, wood floors, stone walls and heavy beams are now joined by leather armchairs, fancy wallpaper and Lloyd Loom furniture. It's an unexpected marriage that works exceedingly well, making this small hotel quite a find in the middle of the Peak District. Airy bedrooms are great value for money. They come in warm colours with spotless bathrooms and excellent beds dressed in crisp linen; those at the back are quietest. As for the food, a good meal waits in the dining room, so scale Arbor Low, then return to wild mushroom soup, loin of venison, white chocolate soufflé.

Price	£132–£188. Singles from £94.
Rooms	22: 15 doubles, 4 twins/doubles, 3 singles.
Meals	Lunch from £4.75. Dinner, 3 courses, about £36.50.
Closed	Never.
Directions	In village at junction of A6187 and B6001, 10 miles west of M1 at Sheffield.

Late checkout (12pm).

Philip Joseph
Main Road, Hathersage,
Hope Valley S32 1BB
Tel   +44 (0)1433 650436
Email   info@george-hotel.net
Web   www.george-hotel.net

Cavendish Hotel

A 20-minute stroll across open fields sweeps you off to Chatsworth House, which sits sublimely between river and hill, a crown jewel of British architecture. Those who potter up find an imperious collection of jaw-dropping art and one of England's finest gardens. Those who amble back to the Cavendish find a welcoming estate hotel that comes in smart country style: sofas in front of a roaring fire, afternoon tea on the lawn in summer, views from the garden of fine open country, art from the 'big house' hanging on the walls. Super bedrooms come in different shapes and sizes, some with pretty florals and golden carpets, others with period colours and enormous beds. None are small, all but one have fine country views and some are seriously swanky. Back downstairs there's a stone-flagged conservatory for breakfast, a country-house sitting room for an afternoon snooze and a colourful dining room for super food, perhaps terrine of local pheasant, Chatsworth beef, then warm pear Bakewell tart with stilton ice cream. Outside, the glorious Peak District waits for walkers, so bring your boots.

Price	£169–£219. Suite £280. Singles from £133.
Rooms	24: 20 doubles, 2 twins, 1 family room, 1 suite.
Meals	Continental breakfast £9.50, full English £18.50. Lunch from £5.95. Dinner £30–£40.
Closed	Never.
Directions	M1 junc. 29, A617 to Chesterfield, A619 to Baslow. On left in village.

Late checkout (12pm).

Philip Joseph
Church Lane, Baslow,
Bakewell DE45 1SP

Tel   +44 (0)1246 582311
Email   info@cavendish-hotel.net
Web   www.cavendish-hotel.net

The Peacock at Rowsley

The Peacock dates to 1652. It was once the dower house to Haddon Hall and stands by the bridge in the middle of the village. It opened as a coaching inn 200 years ago and its lawns run down to the river Derwent. Fishermen come to try their hand, but those who want to walk can follow the river up to Chatsworth. Later, sweep back over gentle hills and return for a night at this rather swish hotel. Old and new mix harmoniously inside. Imagine mullioned windows, hessian rugs, aristocratic art, then striking colours that give a contemporary feel. French windows in the restaurant open onto a pot-festooned terrace in summer, while the fire in the bar smoulders all year. Rooms come in different shapes and sizes, all with a surfeit of style: crisp linen, good beds, Farrow & Ball colours, the odd antique. Serious food waits in the restaurant, perhaps squab pigeon with chocolate jelly, Derbyshire rib-eye with Madeira sauce, ginger crème brûlée with pear sorbet. Three circular walks start from the front door, so you can walk off any excess in the hills that surround you. *Minimum stay two nights at weekends.*

Price	£155–£257.50. Singles from £85. Half-board from £107.50 p.p.
Rooms	16: 6 doubles, 7 twins, 1 four-poster, 2 singles.
Meals	Breakfast buffet included; cooked dishes £3.95–£7.25. Lunch from £4.25. Dinner, 3 courses, about £52.50. Sunday lunch £20.50–£27.50.
Closed	Rarely.
Directions	A6 north through Matlock, then to Rowsley. On right in village.

10% off room rate Mon-Thurs. Late checkout (12pm). One-night stays on Saturdays.

Jenni MacKenzie
Bakewell Road, Rowsley,
Matlock DE4 2EB

Tel   +44 (0)1629 733518
Email   reception@thepeacockatrowsley.com
Web   www.thepeacockatrowsley.com

Masons Arms

Lose yourself in tiny lanes, follow them down towards the sea, pass the Norman church, roll up at the Masons Arms. It stands in a village half a mile back from the pebble beach surrounded by glorious country, with a stone terrace at the front from which to gaze upon lush hills. It dates back to 1350 – a cider house turned country pub – and the men who cut the stone for Exeter Cathedral drank here, hence the name. Inside, simple, authentic interiors are just the thing: timber frames, low beamed ceilings, pine cladding, whitewashed walls and a roaring fire over which the spit roast is cooked on Sundays. Some bedrooms are above the inn, others are behind on the hill. Those in the pub are small but cosy (warm yellows, check fabrics, leather bedheads, super bathrooms); those behind are bigger, quieter and more traditional; they overlook a garden and share a private terrace with valley views that tumble down to the sea. Footpaths lead out – over hills, along the coast – so follow your nose, then return for super food. seared scallops, lamb cutlets, saffron and honey crème brûlée.

Price	£70–£140. Suites £150–£175.
Rooms	21: 8 doubles, 6 twins/doubles, 4 four-posters, 1 family room, 2 four-poster suites.
Meals	Lunch from £7.50. Bar meals from £9.95. Dinner, 3 courses, £20–£25. Sunday lunch from £9.95.
Closed	Never.
Directions	Branscombe is signed off A3052 between Seaton & Sidmouth. In village.

Paul Couldwell
Branscombe,
Seaton EX12 3DJ

Tel	+44 (0)1297 680300
Email	reception@masonsarms.co.uk
Web	www.masonsarms.co.uk

10% off room rate.

Combe House Devon

Combe is immaculate, an ancient house on a huge estate, the full aristocratic works. You spin up a long drive, pass Arabian horses running wild in the distance, then skip through the front door and enter a place of architectural splendour. A fire roars in the magnificent hall, the muralled dining room gives huge views, the sitting room/bar in racing green opens onto the croquet lawn. Best of all is the way things are done: the feel is more home than hotel and you may mistake yourself for lord of the manor – a battalion of household staff to attend to your every whim. Wander around and see 600-year old flagstones, original William Morris wallpaper, Victorian kitchen gardens that provide much for the table, beehives for breakfast honey. Rooms are fabulous, expect the best: stately fabrics, wonderful beds, gorgeous bathrooms, outstanding views. The vast suite, once the laundry press, is now the stuff of fashion shoots and comes with an enormous copper bath. There are 3,500 acres to explore and fabulous food to keep you going, but it's Ruth and Ken who win the prize; they just know how to do it. *Min. two nights at weekends.*

Price	£199–£364. Singles from £169. Suites £399–£419. Half-board from £148.50 p.p. Cottage £399–£419 (B&B per night).
Rooms	15 + 1: 10 twins/doubles, 1 four-poster, 4 suites. Self-catering cottage for 2.
Meals	Lunch £27–£32. Dinner £49; tasting menu, £69, on request.
Closed	Rarely.
Directions	M5 junc. 29, then A30 to Honiton. Here, leave A30 for Heathpark and Gittisham. Hotel signed in village.

Bottle of wine in your room.

Ruth & Ken Hunt
Gittisham, Honiton EX14 3AD
Tel   +44 (0)1404 540400
Email   stay@combehousedevon.com
Web   www.combehousedevon.com

The Lamb Inn

This 16th-century inn is nothing short of perfect, a proper local in the old tradition with gorgeous rooms and the odd touch of scruffiness to add authenticity to earthy bones. It stands on a cobbled walkway in a village lost down Devon's tiny lanes, and those lucky enough to chance upon it will leave reluctantly. Outside, all manner of greenery covers its stone walls; inside there are beams, but they are not sandblasted, red carpets with a little swirl, sofas in front of an open fire and rough-hewn oak panels painted black. Boarded menus trumpet wonderfully priced food – carrot and orange soup, whole baked trout with almond butter, an irresistible tarte tatin. There's a cobbled terrace, a walled garden, an occasional cinema, an open mic night… and a back bar, where four ales are hand-pumped. Upstairs, six marvellous bedrooms elate. One is large with a bath and a wood-burner in the room, but all are lovely with super-smart power showers, sash windows that give village views, hi-fis, flat-screen TVs, good linen and comfy beds. Dartmoor waits but you may well linger. There's Tiny, the guard dog, too.

Price	£65–£105.
Rooms	6: 5 doubles, 1 twin/double.
Meals	Lunch from £8. Dinner, 3 courses, £15–£25.
Closed	Rarely.
Directions	A377 north from Exeter. 1st right in Crediton, left, signed Sandford. 1 mile up & in village.

Mark Hildyard & Katharine Lightfoot
Sandford, Crediton EX17 4LW

Tel	+44 (0)1363 773676
Email	thelambinn@gmail.com
Web	www.lambinnsandford.co.uk

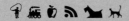

Heasley House

The sort of place you chance upon, only to return again and again. Everything here is lovely. It's a beautiful house in a sleepy village lost in a wild Exmoor valley, with stylish interiors, delicious food and very attractive prices. Inside, Paul and Jan have overseen a total refurbishment, recovering the grandness of a Georgian mine captain's house, then dressing it up in contemporary clothes. You find stripped boards, stone walls, timber frames, a frieze on the fireplace. Harmonious colours run throughout, fires burn in the sitting rooms, there is original art, a fancy bar and fresh flowers everywhere. Airy bedrooms are more than comfy with big beds, good linen and lovely bathrooms. Those at the front have country views, those in the eaves have beams. All have flat-screen TVs, DVD players, bathrobes and armchairs. Spin down to the restaurant for a feast of local Devon produce, perhaps fennel soup with smoked salmon, Exmoor lamb with puy lentils, rhubarb and orange crumble with clotted cream. Paths lead out, so follow the river into the woods or head north for cliffs at the coast. Brilliant – and so hospitable.

Price	£150. Suite £170. Singles from £115.
Rooms	7: 6 twins/doubles, 1 suite.
Meals	Dinner £26-£32.
Closed	Christmas Day, Boxing Day & February.
Directions	M5 junc. 27, A361 for Barnstaple. After South Molton right for North Molton, then left for Heasley Mill.

Paul & Jan Gambrill
Heasley Mill,
South Molton EX36 3LE
Tel   +44 (0)1598 740213
Email   enquiries@heasley-house.co.uk
Web   www.heasley-house.co.uk

The Old Rectory Hotel Exmoor

The coastal road from Lynton is a great way in, a rollercoaster lane that sweeps though woods clinging to the hill with the sea below. Wash up at the Old Rectory and find a warmly stylish hotel that must qualify as one of the quietest in England. Three acres of matured gardens wrap around you, only birdsong disturbs you, though Exmoor deer occasionally come to drink from the pond. Inside, Huw and Sam, corporate escapees who have taken to the hills, have put their elegant mark on the place: uncluttered interiors, Farrow & Ball colours and a revamp of the marvellous conservatory, where a 200-year old vine provides grapes for the cheese board. There are books, an open fire in the snug sitting room and wonderful bedrooms scattered about with big beds, crisp linen, cool colours and flat-screen TVs; one has a balcony, most have super-cool bathrooms. Spin into the restaurant for an excellent meal, perhaps local asparagus, Exmoor pork, bread and butter pudding. Afternoon tea is on the house and served in the garden in good weather. *Minimum stay two nights at weekends in high season.*

Price	£155. Suites £185. Half-board £95-£115. p.p.
Rooms	10: 3 doubles, 4 twins/doubles, 3 suites.
Meals	Dinner, 4 courses, £36.
Closed	November-March.
Directions	M5 junc. 27, A361 to South Molton, then A399 north. Right at Blackmore Gate onto A39 for Lynton. Left after 3 miles, signed Martinhoe. In village, next to church.

	Huw Rees & Sam Prosser
	Martinhoe, Parracombe,
	Barnstaple EX31 4QT
Tel	+44 (0)1598 763368
Email	info@oldrectoryhotel.co.uk
Web	www.oldrectoryhotel.co.uk

Bottle of wine with dinner on first night for stays of 2 or more nights.

Northcote Manor

A divine retreat at the top of a hill built on the site of a 15th-century monastery. Those who want peace in glorious country will be in heaven. You wind up a one-mile drive, through a wood that bursts with colour in spring, then emerge onto a plateau of lush rolling hills. The house is as lovely as the land that surrounds it, built of local stone, wisteria wanders along the walls. There are sweeping lawns, a walled garden and a tennis court with country views. Inside, fires roar: in the airy hall, which doubles as the bar; in the country-house drawing room that floods with light; in the sitting room where you gather for pre-dinner drinks. Super food waits in a lovely dining room, steps lead down to a pretty conservatory, and doors open onto a gravelled terrace for summer breakfasts and exquisite views. Bedrooms are no less appealing, all recently refurbished in contemporary country-house style. Expect padded bedheads, mahogany dressers, flat-screen TVs, silky throws. Lovely walks start from the front door; Exmoor and North Devon's coasts are fabulously close. *'The Sanctuary', a new licensed venue, is available for weddings.*

Price	£160–£215. Suites £260. Singles £110. Half-board (min. 2 nights) from £115 p.p. per night.
Rooms	11: 4 doubles, 2 twins/doubles, 1 four-poster, 4 suites.
Meals	Lunch from £5.75. Dinner £42.
Closed	Rarely.
Directions	M5 junc. 27, A361 to S. Molton. Fork left onto B3227; left on A377 for Exeter. Entrance 4.1 miles on right, signed.
	Use your Sawday's Gift Card here.

Glass of of champagne before dinner.

Cheryl King
Burrington,
Umberleigh EX37 9LZ

Tel +44 (0)1769 560501
Email rest@northcotemanor.co.uk
Web www.northcotemanor.co.uk

Percy's Country Hotel

There are days in summer when all the food you eat at dinner has come from the land that surrounds you. Tony and Tina came west not merely to cook but to grow their own; now even the meat is home-reared. Percy's – a restaurant with rooms on an organic farm – teems with life: pigs roam freely through 60 acres of woodland, Jacob sheep graze open pasture, ducks and chickens supply the tastiest eggs. A kitchen garden is planted seasonally but much is harvested wild from the woods, a natural larder of mushrooms, juniper, crab apples and elderflower. Tina conjures up soups and salads, terrines and sausages, curing her own bacon and delicious hams: a meal at Percy's is no ordinary event. Bedrooms in the converted granary are lovely (super-comfortable beds, chic leather sofas, spotless bathrooms, flat-screen TVs), but Percy's is about more than just a bed. Grab a pair of wellies and lose yourself in the estate, or hitch a lift and lend a hand with the morning feed. Woodpeckers and kingfishers, deer and badger, old hedgerows, wild flowers, a huge sky wait. And a resident otter, who shares his pond with snow geese.

Price	From £155.
Rooms	7: 6 twins/doubles, 1 suite.
Meals	Dinner, 3 courses, £40.
Closed	Never.
Directions	From Okehampton A3079 for Metherell Cross. After 8.3 miles, left. Hotel on left after 6.5 miles.

	Tina & Tony Bricknell-Webb
	Coombeshead Estate, Virginstow,
	Beaworthy EX21 5EA
Tel	+44 (0)1409 211236
Email	info@percys.co.uk
Web	www.percys.co.uk

Book 3 days half-board, get a free room on the fourth night.

Tor Cottage

At the end of the track, a blissful valley lost to the world. This is an indulging hideaway, wrapped up in 28 acres of majestic country, and those who like to be pampered in peace will find just that. Hills rise, cows sleep, streams run, birds sing. Bridle paths lead onto the hill and wild flowers carpet a hay meadow, but you might not stray too far as big rooms in converted outbuildings are the lap of rustic luxury. Each comes with a wood-burner and private terrace: one is straight out of *House and Garden*, another is whitewashed with ceilings open to the rafters. Best of all is the cabin in its own valley — a wonderland in the woods — with hammocks hanging in the trees, a stream passing below, the odd deer pottering past in the forest. Breakfast is served in the conservatory, but you can sit on the terrace in good weather and scoff homemade muesli, local sausages and farm-fresh eggs; and if you get peckish during the day, wash down smoked salmon sandwiches with a glass of sangria while sunbathing by the pool. Maureen spoils you rotten, her staff couldn't be nicer. A wonderful place. *Minimum stay two nights.*

Price	£150. Singles £98. Cabin £155.
Rooms	5: 2 doubles, 1 twin/double, 1 suite, 1 woodland cabin for 2.
Meals	Picnic platters £16. Pubs/restaurants 3 miles.
Closed	Mid-December to end of January.
Directions	In Chillaton keep pub & PO on left, up hill towards Tavistock. After 300 yards right down bridleway (ignore No Access signs).

Cornish pasties & Devonshire chutney on arrival.

	Maureen Rowlatt
	Chillaton, Lifton PL16 0JE
Tel	+44 (0)1822 860248
Email	info@torcottage.co.uk
Web	www.torcottage.co.uk

Browns Hotel

This is a popular spot. The Romans came first and left a well: you can stand on a sheet of glass in the conservatory and peer into it. Then came the Benedictines, who built an abbey: old carved stones are on show in the bar. If tradition holds they'll find Roberts radios and leather sofas when they rebuild in 200 years. The house goes back to 1700 and was Tavistock's first coaching inn. It's still the best place to stay in town with a lively bar, wood floors in the restaurant and a stone-flagged conservatory for delicious breakfasts. You get armchairs in front of the fire, and Lloyd Loom wicker out in the courtyard. Clutter-free bedrooms have a clipped elegance: Farrow & Ball colours, latticed windows, luxurious linen, comforting bathrobes. Some in the coach house are huge, with cathedral ceilings. You dine under beams on serious food, perhaps potted rabbit with pea mousse and hazelnuts, Newlyn hake with black olives and anchovy, passion fruit jelly with coconut sorbet. Tavistock, an old market town, is famous for its October goose fair. Don't miss Dartmoor for uplifting walks.

Price	£109–£219. Suite £259. Singles from £79.
Rooms	29: 16 doubles, 3 twins, 3 singles, 1 four-poster, 6 family rooms.
Meals	Continental breakfast included; cooked dishes £6.95–£12.50. Lunch from £9. Dinner £34–£39.50. Tasting menu, 5 courses, £59.
Closed	Never.
Directions	Leave A386 for Tavistock. Right at statue for town centre. Left at T-junction, them immed. left into West Street. Hotel on right.

Helena King & Phil Biggin
80 West Street, Tavistock PL19 8AQ

Tel	+44 (0)1822 618686
Email	enquiries@brownsdevon.co.uk
Web	www.brownsdevon.co.uk

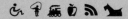 10% off stays of 2 or more nights.

The Horn of Plenty

This country-house hotel has been thrilling guests for 40 years and it doesn't take long to work out why; the view, the food, the staff and the rooms: all deliver in spades. The house goes back to 1860 and was built for the captain of the mines, who could peer down the valley and check his men were at work; these days it's the Tamar snaking through the hills below that catches the eye. Inside you find the essence of graceful simplicity: stripped floors, gilt mirrors, exquisite art and flowers everywhere. Bedrooms are just as good. Some have terraces that look down to the river, others come in country-house style with vast beds, old armoires, shimmering throws and rugs on stripped floors; bathrooms are predictably divine. As for the food, well, it's the big draw, so expect to eat well, perhaps Falmouth Bay scallops with a carrot purée, Devonshire lamb with a Madeira sauce, then nougat parfait with caramelised pineapple and a coconut sorbet. Best of all are the staff, who couldn't be more helpful. Tavistock, Dartmoor and The Eden Project are all within striking distance.

Price	£95–£295. Singles from £85. Half-board from £82.50 p.p.
Rooms	10 twins/doubles.
Meals	Lunch £19-50–£24.50. Dinner, 3 courses, £49.50.
Closed	Never.
Directions	West from Tavistock on A390 following signs to Callington. Right after 3 miles at Gulworthy Cross. Signed left after 0.75 miles.

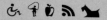 10% off room rate Mon-Thurs.

Julie Leivers & Damien Pease
Gulworthy,
Tavistock PL19 8JD
Tel   +44 (0)1822 832528
Email   enquiries@thehornofplenty.co.uk
Web   www.thehornofplenty.co.uk

Plantation House

Magdalena's eye for interior design has turned this old rectory into a small-scale pleasure dome. Add Richard's ambrosial cooking to the mix and you have an irresistible small hotel that shines from top to toe. Fine Georgian windows frame sublime views of hill and forest, flooding the house with light. An effortless style runs throughout: Lloyd Loom furniture and an open fire in the sitting room/bar; vibrant art and delicious food in Richard's restaurant. Bedrooms are equally lovely. All come with gorgeous travertine marble bathrooms, super-comfy beds, crisp white linen and cool contemporary colours. Two are huge, you get padded bedheads, sound systems and great views. Supper is the main event, so spin down for something heavenly, perhaps seared scallops cooked with champagne, roast duckling in a calvados sauce, a plate of west country cheeses, then caramelised lemon tart with Seville orange ice cream; breakfast is just as good. The river Erme passes across the road; follow it down to the sea and discover Wonwell Beach, one of Devon's best-kept secrets.

Price	£115–£175. Suite £240. Singles from £69.
Rooms	8: 6 doubles, 1 single, 1 suite.
Meals	Dinner, 5 courses, £39.
Closed	Never.
Directions	A38, then A3121 for Ermington. In village on western fringe.

Richard & Magdalena Hendey
Totnes Road, Ermington,
Ivybridge PL21 9NS

Tel	+44 (0)1548 831100
Email	info@plantationhousehotel.co.uk
Web	www.plantationhousehotel.co.uk

 10% off stays of 2 or more nights.

The Henley Hotel

A small house above the sea with fabulous views, super bedrooms and some of the loveliest food in Devon. Despite such credentials it's Martyn and Petra who shine most brightly, and their kind, generous approach makes this a memorable place to stay. Warm Edwardian interiors come with stripped wood floors, seagrass matting, Lloyd Loom wicker chairs, the odd potted palm. Below, the Avon estuary slips gracefully out to sea: at high tide surfers ride the waves; at low tide you can walk on the sands. There's a pretty garden with a path tumbling down to the beach, binoculars in each room, a wood-burner in the snug and good books everywhere. Bedrooms are a steal (one is huge). Expect warm yellows, crisp linen, tongue-and-groove panelling and robes in super little bathrooms. As for Martyn's table d'hôte dinners, expect something special. Fish comes daily from Kingsbridge market, you might have warm crab and parmesan tart, roast monkfish with a lobster sauce, then hot chocolate soufflé with fresh raspberries. Gorgeous Devon is all around. Don't miss it. *Minimum stay two nights at weekends.*

Price	£120–£144. Singles from £80. Half-board option.
Rooms	5: 3 doubles, 2 twins/doubles.
Meals	Dinner £36.
Closed	November–March.
Directions	From A38, A3121 to Modbury, then B3392 to Bigbury-on-Sea. Hotel on left as road slopes down to sea.

Martyn Scarterfield & Petra Lampe
Folly Hill, Bigbury-on-Sea,
Kingsbridge TQ7 4AR

Tel	+44 (0)1548 810240
Email	thehenleyhotel@btconnect.com
Web	www.thehenleyhotel.co.uk

Burgh Island Hotel

Burgh is unique – grand English Art Deco trapped in aspic. Noel Coward loved it, Agatha Christie wrote here. It's much more than a hotel – you come to join a cast of players – so bring your pearls and come for cocktails under a stained-glass dome. By day you lie on steamers in the garden, watch gulls wheeling above, dip your toes into Mermaid's pool or try your hand at a game of croquet. At night you dress for dinner, sip vermouth in a palm-fringed bar, then shuffle off to the ballroom and dine on delicious organic food while the sounds of swing and jazz fill the air. Follow your nose and find flowers in vases four-feet high, bronze ladies thrusting globes into the sky, walls clad in vitrolite, a 14th-century smugglers inn. Art Deco bedrooms are the real thing: Bakelite telephones, ancient radios, bowls of fruit, panelled walls. Some have claw-foot baths, others have balconies, the Beach House suite juts out over rocks. There's snooker, tennis, massage, a sauna. You're on an island; either sweep across the sands at low tide or hitch a ride on the sea tractor. *Minimum stay two nights at weekends.*

Ethical Collection: Food. See page 386 for details

Price	Half-board £390-£420 per room; suite £460-£620.
Rooms	25: 10 doubles, 3 twins/doubles, 12 suites.
Meals	Lunch £45. Dinner included; non-residents, £60. 24-hour residents' menu from £10.50.
Closed	Rarely.
Directions	Drive to Bigbury-on-Sea. At high tide you are transported by sea tractor, at low tide by Landrover. Walking over the beach takes 3 minutes. Eco-taxis can be arranged.

Deborah Clark & Tony Orchard
Burgh Island, Bigbury-on-Sea,
Kingsbridge TQ7 4BG

Tel	+44 (0)1548 810514
Email	reception@burghisland.com
Web	www.burghisland.com

Hazelwood House

Crest the hill, drop down the drive and dive into a hidden valley. If you are looking to escape the outside world, you can here. Sixty-seven wild acres wrap around you with a river galloping through. You'll find native woodlands, ancient rhododendrons, fields of wild flowers, a shepherdess grazing her flock. Hazelwood isn't your standard hotel or B&B, it's a country venue with a bed for all who wish to rest, retreat and recoup; occasionally you'll find yourself among guests on a residential course. It's a comfy, no frills house with open fires, sublime peace and a large drawing and dining room. Bedrooms — some simple, others more fancy — are homely with an assortment of furniture. Some have huge views over the valley, some face the back, others have brass beds and quilted bedcovers or big mirrors and a Victorian fireplace. Cream teas on the wisteria-shaded veranda are wonderful and there are lectures, exhibitions, courses and recitals. Wellington boots wait at the front door. Pull on a pair, pick up a map, lope past a Frederick Frank sculpture in the garden and a boathouse on the river.

Price	£80–£160. Singles £48–£115.
Rooms	14: 4 doubles, 2 twins, 1 family room, all en suite; 2 doubles, 2 twins, 2 family rooms, 1 single, sharing 4 baths.
Meals	Lunch £14–£20. Dinner £20–£30.
Closed	Never.
Directions	Leave A38 for A3121 south. Left onto B3196 south. At California Cross 1st left after petrol station. Signed left after 0.75 miles.

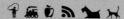
10% off room rate Mon-Thurs.
10% off stays of 2 or more nights.

Janie Bowman, Gillian Kean &
Anabel Watson
Hazelwood, Loddiswell, Kingsbridge TQ7 4EB
Tel   +44 (0)1548 821232
Email   info@hazelwoodhouse.com
Web   www.hazelwoodhouse.com

Seabreeze

A 16th-century teahouse with rooms on Slapton Sands: only in England. The sea laps ten paces from the front door, the rolling hills of Devon soar behind, three miles of beach shoot off before your eyes. Seabreeze is a treat: cute, relaxed, a comforting dash of homespun magic. Step inside and the first thing you notice is a mountain of irresistible cakes. Carol and Bonni bake the old-fashioned way. It's all homemade and utterly delicious: hot scones, Victoria sponge, banana and chocolate chip brownies. The tearoom itself – white walls, pretty art, tables topped with maps – is warmed by a wood-burner in winter, but in summer you decamp onto the terrace, where sea and sky fuse before you. Both rooms have the view and come in seaside colours with jars of driftwood, padded bedheads and window seats. Outside, there's loads to do: buckets and spades on the beach, cliff walks to great pubs, kayaks for intrepid adventures. Epic breakfasts set you up for the day, while the Start Bay Inn for tasty seafood suppers is yards away. There's surf school at Bigbury or sailing at Salcombe. *Min. stay 2 nights at weekends in high season.*

Price	£95-£135.
Rooms	2: 1 double, 1 twin/double.
Meals	Lunch from £4. Dinner by arrangement. Restaurants in village.
Closed	Never.
Directions	A379 south from Dartmouth to Torcross. House on seafront in village.

Carol Simmons & Bonni Lincoln
Torcross, Kingsbridge TQ7 2TQ

Tel	+44 (0)1548 580697
Email	info@seabreezebreaks.com
Web	www.seabreezebreaks.com

Free cream tea.

Fingals

People love the individualism of Fingals and the easy-going among us are the happiest there. Richard runs things in a rare laissez-faire style; Sheila is impossibly kind. Guests wander around as if at home, children and dogs potter about. Dinner (local and mostly organic) is served in one of two panelled dining rooms and you can choose to eat with fellow guests if you fancy. You may find yourself next to an earl, a comedian or a fascinating 'nobody', all drawn in by the charm of this place. Breakfast is served until 11am — a nice touch if you've stayed up late making friends in the honesty bar. The setting is a handsome Queen Anne farmhouse next to a stream with a small indoor pool, a sauna, a grass tennis court and books and art all over the place. Rooms are full of personality and have been spruced up in a mix of styles; most bathrooms have been updated recently. The new eco suite with its sunken bath overlooking the stream is impeccable. It is generous, engaging, occasionally chaotic and, although it may not appeal to everyone, there are legions of devoted fans. *Min. stay two nights at weekends.*

10% off room rate Mon-Thurs.

Price	£75–£210. Barn & mill £400–£1,000 per week.
Rooms	11 + 2: 8 doubles, 2 twins, 1 family room. 1 self-catering barn for 4, 1 self-catering mill for 5.
Meals	Dinner £30.
Closed	Mid-January to mid-March.
Directions	From Totnes A381 south; left for Cornworthy; right at x-roads for Cornworthy; right at ruined priory towards Dittisham. Down steep hill, over bridge. Sign on right.

Richard & Sheila Johnston
Dittisham,
Dartmouth TQ6 0JA

Tel   +44 (0)1803 722398
Email   info@fingals.co.uk
Web   www.fingals.co.uk

Browns Hotel

Browns is all things to all men, a trendy little eatery bang in the middle of town. You can pop in for coffee, stay for lunch, drop by for a beer or book in for a slap-up dinner. The building goes back to 1812 but the interiors are unmistakably contemporary, with sofas by the fire in the bar and Philippe Starck chairs in the airy restaurant. An open-plan feel runs throughout and fine Georgian windows look onto the high street, so sink into a comfy armchair and watch the world go by. Colours come courtesy of Farrow & Ball, big seaside oils hang on the walls, flames leap from a pebbled fire, stripped floors mix with sandstone tiles. Bedrooms upstairs may not be huge but they're clean, comfortable and pretty. Expect padded bedheads, flat-screen TVs, tub leather armchairs and warm colours. Rooms at the back are quieter, but all have radios, good bathrooms and a book that spills local secrets (the best walks and beaches, which ferries to use). Bistro-style food waits in the restaurant: super paella, local sea bass, fish tagine. And the river is close. *Minimum stay two nights at weekends.*

Price	£95–£165. Four-poster £185. Singles from £75 (Sunday-Thursday).
Rooms	10: 8 doubles, 1 twin, 1 four-poster.
Meals	Lunch from £6.95. Dinner, 3 courses, about £25.
Closed	First 2 weeks in January.
Directions	Into Dartmouth on A3122. Left at 1st r'bout, straight over 2nd r'bout, then 3rd right (Townstal Road). Down into town. On right.

James & Clare Brown
27-29 Victoria Road,
Dartmouth TQ6 9RT

Tel	+44 (0)1803 832572
Email	enquiries@brownshoteldartmouth.co.uk
Web	www.brownshoteldartmouth.co.uk

The Cary Arms at Babbacombe Bay

The Cary Arms hovers above Babbacombe Bay with huge views of water and sky that shoot off to Dorset's Jurassic coast. It's a cool little place – half seaside pub, half dreamy hotel – and it makes the most of its spectacular position: five beautiful terraces drop downhill towards a small jetty, where locals fish. The hotel has six moorings in the bay, you can charter a boat and explore the coast. Back on dry land the bar comes with stone walls, wooden floors and a fire that burns every day. In good weather you eat on the terraces, perhaps a pint of prawns, Dover sole, wet chocolate cake; groups of friends can enjoy their own barbecues, too. Dazzling bedrooms come in New England style. All but one opens onto a private terrace or balcony, you get decanters of sloe gin, flat-screen TVs, fabulous beds, super bathrooms (one has a claw-foot bath that looks out to sea). Back outside, you can snorkel on mackerel reefs or hug the coastline in a kayak. If that sounds too energetic, either head to the treatment room (do book) or sink into a deck chair on the residents' sun terrace. *Minimum stay two nights at weekends.*

Price	£155–£260. Suite £310–£360. Singles from £105. Cottages £770–£2,565 per week.
Rooms	8 + 3: 6 doubles, 1 twin/double, 1 family suite. 4 self-catering cottages for 2-8.
Meals	Lunch from £7.95. Dinner, 3 courses, £25–£35.
Closed	Never.
Directions	From Teignmouth south on A379; 5 miles to St Mary Church, thro' lights, left into Babbacombe Downs Rd. Follow road right; left downhill.

A plate of local cheeses in your room on arrival. A bottle of wine with dinner on first night.

Jen Podmore
Beach Road, Torquay TQ1 3LX
Tel   +44 (0)1803 327110
Email enquiries@caryarms.co.uk
Web   www.caryarms.co.uk

Kingston House

It's hard to know where to begin with this stupendous house – the history in one bathroom alone would fill a small book. "It's like visiting a National Trust home where you can get into bed," says Elizabeth, your gentle, erudite host. Set in a flawless Devon valley, completed in 1730 for a wealthy wool merchant, Kingston is one of the finest surviving examples of early 18th-century English architecture and stands in 16 acres of blissful peace. Many original features remain, including numerous open fires, murals peeling off the walls, a sitting room in the old chapel (look for the drunken cherubs). The craftsman who carved the marble hallway later worked on the White House, the marquetry staircase is the best in Europe, and the magnificent bed in the Green Room has stood there since 1830. The cooking is old school as befits the house, perhaps smoked salmon soufflé, rack of lamb, tarte au citron; vegetables come from the garden, free-range hens provide for breakfast. Come in May for 6,000 tulips in the gardens. And there's a small pool with a jet stream so you can swim 20 miles.

Price	£180–£200. Singles from £110.
Rooms	3: 2 four-posters; 1 twin/double with separate bath.
Meals	Dinner, 3 courses, £38.
Closed	Christmas & New Year.
Directions	From A38, A384 to Staverton. At Sea Trout Inn left fork for Kingston; halfway up hill right fork; at top, ahead at x-roads. Left thru' pillars at formal gardenn.

Michael & Elizabeth Corfield
Staverton, Totnes TQ9 6AR

Tel	+44 (0)1803 762235
Email	info@kingston-estate.co.uk
Web	www.kingston-estate.co.uk

2 nights for the price of 1 or 3 nights for the price of 2. Dinner must be booked and paid for on first evening.

Bickley Mill

A small inn full of good things. David and Tricia recently orchestrated a total refurbishment and their stylishly cosy interiors are just the ticket. Come for wood floors, stone walls, hessian rugs, cushioned sofas. Three fires burn in winter, there are Swedish benches, colourful art and a panelled breakfast room in creamy yellow. Everywhere you look something lovely catches the eye, be it a huge sofa covered with mountainous cushions, old black and white photos hanging on the walls or a decked terrace at the side for a pint or two in the summer sun. Bedrooms have a simple beauty in warm colours, pretty pine, trim carpets, crisp white linen – and with reasonable prices they're an absolute steal. Downstairs you'll find helpful staff, local ales and loads to eat (light bites to a three-course feast) perhaps devilled kidneys, salmon fishcakes, banana and toffee pancakes; there's a menu for children and baby chairs, too. You're in the lush Stoneycombe valley with Dartmouth, Dartmoor and the south Devon coast all close. A very generous place, so don't delay.

Price	£80–£95. Family room £130–£140. Singles £67.50.
Rooms	9: 7 doubles, 1 twin, 1 family room.
Meals	Lunch from £5. Dinner from £11.
Closed	Rarely.
Directions	South from Newton Abbot on A381. Left at garage in Ipplepen. Left at T-junction after 1 mile. Down hill, left again, pub on left.

Bottle of house wine with dinner on first night.

David & Tricia Smith
Stoneycombe, Newton Abbot TQ12 5LN
Tel   +44 (0)1803 873201
Email   info@bickleymill.co.uk
Web   www.bickleymill.co.uk

Mill End

Another Dartmoor gem. Mill End is flanked by the Two Moors Way, one of the loveliest walks in England. It leads along the river Teign, then up to Castle Drogo – not a bad way to follow your bacon and eggs. As for the hotel, inside is an elegant country retreat. There are timber frames, nooks and crannies, bowls of fruit, pretty art. Warm, uncluttered interiors are just the ticket, with vases of flowers on plinths in the sofa'd sitting room and smartly upholstered dining chairs in the airy restaurant. Bedrooms come in country-house style: white linen, big beds, moor views, the odd antique. You might find a chandelier, a large balcony or padded window seats. All come with flat-screen TVs, some have big baths stocked with lotions. Back down in the restaurant, where the mill wheel turns in the window, you find delicious food, perhaps mushroom and tarragon soup, Dartmoor lamb with fondant potato and rosemary jus, chocolate tart. Little ones have their own high tea at 6pm. In the morning there's porridge with cream and brown sugar, as well as the usual extravagance. Dogs are very welcome. *Children over 12 welcome in dining room.*

Price	£135-£155. Suites £170-£230. Singles from £67.50. Half-board from £100 p.p.
Rooms	15: 9 doubles, 2 twins, 1 family, 3 suites.
Meals	Lunch by arrangement. Sunday lunch from £15.95. Dinner £36-£39.50.
Closed	2 weeks in January.
Directions	M5, then A30 to Whiddon Down. South on A382, through Sandy Park, over small bridge and on right.

Peter & Sue Davies
Chagford, Newton Abbot TQ13 8JN

Tel	+44 (0)1647 432282
Email	info@millendhotel.com
Web	www.millendhotel.com

10% off room rate. Upgrade subject to availability.

Lydgate House Hotel

You're in 36 acres of heaven, so come for the wonder of Dartmoor: deer and badger, fox and pheasant, kingfisher and woodpecker, all live here. A 30-minute circular walk takes you over the East Dart river, up to a wild hay meadow where rare orchids flourish, then back down to a 12th-century clapper bridge: utterly sensational. Herons dive in the river by day; you may get a glimpse from the conservatory as you dig into your locally cured bacon and eggs. The house is a dream, a nourishing stream of homely comforts: a drying room for walkers, deep white sofas, walls of books, a wood-burner in the sitting room, the sound of the river when the river is full. Karen cooks the sort of food you'd hope for after a day on the moors, perhaps leek and potato soup, whole lemon sole, a raspberry and cinnamon torte or a plate of Tavistock cheeses. Bedrooms — two are huge — are warm and cosseting with crisp florals, comfy beds and Radox in the bathrooms. Finally, moonwort grows in the hay meadow. Legend says if gathered by moonlight it unleashes magical properties; clearly someone has.

Price	£100–£120. Singles £45–£55.
Rooms	7: 4 doubles, 1 twin/double, 2 singles.
Meals	Dinner, 3 courses, £27.50.
Closed	January.
Directions	From Exeter A30 west to Whiddon Down, A382 south to Moretonhampstead, B3212 west to Postbridge. In village, left at pub. House signed straight ahead.

Stephen & Karen Horn
Postbridge,
Yelverton PL20 6TJ

Tel	+44 (0)1822 880209
Email	info@lydgatehouse.co.uk
Web	www.lydgatehouse.co.uk

Entry 90   Map 2

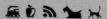

Prince Hall Hotel

An avenue of beech trees sweeps you down to this peaceful hotel, which stands in six acres of woodland and lawns with views to the back across majestic Dartmoor. Inside, a warm and welcoming country house comes with colour and comfort in equal measure, a great spot to escape the city. Follow your nose and find beautiful sofas in front of the fire, an airy bar where doors open onto a smart terrace, then wooden floors in a refurbished restaurant, where you dine on super food from the finest local suppliers – perhaps honey glazed pork belly with pear purée, venison loin with fondant potato and braised cabbage, white chocolate cheesecake with spearmint jelly. Bedrooms come in different shapes and sizes. Expect wallpaper, white linen, dressing mirrors and warm florals. The more expensive rooms have the view and a couple have fancy bathrooms too. Outside, lawns run down to paddocks, the river passes beyond, then nothing but moor and sky. Foxgloves and primroses bring colour in spring. Dogs are very welcome. *Minimum stay two nights at weekends.*

Price	£100–£180. Singles from £80.
Rooms	8: 4 doubles, 4 twins/doubles.
Meals	Lunch from £5.95. Dinner £33.95–£39.95.
Closed	Never.
Directions	A38 to Ashburton, then follow signs through Poundsgate & Dartmeet. Hotel signed on left 1 mile before Two Bridges.

Fi & Chris Daly
Two Bridges, Princetown,
Yelverton PL20 6SA

Tel   +44 (0)1822 890403
Email info@princehall.co.uk
Web   www.princehall.co.uk

Bottle of house wine with dinner on first night.

Alexandra Hotel & Restaurant

Everything here is lovely, but the view is hard to beat, a clean sweep up the Jurassic coast towards Portland Bill. The hotel overlooks Lyme Bay; the only thing between you and it is the lawn. Below, the Cobb curls into the sea, the very spot where Meryl Streep withstood the crashing waves in *The French Lieutenant's Woman*; in summer, steamers pepper the garden and guests fall asleep, book in hand, under an English sun. As for the hotel, it's just as good. Kathryn, ex-Firmdale, bought it from her mother and has refurbished brilliantly. You get stripped wood floors, windows everywhere, an airy bar for pre-dinner drinks, an attractive sitting room with plenty of books. The dining room could double as a ballroom, the conservatory brasserie opens onto a terrace; both provide excellent sustenance; try crab and lime fishcakes, saddle of venison, pear tart tatin with vanilla ice cream. Beautiful rooms are the final treat, most have the view. Expect super beds, padded headboards, robes in wonderful bathrooms. Lyme, the beach and the fossil-ridden coast all wait.

Price	£125–£215. Singles from £80. Half-board £55–£137.50 p.p.
Rooms	24: 19 twins/doubles, 2 singles, 3 family rooms.
Meals	Lunch from £9. Dinner in brasserie from £9; in restaurant, 3 courses, £39.50.
Closed	Last Sunday before Christmas to last Sunday in January.
Directions	In Lyme Regis up hill on high street; keep left at bend; on left after 200m.

Kathryn Haskins
Pound Street, Lyme Regis DT7 3HZ
Tel   +44 (0)1297 442010
Email   enquiries@hotelalexandra.co.uk
Web   www.hotelalexandra.co.uk

The Bull Hotel

With Dorset's star firmly on the rise, it was only a matter of time before a funky hotel appeared on the radar. Step forward The Bull, a sparkling bolthole that comes in cool hues and which stands on the high street in the middle of town. It's smart enough for a masked ball on New Year's Eve, and informal enough for ladies who lunch to pop in unannounced. It's a big hit with the locals and lively most days; at weekends the bar rocks. All of which makes it a lot of fun for guests passing through. Gorgeous rooms wait upstairs; French and English country elegance entwine with a touch of contemporary flair. Expect beautiful beds, pashmina throws, old radiators, perhaps an armoire. Most come in airy whites, some have striking wallpaper, maybe a claw-foot bath at the end of the bed. There are digital radios, flat-screen TVs, super little bathrooms. Back downstairs – stripped floorboards, Farrow & Ball walls, sofas in the bar, candles everywhere – dig into brasserie-style food; moules frites is on the menu every Wednesday night. Lyme Regis and Chesil Beach are close. *Minimum stay two nights at weekends.*

Price	£85–£195. Four-poster £155–£195. Family room £170–£210. Single £75–£115. Suite £205–£265.
Rooms	19: 6 doubles, 1 twin, 3 four-posters, 3 family rooms, 1 single, 5 suites.
Meals	Lunch, 2 courses, from £12. Dinner, 3 courses, around £30. Sunday lunch £19.
Closed	Never.
Directions	On main street in town. Car park at rear.

Aperitif before dinner.

Nikki & Richard Cooper
34 East Street, Bridport DT6 3LF

Tel	+44 (0)1308 422878
Email	info@thebullhotel.co.uk
Web	www.thebullhotel.co.uk

The Greyhound Inn

It's hard to fault this fabulous inn. It sits in one of Dorset's loveliest villages, lost in a lush valley with big views that shoot uphill. Outside, roses, clematis and lavender add the colour; inside rustic interiors have a warm traditional feel. You find stone walls, old flagstones, gilt mirrors and a wood-burner to keep things cosy. There's a lively locals' bar where you can grab a pint of Butcombe and sink into a chesterfield, then a lovely little restaurant with old beams and curios, where you dig into delicious food. The feel here is delightfully relaxed and you can eat wherever you want, so spin onto the terrace in good weather and feast on local food, perhaps clam chowder, venison Wellington, almond tart with vanilla ice cream. Six lovely rooms wait in an old skittle alley. They're not huge, but nor is their price, and what they lack in space, they make up for in comfort and style with fluffy duvets, crisp white linen, iPod docks and painted beams. Not that you'll linger, you'll be too busy having fun in the pub. The Cerne Abbas giant is close, the walking exceptional.

Price	£80–£90. Singles from £70.
Rooms	6 doubles.
Meals	Lunch from £6. Dinner, 3 courses, about £30 (not Sunday evening).
Closed	Never.
Directions	South from Sherborne on A352. In Cerne Abbas right for Sydling. Left at ford for village.

Bottle of wine with dinner on first night.

Martin Frizell & Fiona Phillips
26 High Street, Sydling St Nicholas,
Dorchester DT2 9PD

Tel	+44 (0)1300 341303
Email	info@dorsetgreyhound.co.uk
Web	www.dorsetgreyhound.co.uk

BridgeHouse Hotel

Beaminster — Emminster in Thomas Hardy's *Tess* — sits in a lush Dorset valley. From the hills above, rural England goes on show: quilted fields lead to a country town, the church tower soars towards heaven. At BridgeHouse stone flags, mullioned windows, old beams and huge inglenooks sweep you back to a graceful past. This is a comfortable hotel in a country town — intimate, friendly, quietly smart. There are rugs on parquet floors, a beamed bar in a turreted alcove, a sparkling dining room with Georgian panelling. Breakfast is served in the brasserie, where huge windows look onto the lawns, so watch the gardener potter about as you scoff your bacon and eggs. Delicious food — local and organic — is a big draw, perhaps seared scallops, Gressingham duck, champagne sorbet. And so to bed. Rooms in the main house are bigger and smarter, those in the coach house are simpler and less expensive; all are pretty with chic fabrics, crisp linen, flat-screen TVs and stylish bathrooms. There are river walks, antique shops and Dorset's Jurassic coast. *Minimum stay two nights at weekends.*

Price	£116–£200. Singles from £76. Half-board (min. 2 nights) from £83 p.p.
Rooms	13: 6 twins/doubles, 2 four-posters, 1 single. Coach House: 3 doubles, 1 family room.
Meals	Brasserie lunch & dinner from £12. Dinner, à la carte, £27.50–£40.
Closed	Never.
Directions	From Yeovil A30 west; A3066 for Bridport to Beaminster. Hotel at far end of town as road bends to right.

Mark & Jo Donovan
3 Prout Bridge,
Beaminster DT8 3AY

Tel   +44 (0)1308 862200
Email   enquiries@bridge-house.co.uk
Web   www.bridge-house.co.uk

10% off room rate Sunday-Thursday, October-March. Upgrade subject to availability.

Summer Lodge Country House Hotel, Restaurant & Spa

An architect called Thomas Hardy once helped redesign the drawing room of this beautiful country house. Dorset's most famous son went on to even greater things and you can now pick up a copy of one of his books, and curl up to read on the sofa in front of the fire. Outside, four acres of formal gardens include terraces, fountains, a kitchen garden, a tennis court, even a heated indoor swimming pool at the spa; there are treatments rooms, too. Back in the main house every wall is covered in fabric (Prince of Wales check on the stairs). There are stripped floors and a fire in the library/bar, then a beautiful conservatory for delicious breakfasts, but best of all is the country-house dining room where you eat some of the tastiest food in Dorset, perhaps crab and lobster with lime salad, roast loin of Dorset lamb with rosemary jus, rhubarb and custard soufflé. Bedrooms are scattered about, some in the main house, others in the coach house, there's even a cottage with a hot tub in the garden. All come in grand country-house style: plush fabrics, super beds, wonderful art, excellent bathrooms. *Min. two nights summer weekends.*

Price	£200-£340. Suites £325-£445. Family rooms £545-£785.
Rooms	24: 19 twins/doubles, 4 suites, 1 family room.
Meals	Lunch £20-£25. Dinner, 3 courses, £55. 8-course tasting menu £65.
Closed	Never.
Directions	South from Yeovil on A37 towards Dorchester. After about 8 miles right, signed Evershot. 1st left in village into Summer Lane. Hotel signed right.

Bottle of champagne for bookings of 2 nights or more. Late checkout (12pm). Free pick-up from local bus/train station.

Charles Lotter
Summer Lane, Evershot DT2 0JR
Tel   +44 (0)1935 482000
Email   summerlodge@rchmail.com
Web   www.summerlodgehotel.co.uk

The Eastbury Hotel

Sleepy Sherborne's heyday passed a thousand years ago. It has an ancient abbey and a couple of castles, one of which was home to Walter Raleigh. These days it's one of the loveliest towns in the south, a great place to wash up for a day or two. As for The Eastbury, it stands a stone's throw from the abbey. Its vast garden is the big surprise, utterly serene and English to its core, a perfect spot in good weather. Inside you find warm interiors that fit the mood perfectly. The daily papers wait in the sitting room, there's a snug bar for an evening snifter, an airy restaurant that overlooks the garden. Spotless bedrooms are a treat. Some come in contemporary splendour (fancy wallpaper, Lloyd Loom wicker, super bathrooms), others are warmly traditional (thick fabrics, garden views, padded window seats); one room has a private terrace. Back in town you'll find medieval architecture, Tudor almshouses and antique shops by the dozen, so wander the streets, then return for a good dinner, perhaps smoked salmon, Dorset lamb, hot chocolate fondant with orange sorbet. *Minimum stay two nights at weekends.*

Price	£139-£189. Singles from £70.
Rooms	23: 18 twins/doubles, 5 singles.
Meals	Lunch from £6.25. Dinner, 3 courses, £25-36. Tasting menu £45.
Closed	Never.
Directions	West into Sherborne and hotel signed from A30; or due east from Abbey and on right.

	Paul & Nicky King
	Long Street, Sherborne DT9 3BY
Tel	+44 (0)1935 813131
Email	reservations@theeastburyhotel.co.uk
Web	www.theeastburyhotel.co.uk

25% off DBB rate for stays of 2 or more nights.

Plumber Manor

A grand stone house lost in Dorset's sleepy lanes. It stands in 60 acres of lawns, field and woodland with the river Develish running through. It dates from 1650 and comes with mullioned windows, huge stone flags and a fine terrace for afternoon tea. An avenue of horse chestnuts leads up to the front door, inside which a pair of labradors rule the roost. Interiors pay no heed to designer trends – Plumber is not the place to come to glimpse the latest fashions – but the first-floor landing has the biggest velvet sofa you are ever likely to see, plus a gallery of family oils covering the walls and a grand piano for good measure. Bedrooms are split between the main house and converted barns. The latter tend to be bigger and are good for people with dogs. Décor is dated – 1980s florals – as are the bathrooms, but the family triumvirate of Brian (in the kitchen), Richard (behind the bar) and Alison (simply everywhere) excel in the art of old-fashioned hospitality. Delicious country food waits in the restaurant. Bulbarrow Hill is close. *Pets by arrangement.*

Price	£140–£210. Singles from £120.
Rooms	16: 2 doubles, 13 twins/doubles, all en suite; 1 twin/double with separate bath.
Meals	Sunday lunch £25. Dinner £28–£35.
Closed	February.
Directions	West from Sturminster Newton on A357. Across traffic lights, up hill & left for Hazelbury Bryan. Follow brown tourism signs. Hotel signed left after 2 miles.

Richard, Alison &
Brian Prideaux-Brune
Plumber, Sturminster Newton DT10 2AF
Tel   +44 (0)1258 472507
Email   book@plumbermanor.com
Web   www.plumbermanor.com

Stapleton Arms

A great village inn: lots of style, cheerful staff, great food, excellent prices. The Stapleton started life as a Georgian home, becoming an inn after the war. A recent face lift has given it a streak of country glamour; expect warm colours and a happy vibe. Downstairs, the daily papers are spread across a table, there are sofas in front of the fire, a piano for live music and a restaurant with shuttered windows and candles in the fireplace. You can eat whatever you want, wherever you want – delicious pork pies wait at the bar, but it's hard to resist a three-course feast, perhaps crispy salt and pepper squid, pan-fried duck breast with blood orange jus, steamed treacle sponge with homemade custard. There's a beer menu (ale matters here), on Sundays groups can order their own joint of meat and there's always a menu for kids. Super rooms are soundproofed to ensure a good night's sleep. They're comfy-chic with Egyptian linen, fresh flowers, happy colours, fantastic showers. Also: maps and wellies if you want to walk, games for children, DVDs for all ages. Wincanton is close for the races.

Price	£80–£120. Singles £72–£96.
Rooms	4: 3 doubles, 1 twin/double.
Meals	Lunch from £5.50. Bar meals from £7.50. Dinner from £9.50.
Closed	Rarely.
Directions	A303 to Wincanton. Into town right after fire station, signed Buckhorn Weston. Left at T-junction after 3 miles. In village, pub on right.

Rupert & Victoria Reeves
Church Hill, Buckhorn Weston,
Gillingham SP8 5HS

Tel	+44 (0)1963 370396
Email	relax@thestapletonarms.com
Web	www.thestapletonarms.com

Glass of champagne on arrival. Late checkout (12pm). Free pick-up from local bus/train station.

Castleman Hotel and Restaurant

It's a little like stepping into the pages of a Hardy novel: an untouched corner of idyllic Dorset, a 400-year-old bailiff's house, sheep grazing in lush fields and a rich cast of characters. The Castleman – a country-house restaurant with rooms – is a true one-off: quirky, intimate, defiantly English. It pays no heed to prevailing fashions, not least because the locals would revolt if it did. Edward and Barbara run the place with relaxed informality, though touches of grandeur are hard to miss: a panelled hall, art from Chettle House, a magnificent Jacobean ceiling in one of the sitting rooms. Potter about and find a cosy bar, fresh flowers everywhere, books galore. The restaurant has garden views though your eyes will attend only to Barbara's deliciously old-fashioned English food, perhaps potted shrimp terrine, haunch of local venison, meringues with chocolate mousse and toasted almonds. Smart homely bedrooms fit the bill perfectly: eminently comfortable, delightfully priced; a couple have claw-foot baths. Magical Dorset will fill your days with splendour.

Price	£85–£100.
Rooms	8: 4 doubles, 1 four-poster, 1 twin, 1 twin/double, 1 family.
Meals	Sunday lunch £22. Dinner, 3 courses, about £25.
Closed	February.
Directions	A354 north from Blandford Forum. 3rd left (about 4 miles up) and on left in village.

Edward Bourke & Barbara Garnsworthy
Chettle, Blanford Forum DT11 8DB

Tel	+44 (0)1258 830096
Email	enquiry@castlemanhotel.co.uk
Web	www.castlemanhotel.co.uk

The King John Inn

You're on the Dorset/Wiltshire border, lost in blissful country, with paths that lead into glorious hills. Tumble back down to this super inn. Alex and Gretchen have refurbished every square inch and the place shines. Expect airy interiors, a smart country feel, a sun-trapping terrace and a fire that crackles in winter. Originally a foundry, it opened as a brewery in 1859, and, when beer proved more popular than horseshoes, the inn was born. You'll find three local ales on tap but great wines, too – Alex loves the stuff and has opened his own shop across the courtyard; take home a bottle if you like what you drink. As for the food, it's as local as can be with game straight off the Rushmore estate and meat from over the hill; the sausages are a thing of rare beauty. Country-house bedrooms are the final treat. Some are bigger than others, three are in the Coach House, all come with wonderful fabrics, padded headboards, crisp white linen and super bathrooms (one has a slipper bath). In summer, a terraced lawn gives views over a couple of rooftops onto the woods. A perfect spot.

Price	£115–£165.
Rooms	8: 6 doubles, 2 twins/doubles.
Meals	Lunch from £6.95. Bar meals from £8.95. Dinner, 3 courses, £25–£30. Sunday lunch £30.
Closed	Rarely.
Directions	South from Salisbury on A354, then right onto B3081 at roundabout after 8 miles. In village on right.

Alex & Gretchen Boon
Tollard Royal, Salisbury SP5 5PS

Tel	+44 (0)1725 516207
Email	info@kingjohninn.co.uk
Web	www.kingjohninn.co.uk

 Late checkout (12pm).

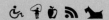

The Bull

A sleepy village, a gorgeous inn, a winning position in the Cranborne Chase: in short, England at its loveliest. Mark, who once played rugby for Harlequins, came west a few years ago and rescued the Bull from neglect. These days all is lovely. Water meadows stretch out to the front, the odd tractor rumbles past, there's a smart garden for a pint in summer. Airy open-plan interiors are just the ticket with sofas and armchairs in front of the fire, local ales waiting at the bar and smart wooden tables scattered about, where you dig into excellent food. When things get busy, life spills into an elegant conservatory which opens onto a smart terrace – a nice little dining spot in good weather. Bedrooms above the shop are smartly uncluttered: India Jane furniture, a wall of paper, crisp white linen and coffee machines; all have good bathrooms. Not that you'll linger. Matt Davey's food is too good to miss, so spin down for a feast, perhaps potato and watercress soup, shoulder of spring lamb, ricotta and honey cake with marinated figs; much comes from a kitchen garden in the village. Brilliant.

Price	£110-£130. Singles from £65.
Rooms	5: 4 doubles, 1 single.
Meals	Lunch from £6.50. Dinner, 3 courses, £25-£30.
Closed	Christmas.
Directions	M27 and A31 west, then B3081 north. Village signed left 1 mile south of Cranborne.

3 nights for the price of 2 (Sun-Wed).

Mark Thornton
Wimborne St Giles,
Wimborne BH21 5NF
Tel   +44 (0)1725 517300
Email   bullwsg@btconnect.com
Web   www.bullinnwsg.com

La Fosse at Cranborne

Cranborne was home to Robert Cecil, Earl of Salisbury, the Tudor spymaster who moved King James onto the throne when Elizabeth died in 1603. Under his patronage the village grew into a market town with a garrison to protect a plentiful supply of royal visitors; these days the village has returned to its sleepy roots and is all the better for it. Mark and Emmanuelle arrived three years ago, he to cook, she to polish and shine. It's a small affair, a restaurant with rooms that has resisted the urge for all-out contemporary design. Instead, you find something more homespun: a bar that doubles as reception; sofas in front of a wood-burner; travel books to sweep you away; maps galore for glorious walking. Bedrooms upstairs, recently refurbished, have a super style: warm yellows, pretty fabrics, comfy beds and crisp white linen, smart little bathrooms with underfloor heating. Best of all is the restaurant for Mark's rustic cooking... game terrine, roast shoulder of veal, Capricorn goat's cheese with plum compote. Spin west a few miles to Hambledon Hill (a prehistoric hill fort) for huge country views.

Price	£85. Singles from £49.
Rooms	6: 3 doubles, 2 twins/doubles, 1 suite.
Meals	Dinner (Mon-Sat) & Sunday lunch £19.95-£25.95.
Closed	Never.
Directions	A338 to Fordingbridge, then B3078 into Cranborne. Right at village shop and on right.

Emmanuelle & Mark Hartstone
The Square, Cranborne,
Wimborne BH21 5PR

Tel	+44 (0)1725 517604
Email	lafossemail@gmail.com
Web	www.la-fosse.com

10% off room rate Mon-Thurs. Late checkout (12pm).

The Priory Hotel

The lawns of this 16th-century priory run down to the river Frome. Behind, a church rises, beyond, a neat Georgian square, and a stone-flagged courtyard leads up to the hotel. Step in to warm country-house interiors: a grand piano in the drawing room, a first-floor sitting room with garden views, and a stone-vaulted dining room in the old cellar. Best of all is the terrace, where you can sit in the sun and watch yachts drift past – a perfect spot for lunch in summer. Bedrooms in the main house come in different sizes, some cosy under beams, others grandly adorned in reds and golds. Also: mahogany dressers, padded window seats, bowls of fruit, the odd sofa. Bathrooms – some dazzlingly opulent – come with white robes. Eight have river views, others look onto the garden or church. Rooms in the boathouse, a 16th-century clay barn, are lavish, with oak panelling, stone walls, the odd chest and sublime views. Four acres of idyllic gardens have climbing roses, a duck pond and banks of daffs. Corfe Castle and Studland Bay are close. A wonderful slice of old England. *Minimum stay two nights at weekends.*

Price	£205–£295. Suites £330–£360. Half-board (obligatory at weekends) from £127.50 p.p.
Rooms	18: 13 twins/doubles, 5 suites.
Meals	Lunch from £29. Dinner £42.50.
Closed	Never.
Directions	West from Poole on A35, then A351 for Wareham and B3075 into town. Through lights, 1st left, right out of square, then keep left. Entrance on left beyond church.

10% off room rate Mon-Thurs.
Bottle of wine in your room.
Late checkout (12pm).

Jeremy Merchant
Church Green, Wareham BH20 4ND
Tel   +44 (0)1929 551666
Email   reservations@theprioryhotel.co.uk
Web   theprioryhotel.co.uk

urban beach hotel

Urban beach operates to different rules. The spirit here is infectious: very friendly with buckets of style – surfer chic in Bournemouth with seven miles of sandy beach waiting at the end of the road. Inside, gaze upon a total renovation. Walls have been removed downstairs to create one large airy room and the bar/restaurant now comes with a ceiling rose and plaster moulding to complement chrome stools and the odd decorative surf board. There are big circular leather booths, driftwood lamps, a house guitar and surf movies projected onto a wall in the bar. In summer, doors open onto a decked terrace for cocktails, fresh fruit smoothies and barbecues in the sun. Lovely bedrooms, some big, some smaller, are all fitted to the same spec: flat-screen TVs, crushed velvet curtains, wonderful bathrooms. Drop down for a good breakfast: freshly squeezed orange juice, hot croissants, the full cooked works. A brasserie-style menu runs all day. It's a 20-minute seaside walk into Bournemouth town centre. *Min. stay 2 nights at weekends (3 nights bank holidays).*

Price	£97–£180. Singles from £72.
Rooms	12: 9 doubles, 1 twin/double, 2 singles.
Meals	Lunch & dinner £5–£25.
Closed	Never.
Directions	South from Ringwood on A338; left for Boscombe (east of centre). Over railway, right onto Centenary Way. Keep with the flow (left, then right) to join Christchurch Rd; 2nd left (St John's Rd); 2nd left.

Mark & Fiona Cribb
23 Argyll Road, Bournemouth BH5 1EB
Tel   +44 (0)1202 301509
Email   reception@urbanbeach.co.uk
Web   www.urbanbeach.co.uk

 Bottle of house wine with dinner.

Captain's Club Hotel

A sparkling hotel on the banks on the Stour, where a tiny ferry potters along the river dodging swans and ducks. The hotel has its own launch and those who want to skim across to the Isle of White can do so in style. Back on dry land, locals flock in day and night and the big bar hums with merry chatter as they sink into sofas, sip cocktails or dig into a crab sandwich. There's live music every night, newspapers at reception and doors that open onto a pretty terrace, perfect in good weather. Bedrooms all have river views and come in an uncluttered contemporary style, with low-slung beds, crisp white linen, neutral colours and excellent bathrooms. None are small, some are huge with separate sitting rooms, apartments have more than one bedroom, thus perfect for families and friends. Residents have free access to the spa (hydrotherapy pool, sauna, four treatment rooms). Dinner comes in an ultra-airy restaurant, where you dig into tasty brasserie-style food, perhaps goats cheese soufflé, Gressingham duck, pear mousse with Kir royale sorbet. Pretty Christchurch is a short walk upstream. *Minimum two nights at weekends.*

Price	£199–£259. Apartments £289–£649.
Rooms	29: 17 doubles, 12 apartments for 2–6.
Meals	Bar meals all day from £6. Restaurant lunch from £14.50; à la carte dinner £30–£35.
Closed	Never.
Directions	M27/A31 west, then A338/B3073 south into Christchurch. At A35 (lights at big r'about) follow one-way system left. Double back after 100m. Cross r'about heading west and 1st left into Sopers Lane. Signed left.

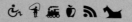 Bottle of wine in your room.

Timothy Lloyd & Robert Wilson
Wick Lane, Christchurch BH23 1HU
Tel   +44 (0)1202 475111
Email   reservations@captainsclubhotel.com
Web   www.captainsclubhotel.com

Rose & Crown

An idyllic village of mellow stone where little has changed in 200 years. The Rose and Crown dates from 1733 and stands on the green, next to the village's Saxon church. Roses ramble above the door in summer, so pick up a pint and search out the sun on the gravelled forecourt. Inside you can sit at settles in the tiny locals' bar and roast in front of the fire while reading the *Teesdale Mercury*, or seek out sofas in the peaceful sitting room and tuck into afternoon tea. Bedrooms are lovely. Those in the converted outbuildings have padded headboards and tumble with colour; in the main house they come with antique pine, padded window seats and warm country colours. All have Bose systems and spotless bathrooms. Fabulous food can be eaten informally in the brasserie (Wensleydale cheese soufflé, steak and kidney pie, sticky toffee pudding) or grandly in the panelled dining room (farmhouse ham with fresh figs, fillet of Teesdale lamb, coconut panna cotta). Hadrian's Wall, the Dales and High Force waterfall are all close and there's a drying room for walkers.

Price	£135–£185. Suites £195–£210. Singles from £95. Half-board from £107 p.p.
Rooms	12: 6 doubles, 4 twins, 2 suites.
Meals	Lunch & bar meals from £12. Dinner, 3 courses, from £35. Sunday lunch £18.50.
Closed	24–26 December.
Directions	From Barnard Castle B6277 north for 6 miles. Right in village towards green. Inn on left.

Christopher & Alison Davy
Romaldkirk, Barnard Castle DL12 9EB

Tel	+44 (0)1833 650213
Email	hotel@rose-and-crown.co.uk
Web	www.rose-and-crown.co.uk

Glass of champagne on first night.

The Sun Inn

An idyllic village made rich by mills in the 16th century. These days you can hire boats on the river, so order a picnic at the inn, float down the glorious Stour, then tie up on the bank for lunch al fresco. You're in the epicentre of Constable country; the artist attended school in the village and often returned to paint St Mary's with its soaring tower; it stands directly opposite. As for The Sun, you couldn't hope to wash up in a better place. Step in to find open fires, stripped floors, timber frames and an easy elegance. A panelled lounge comes with sofas and armchairs, the bar is made from a slab of local elm and the dining room is beamed and airy, so come for fabulous food inspired by Italy: fresh seafood, wild boar, slow-cooked lamb, Tuscan sausage, fabulous East Anglian cheeses. Rooms are gorgeous: creaking floorboards, a panelled four-poster, timber-framed walls. You get light colours on the walls, crisp linen on the beds, super power-showered bathrooms. There's afternoon tea on arrival and a garden for summer barbecues. *Two new rooms planned for July 2011.*

Price	£95–£150. Singles from £70.
Rooms	5: 4 doubles, 1 four-poster.
Meals	Lunch & dinner from £12. Bar meals from £6.85. Sunday lunch £24.
Closed	25 & 26 December.
Directions	A12 north past Colchester. 2nd exit, signed Dedham. In village opposite church.

 Afternoon tea on arrival.

Piers Baker
High Street, Dedham,
Colchester CO7 6DF

Tel	+44 (0)1206 323351
Email	office@thesuninndedham.com
Web	www.thesuninndedham.com

Maison Talbooth

Exceptional service, beautiful interiors, a sublime position overlooking Dedham Vale. This small country house packs a polished punch. Once a rectory, it is now a pleasure dome, so step into a golden hall where plump sofas come dressed in fine fabrics and big windows frame the view. The suites are equally majestic. Some on the ground floor have doors onto terraces where hot tubs wait, others at the front have huge views over Constable country. All come primed to pamper you rotten: exceptional bathrooms, fabulous beds, vintage wallpaper, gilt-framed mirrors. But don't linger. The pool house is magnificent, its pool heated to 85°F every day of the year. There's an open fire on the terrace, an honesty bar inside, a steam room and sauna, even a tennis court with the view. In the evening you're chauffeured to the family's restaurants (both within half a mile): Milsoms for bistro food served informally; Le Talbooth for something more serious overlooking the river. There are treatment rooms back at the hotel and breakfast is served in bed.

Price	£200–£395. Singles from £150.
Rooms	12 suites.
Meals	Dinner at Milsoms £25; at Le Talbooth £35–£50.
Closed	Never.
Directions	North on A12 past Colchester. Left to Dedham, right after S bend. Maison Talbooth is on right; follow brown signs.

Paul & Geraldine Milsom
Stratford Road, Dedham,
Colchester CO7 6HN

Tel +44 (0)1206 322367
Email maison@milsomhotels.com
Web www.milsomhotels.com

Bottle of champagne for bookings of 2 nights or more; free pick-up from local bus/train station. Free upgrade.

The Mistley Thorn

This Georgian pub stands on the high street and dates back to 1746, but inside you find a fresh contemporary feel that will tickle your pleasure receptors. The mood is laid-back with a great little bar, an excellent restaurant and bedrooms that pack an understated punch. Downstairs, an open-plan feel sweeps you through high-ceilinged rooms that flood with light. Expect tongue-and-groove panelling, Farrow & Ball colours, blond wood furniture and smart wicker chairs. Climb up to excellent rooms for smartly dressed beds, flat-screen TVs, DVD players and iPod docks. You get power showers above double-ended baths, those at the front have fine views of the Stour estuary, all are exceptional value for money. Back down in the restaurant dig into delicious food; Sherri runs a cookery school next door and has a pizzeria in town. Try smoked haddock chowder, Debden duck with clementine sauce, chocolate mocha tart (if you stay on a Sunday or Monday, dinner is free). Constable country is all around. There's history, too; the Witch-Finder General once lived on this spot.

Price	£80–£105. Singles from £65.
Rooms	7: 4 doubles, 3 twins/doubles.
Meals	Lunch from £7.95. Dinner, 3 courses, about £25.
Closed	Rarely.
Directions	From A12 Hadleigh/East Bergholt exit north of Colchester. Thro' East Bergholt to A137; signed Manningtree; continue to Mistley High St. 50 yards from station.

10% off room rate Tuesday-Thursday. Bottle of wine in your room. Late checkout (12pm).

David McKay & Sherri Singleton
High Street, Mistley CO11 1HE
Tel   +44 (0)1206 392821
Email info@mistleythorn.co.uk
Web   www.mistleythorn.co.uk

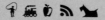

The Pier at Harwich

You're bang on the water, overlooking the historic Ha'penny Pier, with vast skies and watery views that shoot across to Felixstowe. The hotel was built in 1862 in the style of a Venetian palazzo and has remained in continuous service ever since. Inside are boarded floors, big arched windows, a granite bar and travel posters framed on the walls. Eat informally in the bistro downstairs (fish pie, grilled bream, beef stew and dumplings) or grab a window seat in the first-floor dining room and tuck into lobster bisque while huge ferries glide past outside. The owners took over the adjoining pub several years ago and have carved out a pretty lounge with port-hole windows, leather sofas, coir matting, timber frames, even a piano. Bedrooms are scattered about, some above the sitting room, others in the main house. All are pretty, with padded bedheads, seaside colours, crisp white linen, super bathrooms; if you want the best view in town, splash out on the Mayflower suite. Don't miss the blue flag beach at Dovercourt for exhilarating walks, or the Electric Palace, the second oldest cinema in Britain.

Price	£110–£130. Suite £190. Singles from £80.
Rooms	14: 13 doubles, 1 suite.
Meals	Lunch from £9.95. Sunday lunch £29. Dinner à la carte, £25–£40.
Closed	Never.
Directions	M25 junc. 28, A12 to Colchester bypass, then A120 to Harwich. Head for quay. Hotel opposite pier.

Chris & Vreni Oakley & Nick Chambers
The Quay, Harwich CO12 3HH

Tel	+44 (0)1255 241212
Email	pier@milsomhotels.com
Web	www.milsomhotels.com

Bottle of champagne for bookings of 2 nights or more.

Tudor Farmhouse Hotel

The Forest of Dean is one of England's best-kept secrets, a magical world of woodland walks, medieval castles, meandering rivers and bleating sheep. This pretty hotel stands in a pocket of silence, a great base from which to explore. You're in the middle of a tiny village, but views from a gorgeous garden – stone walls, postage-stamp lawn, a couple of cottages forming a courtyard – are of field and woods. Inside, airy interiors, exposed stone and whitewashed walls are the order of the day, though timber frames and low beams in the house bear testament to its Tudor roots. Bedrooms are scattered about. An ancient staircase leads up to a half-tester and a four-poster; those in a converted barn are simpler altogether; super garden suites come in beautiful cottages. All mix stone walls, the odd beam, trim carpets and good bathrooms. Back downstairs, you'll find delicious food in the restaurant, perhaps smoked salmon, fillet of beef, a fabulous plate of local cheese. Don't miss Puzzle Wood or Clearwell Caves. You can also kayak on the Wye or join a guide and forage in the forest.

Price	£90–£150. Suites £160–£190. Singles from £80.
Rooms	20: 10 doubles, 3 twins, 2 four-posters, 3 singles, 2 suites.
Meals	Lunch from £4. Sunday lunch from £14.50. Dinner, 3 courses, £30–£35.
Closed	24–26 December.
Directions	West from Gloucester on A40, south for Monmouth on A4136. Left onto B4028. Leave Coleford for Chepstow on B4228 and Clearwell signed right after a mile.

10% off dinner, bed & breakfast bookings Sunday-Thursday.

Colin & Hari Fell
High Street, Clearwell GL16 8JS
Tel   +44 (0)1594 833046
Email   info@tudorfarmhousehotel.co.uk
Web   www.tudorfarmhousehotel.co.uk

Three Choirs Vineyards

England's answer to the Napa Valley. After 15 years tilling the soil (very sandy, good drainage), Thomas's 75 acres of Gloucestershire hillside now produce 300,000 bottles a year. This is no mean feat and locals love it; the restaurant was packed for lunch the day we visited. There's a shop where you can buy a bottle and paths that weave through the vines – a perfect stroll after a good meal. What's more, three fabulous lodges have recently been built down by the lake, all with decks and walls of glass, so you can camp out in savannah style and listen to the woodpeckers. Rooms up at the restaurant are extremely spacious with terraces that overlook the vineyard. Delightful interiors reveal padded bedheads, walls of colour, leather armchairs, flat-screen TVs, super little bathrooms. Up at the restaurant (squashy sofas, claret walls and big views) a good meal is assured, perhaps ravioli of fresh salmon, Gressingham duck with buttered cabbage, warm treacle tart. World wines are on the list, but you can drink from the vines that surround you; there's a microbrewery, too. *Minimum stay two nights at weekends.*

Price	£125–£185. Singles from £105. Half-board from £100 p.p. (min. 2 nights).
Rooms	11: 6 doubles, 2 twins, 3 vineyard lodges.
Meals	Lunch from £21. Dinner à la carte about £35.
Closed	Christmas & New Year.
Directions	From Newent north on B4215 for about 1.5 miles. Follow brown signs to vineyard.

Thomas Shaw
Castle Tump, Newent GL18 1LS

Tel	+44 (0)1531 890223
Email	info@threechoirs.com
Web	www.threechoirs.com

Corse Lawn House Hotel

Baba is old-school, so is Corse Lawn. The service is excellent, the food is delicious and generous prices make it a must for those in search of an alternative to contemporary minimalism. This fine Queen Anne manor house was built on the ruins of a Tudor inn where Cromwell is thought to have slept before the battle of Worcester (1651). It is now the hub of a small community. The Rotary Club dine once a week, shooting parties gather in winter, locals come to celebrate. At the front, a willow dips its branches into the country's last surviving coach-wash; in summer you can sit out under parasols and dig into a cream tea while ducks glide by. Inside, slightly eccentric furnishings prevail. There are palms in the swimming pool, a sofa'd bistro for light meals, an open fire in the sitting room, a paddock at the back for visiting horses. Big bedrooms are eminently comfortable and come in warm colours with crisp linen, bowls of fruit, fresh milk and leaf tea; the four-poster looks onto the pond. As for the food, it's utterly delicious: game terrine, grilled lobster, sticky toffee pudding.

Price	£150–£170. Suites £185. Singles £95. Half-board from £80 p.p.
Rooms	18: 13 twins/doubles, 2 four-posters, 3 suites.
Meals	Lunch & dinner £10–£35.
Closed	Christmas Day & Boxing Day.
Directions	West from Tewkesbury on A438 for Ledbury. After 3 miles left onto B4211. Hotel on right after 2 miles.

25% off room rate.

Baba Hine
Corse Lawn,
Gloucester GL19 4LZ

Tel	+44 (0)1452 780771
Email	enquiries@corselawn.com
Web	www.corselawn.com

Beaumont House

Beaumont House delivers exactly what you'd want of a small B&B hotel: stylish bedrooms, excellent breakfasts, good value for money, owners who care. Fan and Alan have lived all over the world and came back to England to set up the sort of hotel they like to stay in themselves. After a fine refurbishment, the house shines. Outside, a trim garden gives plenty of scope for summer sundowners before heading into town for an excellent meal. Inside, there's a beautiful sitting room with huge windows and a rather tempting honesty bar. Spotless bedrooms come over three floors. Some are simpler with attractive prices, others are nothing short of extravagant, but all have good bathrooms, so every budget will be happy here. Compact, airy doubles on the lower ground floor are perfect for short stays, while rooms above come with striking design, vast padded headboards, blond-wood furniture and flat-screen TVs. Breakfast is served in an elegant dining room (high ceilings, garden views), while Cheltenham is a 15-minute stroll; there's room service off a short menu in the week in case you want to stay put.

Price	£89-£249. Singles from £69.
Rooms	16: 10 doubles, 3 twins/doubles, 1 family room, 2 singles.
Meals	Restaurants within walking distance. Room service Mon–Thurs eves.
Closed	Rarely.
Directions	Leave one-way system in centre of town for Stroud (south) on A46. Straight ahead, through lights and right at 1st mini-roundabout. On left after 500m.

Alan & Fan Bishop 56 Shurdington Road, Cheltenham GL53 0JE	Bottle of wine in your room. Late checkout (12pm).
Tel	+44 (0)1242 223311
Email	reservations@bhhotel.co.uk
Web	www.bhhotel.co.uk

The Bradley

An early Victorian villa, three windows wide. It was bought in 1918 by Chris's great aunt Madge, who ran it as a home for poor widows returning from the colonies. In the mid-50s an uncle turned it into studios. Now Chris and Sue are continuing the family tradition, restoring it to former glories as a delightful guest house emerges. Downstairs, a couple of vast reception rooms act as the hub of the house. Expect high ceilings, sparkling chandeliers, a roaring fire, cabinets stuffed with interesting things. You get period colours, the daily papers, an Arabian landscape painted by General Rodney Brown. Bedrooms upstairs are a treat. The smallest comes with its own decked balcony, the biggest has a vast four-poster. All have fancy bathrooms; four more rooms are planned for the second floor. Breakfast is served in style with local eggs and bacon. As for dining out, Chris and Sue (who couldn't be nicer) have tried every restaurant in town in order to report back. Try Almanac, Flynn's Bistro or The Emerald for great Thai food. There's a welcoming glass of prosecco on arrival, too.

Price	£85–£100. Four-poster £125.
Rooms	3: 1 double, 1 twin/double, 1 four-poster.
Meals	Restaurants within 400m.
Closed	Rarely.
Directions	Leave one-way system to the west, joining St George's Road, signed M5 north. Second left and on left after school.

Chris & Sue Light
19 Royal Parade, Bayshill Road,
Cheltenham GL50 3AY

Tel	+44 (0)1242 519077
Email	thebradleyguesthouse@googlemail.com
Web	www.thebradleyhotel.co.uk

The Montpellier Chapter

The Montpellier Chapter stands at the vanguard of a new movement in cool hotels: loads of style, attractive prices, excellent service from staff who care. It mixes old-fashioned hospitality (you are met in reception and shown to your room) with new technology (you browse the wine list on an iPad). More than anything else, it's a great place to be as it fills with happy locals who bring an infectious buzz. Follow your nose and find a library bar, a Victorian conservatory and a funky interior courtyard for breakfast in good weather. The style is contemporary, the building is a grand Victorian townhouse that's been meticulously restored. Bedrooms – some big, others smaller – spoil you all the way with super-comfy beds, an excess of technology and bathrooms that take your breath away. You get iPods full of local info, Nespresso coffee machines, even a complimentary mini-bar. Excellent comfort food waits in the restaurant, perhaps scallops cooked with garlic and herbs, Shepherd's pie with swede mash, tarte tatin with crème chantilly. And there's an electric car to whisk you around town.

Price	£140–£245. Suite £400.
Rooms	61: 55 doubles, 5 twins/doubles, 1 suite.
Meals	Bar lunch from £7. Restaurant lunch & dinner £12.50–£15. A la carte from £25.
Closed	Never.
Directions	Leave one-way system to the west, joining St George's Road, signed M5 north. Second left and hotel on right at top.

James Partridge
Bayshill Road, Montpellier,
Cheltenham GL50 3AS

Tel	+44 (0)1242 527788
Email	info@chapterhotels.com
Web	www.chapterhotels.com

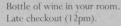
Bottle of wine in your room. Late checkout (12pm).

The Dial House Hotel

Bourton – Venice of the Cotswolds – is bisected by the river Windrush; willow branches bathe in its waters, ducks preen for tourists. Dial House is equally alluring, a sublime retreat set back from the high street. It dates from 1698, but skip past the trim lawns and hanging baskets and find the old world made new. Mullioned windows and stone fireplaces shine warmly, the fire crackles, armchairs are dressed in Zoffany, Cole & Son wallpaper sparkles on some walls. You're in the heart of the village with a peaceful garden at the back in which to escape the summer hordes. You can eat here in good weather or just pull up a deckchair and read in the sun. Stripped floors in the restaurant, cool colours in the bar and bedrooms in different shapes and sizes: grand four-posters and cool colours in the main house; airy pastels and silky quilts in the coach house; small but sweet garden rooms with fancy little bathrooms. There's fabulous food, too, perhaps hand-dived scallops, Scottish beef, then a magnificent caramel soufflé. *Minimum stay two nights at weekends.*

Price	£130–£240.
Rooms	14: 11 doubles, 2 four-posters, 1 suite.
Meals	Lunch from £5.95. Dinner, 3 courses, about £40.
Closed	Rarely.
Directions	From Oxford A40 to Northleach, then right onto A429 for Bourton. Right into village and hotel set back from High St opp. main bridge.

10% off room rate. Bottle of wine with dinner on first night.

Martyn & Elaine Booth
The Chestnuts, Bourton-on-the-Water,
Cheltenham GL54 2AN

Tel	+44 (0)1451 822244
Email	info@dialhousehotel.com
Web	www.dialhousehotel.com

Lords of the Manor

A 1650 mansion fit for a king that was originally built for a rector. The setting is spectacular, eight acres of lush lawns and formal gardens flanked by the river Eye; there's a 19th-century skating pond, too. Inside, interiors glisten after a recent facelift, so step in to find parquet flooring, mullioned windows, roaring fires and porters' chairs in a sitting-room bar. Fabrics come courtesy of Osborne & Little, views from the drawing room spin down to the river, old oils adorn the walls. There's a complimentary wine tasting for guests on Saturday evenings, not a bad way to choose your tipple before sitting down to a Michelin-starred dinner… perhaps crab tian with smoked salmon and lemon, roast loin of lamb with a rosemary jus, pistachio and chocolate soufflé with bitter chocolate sorbet. Super-smart bedrooms come in contemporary country-house style with Egyptian cotton, excellent art, padded bedheads, bowls of fruit. Expect flat-screen TVs and iPods, fancy bathrooms with robes and power showers. Church bells chime on Sunday.

Price	£195–£310. Suites £370. Half-board from £137.50 p.p.
Rooms	26: 22 twins/doubles, 4 suites.
Meals	Dinner, 5 courses, £69. Tasting menu £99.
Closed	Never.
Directions	North from Cirencester on A429 for 17 miles, then left for The Slaughters. In Lower Slaughter left over bridge. Into Upper Slaughter and hotel on right in village.

Paul Thompson
Upper Slaughter,
Cheltenham GL54 2JD
Tel   +44 (0)1451 820243
Email reservations@lordsofthemanor.com
Web   www.lordsofthemanor.com

10% off room rate Mon-Thurs.

Wesley House Restaurant

A 15th-century timber-framed house on Winchcombe's ancient high street; John Wesley stayed in 1755, hence the name. Not satisfied with one excellent restaurant, Matthew has opened another bang next door. The elder statesman comes in traditional style with sofas in front of a roaring fire, candles flickering on smartly dressed tables and a fine conservatory for delicious breakfasts with beautiful views of town and country. Next door, the young upstart is unashamedly contemporary with a smoked-glass bar, faux-zebra-skinned stools and alcoves to hide away in. Both buildings shine with original architecture: timber frames, beamed ceilings, stone flags and stripped boards. Quirky bedrooms up in the eaves tend to be cosy, one has a balcony with views over rooftops to field and hill. All come in a warm country style with good beds, pretty fabrics, small showers, smart carpets and wonky floors. Back downstairs, dig into food as simple or rich as you want, anything from fish cakes or a good burger to a three-course feast. The Cotswolds Way skirts the town, so bring your walking boots.

Price	£90–£100. Singles from £65. Half-board (for 1-night stays on Saturdays) £92.50–£102.50 p.p.
Rooms	5: 1 twin, 1 twin/double, 3 doubles.
Meals	Bar & grill: lunch & dinner from £8.95. Restaurant: dinner £19.95–£39.50. Not Sunday nights.
Closed	Never.
Directions	From Cheltenham B4632 to Winchcombe. Restaurant on right. Drop off luggage, parking nearby.

Matthew Brown
High Street, Winchcombe,
Cheltenham GL54 5LJ

Tel	+44 (0)1242 602366
Email	enquiries@wesleyhouse.co.uk
Web	www.wesleyhouse.co.uk

The Malt House

A wonderfully pretty Cotswold village of sculpted golden stone. The Malt House sits in the middle of it all, delightful inside and out. An impeccable country garden runs down to a stream, beyond which fruit trees blossom in spring. There's a summer house, a croquet lawn and Lloyd Loom furniture: pull up a seat and snooze in the sun. Equally impressive is Judi's kitchen garden which provides freshly cut flowers for beautiful bedrooms and summer fruits for the breakfast table. Inside, clipped country-house interiors are just the thing: parquet flooring, sparkling wallpaper, mullioned windows and a mantelpiece that almost touches the ceiling. There are original beams, books and papers, an honesty bar and sofas by the fire. Spotless bedrooms are warmly elegant and hugely comfortable: big mirrors, Jane Churchill silks, Italian fabrics, crisp white linen. You'll find maps for walkers, a list of local restaurants, hot water bottles and umbrellas to keep you dry. Breakfast is a feast: fresh fruit salad, homemade granola, hot bread straight from the oven, the full cooked works. *Minimum stay two nights at weekends April-October.*

Price	£120–£150. Suite from £160.
Rooms	7: 1 double, 4 twins/doubles, 1 four-poster, 1 suite.
Meals	Pub 200 yards. Dinner by arrangement (min. 12 guests).
Closed	One week over Christmas.
Directions	From Oxford A44 through Moreton-in-Marsh; right on B4081 for Chipping Campden. Entering village 1st right for Broad Campden. Hotel 1 mile on left.

Judi Wilkes
Broad Campden,
Chipping Campden GL55 6UU

Tel	+44 (0)1386 840295
Email	info@malt-house.co.uk
Web	www.malt-house.co.uk

25% off room rate on first night, Mon-Thurs.

Charingworth Manor

This grand old Cotswold manor house stands in blissful country with huge views from its lovely garden shooting south for three miles. Outside, creepers roam on 14th-century walls, while inside you find ancient beams and a roaring fire, painted panelling in the sitting room, mullioned windows in the drawing room, and flickering candles by the score in the low-ceilinged restaurant. Bedrooms – all recently refurbished – come in the same soothing contemporary style: neutral colours, padded headboards, excellent linen, flat-screen TVs. Some open onto private terraces, others have the odd beam, all have white robes in excellent bathrooms. Those in the main house tend to be elegantly traditional – old armoires, window seats, fine views. Elsewhere, there's lots to do: tennis, croquet on the lawn, a small gym, an indoor pool, a steam room and sauna, sun loungers too. Parasols shade pretty tables and chairs on the terrace, perfect for cream teas. As for dinner, try asparagus soup, chump of lamb, lemon mousse with a black pepper sorbet. Sunday night prices are a steal, and Stratford is close.

Price	£145–£205. Suites £245–£350. Singles from £110. Half-board from £105 p.p.
Rooms	26: 20 twins/doubles, 6 suites.
Meals	Lunch from £14.95. Sunday lunch £14.95–£19.95. Dinner, 3 courses, about £35.
Closed	Never.
Directions	East out of Chipping Campden on B4035 and house signed left after three miles.

25% off stays of 2 or more nights.

Michael Eastick
Charingworth,
Chipping Campden GL55 6NS

Tel	+44 (0)1386 593555
Email	info.charingworthmanor@classiclodges.co.uk
Web	www.classiclodges.co.uk

Lower Brook House

The village is a Cotswold jewel, saved from tourist hordes by roads too narrow for coaches. Lower Brook is no less alluring, a fine example of a small 21st-century country-house hotel. It was built in 1624 to house workers from one of the 12 silk mills that made Blockley rich. Step in and find the past on display: flagged floors, mullioned windows, timber-framed walls and heaps of vintage luggage. Logs smoulder in a huge inglenook in winter, while excellent bedrooms (one is small) come in crisp country-house style with beautiful fabrics, pristine linen and bowls of fresh fruit. All but one overlook the garden, views fly up the hill. Back outside, roses climb on golden walls, colour bursts from beds in summer and a small lawn runs down to a shaded terrace for afternoon tea in good weather. Walks start from the front door, so scale the ridge and dive into the country. Come home to Anna's delicious cooking, perhaps squid with a chilli jam, chicken with a Muscat jus, chocolate fondant with clotted cream; breakfast treats include smoothies, croissants and freshly squeezed juice. *Minimum stay two nights at weekends.*

Price	£80–£190.
Rooms	6: 3 doubles, 2 twins, 1 four-poster.
Meals	Dinner £15–£30.
Closed	Christmas.
Directions	A44 west from Moreton-in-Marsh. At top of hill in Bourton-on-the-Hill, right, signed Blockley. Down hill to village; on right.

🎁 Use your Sawday's Gift Card here.

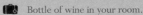
Bottle of wine in your room.

Julian & Anna Ebbutt
Lower Street, Blockley,
Moreton-in-Marsh GL56 9DS

Tel   +44 (0)1386 700286
Email   info@lowerbrookhouse.com
Web   www.lowerbrookhouse.com

Horse & Groom

The Horse and Groom delivers in spades: a warm welcome, stylish interiors, the sort of food you want to eat, and wines and beers for all. The inn stands at the top of the hill with views to the side that pour over the Cotswolds. Inside, cool colours, stripped floors, open fires and the odd stone wall for a modern rustic feel. Outside you can sit under the shade of damson trees and watch chefs gather eggs from the coop or carrots from the kitchen garden. Uncluttered bedrooms are wonderfully plush and come in contemporary country-house style with beautiful linen, pretty art, a padded window seat or two. One room is huge, the garden room opens onto the terrace, and those at the front are soundproofed to minimise noise from the road. This is a hive of youthful endeavour, with two brothers at the helm. Will cooks, Tom pours the ales, and a cheery conviviality flows. Delicious food hits the spot and is much prized by canny locals, so come for pea and ham soup with Moroccan spiced butter, griddled South Devon ox tongue with puy lentils and salsa verde, rhubarb and custard Eton mess. *Minimum stay two nights at weekends.*

Ethical Collection: Community; Food. See page 386 for details

Price	£115-£165. Singles £80. Half-board from £70 p.p.
Rooms	5 doubles.
Meals	Lunch & dinner from £11. Not Sunday eve.
Closed	Christmas Day & New Year's Eve.
Directions	West from Moreton-in-Marsh on A44. Climb hill in Bourton-on-the-Hill; pub at top on left. Moreton-in-Marsh railway station 2 miles away.

Tom & Will Greenstock
Bourton-on-the-Hill,
Moreton-in-Marsh GL56 9AQ
Tel +44 (0)1386 700413
Email greenstocks@horseandgroom.info
Web www.horseandgroom.info

The New Inn at Coln

The New Inn is old – 1632 to be exact – but well-named nonetheless; a top-to-toe renovation has recently swept away past indiscretions. These days, it's all rather smart. The pub stands in a handsome Cotswold village with ivy roaming on original stone walls and a sun-trapping terrace where roses bloom in summer. Inside, airy interiors come with low ceilings, painted beams, flagged floors and fires that roar. There are padded window seats, eastern busts, gilt mirrors and armchairs in the bar. Bedrooms are a treat, all warmly elegant with perfect white linen, flat-screen TVs and good little bathrooms (a couple have claw-foot baths). There are wonky floors and the odd beam in the main house, while those in the old dovecote come in bold colours and have views across water meadows to the river; walks start from the front door. Bibury, Burford and Stow are all close, so spread your wings, then return for a wonderful meal, perhaps grilled goat's cheese with poached pear, roasted lemon sole with pink grapefruit, vanilla panna cotta with plum crumble.

Price	£115–£160. Singles from £105. Half-board from £82.50 p.p.
Rooms	14 doubles.
Meals	Lunch from £5.95. Dinner, 3 courses, about £30. Sunday lunch from £12.50.
Closed	Never.
Directions	From Oxford A40 past Burford, then B4425 for Bibury. Left after Aldsworth to Coln St. Aldwyns.

Stuart Hodges
Main Street, Coln St Aldwyns,
Cirencester GL7 5AN

Tel	+44 (0)1285 750651
Email	info@new-inn.co.uk
Web	www.new-inn.co.uk

2 nights for the price of 1 Sunday-Thursday; terms apply.

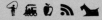

The Woolpack Inn

It's hard to fault this cool little inn. It's one of those rare places that ticks every box: friendly locals, pretty interiors, super food, lovely rooms. It stands blissfully lost in deepest Hampshire in the smallest hamlet in Britain. Its brick and flint exterior dates to 1880 and views from the front shoot across fields to a distant church; there are terraces at the front and the side, perfect for a pint in summer. Inside, you find a clean, contemporary take on a traditional English inn. A fire roars, there are warm colours, rugs on stone floors and the wine cellar is on display behind a wall of glass. Up in the restaurant, rustic charm is the order of the day with lots of wood, smart booths and candles everywhere, and the food is excellent; tuck into crispy fried squid, shoulder of lamb, honey and lemon tart. Bedrooms in the old skittle alley are great value. Expect exposed walls, the odd beam, Farrow & Ball colours and excellent bathrooms. There's a wood-fired oven on the terrace for pizza in summer, while Sunday lunch is madly popular – don't forget to book. Winchester is close.

Price	£85–£105. Family suite £145.
Rooms	7 doubles.
Meals	Lunch & dinner £5–£30. Sunday lunch from £13.50.
Closed	Never.
Directions	On B3046 between Alresford and Basingstoke, 4 miles north of Alresford.

Brian & Jarina Ahearn
Totford, Northington,
Alresford SO24 9TJ

Tel	+44 (0)845 293 8066
Email	info@thewoolpackinn.co.uk
Web	www.thewoolpackinn.co.uk

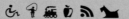

Hotel TerraVina

Few hotels are put under the proverbial microscope as much as this one. Nina and Gerard, co-founders of Hotel du Vin, were all set to decamp to the anonymity of Californian wine fields; when their plans fell through, they brought sunshine colours to the New Forest instead. The long and the short of it is this: if you want to sleep well, eat well and be looked after superbly, this is the place for you. The house sits on the edge of a village and you can walk from the front door, though in summer sunloungers circle the pool, giving every reason to linger. As for the hotel, airy interiors, happy colours and a warm contemporary feel infuse each corner. At its heart is the restaurant where you watch the chefs at work, though distraction comes courtesy of Gerard's wine cellar, which is on display behind a wall of glass. The food is excellent, perhaps seafood broth, chargrilled lamb, hot chocolate mousse with pistachio ice cream. As for some heavenly bedrooms, expect super beds, flat-screen TVs and gorgeous bathrooms. Some have terraces or claw-foot baths in the room. *Minimum stay two nights some weekends.*

Price	£155–£255. Half–board from £110 p.p.
Rooms	11: 9 doubles, 2 twins/doubles.
Meals	Continental breakfast £10.50, full English £13.50. Lunch £29.50–£27.50. A la carte dinner £40–£45.
Closed	Rarely.
Directions	M27 junc. 2, A326 south, then A336 west for Netley Marsh. Left in village at White Horse pub. One mile down and signed on left.

Gerard & Nina Basset
174 Woodlands Road, Woodlands,
Southampton SO40 7GL

Tel	+44 (0)23 8029 3784
Email	info@hotelterravina.co.uk
Web	www.hotelterravina.co.uk

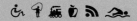

Lime Wood

Lime Wood is the new yardstick for super-cool hotels. Divine from top to toe, it mixes film-star good looks with Georgian splendour, a country house for the modern age. Spin up the drive, then step into dazzling interiors, where fires roar, chandeliers sparkle and contemporary art shines on the walls. Something beautiful catches your eye at every turn: silk wallpaper, a sweeping staircase, painted panelling in the bar. A weather-proofed courtyard doubles as the dance floor on New Year's Eve, there are wellies by the back door and paths that lead into the forest. Bedrooms are faultless: island beds, high ceilings, perhaps a freestanding bath in front of the fireplace. You'll find Bamford toiletries in white marble bathrooms, vast suites come with terraces or balconies. Two restaurants serve delicious food; the full works in the dining room (hand-dived scallops, Dexter beef, passion fruit soufflé); steak and pasta in the Scullery (the loveliest room in the hotel). The Herb House spa has a pool, sauna, steam room and treatment rooms. Best of all is the staff: nothing is too much trouble. *Minimum two nights at weekends.*

Price	£245-£445. Suites £445-£775.
Rooms	29: 14 twins/doubles, 15 suites.
Meals	Breakfast £5-£15. Lunch £18.50-£22.50. Dinner £38-£58; tasting menu £78. Lunch & dinner in brasserie from £12.50.
Closed	Never.
Directions	South from Lyndhurst on B3050 for Beaulieu. Hotel on right after 1 mile.

Justin Pinchbeck
Beaulieu Road,
Lyndhurst SO43 7FZ
Tel   +44 (0)23 8028 7177
Email   info@limewood.co.uk
Web   www.limewoodhotel.co.uk

The Master Builder's House Hotel

The position here is faultless: lawns roll down to the Beaulieu river, curlews race across the water, a vast sky hangs overhead. The house, built in 1729, was home to shipwrights who served the British fleet and Nelson's favourite vessel, *Agamemnon*, was built here. Inside, newly refurbished interiors mix contemporary flair with classical design. Expect earthy colours and a roaring fire in the yachtsman's bar, then huge sofas and watery views in the sitting room. Bedrooms in the main house are nothing short of gorgeous: huge beds, pots of colour, fabulous views, super bathrooms. Those in the annexe are simpler, but cosy – good value for money. Back downstairs, the dining room swings to an informal beat. You get wooden booths, smart rugs and doors that open onto a terrace which looks the right way. You can eat here in summer or barbecue on the lawn, perhaps grilled lobster, a rib-eye steak, then custard tart with nutmeg ice cream. Stride out on the footpaths that sweep along the river, dive into the forest to cycle and ride or lose yourself in acres of silence. *Minimum stay two nights at weekends.*

Price	£135–£180. Annexe: £105–£119. Singles from £95. Half-board from £82.50 p.p.
Rooms	24: 5 doubles, 3 suites. Annexe: 11 doubles, 5 twins/doubles.
Meals	Lunch from £7.50. Dinner, 3 courses, £25–£30.
Closed	Never.
Directions	From Lyndhurst B3056 south past Beaulieu turn-off. 1st left, signed Bucklers Hard. Hotel signed left after 1 mile.

Colin Curran
Bucklers Hard, Beaulieu,
Brockenhurst SO42 7XB

Tel	+44 (0)1590 616253
Email	enquiries@themasterbuilders.co.uk
Web	www.themasterbuilders.co.uk

Bottle of wine with dinner on first night.

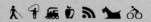

The Montagu Arms Hotel

Beaulieu, an ancient royal hunting ground, was gifted to Cistercian monks by King John in 1204. Their abbey took 40 years to build and you can walk over to see its ruins in the nearby grounds of Palace House, seat of the Montagu family since 1538. As for the village, its tiny high street is a hotchpotch of 17th-century timber-framed houses that totter by the tidal estuary drinking in views of river and sky. The hotel itself dates back to 1742, but was re-modelled in 1925. Interiors reveal a grand country house with roaring fires, painted beams, a library bar and a courtyard garden, where you can eat in summer. Bedrooms, some overlooking the water, come in smart traditional style. Expect thick fabrics, crisp linen, marble bathrooms, the very best beds. Back downstairs, sip pre-dinner drinks in front of the fire in the drawing room, then spin across to the panelled dining room with its Michelin star to feast on hand-dived scallops, roast venison from the Beaulieu estate, milk chocolate mousse with lavender ice cream. Wonderful walking from the front door may help you atone. *Minimum stay two nights at weekends.*

Price	£148-£198. Suites £290-£420. Singles from £140. Half-board from £124 p.p.
Rooms	22: 10 doubles, 3 twins/doubles, 9 suites.
Meals	Lunch £6.50-£25. Sunday lunch £29.50. Dinner, 3 courses, £65.
Closed	Never.
Directions	South from M27, junc. 1 to Lyndhurst on A337, then B3056 for Beaulieu. Left into village and hotel on right.

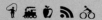 10% off room rate Mon-Thurs.

Philip Archer
Palace Lane, Beaulieu,
Brockenhurst SO42 7ZL
Tel   +44 (0)1590 612324
Email   reservations@montaguarmshotel.co.uk
Web   www.montaguarmshotel.co.uk

The Mill at Gordleton

A 400-year-old mill that sits in two acres of English country garden with Avon Water tumbling over the weir; ducks, lampreys, Indian runners and leaping trout all call it home. It's an idyllic spot, the terrace perfect for summer suppers, with the stream brushing past below. Inside, find low ceilings, wonky walls, busts and mirrors, jars of shells. Colour tumbles from pretty fabrics, a fire roars in reception, a panelled bar serves pre-dinner drinks. Bedrooms are full of character. One is above the wheel house and comes with mind-your-head beams. You get pretty throws, sheets and blankets, bowls of fruit. Three rooms have watery views (you can fall asleep to the sound of the river), two have small sitting rooms, most have fancy new bathrooms, and while a lane passes outside, you are more likely to be woken by birdsong. Downstairs, the size of the restaurant bears testament to its popularity. The seven chefs use the best local produce: look forward to tiger prawns with lemon grass, Hampshire pork braised in cider, an irresistible passion fruit soufflé. The coast is close. *Minimum two nights at weekends April–October.*

Ethical Collection: Environment; Food. See page 386 for details

Price	£140–£195. Suites £150–£235. Singles from £115.
Rooms	8: 3 doubles, 3 twins/doubles, 2 suites.
Meals	Lunch from £6.95. Sunday lunch from £21.50. Dinner £22.50–£27.50; a la carte about £40.
Closed	Christmas Day.
Directions	South from Brockenhurst on A337 for 4 miles. After 2nd roundabout 1st right, signed Hordle. On right after 2 miles.

Liz Cottingham
Silver Street, Sway,
Lymington SO41 6DJ

Tel	+44 (0)1590 682219
Email	info@themillatgordleton.co.uk
Web	www.themillatgordleton.co.uk

Westover Hall

A small-scale country house down by the sea with views from the back that shoot off across the Solent to the Isle of Wight. You can sip champagne cocktails in the garden before supper, spill onto the terrace for afternoon tea or follow a path down to the water and find a private beach hut. Inside, oak panelling astounds, not least in the hall, a controlled explosion of wood. Elsewhere, there's a snug bar with a ribbed ceiling; a private dining room with views of the Needles; a vast sitting room with a log fire where you can sink into claret sofas. Two restaurants keep you going: a bistro with arched windows that flood the room with light; a grandly panelled dining room for serious food at weekends. Bedrooms come in different sizes and not all have the view, but all are terrifically comfortable with seaside colours, padded bedheads, Frette linen and waffle robes in good bathrooms. The smallest room looks out to sea while the big rooms come with sofas, armoires, perhaps a mahogany four-poster. Don't miss the coastal path. You'll find mudflats teeming with birdlife and Hurst Castle, built by Henry VIII.

Price	Half-board £150–£185 p.p.
Rooms	15: 9 doubles, 2 twins, 1 family room, 3 suites.
Meals	Light lunches from £15. Dinner for non-residents: from £15 (bistro), £42 (restaurant: Thurs-Sat).
Closed	Never.
Directions	A337 west from Lymington, then B3058 to Milford-on-Sea. Through village; house on left.

10% off DBB Sunday-Thursday.

Christine & David Smith
Park Lane, Milford On Sea,
Lymington SO41 0PT
Tel   +44 (0)1590 643044
Email   info@westoverhallhotel.com
Web   www.westoverhallhotel.com

Hotel

Chewton Glen

Chewton Glen is one of England's loveliest country-house hotels. It opened in 1964 with eight bedrooms; now it has 58. Despite this growth it still remains wonderfully intimate, and with two staff for every guest there's sublime service too. As for the hotel, it has everything you'd ever want: a pillared swimming pool, a hydrotherapy spa, a golf course, a tennis centre, vast parkland gardens. There's beauty at every turn: stately sitting rooms, roaring fires, busts and oils, flowers everywhere. Bedrooms are exemplary, as their price demands. Some come in country-house style, most bask in contemporary splendour. Expect marble bathrooms, private balconies, designer fabrics, faultless housekeeping. Fires burn, Wellington boots wait at the front door, four gardeners tend the estate. The food in Vetiver, the new restaurant, is predictably exquisite – perhaps twice-baked Emmental soufflé, Thai-spiced Christchurch lobster, Charantais melon soup. You can atone in style: a walk on the beach, mountain biking in the New Forest. Afternoon tea is served on the croquet terrace in summer. Hard to beat. *Min. stay two nights at weekends.*

Price	£269-£468. Suites £448-£1,076.
Rooms	58: 5 doubles, 30 twins/doubles, 23 suites.
Meals	Full English breakfast: £26. Lunch £12-£25. Dinner, 3 courses, £45-£65. Tasting menu 79.50. Light meals available throughout the day.
Closed	Never.
Directions	A337 west from Lymington. Through New Milton for Christchurch. Right at r'bout, signed Walkford. Right again; hotel on right.

Andrew Stembridge
Christchurch Road,
New Milton BH25 6QS
Tel +44 (0)1425 275341
Email reservations@chewtonglen.com
Web www.chewtonglen.com

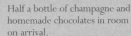 Half a bottle of champagne and homemade chocolates in room on arrival.

Castle House

A supremely elegant hotel that stands close to Hereford's magnificent 11th-century cathedral, home to the Mappa Mundi. Evensong takes place at 5.30pm, miss it at your peril. The hotel, English to the core, has a terraced garden that overlooks what remains of the castle's moat, now a flight pond for visiting geese. The castle itself disappeared long ago, but you can stroll across the park, follow a footpath along the River Wye, then loop back round the cathedral and head for home. Step inside to find warm interiors, a fine staircase, painted panelling in the airy bistro and a serious restaurant that serves the best food in town. Big bedrooms are nothing short of lavish. The top-floor suite runs all the way along the front of the house, but other rooms match its style. Expect fine fabrics, regal colours, gilt-framed mirrors, the odd chaise longue. You get super-comfy beds, crisp white linen, excellent bathrooms, too. Back downstairs, exceptional food waits in the restaurant, perhaps wild mushroom tartlet, fillet of local beef, white chocolate crème brûlée with whisky and marmalade ice cream.

Price	£190–£230. Singles from £130.
Rooms	16: 1 double, 4 singles, 11 suites.
Meals	Lunch from £4.50. Dinner, 3 courses, £25–£42. Tasting menu £50.
Closed	Never.
Directions	Follow signs to Hereford city centre, then City Centre east. Right off Bath St into Union St, through St. Peters Sq to Owen's St, then right into St. Ethelbert St. Hotel on left as road veers right.

Michelle Marriott-Lodge
Castle Street, Hereford HR1 2NW

Tel	+44 (0)1432 356321
Email	info@castlehse.co.uk
Web	www.castlehse.co.uk

The Kilpeck Inn

Kilpeck – best known for its Norman church – now has a second string to its bow, this super little country inn that's recently had a facelift. It stands on the edge of the village overlooking beautiful fields, a mere ten miles south of Hereford. Outside, smart white walls sparkle in the sun. Inside: old stone, slate floors and a warm contemporary feel. There's darts in the locals' bar, the daily papers and a smouldering fire, original beams, candle lanterns and painted panelling in the airy restaurant. Upstairs, super bedrooms come with padded bedheads, crisp white linen and pretty fabrics, while gorgeous travertine bathrooms have underfloor heating and Arran Aromatics; there's a library for your DVD player, too. Back downstairs, dig into the sort of food you hope to find in a country inn: fillet of beef, lemon sole, steak and mushroom pie, fruit crumble. It's as local as possible and, with low food miles, a wood-pellet boiler, hi-spec insulation and a rainwater recovery tank, this a seriously green destination. The Black mountains and Offa's Dyke are close.

Price	£90–£135. Singles from £65.
Rooms	4: 3 doubles, 1 twin/double.
Meals	Lunch from £7.95. Sunday lunch from £9.95. A la carte dinner £25–£30.
Closed	Never.
Directions	South from Hereford on A465. Village signed left after about 7 miles.

	Neil Wadelin
	Kilpeck, Hereford HR2 9DN
Tel	+44 (0)1981 570464
Email	enquiries@kilpeckinn.com
Web	www.kilpeckinn.com

Bottle of wine with dinner on first night.

Glewstone Court Country House Hotel & Restaurant

Those in search of the small and friendly will love it here. Bill and Christine run Glewstone with great style, instinctively disregarding the bland new world in favour of a more colourful landscape. Their realm is this attractive country house, once owned by Guy's Hospital. Inside, an eclectic collection of art and antiques fills the rooms. Eastern rugs cover stripped wood floors, resident dogs snooze in front of the fire, and guests gather in the drawing-room bar to eat, drink and make merry. Outside, there's croquet on the lawn in the shade of an ancient Cedar of Lebanon, while back inside a fine Regency staircase spirals up to a galleried landing. Warmly comfortable bedrooms wait. A couple are huge, those at the front have long views across to the Forest of Dean, those at the back overlook cherry orchards; one room on the ground floor opens onto the garden. Fabulous food, much local, is reason enough to come, with Herefordshire beef served pink with a claret gravy at lunch on Sunday. The Forest of Dean and the Wye valley are close.

Price	£125-£145. Singles £60-£85.
Rooms	9: 6 doubles, 1 four-poster, 1 single, 1 suite.
Meals	Lunch from £12.50. Dinner, 3 courses, about £30. Sunday lunch £20.
Closed	25-27 December.
Directions	From Ross-on-Wye A40 towards Monmouth. Right 1 mile south of Wilton r'bout for Glewstone. Hotel on left after 0.5 miles.

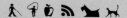 10% off room rate.

Christine & Bill Reeve-Tucker
Glewstone,
Ross-on-Wye HR9 6AW

Tel	+44 (0)1989 770367
Email	glewstone@aol.com
Web	www.glewstonecourt.com

Wilton Court Restaurant with Rooms

A Grade-II listed stone house with a Grade-I listed mulberry tree; in season, its berries are turned in sorbets and pies. The house dates all the way back to 1510 and looks across the river to Wye; herons dive, otters swim, kingfishers nest. Roses ramble on the outside, happy guests potter within. This may not be the fanciest place in the book, but Roger and Helen go the extra mile, and, with good prices, a pretty position on the river and a restaurant for great food; Wilton Court has won itself a devoted following. Bedrooms upstairs come in different shapes and sizes. Splash out on the more expensive ones for watery views, William Morris wallpaper, lots of space, perhaps a four-poster. A couple of rooms are small, but so are their prices and you can lose yourself in the rest of the hotel. Drop down for a drink in the smart panelled bar, then nip across to the airy conservatory/dining room for super food, perhaps langoustine tagliatelli, Raglan lamb, fragipane tart. A small garden across the lane drops down to the river for summer sundowners. Ross is a five-minute stroll. *Minimum stay two nights at weekends.*

Price	£115-£155. Suite £135-£175. Singles from £90. Half-board from £80 p.p. (min. 2 nights).
Rooms	10: 3 doubles, 5 twins/doubles, 1 four-poster, 1 family suite.
Meals	Lunch from £12.75. Sunday lunch £16.50-£18.50. Dinner, 3 courses, about £35. 7-course tasting menu £52.50.
Closed	1st 2 weeks of January.
Directions	South into Ross at A40/A49 Wilton roundabout. 1st right into Wilton Lane. Hotel on right.

Roger & Helen Wynn
Wilton Lane, Wilton,
Ross-on-Wye HR9 6AQ
Tel   +44 (0)1989 562569
Email   info@wiltoncourthotel.com
Web   www.wiltoncourthotel.com

 10% off room rate Sunday-Thursday.

The Wellington

A magical little brasserie with rooms in a pretty village just north of London. Everything here is a treat: an ancient inn, beautiful design, super bedrooms, staff who care. The village dates to Roman times and was mentioned in the Domesday Book. As for the Wellington, Chris, Fiona and Liz have renovated with huge flair. They stripped it back to its bare bones, kept all the lovely old bits, then added 21st-century colour and style. Vast panes of glass connect 700-year-old timber frames, light floods in, so do the locals, who come for good food and wine; both are served informally. Follow their lead and find a zinc-topped bar, raw oak panelling and a fire that burns on both sides. There are beamed ceilings, stripped floors, candles galore, a stone terrace for summer. Bedrooms above are gorgeous: exposed brick walls and timber frames mix with iPod docks and espresso machines. Some have baths in the room, you get big beds, cushioned window seats, local art. Back downstairs, great food waits amid the happy hum, perhaps tiger prawns, rib-eye steak, lemon and thyme crème brûlée. Hatfield House is close.

Price	£100–£120. Singles from £90.
Rooms	6: 1 four-poster, 5 doubles.
Meals	Lunch from £5. Dinner, 3 courses, about £25.
Closed	Never.
Directions	A1(M) junc. 6, then north for 1 mile. At 3rd roundabout left for Welwyn. 1st left (signed Welwyn shops). In village by church.

Fiona & Chris Gerard & Liz Gouldie
1 High Street, Welwyn AL6 9LZ

Tel	+44 (0)1438 714036
Email	info@wellingtonatwelwyn.co.uk
Web	www.wellingtonatwelwyn.co.uk

Priory Bay Hotel

An imperious setting one field up from the sea, with paths that lead down through a ridge of trees to a long private beach. Stone-age axes have been discovered here, medieval monks made this their home, Tudor farmers and Georgian gentry followed. The house dates to the 14th century. Inside, sleeping dogs lie in front of roaring fires. The drawing room comes in grand style with high ceilings, a baby grand and huge windows that frame sea views. Wander freely and find country rugs on parquet flooring, red leather armchairs in the bar, vintage luggage, a children's playroom and golf clubs for the six-hole course. In summer, loungers flank the swimming pool and croquet hoops stand on the lawn. Bedrooms have an uncluttered country-house feel: seaside colours, tongue-and-groove bathrooms, padded bedheads, a sofa if there's room. Some are enormous with timber frames or an exposed stone wall. You can eat in a Regency muralled dining room or the brasserie-style restaurant (there's a terrace for fine weather). Try Isle of Wight asparagus, local lobster, praline chocolate finger. *Minimum stay two nights at weekends.*

Price	£160–£300. Singles from £90.
Rooms	18: 16 twins/doubles, 2 family rooms.
Meals	Lunch £22.50. Dinner, 3 courses, £35.
Closed	Never.
Directions	South from Ryde on B3330. Through Nettlestone and hotel signed left and left again.

10% off room rate Mon-Thurs.

Andrew Palmer
Priory Road, Seaview PO34 5BU
Tel   +44 (0)1983 613146
Email   enquiries@priorybay.co.uk
Web   www.priorybay.co.uk

Seaview Hotel

Everything here is a dream. You're 50 yards from the water in a small seaside village that sweeps you back to a nostalgic past. Locals pop in for a pint, famished yachtsmen float in for a meal, those in the know drop by for a luxurious night in indulging rooms. The bar has nautical curios nailed to its walls, the terrace buzzes with island life in summer, the restaurants hum with the contented sighs of happy diners. The whole show is orchestrated by Andrew and a battalion of kind staff, who book taxis, carry bags, send you off in the right direction. Interior designer Graham Green oversaw the fabulous refurbishment; some rooms come in smart country-house style (upholstered four-posters, padded headboards), others are contemporary (cool colours, fancy bathrooms). Three new apartments have blossomed from a converted bank next door, another is on the way. Don't miss the food. The hotel has its own farm – home-reared meat, home-grown vegetable's, home-laid eggs, while the crab ramekin is an island institution. There's a treatment room, too, for expert pampering. *Minimum stay two nights at weekends.*

Price	£125–£220. Suites from £210.
Rooms	29: 14 twins/doubles, 3 four-posters. New wing: 4 doubles, 3 twins/doubles, 5 family suites.
Meals	Lunch & dinner £5–£35.
Closed	One week at Christmas.
Directions	From Ryde B3330 south for 1.5 miles. Hotel signed left.

Upgrade on arrival subject to availability. Champagne and chocolates in room. 10% off dining in restaurant.

Andrew Morgan
High Street, Seaview PO34 5EX

Tel	+44 (0)1983 612711
Email	reception@seaviewhotel.co.uk
Web	www.seaviewhotel.co.uk

The George Hotel

The George is a kingly retreat; Charles II stayed in 1671 and you can sleep in his room with its panelling and high ceilings. The house, a grand mansion in the middle of tiny Yarmouth, has stupendous views of the Solent; Admiral Sir Robert Holmes took full advantage of them when in residence, nipping off to sack passing ships. These days traditional interiors mix with contemporary flourishes. Ancient panelling and stone flags come as standard in the old house, but push on past the crackling fire in the bar to find an airy brasserie with walls of glass that open onto the terrace. You can eat here in summer, next to the castle walls, with sailboats zipping past – a perfect spot for black truffles and scrambled eggs, New Forest venison with peppercorn butter, fig tart with honey and almond ice cream. Bedrooms come in country-house style, some with crowns above the bed, others with fabulous views. Two rooms have balconies that overlook the water, but smaller rooms at the back have the same homely style. Head off to Osborne House, Cowes for the regatta or The Needles for magical walks. *Minimum stay two nights at weekends.*

Price	£190–£255. Singles from £99.
Rooms	19 twins/doubles.
Meals	Lunch & dinner from £20.
Closed	Rarely.
Directions	Lymington ferry to Yarmouth, then follow signs to town centre.

Jeremy Wilcock
Quay Street, Yarmouth PO41 0PE

Tel	+44 (0)1983 760331
Email	res@thegeorge.co.uk
Web	www.thegeorge.co.uk

The Reading Rooms

The Reading Rooms is a work of art, a statement about the passing of time, its walls stripped back to their Georgian roots with original plaster on display. It is also one of the loveliest places you could ever hope to stay, with each room luxuriously occupying an entire floor. Vast bedrooms at the front peer through beautiful windows while jaw-dropping bathrooms wait behind with free-standing baths and double showers. Design is minimalist, but never short on beauty, with big mirrors, high ceilings, stripped boards and massive beds. Breakfast is brought to you whenever you want – fruit smoothies, strong coffee, porridge with honey, the full cooked works. Liam, a DJ turned architect, and Louise, ex-music industry, are on hand to point you in the right direction. Margate, one of Britain's first holiday resorts, opened reading rooms for its Georgian visitors, hence the name; Keats and Nelson came. These days it's the Turner Contemporary, a spectacular new art gallery overlooking the sea, that's the draw. And where else to stay than this design B&B, a five-minute stroll? London is 90 minutes by train.

Price	£135-£170.
Rooms	3 doubles.
Meals	Restaurants in town.
Closed	Rarely.
Directions	M2, A229, then A28 into Margate. Fork right at clock tower on sea front. Right at lights at T-junction, then square on left.

Louise Oldfield & Liam Nabb
31 Hawley Square,
Margate CT9 1PH

Tel	+44 (0)1843 225166
Email	info@thereadingroomsmargate.co.uk
Web	www.thereadingroomsmargate.co.uk

The Royal Harbour Hotel

A delightfully quirky townhouse hotel that stands on a Georgian crescent with magnificent views of harbour and sea. Simplicity, elegance and a quiet eccentricity go hand in hand. The sitting room is a dream with stripped floors, gorgeous armchairs, a crackling fire and an honesty bar. Beautiful things abound: a roll top desk, super art, potted palms, a miniature orange tree bearing fruit. There are binoculars with which to scan the high seas (Ramsgate was home to the Commander of the Channel Fleet), books by the hundred for a good read (Dickens's Bleak House is up the road in Broadstairs) and a library of DVDs for the telly in your room or the cinema in the basement (home to an inspiring film production company). Bedrooms at the front are tiny, but have the view, those at the back are bigger and quieter. The suite is enormous with a coal fire and French windows that open onto a balcony. All have good linen, excellent shower rooms and flat-screen TVs. Breakfast is a leisurely feast with cured hams from James's brother, a Rick Stein food hero. *Minimum stay two nights at weekends in high season.*

Price	£99–£139. Singles from £79. Suite £198.
Rooms	19: 13 doubles, 2 family rooms, 3 singles, 1 suite.
Meals	Restaurants in town.
Closed	Rarely.
Directions	M2, A299, then A256 into Ramsgate. Follow signs for town centre, pick up coast on right. On left as road drops down hill.

James Thomas
10–11 Nelson Crescent,
Ramsgate CT11 9JF

Tel	+44 (0)1843 591514
Email	info@royalharbourhotel.co.uk
Web	www.royalharbourhotel.co.uk

Late checkout (12pm).

The Bell Hotel

Sandwich, a Cinque port, is England's best-preserved medieval town. It's tiny, dates to the 12th century, and timber-framed houses are found all over town. The Bell stands opposite the old toll gate, where the river Stour glides past on its way to the sea. You can follow it down to Sandwich Bay past the famous Royal St George's golf course. Back at the hotel, oak revolving doors propel you into an elegant world of golden hues, smouldering logs and vintage luggage piled up in a corner. Open-plan interiors flow from restaurant to conservatory to bar. All are smart and airy, with blond wood and halogen lighting giving a contemporary feel. Doors open onto a terrace in summer, while locally sourced seasonal food hits the spot perfectly. Bedrooms come in different sizes and mix comfort and style in equal measure. The bigger ones with river views are fabulous, but all have warm colours, sparkling bathrooms, digital radios and WiFi access. Canterbury is a 20-minute drive, Broadstairs, a pretty seaside town, is worth a peek. *Minimum stay two nights at weekends July/August.*

Price	£110–£165. Suites £190–£210. Singles from £95. Half-board from £80 p.p.
Rooms	37: 29 twins/doubles, 4 family rooms, 2 singles, 2 suites.
Meals	Lunch from £5. Dinner £15–£30. Sunday lunch £15.50.
Closed	Never.
Directions	A2, M2, A299, then A256 south. Follow signs into Sandwich. Over bridge, hotel on left by river.

10% off room rate.

Matt Collins
1 Upper Strand Street,
Sandwich CT13 9EF

Tel	+44 (0)1304 613388
Email	reservations@bellhotelsandwich.co.uk
Web	www.bellhotelsandwich.co.uk

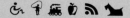

The Salutation

An enchanting house, utterly beguiling. You slip through a gate on the bustling quay, then there you are, peacefully ensconced behind ancient walls. The house, an absolute jaw-dropper, was built by Lutyens in 1911, but it's almost eclipsed by the Secret Gardens, some of the loveliest in England. Gorgeous bedrooms are dotted about in three beautifully restored cottages; two suites in Knightrider House look out across beds of rose and iris. All come with gorgeous sitting rooms, fancy kitchens and super dining rooms, making them perfect boltholes for families or a group of friends. Four rooms share bathrooms, but are only let to the same party, so if you come alone, you may get a whole cottage to yourself. Every conceivable luxury comes in abundance: rich fabrics, antique furnishings, gorgeous linen, French-style beds. There are fresh flowers, too, lots of books and a bar that's 'on the house.' Breakfast is served grandly in the big house; dinner can be arranged for groups over 10. Medieval Sandwich waits, as does Canterbury and its cathedral and the links at Royal St George's. Very special.

Price	£180–£215.
Rooms	Knightrider House: 2 doubles; 2 doubles sharing bath. Coach House: 2 doubles. Garden Cottage: 3 doubles sharing bath & shower. All with kitchens.
Meals	Restaurants 200m.
Closed	Christmas & New Year.
Directions	M2 east, A299 for Ramsgate, A256 south to Sandwich. Over bridge, left along river, then right into Knightrider Street. On left at end of lane.

Dominic & Stephanie Parker
Knightrider Street,
Sandwich CT13 9EW

Tel	+44 (0)1304 619919
Email	dominic@the-salutation.com
Web	www.the-salutation.com

The White Cliffs Hotel & Trading Co.

You're lost in the last folds of England with the beach at the bottom of the hill and the White Cliffs of Dover soaring above, so climb up for views that stretch across to France. This pretty weatherboard hotel stands a mile back from the water with a fine Norman church across the road that's shielded by a curtain of lush trees. Inside, airy interiors come with stripped floors, sandblasted beams, contemporary art and an open fire in the sitting room/bar. Best of all is the walled garden with climbing roses, colourful borders and a trim lawn that plays host to Sunday lunch in summer. Bedrooms are all over the place. Those in the main house are bigger and more sophisticated, and come in bold colours with silky curtains, gilt mirrors and the odd four-poster. Garden rooms are altogether more simple, but good value for money. Expect summer colours, wooden beds, trim carpets and crisp linen. In the restaurant there's meat from Kent, fish from local waters and a children's menu, too. Dover Castle and Sandwich are close and you can use the pool and spa at Wallett's Court, the other half of Gavin's empire.

 25% off room rate Mon-Thurs.

Price	£99–£109. Family suites £129. Singles from £54.
Rooms	15: 4 doubles, 1 triple, 1 four-poster. Mews cottages: 4 doubles, 1 twin, 2 singles, 2 family suites.
Meals	Lunch from £4.50. Dinner, 3 courses, £25–£30.
Closed	Rarely.
Directions	M20/A20 into Dover, then A2 north. At roundabout right for Deal, then right again for St Margaret's. Right in village; hotel on left.

Chris, Lea & Gavin Oakley
High Street, St Margaret's-at-Cliffe,
Dover CT15 6AT
Tel   +44 (0)1304 852229
Email   mail@thewhitecliffs.com
Web   www.thewhitecliffs.com

Wallett's Court Country House Hotel & Spa

A fabulous position at the end of England, with sweeping fields heading south towards white cliffs; you can follow paths across to a lighthouse for rather good views. The hotel stands opposite a Norman church on land gifted by William the Conqueror to his brother Odo. The current building dates from 1627, but recent additions include an indoor swimming pool which opens onto the garden, and cabins for treatments hidden in the trees. Eight acres of grounds include lush lawns, a tennis court, a boules pitch and a climbing frame for kids. Timber-framed interiors come with contemporary art on ancient brick walls, a fire roars in a sitting-room bar and sublime food waits in the whitewashed restaurant – perhaps crab cakes with a chilli sauce, Gressingham duck with a spring onion rösti, a toothsome banana tarte tatin. Bedrooms are scattered about, some grandly traditional with four-posters in the main house, others simpler and quieter in the outbuildings; the suites above the pool come in contemporary style. Canterbury cathedral, Sandwich golf course and Dover Castle are close. *Minimum stay two nights at weekends half-board.*

Price	£129–£199. Singles £109–£139.
Rooms	16: 12 twins/doubles, 4 suites.
Meals	Lunch from £5. Sunday lunch £25. Dinner, 3 courses, £40.
Closed	Christmas.
Directions	From Dover A2 & A20, then A258 towards Deal. Right, signed St Margaret's at Cliffe. House 1 mile on right, signed.

	Chris, Lea & Gavin Oakley
	Dover Road, Westcliffe,
	Dover CT15 6EW
Tel	+44 (0)1304 852424
Email	mail@wallettscourt.com
Web	www.wallettscourt.com

25% off room rate Mon-Thurs.

The Marquis at Alkham

Lying in the peaceful Alkham Valley, The Marquis has the feel of deep country – you'd never think you were minutes from the motorway or Dover's bustling port or the Channel Tunnel (Paris is less than three hours away). Instead, footpaths lead off to rolling downland, cricket graces the green in summer, lofty white cliffs are just over the hill. Recently refurbished, this old village pub is now a chic bolthole, a restaurant with rooms with a cool new look: whitewashed walls, blond wood floors, leather sofas and a laid-back feel. Serious food comes from a menu that evolves with the seasons, perhaps Dover-caught crab, Godmersham pheasant, pear tart tatin with bay leaf ice cream. It's all as local as possible with allotment vegetables often bartered for a bottle of wine. Above, five stylish rooms come with contemporary wallpapers, clean lines and stylish hues. Expect crisp linen on big beds, plasma screens and espresso machines, then swish bathrooms with monsoon showers. Rooms at the front have views of village and valley. Canterbury and Sandwich are close.

Price	£95-£185. Suite £195-£235. Singles from £65. Half board from £67.50 p.p.
Rooms	5: 4 doubles, 1 suite.
Meals	Lunch from £12.50. Sunday lunch from £18.95. Dinner: set menu £18.95-£24.95; à la carte £32.50-£42.50.
Closed	Rarely.
Directions	M20 south for Dover, A20 to first exit, then south for 50m on A260 for Folkestone. 1st left for Alkham. In village, on right, after three miles.

25% off room rate Mon-Thurs.

Ben & Hannah Walton
Alkham Valley Road, Alkham,
Dover CT15 7DF

Tel	+44 (0)1304 873410
Email	info@themarquisatalkham.co.uk
Web	www.themarquisatalkham.co.uk

The Relish

It's not just the super-comfy interiors that make The Relish such a tempting port of call. There's a sense of generosity here: a drink on the house each night in the sitting room; tea and cakes on tap all day; free internet throughout. This is a grand 1850s merchant's house on the posh side of town with warmly contemporary interiors; wind up the cast-iron staircase to find bedrooms that make you smile. Hypnos beds with padded headboards wear crisp white linen and pretty throws. You get a sense of space, a sofa if there's room, big mirrors and fabulous bathrooms. All are great value for money. Downstairs there are candles on the mantelpieces above an open fire, stripped wooden floors and padded benches in the dining room; in summer, you can decamp onto the terrace for breakfast, a four-acre communal garden stretching out beyond. You're one street back from Folkestone's cliff-top front for huge sea views; steps lead down to smart gardens and the promenade. There are takeaway breakfasts for early Eurostar departures and a local restaurant guide in every room. *Minimum stay two nights at weekends in summer.*

Price	£95–£125. Four-poster £145. Singles from £69.
Rooms	10: 2 twins/doubles, 6 doubles, 1 four-poster, 1 single.
Meals	Restaurants nearby.
Closed	22 December–2 January.
Directions	In centre of town, from Langholm Gardens, head west on Sandgate Road. 1st right into Augusta Gardens/Trinity Gardens. Hotel on right.

Chris & Sarah van Dyke
4 Augusta Gardens,
Folkestone CT20 2RR

Tel	+44 (0)1303 850952
Email	reservations@hotelrelish.co.uk
Web	www.hotelrelish.co.uk

Wife of Bath

With Canterbury on your doorstep, you'd guess this restaurant took its name from Chaucer's famous tale, but the wife in question belonged to the original owner, whom he met in Bath. Named in her honour, it opened in 1963 to great acclaim, one of the first restaurants with rooms to appear in the country. Over the years it has reinvented itself several times, always keeping its reputation for fabulous food; current chef, Robert Hymers, has been at the helm for 16 years. A recent refurbishment has brought Georgian interiors back to life. Expect airy whites, timber frames, the odd roll of fancy wallpaper. There's a bar for cocktails, after which you are whisked through to feast on super food, perhaps watercress and nettle soup with grated horseradish, pressed shoulder of lamb with pistachio pesto, warm pear tart with rosemary ice cream. Bedrooms give every reason to make the most of the wine list, so knock back a good claret, then retire to pretty rooms (crisp linen, Farrow & Ball colours, the odd beam and bathrobes). Great walks start from the village; Ashford is close for Eurostar.

Price	£95–£115. Singles from £75.
Rooms	5: 3 doubles, 1 twin, 1 four-poster.
Meals	Lunch £15–£18. Dinner, 3 courses, £30–£35.
Closed	Sunday & Monday nights.
Directions	M20 junc. 10, then A2070 & immediately right for Wye. Follow signs for 3 miles into Wye. Left in village; on left.

 Glass of champagne on arrival.

Gregory Loison
4 Upper Bridge Street, Wye,
Ashford TN25 5AF

Tel	+44 (0)1233 812232
Email	relax@thewifeofbath.com
Web	www.thewifeofbath.com

Elvey Farm

This ancient Kentish farmhouse stands in six acres of blissful peace half a mile up a private drive. It's a deeply rural position, a nostalgic sweep back to old England. White roses run riot on red walls, a cooling vine shades the veranda, trim lawns are flanked by colourful borders. Inside you find timber frames at every turn, but the feel is airy and contemporary with smart furniture sitting amid stripped boards and old beams. Bedrooms come in similar vein. The two in the main house are big and very family-friendly, while those in the stable block are seriously indulging with chunky beds wrapped in crisp cotton, small sitting areas with flat-screen TV/DVDs, and fabulous wet rooms (two have slipper baths). The four-poster suite comes with a hot tub in a secret garden, but all open onto the veranda, beyond which tables and chairs are scattered across the lawn. As for the restaurant, seasonal menus of Kentish fare offer long-lost treats: potted ham, hop-pickers pie... and gypsy tart. Leeds Castle is close; the *Darling Buds of May* was filmed in the village.

Price	£105–£225.
Rooms	11: 2 suites for 4. Stable block: 1 four-poster, 4 suites. Oast house: 2 doubles. Granary: 2 suites.
Meals	Dinner £23–£28. Sunday lunch from £12.95.
Closed	Never.
Directions	M20 junc. 8, then A20 to Lenham. At Charing r'bout 3rd exit for A20 Ashford. Right at the lights to Pluckley. Bypass village, down hill, right at pub, then right and right again.

Jeff Moody & Simon Peek
Pluckley,
Ashford TN27 0SU

Tel	+44 (0)1233 840442
Email	bookings@elveyfarm.co.uk
Web	www.elveyfarm.co.uk

10% off room rate Mon-Thurs.

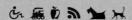

Cloth Hall Oast

Sweep up the rhododendron-lined drive to this immaculate Kentish oast house and barn. For 40 years Mrs Morgan lived in the 15th-century manor next door where she tended both guests and garden; now she has turned her perfectionist's eye upon these five acres. There are well-groomed lawns, a carp-filled pond, pergola, summer house, heated pool and flower beds – two of orange and yellow, four all-white. Light shimmers through swathes of glass in the dining room; there are off-white walls and pale beams that soar from floor to rafter. Mrs Morgan is a courteous hostess and an excellent cook, and will rustle up dinner on request; you dine at an antique table gleaming with crystal and candelabra. There are three bedrooms for guests: a four-poster on the ground floor, a triple and a queen-size double on the first. Colours are soft, fabrics are frilled but nothing is busy or overdone; you are spoiled with good bathrooms and fine mattresses, crisp linen, flowered chintz… and a Michelin starred restaurant in the village. Return to the sitting room for guests, made snug by a log fire on winter nights. *No credit cards.*

Price	£90-£125.
Rooms	3: 1 four-poster, 1 triple, 1 double.
Meals	Dinner from £25, by arrangement. Pub & restaurant 1 mile.
Closed	Christmas.
Directions	Leave village with windmill on left, taking Golford Road east for Tenterden. After a mile right, before cemetery. Signed right.

10% off room rate Mon-Thurs. Late checkout (12pm).

Katherine Morgan
Course Horn Lane, Cranbrook TN17 3NR
Tel +44 (0)1580 712220
Email clothhalloast@aol.com
Web www.clothhalloast.co.uk

The Spread Eagle

If you know a better inn in Britain, let us know. The Spread Eagle is one of those rare places that scores ten out of ten on all counts. First, there's its sublime position on the banks of the Ribble, then there's the pub itself, a pleasure dome for the senses. Its airy interiors draw in locals and walkers alike, and they come for fabulous food, well-kept ales, and happy staff who go the extra mile. Inside: Farrow & Ball colours, sofas and settles, roaring fires, flagstones and beams. An elegant dining room comes with library wallpaper, but this is an informal place and you can eat whatever you want wherever you want, so dig into pressed duck terrine, steak, stout and stilton pudding, pear tarte tatin with cider sorbet. Gorgeous bedrooms are fantastic value for money. Expect style and colour, lavish linen, big beds and fat mattresses. Some have river views, all have fancy showers, one has a bathtub in the room. You're in the glorious Ribble valley, on the southern edge of the Yorkshire Dales: Malham is close for walking, Settle for antiques. To quote a reader: 'I couldn't fault anything.' Wonderful.

Price	£80–£99. Suite £120. Singles from £70.
Rooms	7: 4 doubles, 2 twins/doubles, 1 suite.
Meals	Lunch & dinner £5–£30.
Closed	Never.
Directions	A59 north past Clitheroe. Sawley & Sawley Abbey signed left after 2 miles.

Kate & Gary Peill
Sawley, Clitheroe BB7 4NH

Tel	+44 (0)1200 441202
Email	spread.eagle@zen.co.uk
Web	www.spreadeaglesawley.co.uk

 10% off room rate. Bottle of wine in your room.

The Inn at Whitewell

It is almost impossible to imagine a day when a better inn will grace the English landscape. Everything here is perfect. The inn sits just above the river Hodder with five-mile views across blistering parkland to rising fells; doors in the bar lead onto a terrace where guests sit in a row and gaze upon it. Inside, fires roar, the papers wait, there are beams, sofas, maps and copies of Wisden. Bedrooms are exemplary and come with real luxury, perhaps a peat fire, a lavish four-poster, a fabulous Victorian power shower. All have beautiful fabrics, Egyptian linen and gadgets galore; many have the view – you can fall asleep at night to the sound of the river. There's a restaurant for splendid food (the Queen once popped in for lunch), so dig into seared scallops, Bowland lamb, a plate of cheese or something sweet; there are bar meals for those who want to watch their weight and the Whitewell fish pie is rightly famous. Elsewhere, a small vintners in reception, seven miles of private fishing and countryside as good as any in the land. Magnificent.

Price	£113–£162. Suite £191. Singles from £83.
Rooms	23: 9 twins/doubles, 13 four-posters, 1 suite.
Meals	Bar meals from £8. Dinner £25–£35.
Closed	Never.
Directions	M6 junc. 31A, B6243 east through Longridge, then follow signs to Whitewell for 9 miles.

Charles Bowman
Dunsop Road, Whitewell,
Clitheroe BB7 3AT

Tel	+44 (0)1200 448222
Email	reception@innatwhitewell.com
Web	www.innatwhitewell.com

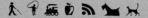

The Ashton

The Ashton offers what most people want: a host who goes the extra mile, beautiful rooms you won't want to leave, super food at the end of the day. James, once a TV set designer, has poured love and money into his new home, making this boutique B&B much more than an overnight stop for those hurtling along the M6. The house, set back from a quiet road, stands in country on the edge of this historic town. Outside chickens strut their stuff, providing eggs for breakfast, while inside classical and contemporary designs mix harmoniously, all the result of a total renovation. There's a small sitting room with candles in the fireplace and piles of glossy books, a dining room in racing green for excellent breakfasts, a treatment room for massage at weekends. Best of all are the bedrooms. Some are bigger than others, but all come with Hypnos beds, crisp white linen, flat-screen TVs and DVD players, white robes in seriously cool bathrooms. Dinner is by arrangement, perhaps homemade soup, shepherds pie, sticky toffee pudding. If you want to eat out, the Bay Horse at Forton is excelllent. Morecambe Bay is close.

Price	£118–£168. Singles from £98.
Rooms	5 twins/doubles.
Meals	Lunch & dinner £24–£39. By arrangement.
Closed	Never.
Directions	M6 junc. 33, then A6 north into Lancaster. Thru' traffic lights at supermarket; 1st right; then right at mini roundabout. Right after 0.5 mile for Clitheroe. On right after 0.3 mile.

James Gray
Wyresdale Road,
Lancaster LA1 3JJ

Tel	+44 (0)1524 68460
Email	stay@theashtonlancaster.com
Web	www.theashtonlancaster.com

The Cartford Inn

Patrick and Julie know how to run a great little inn: whisk up some fabulous food, throw in a pinch of contemporary style, then add distinctly groovy rooms and serve informally. It's a recipe that's proved so popular they've had to expand: the restaurant now overlooks the river Wyre, while nine sizzling new bedrooms have been added above. Not that they've lost an ounce of the magic that makes this place so special. The front bar, with its whitewashed walls, roaring fire and friendly locals, is a great place to stop for a pint of local ale, though a courtyard garden will draw you out in good weather. In typically relaxed style you can eat whatever you want wherever you want: tuck into king prawns with fresh mango and chilli salsa; oxtail, beef and real ale pudding with green beans; glazed lemon tart and raspberry sorbet. Bedrooms are just as good – gilded sleigh beds, funky wallpaper, crisp white linen, river views. One has a claw-foot bath in the room, the penthouse suite has its own balcony. Pull yourself away and follow the river; a two-mile circular walk will spin you round. Fantastic.

Price	£90–£120. Suite £190. Singles from £65 (Sun-Thurs only).
Rooms	15: 13 doubles, 1 twin, 1 penthouse suite.
Meals	Lunch from £8.50. Dinner, 3 courses, £20–£30.
Closed	Christmas Day.
Directions	M6 junc. 32, M55 junc 3, then A585 north. Right at T-junction onto A586 for Garstang. Little Ecclestone signed left.

Patrick & Julie Beaume
Cartford Lane, Little Eccleston,
Preston PR3 0YP

Tel	+44 (0)1995 670166
Email	info@thecartfordinn.co.uk
Web	www.thecartfordinn.co.uk

The Bull & Swan

A magical renovation, an ancient inn that stands a short walk from the middle of glorious Stamford. It is part of the Burghley estate, and the Order of Little Bedlam, a 17th-century aristocratic drinking club, almost certainly popped in for the odd snifter. Not that they had it this good. Step inside and find varnished wood floors, golden stone walls, fires smouldering all over the place, newspapers hanging on poles. At the bar venison Scotch eggs are impossible to resist, as are a raft of local ales and splendid wines. You eat wherever you want, here or in the dining room across the coach arch, where leather-backed settles take the strain and regal oils adorn the walls. As for the beautiful bedrooms, they come in country-house style with huge beds, fabulous linen, warm colours and super-funky bathrooms. Most are big, all are delightful, two interconnect, mattresses are divine. Back downstairs, delicious food waits, perhaps stilton on toast, estate game pie, apple and blueberry crumble. Don't miss Burghley, a five-minute stroll, one of Britain's finest houses.

Price	£80–£110. Half-board from £70 p.p.
Rooms	7: 5 doubles, 2 twins/family.
Meals	Lunch from £6. Dinner, 3 courses, £25–£30.
Closed	Never.
Directions	On the Old London Road, just south of the river and town centre, heading south towards the A1.

	Ben Larter
	St Martins,
	Stamford PE9 2LJ
Tel	+44 (0)1780 766412
Email	enquiries@thebullandswan.co.uk
Web	www.thebullandswan.co.uk

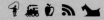 Bottle of wine with dinner on first night.

base2stay Liverpool

This canny small hotel group has a very simple philosophy: find a beautiful building, renovate stylishly, design brilliant bedrooms, add attractive prices. Having taken London by storm they've come north to the epicentre of cultural Liverpool. This 19th-century building, once a beeswax factory, stands in the old RopeWalks district, half a mile up from the Albert Docks. Inside, everything you'd hope for in a cool little bolthole: staff who care, loads of style, city life on your doorstep. Excellent bedrooms vary in size and price, but not style. Rooms at the top have big city views, all have charcoal carpets, super-comfy beds, air con, crisp white linen. Beautiful bathrooms come as standard while HD TVs supply films, free music and internet access (WiFi is 'on the house', too). Some interconnect, duplex suites come over two floors, one has a private terrace. All have mini-kitchens hidden behind wardrobe doors (microwave, sink, fridge, kettle, Nespresso machine), so you can make your own breakfast, have it delivered or nip round the corner to a flurry of local cafés. All this two hours by train from Euston.

Price	£75-£150. Suites £135-£250. Singles from £65.
Rooms	106: 26 doubles, 27 twins, 26 triples/ family, 9 suites, 18 singles. All with kitchenette.
Meals	Breakfast £5-£10. Restaurants nearby (many offer discounts to guests).
Closed	Never.
Directions	Pick up signs for centre of town, then Lime Street station. Pass station on left, then bear right into Berry Street after 800m. Third right; car parks on Seel Street.

Andrea Burton
29-35 Seel Street,
Liverpool L1 4AU

Tel	+44 (0)151 705 2626
Email	info@base2stayliverpool.com
Web	www.base2stay.com

SACO Holborn Serviced Apartments

Lamb's Conduit Street is cool, quirky and pedestrianised with a sprinkling of cafés and restaurants, including the mayor of London's favourite eaterie. A recent refurbishment has made these serviced apartments a great central base for people who want to look after themselves. You get the equivalent of a hotel suite and find super-cool kitchens thrown in for free. Sparkling top-floor apartments open onto vast decked terraces while those below have walls of glass overlooking the street. It's all a big surprise, given the utilitarian 60s exterior: the interiors have both space and style, with open-plan kitchen/sitting rooms, excellent bathrooms, comfy bedrooms and lots of appealing extras such as washing machines, dishwashers and flat-screen TVs. The building stands directly opposite Great Ormond Street Hospital and it's quiet at night, devoid of the crowds. It's also brilliantly central: you can walk to St Paul's, Oxford Street *and* the British Museum. Waitrose for shopping and Russell Square for the tube are both a step away. *Long-stay rates available.*

Price	£150–£367.
Rooms	30 apartments for 2, 4 or 6. 2 penthouse suites.
Meals	Self-catered. Restaurants nearby.
Closed	Never.
Directions	Train: Liverpool Street. Tube: Russell Square. Bus: 19, 38, 55, 243. Private parking from £15 a day.

	Tim Ripman
	72-84 Lamb's Conduit Street, Holborn, London WC1N 3LT
Tel	+44 (0)20 7269 9930
Email	london@sacoapartments.co.uk
Web	london.sacoapartments.co.uk

22 York Street

A 1820s Georgian-style townhouse in W1 – not your average London residence, and one that defies all attempts to pigeonhole it. There are 10 bedrooms, but it is homelier than a hotel, and the price is hard to beat for the centre of town. Breakfast is a meal of great conviviality taken around an impressive curved wooden table in a big kitchen with a pretty dresser. Elsewhere, there's always something to catch your eye, be it the red-lipped oil painting outside the dining room or the old riding boots on the landing. Wooden floors run throughout, a fine stone staircase winds up four flights. The house has a first-floor sitting room (original high ceilings, shuttered windows) with sofas, books and backgammon and a cosy room off it for making tea and coffee. Bedrooms, spotless and comfy, have Provençal eiderdowns, good beds, country rugs, perhaps a square piano or a chaise longue; the rear basement room has skylights only. There's a computer for guests to use, friendly staff to care for you and Marylebone HIgh Street, Regent's Park and Lord's are close. A welcoming bolthole in a superb position.

Price	£129. Singles £89–£109.
Rooms	10: 5 doubles, 2 twins, 3 singles.
Meals	Continental breakfast included. Pubs/restaurants nearby.
Closed	Never.
Directions	Train: Paddington (to Heathrow). Tube: Baker Street (2-minute walk). Bus: 2, 13, 30, 74, 82, 113, 139, 274. Parking: £25 a day, off-street.

Michael & Liz Callis
Marylebone,
London W1U 6PX

Tel	+44 (0)20 7224 2990
Email	mc@22yorkstreet.co.uk
Web	www.22yorkstreet.co.uk

Searcys Roof Garden Bedrooms

Only in old black-and-white films do you sidle straight from the pavement into an ancient lift, losing your pursuer with sublime ease, but that's how it goes at Searcys. Four floors up and you emerge into a quiet corridor with lovely bedrooms waiting and an office that serves as reception. It is altogether low-key and surprising, with no public area, nothing 'hotelly' – other than the rooms themselves – and the charming staff who bring breakfast and drinks and whatever you need. In a quiet area behind busy Knightsbridge, close to Harrods with Hyde Park a short stroll away, this is an unusual hotel and all the better for it. As for the rooms, a recent refurbishment has brought comfort and style back to the middle of London; much is splendid. Breakfasts arrive promptly and elegantly to your room; somehow you feel that you are inhabiting a private space far from the delightful madness of London. Sleep with windows open and be accosted by nobody. If you want to eat in, local restaurants will deliver. Discreet and comfortable, with touches of luxury – a survivor in its own category.

Price	£249. Singles £139. Suite £299.
Rooms	11: 7 twins/doubles, 3 singles, 1 family suite.
Meals	Continental breakfast included. 24-hour room service (light meals). Restaurants nearby.
Closed	Christmas.
Directions	Train: Victoria (to Gatwick). Tube: Knightsbridge (5-minute walk); Sloane Sq. (10-minute walk). Bus: 9, 10, 14, 19, 22, 137. Parking: £58 a day, off-street.

Neringa Zutautaite
30 Pavilion Road, Knightsbridge,
London SW1X 0HJ

Tel	+44 (0)20 7584 4921
Email	rgr@searcys.co.uk
Web	www.searcys.co.uk

 Bottle of wine.

Lime Tree Hotel

You'll be hard pressed to find better value in the centre of town. The Lime Tree – two elegant Georgian townhouses – stands less than a mile from Buckingham Palace, with Westminster, Sloane Square and Piccadilly within walking distance. Add warm interiors, kind owners and one of the capital's loveliest pubs waiting round the corner and you've unearthed a London gem. There's Cole & Son wallpaper in the airy dining room, so dig into an excellent breakfast (included in the price), then drop into the tiny sitting room next door for guide books and a computer for guests to use. Rooms – one on the ground floor with doors onto the garden – are just the ticket: smart without being lavish; this is a great place for a night or a week. Expect warm colours, crisp linen, pretty wallpaper and excellent bathrooms (most have super showers). Those at the front on the first floor have high ceilings and fine windows, those at the top are cosy in the eaves. Charlotte and Matt are hands-on and will point you in the right direction. Don't miss the Thomas Cubitt pub (50 paces from the front door) for seriously good food.

Price	£145-£165. Triple £170-£190. Family room £205. Singles £95-£125.
Rooms	25: 14 doubles, 3 twins, 4 triples, 1 family room, 3 singles.
Meals	Restaurants nearby.
Closed	Never.
Directions	Train: Victoria (to Gatwick). Tube: Victoria or Sloan Square. Bus: 11, 24, 38, 52, 73, C1. Parking: £34 a day off-street.

Charlotte & Matt Goodsall
135 Ebury Street,
London SW1W 9QU

Tel   +44 (0)20 7730 8191
Email info@limetreehotel.co.uk
Web   www.limetreehotel.co.uk

base2stay Kensington

Stylish rooms and attractive prices make this London bolthole a brilliant base. Part hotel, part serviced apartments, the idea is to keep things simple and pass on the savings to guests. You won't find a bar or a restaurant, you will find a tiny kitchen cleverly concealed behind cupboard doors in each room. You get fridges, kettles, sinks and microwaves, so chill drinks, make your own breakfast or zap up an evening meal. Super rooms come in contemporary style and offer a lot for the money: energy-efficient lighting, crisp white linen, air conditioning and flat-screen TVs through which you can google the night away at no cost (free WiFi, too). Watch movies on demand, play games, raid the hotel's music library for 6,000 tracks. Bathrooms are excellent and come with limestone tiles, big white towels and power showers. Bustling Earl's Court is on your doorstep, but there's a directory of local restaurants that deliver to the door. Also: 24-hour reception, a concierge service, good security and a daily maid service. The hotel is family-friendly and local restaurants offer discounts to base guests.

Price	£113–£164. Triples £173–£199. Suites £215–£247. Singles £95–£118.
Rooms	67: 33 twins/doubles, 13 triples, 17 singles, 4 suites. All with kitchenettes.
Meals	Self-catered. Restaurants nearby.
Closed	Never.
Directions	Tube: Earl's Court (3-minute walk). Bus: 74, 328, C1, C3. Parking: £30 a day, off-street.

	Amie Conway 25 Courtfield Gardens, Earl's Court, London SW5 0PG
Tel	+44 (0)20 7244 2255
Email	info@base2stay.com
Web	www.base2stay.com

The Troubadour

Bob Dylan played here in the 1960s, so did Jimi Hendrix, Joni Mitchell, Paul Simon and the Rolling Stones. The Troubadour is a slice of old London cool, a quirky coffee house/bar in Earls Court with a magical garden and a small club in the basement where bands play most nights. Outside, pavement tables make the best of the weather, inside the past lives on: rows of teapots elegantly displayed in the windows date from 1954, when the bar opened. The ceiling drips with musical instruments, you find stripped boards, tables and booths, the odd pew. The kitchen is open all day (if you wear a hat on Tuesday nights, pudding is free), so try Welsh rarebit, bangers and mash, Belgian waffles with chocolate ice cream; in summer, you can eat in the courtyard garden. Next door, two floors above The Gallery, is the Garret, a vibrant suite up in the eaves which gives views to the back of London rooftops. Expect colour, a super-comfy bed, leather armchairs in front of the flat-screen TV, an alcoholic fridge. There's a kitchen, too: wake before 9am and make your own breakfast, or come down after for bacon and eggs served late into the afternoon.

Price	From £175. Singles from £160.
Rooms	1 suite for 2-4.
Meals	Breakfast from £4.25. Lunch & dinner £5-£25.
Closed	25 & 26 December; 1 January.
Directions	Tube: Earl's Court or West Brompton (both 5-minute walk). Bus: 74, 328, 430, C1, C3. Car parks £35 a day.
🎁	Use your Sawday's Gift Card here.

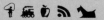 Bottle of wine with dinner on first night. Late checkout (12pm).

Simon & Susie Thornhill
263-267 Old Brompton Road,
London SW5 9JA
Tel   +44 (0)20 7370 1434
Email   susie@troubadour.co.uk
Web   www.troubadour.co.uk

Temple Lodge Club

Temple Lodge, once home to the painter Sir Frank Brangwyn, is sandwiched between a courtyard and a lushly landscaped garden. The peace is remarkable making it a very restful place – simple yet human and warmly comfortable – an extremely nourishing experience. Michael and a small devoted team run it with quiet energy. You breakfast overlooking the garden, there are newspapers to browse, a library instead of TVs. Bedrooms make you smile and come with crisp linen, garden views, good books, excellent prints. They're surprisingly stylish – clean, uncluttered with a hint of country chic – and represent exceptional value for money. Only one double has its own bathroom and loo; if you don't mind that, you'll be delighted. The Thames passes by at the end of the road, the Riverside Studios are close for theatre and film. Nearer still is the Gate Vegetarian Restaurant, ten paces across the courtyard. It's a well-known eatery and was Brangwyn's studio, hence the enormous artist's window. The house is a non-denominational Christian centre with two services a week, which you may take or leave as you choose.

Price	£68-£92. Singles £57-£62.
Rooms	10: 2 doubles en suite (1 with separate wc); 3 twins, 5 twins/singles all sharing 2 baths & 1 shower.
Meals	Continental breakfast included. Vegetarian restaurant across courtyard.
Closed	Never.
Directions	Tube: Hammersmith (5-minute walk). Bus: 9, 10, 27, 295.

Michael Beaumont
51 Queen Caroline Street,
Hammersmith, London W6 9QL

Tel   +44 (0)20 8748 8388
Email   templelodgeclub@btconnect.com
Web   www.templelodgeclub.com

10% off meals at the Gate restaurant; Sunday nights half price January & February.

MIC Hotel & Conference Centre

Central London hotels usually cost a bomb; MIC bucks that trend. It stands around the corner from Euston station in a pretty side street that's quiet at night. Tottenham Court Road, Camden Market and the British Museum are all close. The big surprise is a batch of attractive rooms that come with attractive prices. MIC itself is a social enterprise which supports a village in Kenya and pays for the education of overseas students who wouldn't be able to study without help. It funds this work with its bedrooms, conference suites and meeting rooms, all of which you can use when in town. Inside, you find a large central atrium: very informal, lots of colour. You can tap into free WiFi, order a coffee or a drink at the bar, even dig into good food (the full English for breakfast, paninis at lunch, rack of lamb or spicy salmon for dinner). As for the bedrooms, some are smaller than others, but the same crisp style runs throughout: contemporary panelling, charcoal carpets, pressed white linen, air conditioning, super bathrooms. Become a member (£100) for big discounts. Brilliant.

Price	£130–£149.
Rooms	28: 12 twins, 14 doubles, 2 triples.
Meals	Lunch & dinner £5–£20. Pubs/restaurants nearby.
Closed	Never.
Directions	Train: Euston, St Pancras (Eurostar). Tube: Euston or Warren Street (both 5-min walk). Bus: 10, 18, 24, 29, 30, 59, 68, 73, 91, 134, 168. 253. Car parks £30 a day.

Bottle of wine with dinner on first night.

James Barr
81-103 Euston Street,
London NW1 2EZ
Tel   +44 (0)20 7380 0001
Email reservations@micentre.com
Web   www.micentre.com

Bingham

The Bingham, a super little boutique hotel, stands above the Thames at Richmond Bridge, with a terrace for fabulous food in summer and a small garden that drops down to the towpath, so follow the river into town. This is a lovely spot to escape the London crush and it's easily done – the train from Waterloo whisks you home in seventeen minutes, though you can also travel in kingly style; the riverboat from Westminster to Hampton Court will drop you off in town. Back at the hotel chic interiors abound, not least in the mirrored bar, where you sink into comfy sofas under a grand high ceiling to sip your Kir Royale. Bedrooms are elegant and contemporary, with cool colours, crisp white linen, excellent beds, padded headboards. Some have chandeliers, others have ornamental fireplaces, those at the back overlook the river. All come with flat-screen TVs and robes in excellent bathrooms. Back downstairs ambrosial food waits in the restaurant, perhaps poached brill with razor clams, slow-cooked suckling pig, fig parfait with espresso syrup. Don't miss Kew Gardens or Richmond's magnificent deer park.

Price	£170–£285.
Rooms	15: 10 doubles, 3 singles, 2 four-posters.
Meals	Breakfast £11–£15. Lunch from £22.50. Dinner, 3 courses, from £55.
Closed	Never.
Directions	Train: Richmond (to Waterloo & Victoria). Tube: Richmond. Bus: 65, 371.

Samantha Trinder
61-63 Petersham Road,
Richmond TW10 6UT
Tel +44 (0)20 8940 0902
Email info@thebingham.co.uk
Web www.thebingham.co.uk

Gin Trap Inn

An actor and a lawyer run this old English Inn. Steve and Cindy left London for the quiet life and haven't stopped since, adding a conservatory dining room at the back and giving the garden a haircut. The Gin Trap dates to 1667, while the horse chestnut tree that shades the front took root in the 19th century; a conker championship is in the offing. A smart whitewashed exterior gives way to a beamed locals' bar with a crackling fire and the original dining room in Farrow & Ball hues. Upstairs, you find three delightful bedrooms in smart country style. Two have big bathrooms with claw-foot baths and separate showers, all come with timber frames, cushioned window seats, Jane Churchill fabrics and the odd chandelier; walkers will find great comfort here. Come down for delicious food: Thornham oysters, shoulder of lamb, a plate of local cheeses. Ringstead – a pretty village lost in the country – is two miles inland from the coastal road, thus peaceful at night. You're on the Peddars Way, Sandringham is close and fabulous sandy beaches beckon.

Price	£78-£120. Singles from £39.
Rooms	3 doubles.
Meals	Lunch from £7. Dinner from £20.
Closed	Rarely.
Directions	North from King's Lynn on A149. Ringstead signed right in Heacham. Pub on right in village.

Steve Knowles & Cindy Cook
6 High Street, Ringstead,
Hunstanton PE36 5JU

Tel	+44 (0)1485 525264
Email	thegintrap@hotmail.co.uk
Web	www.gintrapinn.co.uk

Titchwell Manor

A lane nearby leads down to the sea, where a vast sky hangs above huge tracts of sandy beach. In between stands Titchwell's famous RSPB sanctuary; guided tours include the May dawn chorus, stupendous stuff. Back at this brick-and-flint Victorian manor there's a mix of the modern and traditional; the new Eating Rooms and seaview terrace are eclectically bold, while there's the odd tumbling fern in a conservatory dining room that has its own terrace in summer. Open fires smoulder, views from first-floor rooms drift over fields and out to sea. Bedrooms – some simple in the main house – are light and airy, nicely uncluttered, with warm colours, crisp linen and padded headboards. Courtyard rooms open onto a parterre herb garden and come with neutral colours, flat-screen TVs and super bathrooms; some at the back have French windows onto small terraces. There's also a potting shed for two, complete with rustic interiors and a free-standing bath. Spin back to the main house for an excellent meal, perhaps local oysters, Cromer crabs, Dexter beef. There's a walled garden for afternoon tea and golf all along the coast.

Price	£110–£250. Half-board from £75 p.p.
Rooms	27: 7 doubles, 1 family. Cottages: 4 doubles, 2 family. Herb Garden: 6 doubles, 7 twins/doubles.
Meals	Lunch from £7. Sunday lunch £14. Picnic £10. Dinner £30–£35. Tasting menu £45.
Closed	Never.
Directions	20 miles north from King's Lynn on A149 to Titchwell. Hotel in village on right.

Margaret Snaith
Main Road, Titchwell,
King's Lynn PE31 8BB

Tel	+44 (0)1485 210221
Email	margaret@titchwellmanor.com
Web	www.titchwellmanor.com

Glass of champagne on arrival.

The White Horse

You strike gold at The White Horse. For a start, you get one of the best views on the North Norfolk coast – a long, cool sweep over tidal marshes to Scolt Head Island. But it's not just the proximity of the water that elates: the inn, its rooms and the delicious food all score top marks. Follow your nose and find a sunken garden at the front, a local's bar for billiards, a couple of sofas for a game of Scrabble, and a conservatory/dining room for the freshest fish. Best of all is the sun-trapping terrace; eat out here in summer. Walkers pass, sea birds swoop, sail boats glide off into the sunset. At high tide the water laps at the garden edge, at low tide fishermen harvest mussels and oysters from the bay. Inside, the feel is smart without being stuffy: stripped boards, open fires, seaside chic with sunny colours. Beautiful bedrooms in New England style come in duck-egg blue with spotless bathrooms. In the main house some have fabulous views, those in the garden open onto flower-filled terraces. The coastal path passes directly outside. *Minimum stay two nights April-October & all weekends.*

Price	£96–£190.
Rooms	15: 11 doubles, 4 twins.
Meals	Lunch & bar meals from £8.50. Dinner £13.50–£17.75. Sunday lunch £23.15.
Closed	Never.
Directions	Midway between Hunstanton & Wells-next-the-Sea on A149.

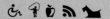 Half bottle of champagne in your room on arrival.

Cliff Nye
Brancaster Staithe,
King's Lynn PE31 8BY
Tel   +44 (0)1485 210262
Email   reception@whitehorsebrancaster.co.uk
Web   www.whitehorsebrancaster.co.uk

The Hoste Arms

Nelson was a local, but now it's farmers, fishermen and film stars who jostle at the bar and roast away on winter evenings in front of a roaring fire. In its 300-year history The Hoste has been a court house, a livestock market, a gallery and a brothel. These days it's more pleasure dome than inn and even on a grey February morning it was buzzing with life. The place has a genius of its own with warm bold colours, armchairs to sink into, panelled walls, a conservatory, its own art gallery. Fabulous food can be eaten anywhere and anytime, so dig into Brancaster mussels, Holkham venison, sticky toffee pudding. In summer life spills out onto tables at the front or you can dine on the Moroccan styled terrace in the garden at the back. Rooms are all different: a tartan four-poster, an oak half-tester, leather sleigh beds in the Zulu wing, or country-house elegance across the road in the Vine House; bathrooms are all predictably over the top. Burnham Market is gorgeous, the north Norfolk coast is on your doorstep, but don't miss afternoon tea – or the ladies' loo!

Price	£122-£271. Singles £122-£241. Suites £170-£312. Half-board from £76.50 p.p.
Rooms	49 + 3: 34 twins/doubles/suites. Vine House: 7 doubles. Railway Inn: 7 doubles, 1 carriage. 3 self-catering railway cottages.
Meals	Lunch from £6. Dinner, 3 courses, £25-£30.
Closed	Never.
Directions	On B1155 for Burnham Market. By green & church in village centre.

Emma Tagg
Market Place, Burnham Market,
King's Lynn PE31 8HD

Tel	+44 (0)1328 738777
Email	reception@hostearms.co.uk
Web	www.hostearms.co.uk

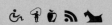

The Blakeney Hotel

The view here is imperious, a clean sweep across the salt marshes up to Blakeney Point. The estuary passes five paces from the front door and guests are prone to fall into graceful inertia and watch the boats slide by. There are plenty of places to do this from: a sun-trapping terrace; a convivial bar; a traditional restaurant for super food; a magnificent first-floor sitting room. Half the bedrooms have recently been refurbished in warm contemporary style (cool creams, stylish fabrics, painted beams, fancy bathrooms), but the traditional rooms are pretty, too (soft chintz, yellows and reds, super beds, the crispest linen). You'll find the daily papers and an open fire in the sitting room; a snooker room; a super-cool indoor swimming pool with steam room and sauna attached. Outside, paths lead down to the marshes, there are seals to spot, birds to peer at, links golf at Sheringham and Cromer. Finally, delicious food awaits your return, perhaps local mussels in white wine, saddle of venison with a port sauce, roasted pineapple with rum and raisin ice cream.

Price	£154–£314. Singles from £77. Half board from £89 p.p.
Rooms	63: 19 doubles, 36 twins/doubles, 8 singles.
Meals	Lunch from £5.95. Dinner, 3 courses, £27.50–£42.
Closed	Never.
Directions	A148 north from Fakenham, then B1156 north to Blakeney. In village on quay.

Michael Stannard
The Quay, Blakeney, Holt NR25 7NE

Tel	+44 (0)1263 740797
Email	reception@blakeneyhotel.co.uk
Web	www.blakeneyhotel.co.uk

Cley Windmill

The setting here is magical with rushes fluttering in the salt marsh, raised paths leading off to the sea and a vast sky that seemingly starts at your feet. The windmill dates to 1713 and was converted into a house in the 1920s. Square rooms are bigger and suit those who prefer to shuffle, while round rooms in the tower are impossibly romantic (one is for mountaineers only). Six rooms are in the mill and you really want to go for these, though the cottage is set up for self-catering and visiting dogs. Inside, you find the loveliest drawing room – low ceiling, open fire, honesty bar, stripped floorboards… and a window seat to beat most others. Bedrooms come in country style with pretty pine, painted wood, colourful walls, super views. Rooms in the tower (with compact shower rooms) get smaller as you rise, but the view improves with every step; there's a viewing platform half way up for all. Meals are taken in a pretty dining room, so drop down for a big breakfast or book for dinner: homemade soups, local-fish pie, sinful puddings. *Minimum stay two nights at weekends.*

Price	£80-£165. Singles from £92. Cottage (min. 3 nights) £275 for first night, extra nights £85.
Rooms	8 + 1: 6 doubles, 2 twins/doubles. 1 self-catering cottage.
Meals	Dinner, 3 courses, £32.50.
Closed	Never.
Directions	Head east through Cley on A149. Mill signed on left in village.

Charlotte Martin
The Quay, Cley, Holt NR25 7RP

Tel	+44 (0)1263 740209
Email	info@cleywindmill.co.uk
Web	www.cleywindmill.co.uk

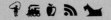

The Wiveton Bell

A dreamy village one mile back from Norfolk's magical coast: you'll find a scattering of cottages, a brick-and-flint church and this super little inn on the village green. This is reclaimed land. 300 years ago the sea ran up to the church and eight trade ships sat in the harbour below; now idyllic views sweep across fields to Cley. As for the Bell, a recent refurbishment has planted it firmly back on the map. Airy interiors shine while old beams, timber frames and stripped boards give a warm rustic feel. You get bright whites, contemporary art and comfy armchairs in front of the wood-burner. Doors open back and front onto garden and green respectully, though super-stylish bedrooms all have their own terrace. You also get fabulous bathrooms, flat-screen TVs and DVD players, then underfloor heating and iPod docks. Breakfast hampers are delivered to your door with a newspaper in the morning, so you can enjoy warm croissants leisurely in the summer sun. Great bistro-style food waits in the restaurant – fresh fish, local meat – while on a clear night shooting stars arch through the sky. *Min. two nights at weekends.*

Price	£95–£140.
Rooms	4 doubles.
Meals	Lunch from £6.95. Dinner, 3 courses, around £30.
Closed	Christmas Day.
Directions	Wiveton signed south off A149 at Blakeney; pub on the green.

 Bottle of wine with dinner on first night.

Berni Morritt & Sandy Butcher
Blakeney Road, Wiveton, Holt NR25 7TL
Tel   +44 (0)1263 740101
Email   wivetonbellroom@me.com
Web   www.wivetonbell.com

Byfords Café, Deli & Posh B&B

A listed deli-store with rooms in a Georgian market town three miles south of the North Norfolk coast. There's a café, too, one that was packed to the gunnels on a Sunday morning in February. Downstairs, labyrinthine interiors weave past red-brick walls and timber-framed alcoves, all of which ooze rustic chic, but it's the bedrooms that take the biscuit: this is 'posh B&B' as the brochure exclaims, without exaggeration. Rooms on the first floor have country rugs on stripped oak boards, Vi-Spring mattresses on half-tester beds, travertine marble bathrooms, Bang & Olufsen TVs. One floor up and you find rooms open to timbered eaves – smaller, but ever so cute and with all the same trappings (speakers in the bathroom ceilings, Egyptian cotton on the beds, vases of lilies liberally displayed, the odd panelled wall). When hunger strikes, drop down to a domed oak restaurant for delicious local food cooked in Mediterranean-style. There's a vaulted cellar bar, and in summer life spills onto the pavement. Don't forget to stop at the deli; delicious things wait. *Minimum stay two nights at weekends.*

Price	£140–£190. Singles from £105.
Rooms	16: 3 twins/doubles, 12 doubles, 1 family room.
Meals	Lunch & dinner from £8.95.
Closed	Never.
Directions	A148 for Cromer and into town. On main street (heading east), left after Barclays Bank into car park.

Iain Wilson
1-3 Shirehall Plain, Holt NR25 6BG

Tel	+44 (0)1263 711400
Email	queries@byfords.org.uk
Web	www.byfords.org.uk

Saracens Head

Lost in the lanes of deepest Norfolk, an English inn that's hard to beat. Outside, Georgian red-brick walls ripple around, encircling a beautiful courtyard where you can sit for sundowners in summer before slipping into the restaurant for a good meal. Tim and Janie came back from the Alps, unable to resist the allure of this inn. A sympathetic refurbishment has brightened things up, but the spirit remains the same: this is a country-house pub with lovely staff who go the extra mile. Downstairs the bar hums with happy locals who come for Norfolk ales and good French wines, while the food in the restaurant is as good as it ever was, perhaps baked camembert, haunch of venison, treacle tart and caramel ice cream. Upstairs you'll find a sitting room on the landing, where windows frame country views, and six pretty bedrooms. All have been redecorated and have smart carpets, blond wood furniture, comfy beds and sparkling bathrooms. Breakfast sets you up for the day, so explore the coast at Cromer, play golf on the cliffs at Sheringham, or visit Blickling Hall, a Jacobean pile. Blissful stuff.

Price	From £95. Singles £65.
Rooms	6: 5 twins/doubles, 1 family room.
Meals	Lunch & dinner £6.50-£20. Not Monday or Tuesday lunch Sept-June.
Closed	25-28 December.
Directions	From Norwich A140 past Aylsham, then 3rd left for Erpingham. Right into Calthorpe, through village, straight out the other side (not right). On right after about 0.5 miles.

 15% off dinner (Tues-Thurs).

Tim & Janie Elwes
Wolterton, Norwich NR11 7LZ

Tel	+44 (0)1263 768909
Email	info@saracenshead-norfolk.co.uk
Web	www.saracenshead-norfolk.co.uk

Strattons

There's nowhere quite like Strattons, a country-house bolthole that doubles as a contemporary art gallery. It's also one of Britain's greenest hotels (arrive by public transport and pay 10% less for your room), so substance and style go hand in hand. Wander about and find cowhide rugs on stripped wood floors, busts and murals by the dozen, art packed tight on the walls. Les and Vanessa met at art school and their Queen Anne villa overflows with beautiful things. Bedrooms are exquisite: a carved four-poster, a tented bathroom, Indian brocade, trompe l'œil panelling. You'll find vintage wallpaper, sofas by a log fire, new suites and apartments that spoil you rotten. Wonderful food in the candlelit restaurant (turn right by the chaise longue) is mostly organic, perhaps wild mushroom risotto, local pheasant, chocolate fondant with nougatine ice cream. Charlie talks you through the cheese board with great panache, and breakfast (smoked salmon, eggs from their own chickens, organic porridge) is equally divine. Don't miss the Brecks for cycle tracks through Thetford forest. *Minimum two nights at weekends.*

Ethical Collection: Environment; Community; Food. See page 386 for details

Price	£155–£180. Suites & apartments £205–£275. Singles from £125.
Rooms	14: 6 doubles, 1 twin/double, 5 suites, 2 apartments.
Meals	Lunch in deli from £6. A la carte dinner about £30. Sunday lunch from £25.
Closed	One week at Christmas.
Directions	Ash Close runs off north end of market place between W H Brown estate agents & fish & chip restaurant.

Vanessa & Les Scott
4 Ash Close, Swaffham PE37 7NH
Tel   +44 (0)1760 723845
Email   enquiries@strattonshotel.com
Web   www.strattonshotel.com

Bottle of Norfolk wine with dinner on first night.

The Mulberry Tree

Attleborough is ancient, mentioned in the Domesday Book. Its weekly market is 800 years old, its monastery suffered at the hands of Henry VIII and a fire swept through in 1559. These days it's a sleepy English country town with a good line in street names: Defunct Passage, Surrogate Precinct and Thieves Lane all bring a smile. It's also well-positioned for Norwich, Snetterton, Thetford Forest and Bury St Edmund's, making the Mulberry Tree a great little base for minor explorations. Airy interiors come in Farrow & Ball colours with stripped floors, big mirrors and contemporary art on the walls. There's a buzzing bar for local ales, a restaurant for super food and a garden that overlooks the bowling green. Best of all are excellent rooms that spoil you rotten: big beds, crisp linen, padded heads, flat-screen TVs. Willow twigs stand six feet high, mirrors lean against the wall, there are cushioned wicker chairs and fabulous tongue-and-groove bathrooms. Back downstairs in the bar, dig into Suffolk ham, free-range eggs and hand-cut chips, or slip into the restaurant for a three-course feast.

Price	£95. Singles £72.50.
Rooms	7: 6 doubles, 1 twin/double.
Meals	Lunch from £7. Dinner, 3 courses, £25–£30.
Closed	Christmas.
Directions	On one-way system around town centre at junction with Station Road.

Philip & Victoria Milligan
Station Road, Attleborough NR17 2AS
Tel   +44 (0)1953 452124
Email   relax@the-mulberry-tree.co.uk
Web   www.the-mulberry-tree.co.uk

Rushton Hall

Rushton Hall, a 15th-century mansion of gargantuan proportions, was home to Francis Tresham, who took part in the Gunpowder Plot; priest holes abound, while a tiny chapel has ornate frescos. The house stands in 25 acres with a small lake and sheep grazing in neighbouring fields. Step inside and the first thing you notice is a vast courtyard around which the house was built; in summer you spill out for lunch in the sun. Elsewhere, you find a cellar bar and a panelled dining room, but it's the Great Hall that takes away your breath – a vast room that soars towards heaven, with old oils crammed on the walls and huge windows that flood the room with light; sink into sofas here and read the papers while flames leap in the enormous fireplace. Bedrooms vary. Some are vast and have loads of character (mullioned windows, oak panelling, ornate ceilings, four-poster beds). Others are simpler altogether, but those in the main house (the place to stay) have an airy contemporary feel and excellent little bathrooms. There's a spa, too: a proper pool, treatment rooms, a steam room and sauna.

Price	£150–£190. Suites £200–£220. Four-poster rooms £250–£350.
Rooms	45: 30 twins/doubles, 6 suites, 4 four-posters.
Meals	Lunch from £6.50. Dinner £32–£39.
Closed	Never.
Directions	A14 to Rothwell, then east, signed Rushton. Left at T-junction and on left.

Valerie Hazelton
Rushton NN14 1RR

Tel	+44 (0)1536 713001
Email	enquiries@rushtonhall.com
Web	www.rushtonhall.com

 10% off room rate.

Northumberland   Hotel

Eshott Hall

An utterly gorgeous Palladian mansion set in 35 acres of medieval woodlands and pasture; its mellow golden stone may have been 'reclaimed' from a castle that stood near by. Wisteria fans out at the front, there's an ancient fernery, paths that weave past rare trees, an extremely productive kitchen garden. Inside is equally grand. You get wing-backed armchairs and leather sofas in front of the library fire; Corinthian columns and a fine ceiling in the yellow drawing room; a restaurant that doubles as a ballroom and which opens onto the garden. Climb the staircase, pass a stained-glass window designed by William Morris and discover a batch of beautiful bedrooms recently refurbished. You'll find high ceilings, pretty views, sumptuous beds, iPod docks. A couple come with free-standing baths in the room and one with a copy of Nelson's bed; stylish bathrooms have natural stone, white robes, spoiling oils. Pull yourself away and discover ancient castles, white beaches, fantastic country, then return for a good meal, perhaps local seafood, game in season, chilled lemon soufflé. Brilliant.

Ethical Collection: Environment; Community; Food. See page 386 for details

Price	£140–£210. Singles from £130.
Rooms	11: 9 doubles, 2 twins.
Meals	Lunch, by arrangement, £19.95. Dinner, 3 courses, £35.
Closed	24 & 25 December.
Directions	East off A1 7 miles north of Morpeth, 9 miles south of Alnwick, at Eshott signpost. Hall gates approx. 1 mile down lane.

Bottle of champagne for bookings of 2 nights or more.

Dan & Louise Ball
Eshott, Morpeth NE65 9EN
Tel   +44 (0)1670 787454
Email   info@eshotthall.co.uk
Web   www.eshotthall.co.uk

Entry 180   Map 9

The Pheasant Inn

A really super little inn, the kind you hope to chance upon. The Kershaws run it with great passion and an instinctive understanding of its traditions. The stone walls hold 100-year-old photos of the local community; from colliery to smithy, a vital record of its past. The bars are wonderful: brass beer taps glow, anything wooden – ceiling, beams, tables – has been polished to perfection and the clock above the fire keeps perfect time. The attention to detail is a delight, the house ales expertly kept: Timothy Taylor's and Northern Kite. Robin cooks with relish, again nothing too fancy, but more than enough to keep a smile on your face – cider-baked gammon, grilled sea bass with herb butter, wicked puddings, Northumbrian cheeses; as for Sunday lunch, *The Observer* voted it the best in the North. Bedrooms in the old hay barn are as you'd expect: simple and cosy, good value for money. You are in the glorious Northumberland National Park – no traffic jams, no rush. Hire bikes and cycle round the lake, canoe or sail on it, or saddle up and take to the hills. *Minimum stay two nights at weekends.*

Price	£90–£100. Singles £50–£65. Half-board from £70 p.p.
Rooms	8: 4 doubles, 3 twins, 1 family room.
Meals	Bar meals from £8.95. Dinner, 3 courses, £18–£22.
Closed	25-27 December.
Directions	From Bellingham follow signs west to Kielder Water & Falstone for 9 miles. Hotel on left, 1 mile short of Kielder Water.

Walter, Irene & Robin Kershaw
Stannersburn, Hexham NE48 1DD

Tel	+44 (0)1434 240382
Email	stay@thepheasantinn.com
Web	www.thepheasantinn.com

10% off stays of 2 or more nights. Bottle of wine with dinner on first night.

Hart's Nottingham

A small enclave of good things. You're on the smart side of town at the end of a cul-de-sac, thus remarkably quiet. You're also at the top of the hill and close to the castle with exceptional views that sweep south for ten miles; at night, a carpet of light sparkles. Inside, cool lines and travertine marble greet you in reception. Bedrooms are excellent, not huge, but perfectly adequate and extremely well designed. All come with wide-screen TVs, Bose sound systems, super little bathrooms and king-size beds wrapped in Egyptian cotton. Those on the ground floor open onto a fine garden, each with a terrace where you can breakfast in good weather; rooms on higher floors have better views (six overlook the courtyard). A cool little bar, the hub of the hotel, is open for breakfast, lunch and dinner, but Hart's Restaurant across the courtyard offers fabulous food, perhaps pan-fried wood pigeon with blackberries, free-range chicken with wild garlic, tarte tatin with caramel ice cream. There's a private car park for hotel guests and a small gym for those who must.

Price	£125–£175. Suites £265.
Rooms	32: 29 doubles, 1 family room, 2 suites.
Meals	Continental breakfast £9, full English £14. Bar snacks from £3.50. Lunch from £14.95. Dinner, 3 courses, £26.
Closed	Never.
Directions	M1 junc. 24, then follow signs for city centre and Nottingham Castle. Left into Park Row from Maid Marian Way. Hotel on left at top of hill.

 25% off room rate Mon-Thurs.

Katinka Rieger
Standard Hill, Park Row,
Nottingham NG1 6FN
Tel   +44 (0)115 988 1900
Email   reception@hartshotel.co.uk
Web   www.hartsnottingham.co.uk

Langar Hall

Langar Hall is one of the most engaging and delightful places in this book – reason enough to come to Nottinghamshire. Imogen's exquisite style and natural joie de vivre make this a mecca for those in search of a warm, country-house atmosphere. The house sits at the top of a hardly noticeable hill in glorious parkland, bang next door to the church. Imo's family came here over 150 years ago, building on the site of Admiral Lord Howe's burned-down home. Much of what fills the house arrived then and it's easy to feel intoxicated by beautiful things: statues and busts, a pillared dining room, ancient tomes in overflowing bookshelves, a good collection of oil paintings. Bedrooms are wonderful, some resplendent with antiques, others with fabrics draped from beams or trompe l'œil panelling. Heavenly food, simply prepared for healthy eating, makes this almost a restaurant with rooms, so come for Langar lamb, fish from Brixham, game from Belvoir Castle and garden-grown vegetables. In the grounds: medieval fishponds, canals, a den-like adventure play area and, once a year, Shakespeare on the lawn.

Price	£95–£185. Suite £210. Singles from £75.
Rooms	12: 7 doubles, 2 twins, 1 four-poster, 1 suite, 1 chalet for 2.
Meals	Lunch from £15. Dinner, 3 courses, £25–£35.
Closed	Never.
Directions	From Nottingham A52 towards Grantham. Right, signed Cropwell Bishop, then straight on for 5 miles. House next to church on edge of village, signed.

Imogen Skirving
Church Lane, Langar,
Nottingham NG13 9HG

Tel   +44 (0)1949 860559
Email   info@langarhall.co.uk
Web   www.langarhall.com

10% off room rate Mon-Thurs. Automatic upgrade subject to availability. Late checkout (12pm).

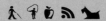

Entry 183   Map 6

The Feathered Nest Country Inn

The village is tiny, the view is fantastic, the bar is lively, the rooms are a treat. This 300-year-old malthouse recently had a facelift and now shines. Interiors mix all the old originals – stone walls, timber frames, beamed ceilings, open fires – with a contemporary, rustic style. The net result is an extremely attractive country inn, one of the best in the south. Downstairs, one room flows into another. You get beautiful bay windows, roaring fires, saddled bar stools, green leather armchairs. Everywhere you go something lovely catches the eye, not least the view – the best in the Cotswolds; it will draw you to the terrace where your eyes drift off over quilted fields to a distant ridge. You get beds of lavender, swathes of lawn, a vegetable garden that serves the kitchen. Bedrooms upstairs are gorgeous. One is enormous, two have the view, beds are dressed in crisp linen. Most have power showers, one has a claw-foot bath, all have robes. There are coffee machines and iPod docks, too. Super food waits downstairs: Old Spot terrine, Fairford chicken, rhubarb and champagne jelly. *Minimum stay two nights at weekends.*

Price	£120-£145. Suite £170.
Rooms	4: 1 double, 1 twin, 1 family, 1 suite.
Meals	Lunch & dinner £6.50-£30.
Closed	Never.
Directions	North from Burford on A424 for Stow-on-the-Wold. After 4 miles right for Nether Westcote. In village.

Tony & Amanda Timmer
Nether Westcote,
Chipping Norton OX7 6SD

Tel	+44 (0)1993 833030
Email	reservations@thefeatherednestinn.co.uk
Web	www.thefeatherednestinn.co.uk

The Kingham Plough

You don't expect to find locals clamouring for a table in a country pub on a cold Tuesday in February, but different rules apply at the Kingham Plough. Emily, once junior sous chef at the famous Fat Duck in Bray, is now doing her own thing and it would seem the locals approve. You eat in the tithe barn, now a splendid dining room, with ceilings open to ancient rafters and excellent art on the walls. Attentive staff bring sublime food. Dig into game broth with pheasant dumplings, fabulous lamb hotpot with crispy kale, and hot chocolate fondant with blood orange sorbet. Interiors elsewhere are equally pretty, all the result of a delightful refurbishment. There's a piano by the fire in the locals' bar, a terrace outside for summer dining, fruit trees, herbs and lavender in the garden. Bedrooms, three of which are small, have honest prices and come with super-comfy beds, flat-screen TVs, smart carpets, white linen, the odd beam; one has a claw-foot bath. Arrive by train, straight from London, to be met by a bus that delivers you to the front door. The Daylesford Organic farm shop/café is close.

Price	£90–£130. Singles from £75.
Rooms	7 twins/doubles.
Meals	Lunch from £15. Bar meals from £5. Dinner, 3 courses, about £30. Sunday lunch from £17.
Closed	Christmas Day.
Directions	In village, off B4450, between Chipping Norton & Stow-on-the-Wold.

Emily Watkins & Miles Lampson
The Green, Kingham,
Chipping Norton OX7 6YD
Tel   +44 (0)1608 658327
Email   book@thekinghamplough.co.uk
Web   www.thekinghamplough.co.uk

10% off room rate Mon-Thurs.
10% off stays of 2 or more nights.

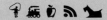

The Kings Head Inn

The sort of inn that defines this country: a 16th-century cider house made of ancient stone that sits on the green in a Cotswold village with free-range hens strutting their stuff and a family of ducks bathing in the pond. Inside, locals gather to chew the cud, scoff great food and wash it down with a cleansing ale. The fire burns all year, you get low ceilings, painted stone walls, country rugs on flagstone floors. Bedrooms, all different, are scattered about; all are well priced. Those in the main house have more character, those in the courtyard are bigger (and quieter). You'll find painted wood, lots of colour, pretty fabrics, spotless bathrooms; most have great views, too. Breakfast and supper are taken in a pretty dining room (exposed stone walls, pale wood tables), while you can lunch by the fire in the bar on Cornish scallops, steak and ale pie, then a plate of British cheeses. There are lovely unpompous touches like jugs of cow parsley in the loo, and loads to do: antiques in Stow, golf at Burford, walking and riding through gorgeous terrain. The front terrace teams with life in summer.

Price	£90–£125. Singles from £70.
Rooms	12: 10 doubles, 2 twins/doubles.
Meals	Lunch from £6. Bar meals from £7. Dinner from £12. Sunday lunch £26.
Closed	Christmas Day & Boxing Day.
Directions	East out of Stow-on-the-Wold on A436, then right onto B4450 for Bledington. Pub in village on green.

Archie & Nicola Orr-Ewing
The Green, Bledington,
Chipping Norton OX7 6XQ

Tel   +44 (0)1608 658365
Email   info@kingsheadinn.net
Web   www.kingsheadinn.net

The Feathers Hotel

Woodstock is hard to beat, its golden cottages stitched together seamlessly. It's intrinsically linked to Blenheim Palace, one of Britain's finest houses, seat of the Dukes of Marlborough, birthplace of Winston Churchill. You can stroll up in five minutes, drop your jaw, then return to this wonderfully indulging hotel. It sits serenely on the high street with a carriage arch leading through to a stone courtyard where you sit in summer sipping your Pimms; just heavenly. Inside, a total refurbishment has poured in colour and style. You get old stone walls, parquet flooring, a roaring wood-burner, ancient windows that flood the place with light. Bedrooms are dreamy, big or small, with beautiful fabrics, lovely beds, mohair throws, delicious wallpapers. Some have sofas, all come with robes in gorgeous bathrooms. Back downstairs, the bar has over 100 varieties of gin – there's even a tasting menu with a different shot at each course. They'll help you wash down some wonderful food, perhaps scallop ravioli, slow-cooked Tamworth pork, passion fruit soufflé with its own sorbet. Oxford is close. *Min. two nights at weekends in summer.*

Price	£169–£229. Suites £259–£319. Singles from £129.
Rooms	21: 13 doubles, 3 twins/doubles, 5 suites.
Meals	Lunch from £5. Dinner £39.95–£49.95 (not Sunday eve).
Closed	Never.
Directions	North from Oxford on A44. In Woodstock left after traffic lights & hotel on left.

Luc Morel
Market Street,
Woodstock OX20 1SX

Tel   +44 (0)1993 812291
Email   enquiries@feathers.co.uk
Web   www.feathers.co.uk

10% off room rate Mon-Thurs.

Kings Arms Hotel

Woodstock is the estate village to Blenheim Palace, home to the Dukes of Marlborough, birthplace of Winston Churchill, and one of the country's architectural gems. It is open most of the year and there is no better way to arrive than by foot after a good breakfast at a local inn. Cue the King's Arms, a late Georgian hostelry which stands on the corner of Market Place and the Oxford Street. In summer, tables and chairs line up smartly outside, while in winter the wood-burner works overtime in the bar, the logs jammed into alcoves all over the place. Airy, open-plan interiors drift easily from one room to another. You get leather stools at a marble bar, stripped floors in the restaurant, huge hanging lampshades in the breakfast room. There are clean lines, contemporary art, big antique mirrors, the odd settle – a cute mix of old and new. Uncluttered bedrooms come in cool colours and all sizes, many with high ceilings, all with crisp linen, wooden bedheads, black and white photographs and nice little bathrooms. One room is huge with exposed timbers. Posh pub grub waits downstairs. Oxford is close.

Price	£140–£150. Singles from £75.
Rooms	15: 14 doubles, 1 twin.
Meals	Lunch from £8.75. Dinner, 3 courses, about £30.
Closed	Never.
Directions	In Woodstock on A44 at corner of Market Street in town centre.

25% off stays of 2 or more nights.

David & Sara Sykes
19 Market Street, Woodstock OX20 1SU

Tel	+44 (0)1993 813636
Email	stay@kingshotelwoodstock.co.uk
Web	www.kingshotelwoodstock.co.uk

The Swan

This ancient country pub sits in glorious country with the river Windrush passing yards from the front door and a cricket pitch waiting beyond. It started life as a water mill and stands on the Devonshire estate (the Duchess advised on its restoration). Outside, wisteria wanders along stone walls and creepers blush red in the autumn sun. Interiors come laden with period charm: beautiful windows, open fires, warm colours, the odd beam. Over the years thirsty feet have worn grooves into 400-year-old flagstones, so follow in their footsteps and stop for a pint of Hook Norton at the bar, then eat from a seasonal menu that brims with local produce: deep-fried Windrush goat's cheese, Foxbury Farm chargrilled steak, rich chocolate tart with orange sorbet. Fires roar in winter while doors in the conservatory restaurant open to a pretty garden in fine weather. Bedrooms in the old forge are the most recent addition. Expect 15th-century walls and 21st-century interior design. You get pastel colours to soak up the light, smart white linen on comfy beds and a pink chaise longue in the suite.

Price	£110–£180. Singles from £70.
Rooms	6: 4 doubles, 1 twin, 1 suite.
Meals	Lunch from £7.50. Sunday lunch £25. Dinner from £12.
Closed	Christmas Day & Boxing Day.
Directions	West from Oxford on A40 for Cheltenham/Burford. Past Witney and village signed right at 1st r'bout.

Archie & Nicola Orr-Ewing
Swinbrook, Burford OX18 4DY

Tel	+44 (0)1993 823339
Email	info@theswanswinbrook.co.uk
Web	www.theswanswinbrook.co.uk

25% off room rate Mon-Thurs.

Burford House

Burford was made rich by 14th-century mill owners. Its golden high street slips downhill to the river Windrush, where paths lead out into glorious country, passing a church that dates to Norman times; Cromwell held a band of Levellers here in 1649 and their murals survive inside. Halfway up the hill, this 17th-century timber-framed house stands bang in the middle of town. Interiors sweep you back to the soft elegance of old England: a couple of cosy sitting rooms, a fire that roars, exposed stone walls, a courtyard for summer dining. Slip into the restaurant and find Farrow & Ball colours, freshly cut flowers, rugs on wood boards, theatre posters hanging on the wall. Lunch is offered six days a week — and now dinner at weekends — so try salmon fishcakes, Cotswold lamb, spiced plum cheesecake. Bedrooms are delightful, two across the courtyard in the coach house. Some have oak beams, others a claw-foot bath. All come with super beds, woollen blankets, robes in good bathrooms and those at the back have rooftop views. Wake on Sunday to the sound of pealing bells. *Minimum stay two nights at weekends.*

Price	£159-£199. Singles from £124.
Rooms	8: 3 doubles, 2 twins/doubles, 3 four-posters.
Meals	Light lunch from £4.95 (not Sundays). Dinner (Thurs-Sat) about £35.
Closed	Rarely.
Directions	In centre of Burford, halfway down hill. Free on-street parking, free public car park nearby.

 Glass of champagne on arrival.

Ian Hawkins & Stewart Dunkley
99 High Street, Burford OX18 4QA
Tel +44 (0)1993 823151
Email stay@burfordhouse.co.uk
Web www.burfordhouse.co.uk

The Plough at Clanfield

A country-house inn with a sitting-room bar, a great place to wash up for a couple of nights. It dates to 1550 and was once a wool merchant's house, but changed its colours to welcome travellers crossing the Thames at nearby Radcot Bridge. Outside, a lawn runs up to a smart terrace, where you sit in summer sipping something from the gin pantry with a plume of wisteria resplendent on the golden walls behind. Inside, you get all the old stuff – ancient beams, mullioned windows, original stone floors – but Martin's eye for beautiful things has added oodles of style. You find sofas in front of a roaring fire, bold colours and country rugs, eclectic art crammed on the walls, games to be played in the sitting room. Bedrooms – some huge in an attractive extension, others smaller with wonky floors above the shop – are all delightful and come with excellent bathrooms. What's more, they're free on Sunday nights if you spend £75 in the restaurant, a hugely popular ruse, so book early. As for the food, expect, delicious country cooking: lots of game, fantastic seafood, irresistible puddings. Badbury Hill, an Iron Age hill fort, is close.

Price	£115–£160. Four-poster £150–£175. Half-board from £81.25 p.p.
Rooms	11: 6 doubles, 2 twins/doubles, 3 four-posters.
Meals	Lunch & dinner £5–£35.
Closed	Christmas Day.
Directions	North from Farringdon on A4095. In village on left.

Martin Agius
Bourton Road, Clanfield OX18 2RB

Tel	+44 (0)1367 810222
Email	bookings@theploughclanfield.co.uk
Web	www.theploughclanfield.co.uk

The Trout at Tadpole Bridge

A 17th-century Cotswold inn on the banks of the Thames; pick up a pint, drift into the garden and watch life float by. Gareth and Helen bought The Trout after a two-year search and have cast their fairy dust into every corner: expect super bedrooms, oodles of style, delicious local food. The downstairs is open plan and timber-framed, with stone floors, gilt mirrors, wood-burners and logs piled high in alcoves. Bedrooms at the back are away from the crowd; three open onto a small courtyard where wild roses ramble on creamy stone – but you may prefer to stay put in your room and indulge in unabashed luxury. You get the best of everything: funky fabrics, trim carpets, monsoon showers (one room has a claw-foot bath), DVD players, flat-screen TVs, a library of films. Sleigh beds, brass beds, beautifully upholstered armchairs... one room even has a roof terrace. You can watch boats pass from the breakfast table, feast on local sausages, tuck into homemade marmalade courtesy of Helen's mum. Food is as local as possible, there are maps for walkers to keep you thin. *Minimum stay two nights at weekends May-October.*

Price	£120. Suite £150. Singles from £80.
Rooms	6: 2 doubles, 3 twins/doubles, 1 suite.
Meals	Lunch & dinner £10.95–£19. Sunday lunch from £10.95.
Closed	Never.
Directions	A420 southwest from Oxford for Swindon. After 13 miles right for Tadpole Bridge. Pub on right by bridge.

10% off room rate Mon-Thurs.

Gareth & Helen Pugh
Buckland Marsh, Faringdon SN7 8RF
Tel   +44 (0)1367 870382
Email   info@trout-inn.co.uk
Web   www.trout-inn.co.uk

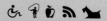

Old Parsonage Hotel

A country house in the city, with a lively bar for a drop of champagne, a rooftop terrace for afternoon tea and a hidden garden where you can sit in the shade and listen to the bells of St Giles. Logs smoulder in the original stone fireplace, the daily papers wait by an ancient window and an extensive collection of exquisite art hangs on the walls. You feast in the restaurant on meat from the owner's Oxfordshire farm or fish from the Channel Islands, then retire to warm stylish bedrooms which are scattered all over the place – some at the front (where Oscar Wilde entertained lavishly when he was sent down), others at the back in a sympathetic extension where some suites have French windows onto tiny balconies and a couple of the less-expensive rooms open onto private terraces. Expect Vi-Spring mattresses, flat-screen TVs, crisp white linen, spotless bathrooms. Daily walking tours led by an art historian are 'on the house', while the hotel can book a punt on the Cherwell, then pack you a picnic, so glide effortlessly past spire and meadow before tying up for lunch. *Minimum stay two nights at weekends.*

Price	£132-£225. Suites £202-£295.
Rooms	30: 22 twins/doubles, 7 suites for 3, 1 for 4.
Meals	Breakfast £12.95-£14. Lunch & dinner £10-£45.
Closed	Never.
Directions	From A40 ring road, south onto Banbury Road thro' Summertown. Hotel on right just before St Giles Church.

Deniz Bostanci
1 Banbury Road, Oxford OX2 6NN

Tel	+44 (0)1865 310210
Email	info@oldparsonage-hotel.co.uk
Web	www.oldparsonage-hotel.co.uk

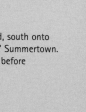

Old Bank Hotel

You're in the heart of old Oxford. Stroll south past Corpus Christi to Christ Church meadows, head north for the Radcliffe Camera and the Bodleian Library. Back at the Old Bank warm contemporary elegance comes with an important collection of modern art and photography. It adorns most walls, even in bedrooms, and catalogues can be perused. Downstairs the old tiller's hall is now a vibrant bar/brasserie with fine arched windows giving views onto the high street; come for cocktails before a convivial meal (fish from the Channel Islands, meat from the owner's farm). Bedrooms upstairs are exemplary, with fine new beds, piles of cushions, Denon CD players, flat-screen TVs. Bigger rooms have sofas, you get robes in super bathrooms, there's free broadband access throughout. Service is friendly and serene: curtains are pleated, beds are turned down, the daily papers delivered to your door. There's room service, too. Breakfast is served in the tiller's hall or on the deck in the courtyard in summer. Off-street parking is priceless, daily walking tours led by an art historian are free for guests. *Min. stay two nights at weekends.*

Price	£132-£420.
Rooms	42: 12 twins/doubles, 29 doubles, 1 suite for 2-5.
Meals	Breakfast £12.50-£13.95. Lunch & dinner £10-£30.
Closed	Never.
Directions	Cross Magdalen Bridge for city centre. Straight through 1st set of lights, then left into Merton St. Follow road right; 1st right into Magpie Lane. Car park 2nd right.

Ben Truesdale
92-94 High Street,
Oxford OX1 4BJ

Tel	+44 (0)1865 799599
Email	info@oldbank-hotel.co.uk
Web	www.oldbank-hotel.co.uk

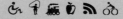

Miller of Mansfield

This handsome coaching inn looms on the high street, a timeless model of Georgian splendour, or so it seems. But step inside and worlds collide, with 18th-century exteriors giving way to 21st-century fixtures and fittings. You'll find sand-blasted beams, black suede stools, silver-leaf wallpaper above open fires, fairylight chandeliers dangling from the ceiling. Upstairs, bedrooms are equally lively. The chrome four-poster has a leather headboard, there are cow-hide rugs on white wood floors and the occasional block of Cole & Son wallpaper. Colours are electric – pink, orange and green, and plasma screens and bathrobes come as standard. Bathrooms are extravagant, some with monsoon showers, others with free-standing stone baths. One has a Japanese tub for two, two have no door from the bedroom. There's seriously good food in the airy restaurant or relaxed bar, so walk by the Thames or take to the Berkshire Downs, then return for fresh lobster, braised shoulder of lamb, caramelised lemon tart. Bells peal at the Norman church. One for the young at heart.

Price	£80-£170. Suites £160-£195. Singles (Sun-Thurs only) from £70.
Rooms	13: 10 doubles, 1 twin/double, 2 suites.
Meals	Bar meals all day. Lunch from £14.95. Dinner, 3 courses, £25-£35.
Closed	Never.
Directions	North from Reading on A329. In Streatley right onto B4526. Over bridge; hotel on left.

Paul Suter
High Street, Goring-on-Thames,
Reading RG8 9AW
Tel +44 (0)1491 872829
Email reservations@millerofmansfield.com
Web www.millerofmansfield.com

25% off room rate Sunday-Thursday. 50% off room rate on Sunday if Friday & Saturday booked.

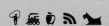

Hambleton Hall Hotel

A sublime country house, one of the loveliest in England. The position here is matchless. The house stands on a tiny peninsular that juts into Rutland Water. You can sail on it or cycle around it, then come back to the undisputed wonders of Hambleton: sofas by the fire in the panelled hall, a pillared bar in red for cocktails and a Michelin star in the dining room. French windows in the sitting room (beautiful art, fresh flowers, the daily papers) open onto idyllic gardens. Expect clipped lawns and gravel paths, a formal parterre garden that bursts with summer colour and a walled swimming pool with views over grazing parkland down to the water. Bedrooms are the very best. Hand-stitched Italian linen, mirrored armoires, fabulous marble bathrooms – and Stefa's eye for fabrics, some of which coat the walls, is faultless; the Croquet Pavilion, a supremely comfortable two-bedroom suite, has its own terrace. Polish the day off with incredible food, perhaps sautéed scallops with lemon grass, fallow venison with gin and tonic jelly, passion fruit soufflé with banana sorbet. *Minimum stay two nights at weekends.*

Price	£245–£415. Singles from £195. Pavilion £525–£625 for 4.
Rooms	17: 15 twins/doubles, 1 four-poster. Pavilion: 1 suite (1 four-poster, 1 twin/double) for 4.
Meals	Lunch, 2 courses, from £22. Dinner £38.50–£70.
Closed	Never.
Directions	From A1, A606 west towards Oakham for about 8 miles, then left, signed Hambleton. In village bear left and hotel signed right.

Bottle of champagne for bookings of 2 nights or more. Late checkout (12pm). Bottle of wine with dinner on first night.

Tim & Stefa Hart
Ketton Road, Hambleton,
Oakham LE15 8TH

Tel   +44 (0)1572 756991
Email   hotel@hambletonhall.com
Web   www.hambletonhall.com

The Olive Branch

A Michelin-starred pub in a sleepy Rutland village, where bridle paths lead out across peaceful fields. The inn dates to the 17th century and is built of Clipsham stone. Inside, a warm, informal rustic chic hits the spot perfectly; come for open fires, old beams, exposed stone walls and choir stalls in the bar. Chalk boards on tables in the restaurant reveal the names of the evening's diners, while the food — seared scallops with black pudding fritter, slow-roast pork belly with creamed leeks and apple sauce — elates. As do the hampers that you can whisk away for picnics in the country. Bedrooms in Beech House across the lane are impeccable. Three have terraces, one has a free-standing bath, all come with crisp linen, pretty beds, Roberts radios, real coffee. Super breakfasts — smoothies, boiled eggs and soldiers, the full cooked works — are served in a smartly renovated barn, with flames leaping in the wood-burner. The front garden fills in summer, the sloe gin comes from local berries, and Newark is close for the biggest antiques market in Europe. A total gem. *Ask about cookery demos.*

Ethical Collection: Community; Food. See page 386 for details

Price	£115–£195. Suite £175–£260. Singles from £97.50.
Rooms	6: 5 doubles, 1 family suite.
Meals	Bar meals from £10.50. Dinner from £14.50. Sunday lunch £24.95.
Closed	Rarely.
Directions	A1 five miles north of Stamford, then exit onto B668. Right and right again for Clipsham. In village (Beech House across the road from The Olive Branch).

Ben Jones & Sean Hope
Main Street, Clipsham,
Oakham LE15 7SH

Tel	+44 (0)1780 410355
Email	info@theolivebranchpub.com
Web	www.theolivebranchpub.com

25% off B&B in superior rooms Sunday-Thursday (not bank holidays).

The Lion at Leintwardine

The position here is lovely with the river Teme streaming under a packhorse bridge and long views shooting west across water meadows. Lawns run down to the water, so sit with a glass of Pimm's in summer and watch the swans glide by. Inside, you find the fruits of an attractive renovation. There are sofas in the hall, a wood-burner in the bar, lime greens and timber frames in the pretty restaurant. An airy, open-plan feel runs throughout. The odd chandelier dangles from the ceiling, while walls everywhere host a fantastic collection of black-and white photos, a hundred years of village life on display; just magical. Super bedrooms upstairs aren't huge, but nor are their prices and they don't stint on style. Expect sleigh beds, a wall of paper, pretty fabrics, crisp linen; bathrooms are equally good. Outside, there's lots to do: Offa's Dyke, Ludlow and its castle, you can even hire bikes and take to the hills. Back at the inn, delicious food waits, perhaps crab and lemongrass mousse, local duck with Pear William confit, spiced pineapple with elderflower sorbet.

Price	£90–£120. Singles from £65.
Rooms	8: 6 doubles, 1 twin, 1 single.
Meals	Lunch from £4.95. Dinner, 3 courses, about £30. Sunday lunch from £13.45.
Closed	Never.
Directions	West from Ludlow on A4113. On left in village by bridge.

10% off room rate Mon-Thurs.

Jessica Griffiths
Leintwardine, Craven Arms SY7 0JZ
Tel   +44 (0)1547 540203
Email   enquiries@thelionleintwardine.co.uk
Web   www.thelionleintwardine.co.uk

Pen-y-Dyffryn Country Hotel

In a blissful valley lost to the world, this small, traditional country house sparkles on the side of a peaceful hill. To the front, beyond the stone terraces that drip with aubretia, fields tumble down to a stream that marks the border with Wales. Outside, daffodils erupt in spring, the lawns are scattered with deckchairs in summer, paths lead onto the hill for excellent walks. Inside, colourful interiors are warmly attractive: Laura Ashley wallpaper and an open fire in the quirky bar; shuttered windows and super food in the yellow restaurant; the daily papers and a good collection of art in the sitting room. Bedrooms are stylish without being grand. Most have great views, one has a French sleigh bed, good bathrooms come with fluffy towels. Four rooms are dog-friendly and have their own patios, you get crisp white linen, silky curtains, padded bedheads. There's plenty of space, ideal for a gathering, and super food to help you celebrate, perhaps Shetland mussels, Welsh beef, a plate of local cheese; the smoked haddock at breakfast is divine. Offa's Dyke and Powys Castle are close. *Minimum stay two nights at weekends.*

Price	£114–£166. Singles £86.
Rooms	12: 8 doubles, 4 twins.
Meals	Light lunch (for residents) by arrangement. Dinner £30–£37.
Closed	Rarely.
Directions	From A5 head to Oswestry. Leave town on B4580, signed Llansilin. Hotel 3 miles up. Approach Rhydycroesau, left at town sign, first right.

Miles & Audrey Hunter
Rhydycroesau, Oswestry SY10 7JD
Tel   +44 (0)1691 653700
Email   stay@peny.co.uk
Web   www.peny.co.uk

10% off room rate Sunday-Thursday, 5% at weekends.

The Inn at Grinshill

A ridge of pine soars high above the village; so bring your boots and take to the hills. Down at the inn, nothing but good things. Wander at will and find an 18th-century panelled family room, a 19th-century bar with crackling fire and a 21st-century champagne bar where you can stop for lunch or coffee. Best of all is the elegant dining room, which floods with light courtesy of original coach-house arches. Ambrosial delights pour from the kitchen, perhaps king scallops and black pudding with garlic foam, pan-fried duck with parsnip purée and apple tarte tatin, or chocolate and marzipan gateau and red wine jelly; there's brasserie-style food in the bar if you fancy something simpler. Bedrooms upstairs are equally delicious. You get comfy beds, piles of pillows, crisp white linen and wispy mohair blankets. You also find TVs hidden behind mirrors, DVD players and great little bathrooms. Back downstairs, life spills into the garden in summer, church bells peal, roses ramble. There's cricket in the village at weekends and the Shropshire Way passes outside. Don't miss the magical follies at Hawkstone Park. Brilliant.

Price	£120. Singles £90.
Rooms	6 twins/doubles.
Meals	Lunch from £4.50. Sunday lunch from £13.95. Dinner (not Sun/Mon) £25–£35.
Closed	Sunday evenings and Mondays.
Directions	A49 north from Shrewsbury. Grinshill signed left after 5 miles, just past Hadnall.

10% off stays of 2 or more nights.

Kevin & Victoria Brazier
High Street, Grinshill,
Shrewsbury SY4 3BL
Tel   +44 (0)1939 220410
Email   info@theinnatgrinshill.co.uk
Web   www.theinnatgrinshill.co.uk

Soulton Hall

There's been a house on this land since 1066, but Soulton goes back to 1430, a fortified house that was home to the first Protestant mayor of London. It stands magnificently in 500 acres of pasture and woodland, yours to roam. It's a family affair: John farms, Ann looks after the house. Climb the steps, slip through a spectacular stone doorway, arrive in the hall, sink in a sofa in front of a fire. Potter about and find an attractive dining room and a cosy bar, but it's the bedrooms in the main house that leave the big impression. You'll find them up an old oak staircase (and you glimpse a section of original wattle and daub on your way up). Four grand country-house bedrooms wait. They come with timber frames, mullioned windows, the odd panelled wall and polished floors; three have fancy bathrooms. It's all splendidly regal, and while simpler bedrooms are also available, it's worth bagging one of these. Back downstairs, you eat in style, perhaps carrot and coriander soup, lemon sorbet with sparkling wine, chicken cooked with hazelnuts and cream, sticky toffee pudding.

Price	£110–£125.
Rooms	7: 3 doubles, 1 twin/double. Carriage House: 2 doubles. Garden room: 1 four-poster.
Meals	Dinner, 4 courses, £35.
Closed	Rarely.
Directions	North from Shrewsbury on A49. Left in Prees Green onto B5065 for Wem. House on left after two miles.

Ann & John Ashton
Shrewsbury SY4 5RS

Tel	+44 (0)1939 232786
Email	enquiries@soultonhall.co.uk
Web	www.soultonhall.co.uk

The Castle at Taunton

A Saxon castle took root on this land 1,300 years ago. Its fortunes fluctuated with the centuries and it fell into disrepair, but when the hotel came along, in 1830, it was crenellated in keeping with the old battlements around it (now the museum). The best spot to take it all in is the garden, once the Norman keep. Spin through the revolving doors and you find the sort of place that befits this gracious county town. At times it's as if you've entered a gentleman's club, but it manages to bridge the spirit of the past with the needs of the present, hence the the ever-busy brasserie, a cool little bar for a pre-dinner snifter, a grand function room for private parties and nooks and crannies in which to hide away in. Best of all is the music. Five weekends a year are given over to chamber music with musicians from all over the world flying in to perform: stupendous stuff. Country-house bedrooms are sprinkled about and come with pretty fabrics, the odd antique, huge beds dressed in white linen. The cricket ground is a short stroll, the best of the West Country is on your doorstep.

Price	£225. Garden rooms £335. Singles from £145.
Rooms	44: 27 twins/doubles, 12 singles, 5 garden rooms.
Meals	Lunch & dinner £5-£30.
Closed	Never.
Directions	M5 junc. 25 or 26, then centre of town. In town, pick up brown signs to hotel and follow them in.

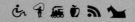 10% off stays of 2 or more nights.

Kit Chapman
Castle Green, Taunton TA1 1NF
Tel   +44 (0)1823 272671
Email   reception@the-castle-hotel.com
Web   www.the-castle-hotel.com

Hotel

Combe House Hotel

A country lane winds up to this hotel, which basks peacefully in the first folds of the Quantocks. Woodlands rise, a stream pours past and paths lead out for uplifting walks, though with the recent addition of a couple of treatments rooms and a hot tub, you might want to stay put. The hotel, an old mill, dates back to the 17th century and couldn't be in better hands; Gareth and Catherine came to look after the place and have done just that. Outside, free-range chickens stroll around a very productive kitchen garden, while inside you find airy interiors, smart carpets, a wood-burner in the inglenook, the odd exposed wall. Sofas take the strain in the sitting room, armchairs do the job in the bar and you eat under beams in the restaurant, where seriously good local food does the trick: seared scallops with cauliflower purée, Exmoor lamb with dauphinoise potatoes, passion fruit brûlée with mango sorbet. Bedrooms have all been refurbished. Expect a contemporary country style with warm colours, silky throws, flat-screen TVs, and robes in super new bathrooms. There are deer on the hill, too.

Price	£125–£150. Suites £175. Singles from £65. Half-board from £80 p.p.
Rooms	15: 11 twins/doubles, 2 singles, 2 suites.
Meals	Lunch from £6.95. Sunday lunch £16–£20. Dinner, 3 courses, about £30.
Closed	Never.
Directions	From Bridgwater A39 to Minehead. At Holford left in front of Plough Inn; follow lane thro' village. Bear left at fork signed Holford Combe; on right.

Gareth & Catherine Weed
Holford, Bridgwater TA5 1RZ

Tel	+44 (0)1278 741382
Email	enquiries@combehouse.co.uk
Web	www.combehouse.co.uk

10% off room rate Mon–Thurs.
10% off stays of 2 or more nights.

The Three Horseshoes

A magnificent spot, England at its best. You get the full works here: a beautiful valley lost to the world, an English village impeccably preserved, a great little inn in the shade of an ancient church tower. Inside, fires burn at both ends of the bar, there are low ceilings, window seats and a warm mix of traditional and contemporary design. Rustic food hits the spot perfectly. Westcombe Cheddar sandwiches come with a real ale chutney, and if you want something fancier, try cucumber gazpacho with Bloody Mary sorbet, roasted chicken with basil mousse and spring onions, Earl Grey jelly with milk ice cream. In summer you slip outside and take your choice from a pretty courtyard where walls are clad in wisteria or a lawned garden, where you can sip your pint while church bells chime. Back inside, three bedrooms wait for those wise enough to linger. Two are cosy, one is open to the rafters, all have crisp linen, comfy beds and attractive prices. Kids are very welcome, there's a locals' bar for a game of darts and great walks start from the front door. Glastonbury is close. Wonderful.

Price	£70-£85. Singles from £65.
Rooms	3 doubles.
Meals	Lunch from £8.90. Dinner, 3 courses, £25-£30. Sunday lunch from £11.50.
Closed	Rarely.
Directions	Off A359 between Frome & Bruton, 7 miles south west of Frome, 4 miles east of Royal Bath & West Showground.

Kaveh Javvi
Batcombe, Frome BA4 6HE

Tel	+44 (0)1749 850359
Email	info@thethreehorseshoesinn.com
Web	www.thethreehorseshoesinn.com

The Pilgrim's at Lovington

A slightly eccentric dining pub within striking distance of Wells and Glastonbury. Interiors have a warm, unpretentious, rustic style: timber frames, old flagged floors, panelled walls and painted ceilings. There are alcoves to hide away in or leather armchairs in front of the fire; you'll find games and books, Farrow & Ball colours and photos of New York lined up on the walls. If the bar is earthy, then the rooms are decidedly fancy. They're out at the back in what was the skittle alley, quietly idling away from the road. Three have cathedral ceilings, all come with exposed stone walls, flat-screen TVs, lovely beds wrapped up in good linen, perhaps a faux-leopard-skin chaise longue. As for the bathrooms, expect the best: double-ended baths, separate power showers, fancy tiles and cotton robes. Spin back to the restaurant – fresh flowers, big mirrors, candles galore – and dig into delicious food, perhaps west country mussels, local lamb, Somerset rhubarb crumble. Breakfast is equally indulging and you can scoff your Gloucester Old Spot sausages on the decked terrace in summer.

Price	£80–£120.
Rooms	5: 4 doubles, 1 twin/double.
Meals	Lunch from £8. Dinner, 3 courses, about £30. Sunday lunch £25. Not Monday.
Closed	Rarely.
Directions	On B3153 between Castle Cary & Somerton. In village by traffic lights.

Use your Sawday's Gift Card here.

Special rate for stays of 2 or more nights.

	Julian & Sally Mitchison
	Lovington, Castle Cary BA7 7PT
Tel	+44 (0)1963 240597
Email	jools@thepilgrimsatlovington.co.uk
Web	www.thepilgrimsatlovington.co.uk

The Queen's Arms

It's all rather blissful here: a hip little inn, a pretty village, stupendous country all around. You're halfway up a hill with paddocks soaring up to a high ridge on one side and views shooting across a quilt of fields on the other. Wellington boots wait at the front door, so pull on a pair and explore. Return to the pub – rescued from neglect, now shining in relaxed country style – to find a high-ceilinged bar with rugs on flagstone floors, leather sofas on stripped boards, the odd armchair next to the fire. In summer life spills onto a sun-trapping courtyard. Bedrooms upstairs are a treat: small chandeliers, contemporary art, beautiful beds, iPod docks, perhaps vibrant silk curtains or a sofa. Pretty bathrooms come with robes and underfloor heating; one has a painted cast iron bath. Back downstairs, dig into delicious country food, much sourced locally, and wash it down with a pint of ale or a bottle of good wine; there's also a brilliant cider and apple juice list. Breakfast is taken communally: pub-reared pork for your bacon, home-laid eggs. Staff are lovely, too.

Price	£85–£120. Singles from £75.
Rooms	5: 3 doubles, 1 twin, 1 four-poster.
Meals	Lunch from £6.50. Dinner, 3 courses £25–£30.
Closed	Never.
Directions	From A303 take Chapel Crosse turning. Through South Cadbury then next left & follow signs to Corton Denham. Pub at end of village on right.

Free pick-up from local bus/train station.

Gordon & Jeanette Reid
Corton Denham, Sherborne DT9 4LR
Tel   +44 (0)1963 220317
Email   relax@thequeensarms.com
Web   www.thequeensarms.com

The Devonshire Arms

A lively English village with a well-kept green; the old school house stands to the south, the church to the east and the post office to the west. The inn (due north) is over 400 years old and was once a hunting lodge for the Dukes of Devonshire; a rather smart pillared porch survives at the front. These days open-plan interiors are warmly contemporary with high ceilings, shiny blond floorboards and fresh flowers everywhere. Hop onto brown leather stools at the bar and order a pint of Moor Revival, or sink into sofas in front of the fire and crack open a bottle of wine. In summer, life spills onto the terrace at the front, the courtyard at the back and the lawned garden beyond. Super bedrooms run along at the front; all are a good size, but those at each end are huge. You get low-slung wooden beds, seagrass matting, crisp white linen and freeview TV. One has a purple claw-foot bath, some have compact showers. Delicious food is on tap in the restaurant – chargrilled scallops, slow-cooked lamb, passion fruit crème brûlée – so take to the nearby Somerset levels and walk off your indulgence in style.

Price	£87.50–£135. Singles from £77.50.
Rooms	9: 8 doubles, 1 twin.
Meals	Lunch from £5.95. Dinner from £25–£30.
Closed	Rarely.
Directions	A303, then north on B3165, through Martock to Long Sutton. On village green.

Philip & Sheila Mepham
Long Sutton, Langport TA10 9LP
Tel   +44 (0)1458 241271
Email   mail@thedevonshirearms.com
Web   www.thedevonshirearms.com

Little Barwick House

A dreamy restaurant with rooms lost in the hills three miles south of Yeovil. Tim and Emma rolled west ten years ago and have gathered a legion of fans who come to feast on their ambrosial food. The stage is this small Georgian country house which stands in three acres of peace. A curtain of trees shields it from the outside world, horses graze in the paddock below and afternoon tea is served in the garden in summer, so sip your Earl Grey accompanied by birdsong. Inside, graceful interiors flood with light courtesy of fine windows that run along the front. There's an open fire in the cosy bar, eclectic reading in the pretty sitting room, and hessian-style carpets in the high-ceilinged dining room. Upstairs, super bedrooms hit the spot with warm colours, silk curtains and a country-house feel. But dinner is the main event, heaven in three courses. Everything is homemade and cooked by Tim and Emma, an equal partnership in the kitchen. Try twice-baked cheese soufflé, pan-fried fillet of Cornish sea bass, apple strudel with calvados ice cream. A treat. *One-night weekend bookings occasionally refused.*

Price	Half-board £105–£130 p.p.
Rooms	6: 4 doubles, 2 twins.
Meals	Lunch £23.95–£27.95 (not Mon/Tues). Sunday lunch £29.95. Dinner for non-residents, £43.95 (not Sun/Mon).
Closed	Sundays & Mondays. 2 weeks in January.
Directions	From Yeovil A37 south for Dorchester; left at 1st r'bout. Down hill, past church, left in village and house on left after 200 yds.

Bottle of champagne for bookings of 2 nights or more.

Emma & Tim Ford
Rexes Hollow Lane, Barwick,
Yeovil BA22 9TD

Tel   +44 (0)1935 423902
Email   reservations@barwick7.fsnet.co.uk
Web   www.littlebarwickhouse.co.uk

Lord Poulett Arms

In a ravishing village, an idyllic inn, French at heart and quietly groovy. Part pub, part country house, with walls painted in reds and greens and old rugs covering flagged floors, the Lord Poulett gives a glimpse of a 21st-century dream local, where classical design fuses with earthy rusticity. A fire burns on both sides of the chimney in the dining room; on one side you can sink into leather armchairs, on the other you can eat under beams at antique oak tables while candles flicker. Take refuge with the daily papers on the sofa in the locals' bar or head past a pile of logs at the back door and discover an informal French garden of box and bay trees, with a piste for boules and a creeper-shaded terrace. Bedrooms upstairs come in funky country-house style, with fancy flock wallpaper, perhaps crushed velvet curtains, a small chandelier or a carved-wood bed. Two rooms have slipper baths behind screens in the room; two have claw-foot baths in bathrooms one step across the landing; Roberts radios add to the fun. Delicious food includes summer barbecues, Sunday roasts and the full works at breakfast.

Price	£85–£95. Singles £60–£65.
Rooms	4: 2 doubles en suite; 2 doubles, each with separate bath.
Meals	Lunch & dinner £10–£20.
Closed	Never.
Directions	A303, then A356 south for Crewkerne. Right for West Chinnock. Through village, 1st left for Hinton St George. Pub on right in village.

Steve & Michelle Hill
High Street,
Hinton St George TA17 8SE

Tel	+44 (0)1460 73149
Email	reservations@lordpoulettarms.com
Web	www.lordpoulettarms.com

The Crown

Everything here is good: a lovely country pub, a very pretty village, a sublime position in Constable country. The Crown dates back to 1560 and has old beams, timber frames and roaring fires, but the warm country interiors have youthful good looks – tongue-and-groove bars, terracotta-tiled floors, a fancy wine cellar that stands behind a wall of glass. Also: rugs and settles, the daily papers, leather armchairs in front of a wood-burner. Four ales wait at the bar, 30 wines come by the glass and seasonal rustic food has a big local following; try buck rarebit with fried quail's eggs, confit of Blythburgh pork with honey and apricots, steamed marmalade pudding with custard. In summer you can eat on the terrace. Airy bedrooms – peacefully hidden away at the bottom of the garden – are exemplary, with bathrooms as good as any you'll find. There are excellent beds, lovely linen, underfloor heating, a dash of colour. All have armchairs or sofas, three have French windows that open onto private terraces. Outside, fields stretch off to a distant ridge, birds soar high in the sky. A great place to eat, sleep and potter.

Price	£80–£185. Suite £135–£200. Singles from £80.
Rooms	11: 10 doubles, 1 suite.
Meals	Lunch & dinner £5–£19.95.
Closed	Rarely.
Directions	North from Colchester on A134, then B1087 east into Stoke-by-Nayland. Right at T-junction; pub on left.

10% off room rate Mon-Thurs.

Richard Sunderland
Park Street, Stoke-by-Nayland,
Colchester CO6 4SE
Tel   +44 (0)1206 262001
Email   enquiries@crowninn.net
Web   www.crowninn.net

The Great House

Lavenham is a Suffolk gem, a showpiece town made prosperous by medieval wool merchants, hence the timber-framed houses. The Great House stands across the market place from the Guildhall, its Georgian façade giving way to airy 15th-century interiors which mix timber frames and old beams with contemporary colours and varnished wood floors. The poet Stephen Spender once lived here and the house became a meeting place for artists, but these days it's irresistible cooking that draws the crowd. Try smoked salmon sushi with cucumber and dilll yogurt sauce, confit of Suffolk pork belly and caramelised balsamic vinegar, hot chocolate soufflé and a raspberry milkshake; as for the cheese board, it's a work of art. Fabulous bedrooms – all recently refurbished in lavish style – come with Egyptian cotton, suede sofas, coffee machines, and robes in magnificent bathrooms. Four are huge, but even the tiniest is a dream. One has a regal four-poster, another has a 14th-century fireplace in its bathroom. All come with an array of gadgets: hi-fis, surround-sound, flat-screen TVs. *Minimum stay two nights at weekends.*

Price	£99–£220. Singles from £95. Half-board from £115 p.p.
Rooms	5: 4 doubles, 1 twin/double.
Meals	Continental breakfast £10, full English £15. Lunch from £17.50. Dinner from £31.95. Not Sunday nights & Mondays.
Closed	First 3 weeks in January.
Directions	A1141 to Lavenham. At High Street 1st right after The Swan or up Lady Street into Market Place.

Régis & Martine Crépy
Market Place, Lavenham,
Sudbury CO10 9QZ

Tel	+44 (0)1787 247431
Email	info@greathouse.co.uk
Web	www.greathouse.co.uk

Bowl of fresh fruit & decanter of sherry.

The Bildeston Crown

The Bildeston Crown has been around for nearly 500 years and given her gorgeous good looks you may well wonder if the secret of eternal life is lodged in her old timbers or flagstone floors. This is a very pretty inn, part locals' bar, part country house, part restaurant with rooms. Inside, you find beautiful colours sitting between ancient timer frames, a Chesterfield sofa reclining in front of a roaring fire, a fine bar made of wood which came out of a local church, a small terrace for a pint in summer. Gorgeous bedrooms come with striking fabrics, pressed linen and delightfully funky bathrooms. Some have padded headboards, all have hi-tech music systems, the suite has a gilt-framed oil painting hanging above a free-standing bath. Remarkably, it's the food that takes the biscuit – this is clearly one of the best tables in East Anglia – so come for something special, perhaps lobster with quail's eggs, local venison with pear and parsnips, tarte tatin with sage and apple doughnut. Constable country is all around, the tiny Georgian square is worth a look. Not to be missed.

Price	£150–£225. Singles from £70.
Rooms	12: 10 doubles, 2 twins.
Meals	Lunch & dinner £24–£50. Bar meals from £5. Sunday lunch £25.
Closed	Never.
Directions	A12 junc. 31, then B1070 to Hadleigh. A1141 north, then B1115 into village & on right.

10% off room rate Mon-Thurs.
10% off stays of 2 or more nights.
Late checkout (12pm).

	Hayley Lee
	104 High Street, Bildeston,
	Ipswich IP7 7EB
Tel	+44 (0)1449 740510
Email	info@thebildestoncrown.co.uk
Web	www.thebildestoncrown.co.uk

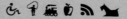

Kesgrave Hall

This Georgian mansion sits in 38 acres of woodland with a sweeping drive that cuts through the trees. It was built for an MP in 1812, served as home to US airmen during WWII, then became a prep school; recently refurbished, it shines in contemporary splendour. Despite its county-house good looks, it is more a restaurant with rooms, and its emphasis on good food served informally is a big hit with locals; the place was crammed on a February afternoon. Inside, find Wellington boots lined up in the entrance, high ceilings in the huge sitting room, stripped boards in the humming bistro and doors onto a terrace that is used all summer. Excellent bedrooms have attractive prices. One is huge and comes with a little bling (faux-leopard skin sofa, free-standing bath), but all are lovely, some in the eaves, others overlooking the lawn. Expect warm colours, crisp linen, super bathrooms. Back downstairs you can watch the cooks at work in the restaurant, so dig into something tasty, perhaps crab linguine, steak and kidney pudding, treacle tart with clotted cream ice cream. Suffolk's magical coast is close.

Price	£110–£199. Suites £230. Singles from £97.
Rooms	23: 10 doubles, 7 twins/doubles, 6 suites.
Meals	Breakfast £9–£15. Lunch & dinner, 3 courses, £25.
Closed	Never.
Directions	Skirt Ipswich to the south on A14, then head north on A12. Left at 4th roundabout; signed right after 0.25 miles.

Bottle of champagne for bookings of 2 nights or more.

Garth Wray
Hall Road, Kesgrave,
Ipswich IP5 2PU

Tel	+44 (0)1473 333741
Email	reception@kesgravehall.com
Web	www.milsomhotels.com

The Crown at Woodbridge

Woodbridge's long wait for a classy inn with great food, urbane bedrooms and a cosmopolitan air is over. The 400-year-old Crown emerged from the shadows in 2009 and it's the talk of the town. Everyone loves the new Crown, from its pastel façade to its cool laid-back interiors and humorous touches: beneath a glass roof a wooden skiff is suspended above a long granite-topped bar. In intimate dining rooms, chef-patron Stephen David's menu trawls Europe for inspiration and draws on Suffolk's natural larder. Look forward to hearty dishes full of flavour and some amazing taste combinations: Cromer crab cakes with pickled ginger; braised shin of beef in chocolate beer; Brancaster mussels; blueberry and almond tart. Wash it all down with Adnams or Meantime beers or delve into the impressive list of wines. Cosseting bedrooms decorated in simple, Nantucket style and themed in white and grey are a further attraction. There are big beds, quirky touches and a host of extras, from fruit, fresh coffee and homemade shortbread to soft bathrobes and heated bathroom floors. A chic Suffolk bolthole – unmissable!

Price	£140–£180. Singles from £95.
Rooms	10: 8 twins/doubles, 2 family rooms.
Meals	Lunch & dinner £9.50–£30. Sunday lunch from £16.
Closed	Rarely.
Directions	A12 north from Ipswich, then B1438 into town. Pass station and left into Quay St. On right.

Stephen David
Thoroughfare, Woodbridge IP12 1AD
Tel   +44 (0)1394 384242
Email   info@thecrownatwoodbridge.co.uk
Web   www.thecrownatwoodbridge.co.uk

Crown & Castle Hotel

The road runs out at sleepy Orford, so saddle up and head into the forest; cycle tracks and bridle paths sweep you in and you can return to the splendour of the Crown, a red-brick inn that stands close to a 12th-century castle. Today the feel is warm and airy with stripped wood floors, open fires, big colours and eclectic art: this is a very comfortable hotel. Beautiful bedrooms come with pretty fabrics, light colours, Vi-Spring beds and super bathrooms. Four in the main house have watery views, the suite is gorgeous and the garden rooms (dull on the outside, lovely within) are big and airy, with padded headboards, seagrass matting and doors onto a communal garden. All have crisp white linen, TVs, DVDs, digital radios. Wellington boots wait at the back door, so pull on a pair and discover Suffolk, then return for some seriously good food, perhaps half a dozen oysters with shallot and thyme vinegar, rump of Suffolk lamb with spiced barberry and pistachio pilaf, a flourless bitter chocolate cake with cream. A treat. *Children over eight welcome.*

Price	£125–£170. Suite £225–£270. Half-board from £85 p.p.
Rooms	19: 16 doubles, 2 twins, 1 suite.
Meals	Lunch from £7.50. À la carte dinner around £30.
Closed	Never.
Directions	A12 north from Ipswich, A1152 east to Woodbridge, then B1084 into Orford. Right in square for castle. On left.

David & Ruth Watson
Orford, Woodbridge IP12 2LJ
Tel   +44 (0)1394 450205
Email   info@crownandcastle.co.uk
Web   www.crownandcastle.co.uk

The Old Rectory

An old country rectory with contemporary interiors; what would the rector think? You get stripped floors in the dining room, a 21st-century orange chaise longue by the honesty bar and windows dressed in fabulous fabrics. Michael and Sally swapped Hong Kong for Suffolk and the odd souvenir came with them: wood carvings from the Orient and framed Burmese chanting bibles. In winter, a fire smoulders at breakfast; in summer, you feast in a huge stone-flagged conservatory where doors open onto two acres of orchard and lawns. A warm country-house informality flows within, so help yourself to a drink, sink into a sofa or spin onto the terrace in search of sun and birdsong. Smart bedrooms are warmly decorated; one is up in the eaves, one overlooks the church, another has a claw-foot bath. Delicious food includes organic sausages and homemade jams at breakfast, perhaps parsnip soup and roast loin of Suffolk pork at dinner, then almond and lemon tart. Sutton Hoo is close as is Snape Maltings (opera singers occasionally stay and warm up for work in the bedrooms). A happy house. *Minimum stay two nights at weekends April-October.*

10% off room rate Mon-Thurs.

Price	£95–£140. Singles from £75.
Rooms	7: 5 doubles, 1 twin/double, 1 four-poster.
Meals	Dinner, 3 courses, £28. Not Saturday or Sunday (except for parties of 10 or more).
Closed	Occasionally.
Directions	North from Woodbridge on A12 for 8 miles, then right onto B1078. In village, over railway line; house on right just before church.

Michael & Sally Ball
Station Road, Campsea Ashe,
Woodbridge IP13 0PU
Tel   +44 (0)1728 746524
Email   mail@theoldrectorysuffolk.com
Web   www.theoldrectorysuffolk.com

Wentworth Hotel

The Wentworth has the loveliest position in town, the beach, quite literally, a pebble's throw from the garden, the sea rolling east under a vast sky. Inside, fires smoulder, clocks chime and seaside elegance abounds. It's all terrifically English, with Zoffany wallpapers, kind local staff and an elegant bar that opens onto a terrace garden. The restaurant looks out to sea, comes in Georgian red and spills onto the sunken terrace in summer for views of passing boats. What's more, it serves up delicious English fare, perhaps cauliflower soup, confit of pork, then lemon meringue pie. The hotel has been in the same family since 1920 and old-fashioned values mix harmoniously with new-fangled necessities. Bedrooms are extremely comfortable, those at the front have huge sea views (and binoculars). Expect warm colours, wicker armchairs, padded headboards and comfortable beds. Bathrooms, all refurbished, are excellent. Sofas galore wait in the sitting room, but you may want to spurn them to walk by the sea. Joyce Grenfell was a regular. The Snape Maltings are close. *Minimum stay two nights at weekends.*

Price	£130–£186. Single from £71. Half-board £70–£105 p.p.
Rooms	35: 24 twins/doubles, 4 singles. Darfield House: 7 doubles.
Meals	Bar meals from £5. Lunch from £10. Dinner, 3 courses, £23.
Closed	Never.
Directions	A12 north from Ipswich, then A1094 for Aldeburgh. Past church, down hill, left at x-roads; hotel on right.

Michael Pritt
Wentworth Road,
Aldeburgh IP15 5BD

Tel	+44 (0)1728 452312
Email	stay@wentworth-aldeburgh.com
Web	www.wentworth-aldeburgh.com

10% off stays of 2 or more nights.

The Brudenell Hotel

The Brudenell stands bang on the beach in one of England's loveliest seaside towns. It makes the most of its view. A dining terrace at the front runs the length of the building; a glass-fronted restaurant swims in light; an elegant sitting room looks the right way. The hotel mixes a contemporary style and an informal feel to great effect: find coastal art, sunny colours, driftwood sculptures on display. Beautiful bedrooms come in different shapes and sizes. Those at the back look onto open country and river marsh, those at the front have hypnotic views of sea and sky. A chic style runs throughout: cool colours, fabulous fabrics, blond wood furniture, sofas if there's room; bathrooms are predictably divine. Back downstairs the open-plan brasserie is the hub of the hotel. There's a cocktail bar where you can wash back oysters with a glass of champagne, then booths and tables for super food, perhaps Parma ham with pan-fried langoustine, Sutton Hoo chicken with tarragon mash, banoffee pie and banana ice cream. As for gorgeous Aldeburgh, you can walk, sail, swim, or shop. *Minimum stay two nights at weekends.*

Price	£147–£314. Singles from £80.
Rooms	44: 30 twins/doubles, 12 doubles, 2 singles.
Meals	Lunch from £10.25. Dinner, 3 courses, about £30.
Closed	Never.
Directions	A1094 into Aldebrough. Right at T-junction, down high street, last left in village before car park & yacht club.

10% off room rate Mon-Thurs.

Sean Morrison
The Parade,
Aldeburgh IP15 5BU

Tel	+44 (0)1728 452071
Email	info@brudenellhotel.co.uk
Web	www.brudenellhotel.co.uk

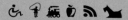

The Westleton Crown

This is one of England's oldest coaching inns, with 800 years of continuous service under its belt. It stands in a village two miles inland from the sea at Dunwich, with Westleton Heath running east towards Minsmere Bird Sanctuary. Inside, you find the best of old and new. A recent refurbishment has introduced Farrow & Ball colours, leather sofas and a tongue-and-groove bar, and they mix harmoniously with panelled walls, stripped floors and ancient beams. Weave around and find nooks and crannies in which to hide, flames flickering in an open fire, a huge map on the wall for walkers. You can eat wherever you want, and a conservatory/breakfast room opens onto a terraced garden for summer barbecues. Fish comes straight off the boats at Lowestoft, local butchers provide local meat. Lovely bedrooms are scattered about and come in cool lime white with comfy beds, Egyptian cotton, flat-screen TVs. Super bathrooms are fitted out in Fired Earth, and some have claw-foot baths. Aldeburgh and Southwold are close by. *Minimum stay two nights at weekends.*

Price	£90–£215. Singles from £80.
Rooms	34: 26 doubles, 2 twins, 3 family rooms, 2 suites, 1 single.
Meals	Lunch & bar meals from £5.50. Dinner from £11.95. Sunday lunch £26.
Closed	Never.
Directions	A12 north from Ipswich. Right at Yoxford onto B1122, then left for Westleton on B1125. On right in village.

Gareth Clarke
The Street, Westleton,
Saxmundham IP17 3AD

Tel	+44 (0)1728 648777
Email	info@westletoncrown.co.uk
Web	www.westletoncrown.co.uk

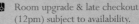 Room upgrade & late checkout (12pm) subject to availability.

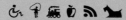

Ounce House

Bury St Edmunds, an ancient English town, is a dream; if you've never been, don't delay. The Romans were here, the barons hatched plans for Magna Carta within the now-crumbled walls of its monastery, and its Norman abbey attracted pilgrims by the cartload. The town was made rich by the wool trade in the 1700s and highlights include the cathedral (its exquisite new tower looks hundreds of years old) and the magnificent Abbey Gardens, perfect for summer picnics. Just around the corner Ounce House, a handsome 1870 red-brick townhouse, overflows with creature comforts, so slump into leather armchairs in front of a carved fireplace and gaze at walls of art. You'll also find a snug library, a lawned garden and homely bedrooms packed with books, mahogany furniture and fresh flowers. Princely breakfasts are served on blue-and-white Spode china at one vast table. This is B&B in a grand-ish home and ever-cheerful Simon and Jenny will pick you up from the station or book a table at a local restaurant. Try The Fox (around the corner) or Maison Bleue (excellent seafood). Don't miss the May arts festival.

Price	£125-£135. Singles £85-£95.
Rooms	5: 4 doubles, 1 twin.
Meals	Restaurants 5-minute walk.
Closed	Rarely.
Directions	A14 north, then central junction for Bury, following signs to historic centre. At 1st r'bout left into Northgate St. On right at top of hill.

Simon & Jenny Pott
13-14 Northgate Street,
Bury St Edmunds IP33 1HP

Tel	+44 (0)1284 761779
Email	enquiries@ouncehouse.co.uk
Web	www.ouncehouse.co.uk

Tuddenham Mill

A super cool boutique hotel in an ancient mill with a swan-strewn pond and meadows all around. Willows dip their branches in the water, tables and chairs wait on dry land. Inside, a beautiful refurbishment has brought old bones back to life, and chic rustic interiors sparkle in contemporary splendour. Whitewashed walls and old timber frames mix harmoniously with Italian design and polished concrete. Downstairs, the old mill wheel is lit up at night, while the first-floor restaurant, with its vast beams and sisal flooring, is a great spot for a good meal, perhaps Cornish crab with lime and coriander, Goosnargh duck with grapefruit and chocolate, fennel panna cotta and iced tea. Fabulous bedrooms don't hold back. Expect huge beds, walk-in showers, double-ended baths, Missoni robes. Some are in the main house, others have fabulous views of the meadows. All give an overdose of luxury: goose down duvets, Bose sound systems, perhaps a private terrace. Dogs are welcome, you can play boules in the garden, Newmarket race course is close. A very spoiling place. *Minimum stay two nights at weekends.*

Price	£185-£295. Suites £345-£395. Singles from £170.
Rooms	15: 5 suites, 10 doubles.
Meals	Lunch from £7. Dinner, 3 courses, about £40. 8-course tasting menu £65.
Closed	Never.
Directions	A14 junc. 38, then A11 for Thetford & Norwich. Right at Herringswell Rd, then on until High Street. Tuddenham Mill on the right.

Lyndon Barrett-Scott
High Street, Tuddenham,
Newmarket IP28 6SQ

Tel	+44 (0)1638 713552
Email	info@tuddenhammill.co.uk
Web	www.tuddenhammill.co.uk

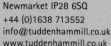 Late checkout. Free upgrade subject to availability.

Park House hotel & spa

A blissful pocket of rural Sussex. Park House sits in 12 acres of glorious English gardens with quilted fields circling the grounds and the South Downs rising beyond. Potter about outside and find a croquet lawn, a grass tennis court and a six-hole golf course that slips into the country. Fine shrubberies burst with colour while Wellington boots wait at the front door for long country walks. You may prefer to stay put; the most recent addition to the Park House empire is its fabulous spa. It comes with a very swanky indoor pool to go with its outside partner, four treatment rooms, a sauna and steam room, then a proper gym and a terraced bar for lazy afternoons. As for the house, it's just as good. Beautiful interiors abound mixing country-house style with contemporary colours. The pavilion bar overlooks the gardens, you breakfast in the conservatory or out on the terrace, there are flagstones in reception, the daily papers in the sitting room, great food in the dining room. Gorgeous bedrooms are the final luxury: heavenly beds, big country views, fancy bathrooms, iMac TVs. Exceptional. *Special rates for Goodwood.*

Price	£160-£215. Family suites & cottage £230-£350.
Rooms	20 + 1: 10 twins/doubles, 6 doubles, 4 family suites. Self-catering cottage for 2-4.
Meals	Lunch, 2 courses, from £20.95. Afternoon tea £19.95. Dinner, 3 courses, £37.50.
Closed	Rarely.
Directions	South from Midhurst on A286. At sharp left bend, right (straight ahead), signed Bepton. Hotel on left after 2 miles.

10% off room rate Mon-Thurs.

	Rebecca Coonan
	Bepton,
	Midhurst GU29 0JB
Tel	+44 (0)1730 819000
Email	reservations@parkhousehotel.com
Web	www.parkhousehotel.com

The Royal Oak Inn

This extremely attractive inn sits in a sleepy Sussex village with the South Downs rising above and the coast at Chichester waiting below. Inside, a modern, rustic feel prevails: stripped floors, exposed brickwork and the odd racing print (the inn was once part of the Goodwood estate). There's a small bar for a pint in front of an open fire, but these days this is a pretty much a dining pub and the restaurant spreads itself far and wide, through the conservatory and out onto the terrace. A small army of chefs conjure up irresistible food, perhaps shallot and goat's cheese tarte tatin, Sussex pork with calvados cream, then glazed lemon tart. Elegant bedrooms are sprinkled about, some in cottages, others upstairs at the back of the pub. All come in elegant, contemporary style with good fabrics, leather armchairs, big comfy beds and fancy bathrooms; CD players, plasma screens, and DVD libraries keep you amused. Staff are attentive, complimentary newspapers arrive with breakfast, a secret garden looks out over cornfields. Chichester Theatre, Bosham and Goodwood are close. *Minimum stay two nights at weekends.*

Price	£110–£185. Cottage rooms £180–£260. Singles from £90.
Rooms	8: 4 doubles, 1 twin, 3 cottage rooms for 2–4.
Meals	Lunch from £6.25. Dinner, 3 courses, £30–£35.
Closed	Rarely.
Directions	From Chichester A286 for Midhurst. First right at first mini roundabout into E. Lavant. Down hill, pass village green, over bridge, pub 200 yds on left. Car park opposite.

Charles Ullmann
Pook Lane, East Lavant,
Chichester PO18 0AX

Tel	+44 (0)1243 527434
Email	rooms@royaloakeastlavant.co.uk
Web	www.royaloakeastlavant.co.uk

20% off stays of 2 nights or more Mon-Thurs.

The Crab & Lobster

This tiny arrowhead of land south of Chichester is something of a time warp, more 1940s than 21st century. The Crab & Lobster is older still – 350 years at last count. It sits on Pagham Harbour, a tidal marsh that teems with preening birds. Outside, you find a smart whitewashed exterior and a small garden for dreamy views across grazing fields to the water. Inside, a glittering refurbishment comes in contemporary style with Farrow & Ball colours, flagstone floors, blond wood furniture, suede armchairs and a smouldering fire. Big mirrors reflect the light, candles flicker in the evening. Upstairs, four super rooms come in duck-egg blue with crisp white linen, flat-screen TVs and gorgeous little bathrooms. Three have views of the water, one is up in the eaves and has a telescope to scan the high seas. There's much to explore: Bosham, where King Canute tried to turn back the waves; Fishbourne, for its imperious Roman palace; the Witterings, for sand dunes and miles of beach. Don't forget dinner, perhaps fresh calamari, Barbary duck, marmalade bread and butter pudding. *Minimum stay two nights at weekends.*

Price	From £140. Cottage from £220.
Rooms	4 + 1: 4 doubles. 1 cottage for 4.
Meals	Lunch from £9.95. Sunday lunch £15.95. Dinner, 3 courses, £30–£35.
Closed	Rarely.
Directions	Mill Lane is off B2145 Chichester to Selsey road, just south of Sidlesham. Pub close to Pagham Harbour.

 Glass of champagne on arrival.

Sam Bakose
Mill Lane, Sidlesham,
Chichester PO20 7NB

Tel   +44 (0)1243 641233
Email   enquiries@crab-lobster.co.uk
Web   www.crab-lobster.co.uk

Burpham Country House & Brasserie

Come for old England in the foothills of the South Downs. Woodpeckers and warblers live in the woods, the church was built in 1167 and when you potter south to Arundel, its magnificent castle looms across the fields. The road runs out in the village and the house stands quietly, with colour tumbling from stone walls and a lawned terrace in front of a Victorian veranda. Originally a Georgian hunting lodge, it served as a vicarage to Tickner Edwardes, the great apiarist, who fought in Gallipoli; John Ruskin knew the house, too. Inside, warmly comfortable interiors are stylish without being style-led. There's an airy sitting-room bar, a panelled restaurant for local food and a brick-and-flint conservatory that opens onto a croquet lawn. Spotless bedrooms are good value for money, some big, some smaller, all with crisp linen, airy colours and flat-screen TVs; most have country views. Collared doves nest in the garden, swans winter on the Arundel wetlands and Alfred the Great extended this ridge 1,200 years ago to defend England from the Vikings. There's cricket in summer, too. *Minimum stay two nights at weekends April-October.*

Price	£80-£140.
Rooms	9: 5 doubles, 4 twins/doubles.
Meals	Dinner, 3 courses, £20-£27 (not Monday).
Closed	Rarely.
Directions	A27 east from Arundel, past station, then left for Burpham. Straight ahead for 2.5 miles; on left.

Jacqueline & Steve Penticost
Burpham,
Arundel BN18 9RJ

Tel	+44 (0)1903 882160
Email	info@burphamcountryhouse.com
Web	www.burphamcountryhouse.com

25% off cheapest night for stays of 4 nights.

Entry 225 Map 3

The Bull

Stepping into The Bull is like travelling back in time to Dickensian England; little seems to have changed in 200 years. OK, so electricity has been introduced, but even that is rationed on aesthetic grounds; as a result, light plays beautifully amid old timbers. Elsewhere, fires roar, beams sag, candles twinkle, tankards dangle. You might call it 'nostalgic interior design', but whatever it is, the locals love it; the place was packed on a Sunday afternoon in late January. Well-kept ales are on tap in the bar, excellent food flies from the kitchen, perhaps caramelised parsnip and apple soup, a magnificent plate of rare roast beef, then chilled white chocolate and vanilla fondue. Upstairs, four pretty rooms await (two are larger, two are above the bar). You may find timber-framed walls, leather sleigh beds or statues of eastern deities, while representation from the 21st century includes digital radios, contemporary art and very good compact bathrooms. Bring walking boots or mountain bikes and take to the high trails on the South Downs National Park, which rise beyond the village. Brighton is close.

Price	£80–£120.
Rooms	4: 3 doubles, 1 twin/double.
Meals	Lunch & dinner £5–£30.
Closed	Never.
Directions	Leave A23 just north of Brighton for Pyecombe. North on A273, then west for Ditchling on B2112. In centre of village at crossroads.

Dominic Worrall
2 High Street, Ditchling,
Hassocks BN6 8TA

Tel	+44 (0)1273 843147
Email	info@thebullditchling.com
Web	www.thebullditchling.com

[handwritten annotations: Sheffield Pm £140 +25 Mon £130   Horselft £80]

The Griffin Inn

A proper inn, one of the best, a community local that draws a well-heeled and devoted crowd. The occasional touch of scruffiness makes it almost perfect; fancy designers need not apply. The Pullan family run it with huge passion. You get cosy open fires, 400-year-old beams, oak panelling, settles, red carpets, prints on the walls... this inn has aged beautifully. There's a lively bar, a small club room for racing on Saturdays and two cricket teams play in summer. Bedrooms are tremendous value for money and full of uncluttered country-inn elegance: uneven floors, lovely old furniture, soft coloured walls, free-standing Victorian baths, huge shower heads, crisp linen, fluffy bathrobes, handmade soaps. Rooms in the coach house are quieter, those in next-door Griffin House quieter still. Smart seasonal menus include fresh fish from Rye and Fletching lamb. On Sundays in summer they lay on a spit-roast barbecue in the garden, with ten-mile views stretching across Pooh Bear's Ashdown Forest to Sheffield Park. Not to be missed. *Minimum stay two nights bank holiday weekends.*

Price	£85-£145. Singles £60-£80 (Sun-Thurs).
Rooms	13: 6 doubles, 7 four-posters.
Meals	Lunch from £11. Dinner, 3 courses, £30-£40.
Closed	Never.
Directions	From East Grinstead A22 south, right at Nutley for Fletching. On for 2 miles into village.

Nigel & James Pullan
Fletching,
Uckfield TN22 3SS

Tel	+44 (0)1825 722890
Email	info@thegriffininn.co.uk
Web	www.thegriffininn.co.uk

25% off room rate Mon-Thurs.

Newick Park Hotel & Country Estate

A heavenly country house that thrills at every turn. The setting – 255 acres of parkland, river, lake and gardens – is spectacular; come in winter and you may wake to find a ribbon of mist entangled in a distant ridge of trees. Inside, majestic interiors never fail to elate, be they colour-coded bookshelves in a panelled study, Doric columns in a glittering drawing room or roaring fires in a sofa-strewn hall. You get all the aristocratic fixtures and fittings – grand pianos, plaster mouldings, a bar that sits in an elegant alcove, views from the terrace that run down to a lake. Oils hang on walls, chandeliers dangle above. Country-house bedrooms are the stuff of dreams: lush linen, thick floral fabrics, marble bathrooms with robes and lotions, views to the front of nothing but country; some are the size of a London flat. A two-acre walled garden provides much for the table, so don't miss exceptional food, perhaps pan-fried Rye Bay scallops, pork belly with black pudding and sage, Earl Grey parfait and almond tuille. Peacocks roam outside, Ashdown Forest is close for pooh sticks. *Min. stay two nights at weekends during Glyndebourne.*

Price	£165–£285. Singles from £125.
Rooms	16 twins/doubles.
Meals	Lunch about £20. Dinner about £30
Closed	New Year's Eve & New Year's Day.
Directions	From Newick village turn off the green & follow signs to Newick Park for 1 mile until T-junction. Turn left; after 300 yds, entrance on right.

20% off Sunday-Thursday, October-April (not Christmas). Local food/produce in your room.

Michael & Virginia Childs
Newick,
Lewes BN8 4SB

Tel	+44 (0)1825 723633
Email	bookings@newickpark.co.uk
Web	www.newickpark.co.uk

Wingrove House

A beautiful house at the end of Alfriston High Street with delightful terraces that give the feel of Provence. A vine runs along an old stone wall, colour bursts from well-kept beds, olive trees shimmer in the sun. In good weather you can breakfast here with the daily papers, so dig into scrambled eggs and croissants, then wash it all down with freshly squeezed orange juice. This is the last house in a pretty red-brick village with the South Downs Way passing directly to the south; strike out across the fields to the cliffs of Beachy Head. Return to find an extremely attractive house: stripped floors, an open fire and leather sofas in the sitting room; a small bar that opens onto the upper terrace; an airy restaurant for super food. You can eat al fresco in summer, on carpaccio of Sussex beef with truffle oil, confit belly of pork with salsa verde, warm chocolate pudding. Big bedrooms are just as good. Those at the front open onto the veranda, those at the side overlook the village church and green. All come in a smart, clipped style: big mirrors, light colours, crisp linen, pretty furniture.

Price	£95–£155.
Rooms	5: 4 doubles, 1 twin.
Meals	Lunch from £7.50. Dinner, 3 courses, £28–£32.
Closed	Rarely.
Directions	M23, A23, then A27 east from Brighton. Past Berwick, then south at r'bout for Alfriston. In village on left.

Nicholas Denyer
High Street, Alfriston,
Polegate BN26 5TD

Tel	+44 (0)1323 870276
Email	info@wingrovehousealfriston.com
Web	www.wingrovehousealfriston.com

The Tiger Inn

The Tiger sits on a village green that has hardly changed in 50 years and in summer life spills onto the terrace to soak up an English sun. It's all part of a large estate that hugs the coast from Beachy Head to Cuckmere Haven with Birling Gap in between; some of the best coastal walking in the south lies on your doorstep. Back at the inn a fabulous renovation has breathed new life into old bones. Downstairs has bags of character with low beams, stone floors, ancient settles and a roaring fire. Beer brewed on the estate pours from the tap, so try a pint of Legless Rambler before digging into hearty food – mussels cooked in Sussex cider, sausage and mash with a sweet onion gravy, treacle tart with vanilla ice cream. Five country-house bedrooms are the big surprise. Find beautiful fabrics, padded bedheads, funky bathrooms, the odd beam. Beds are dressed with lambs' wool throws, warm colours hang on the walls. Back outside, white cliffs wait, as do the South Downs. Finally, Arthur Conan Doyle knew the village and a blue plaque on one of the cottages suggests Sherlock Holmes retired here.

Price	£95.
Rooms	5: 4 doubles, 1 twin.
Meals	Lunch from £4.25. Dinner, 3 courses, £20-£25.
Closed	Never.
Directions	West from Eastbourne on A259. Left in village and on right.

Jo Staveley & Stuart Crook
The Green, East Dean,
Eastbourne BN20 0DA
Tel   +44 (0)1323 423209
Email   tiger@beachyhead.org.uk
Web   www.beachyhead.org.uk

Strand House

Strand House was built in 1425 and originally stood on Winchelsea harbour, though the sea was reclaimed long ago and marshland now runs off to the coast. You can walk down after breakfast, a great way to atone for your bacon and eggs. Back at the house, cosy interiors come with low ceilings, timber frames and ancient beams, all of which give an intimate feel. You'll find warm reds and yellows, sofas galore, a wood-burner in the sitting room and an honesty bar where you help yourself. It's a homespun affair: Hugh cooks breakfast, Mary conjures up delicious dinners… maybe grilled goat's cheese with red onion marmalade, Dover sole with a lemon butter, rhubarb and ginger crumble. Attractive bedrooms are warm and colourful and a couple are small; one has an ancient four-poster, some have wonky floors, all have beamed ceilings, good linen, comfy beds. Tall people are better off with ground-floor rooms as low ceilings are de rigueur on upper floors; all rooms have compact bathrooms. The house, once a workhouse, was painted by Turner and Millais. A short walk through the woods leads up to the village.

Price	£70–£135. Singles from £60.
Rooms	13: 8 doubles, 2 triples, 1 twin/double, 1 twin, 1 suite.
Meals	Dinner, 3 courses, £29.50.
Closed	4 January–12 February: Mon–Thurs.
Directions	A259 west from Rye for 2 miles. House on the left at foot of hill, opposite Bridge Inn pub.

Mary Sullivan & Hugh Davie
Tanyards Lane, Winchelsea,
Rye TN36 4JT
Tel   +44 (0)1797 226276
Email   info@thestrandhouse.co.uk
Web   www.thestrandhouse.co.uk

Bottle of wine with dinner on first night. A Strand House bear to take home.

The Gallivant Hotel

A boutique hotel down by the sea – friendly, stylish, very well priced. Across the road, enormous dunes tumble down to Camber Sands for two miles of uninterrupted beach, so watch the kite-surfing or walk up to the river Rother and follow it into Rye (three miles). Back at The Gallivant pretty interiors have a warm seaside feel: comfy bedrooms come in light colours, you get crisp linen and colourful cushions on big oak beds, driftwood-style furniture, a sofa if there's room; spotless bathrooms provide for a good soak after a hard day on the beach. The airy brasserie opens onto a dining veranda in summer, where you dig into local food, with plaice and mackerel fresh from the market. Try Rye Bay scallops, Romney Marsh Lamb, then chocolate tart with vanilla ice cream – or barbecues in summer on the new decked terrace. There's a good DVD library at reception and big family rooms (very popular in summer). Kite-surfing, golf and wildlife-watching weekends can all be arranged. Lympne Castle is close, as is Dungeness; Derek Jarman's Prospect Cottage is worth a look. *Minimum stay two nights at weekends.*

Price	£85–£245.
Rooms	18: 13 doubles, 1 twin, 3 family rooms, 1 triple.
Meals	Lunch from £5. Dinner, 3 courses, about £30.
Closed	Never.
Directions	A259 east from Rye, then B2075 for Camber & Lydd. On left after 2 miles.

Tudor Hopkins
New Lydd Road, Camber, Rye TN31 7RB
Tel   +44 (0)1797 225057
Email   enquiries@thegallivanthotel.com
Web   www.thegallivanthotel.com

The George in Rye

Ancient Rye has a big history. It's a reclaimed island, a Cinque Port which held its own army yet regularly fell into French hands. Henry James lived here and the oldest church clock in England chimes at the top of the hill. As for The George, it stands serenely on the cobbled high street. It was built in 1575 from reclaimed ships' timbers and its exposed beams and joists remain on display. A contemporary revamp in classical style runs throughout with airy interiors, stripped floors, panelled walls and open fires – Jane Austen in the 21st century. There's a huge leather sofa in the bar by the fire, screen prints of the Beatles on the walls in reception, a first-floor ballroom with a minstrels' gallery. Super bedrooms come in all shapes and sizes, but fabulous fabrics, Frette linen and Vi-Spring mattresses are standard, as are cashmere covers on hot water bottles. Superb food in the restaurant – chargrilled squid, venison Wellington, tarte tatin with gorgonzola ice cream – can be washed back with English wines. Festivals abound: scallops in February, art in September. Exceptional.

Price	£135–£195. Suites £295. Singles from £95.
Rooms	24: 12 doubles, 7 twins/doubles, 5 suites.
Meals	Lunch & dinner £6–£30.
Closed	Never.
Directions	Follow signs up hill into town centre. Through arch; hotel on left, below church. Parking at foot of hill.

Alex & Katie Clarke
98 High Street, Rye TN31 7JT

Tel	+44 (0)1797 222114
Email	stay@thegeorgeinrye.com
Web	www.thegeorgeinrye.com

Free dinner for one night (two nights in winter) for 2-night stays Sunday-Thursday in a superior room or junior suite.

Jeake's House

Rye, one of the Cinque Ports, is a perfect town for whiling away an afternoon; follow the tidal river, wander past old fishing boats, potter around Church Square, visit a gallery. Jeake's House, on a steep, cobbled street in the heart of it all, has a colourful past as wool store, school and home of American poet Conrad Potter Aiken. Carpeted corridors weave along to cosy bedrooms which come with beams and timber frames. They're generously furnished, excellent value. Some have stunning old chandeliers, others four-posters, one has a telly concealed in the wood-burner. A mind-your-head stairway leads up to a generous attic room for views over roof tops and chimneys. The galleried dining room — once an old Baptist chapel, now painted deep red — is full of busts, books, clocks, mirrors and fabric flowers: a fine setting for a full English breakfast. A cosy honesty bar with armchairs, books and papers is a convivial spot for a nightcap, the hearth is lit in winter and musicians will swoon at the working square piano. Jenny, efficient and friendly, has created a lovely atmosphere. *Children over eight welcome.*

Price	£90–£138. Singles £79.
Rooms	11: 7 twins/doubles, 3 four-poster suites, all en suite; 1 double with separate bath.
Meals	Restaurants in Rye.
Closed	Never.
Directions	From centre of Rye on A268, left off High St onto West St, then 1st right into Mermaid St. House on left. Private car park, £3 a day for guests.

Jenny Hadfield
Mermaid Street,
Rye TN31 7ET

Tel	+44 (0)1797 222828
Email	stay@jeakeshouse.com
Web	www.jeakeshouse.com

Prawles Court

Everything here is wonderful: house, gardens, owners, rooms. This is a magnificent country house, a B&B that thrills, as good as any hotel. It stands in 27 acres of peace, lost to the world in idyllic country (you can walk across fields to Bodiam Castle). It started out as an Elizabethan farmhouse, but was remodelled by Nathaniel Lloyd in Arts & Crafts style in the 1920s; on completion, it featured in *Country Life*. These days, after a fine refurbishment, it must qualify as one of the loveliest places to stay in Sussex. Potter about and find half-panelling in an exquisite drawing room, timber frames in the gorgeous dining room, an honesty bar stashed away in an elegant armoire. Bedrooms upstairs are divine: wonderful beds, beautiful fabrics, super colours, bowls of fruit. Two are huge, all have robes in exceptional bathrooms. You breakfast in the orangery on home-laid eggs and local bacon washed down with Sussex apple juice; at night, the vegetable garden provides much for dinner, served grandly in the dining room. Magical Sussex is all around. *Min. two nights at weekends in summer.*

Price	£130–£150. Singles from £90.
Rooms	3: 1 double, 2 twins/doubles.
Meals	Dinner, by arrangement, £25–£30.
Closed	Christmas & New Year.
Directions	A21 south thro' Hurst Green, then left, opp. pub, for Bodiam. Over x-roads, through Bodiam, over steam railway, then 2nd left into Shoreham Lane. 2nd drive on right.

Candida & Rob Machin
Shoreham Lane, Ewhurst Green,
Robertsbridge TN32 5RG

Tel	+44 (0)1580 830136
Email	info@prawlescourt.com
Web	www.prawlescourt.com

10% off stays of 3 or more nights.
Local produce in your room.

Fulready Manor

Fulready is majestic, a castle in the fields. It took 12 years to build from 2,000 pieces of hand-cut stone and is designed to last 500 years. It stands in 120 acres of quiet green country, with soothing views at the back over lamb-dotted fields to rippling hills. There's a lake, too, with a rowing boat for excursions to the island. All this you gaze upon dreamily from a glorious drawing room (muralled walls, huge sofas, roaring fire) where mullioned windows from floor to ceiling frame perfect views. Upstairs, bedrooms are just as you'd expect: sublimely decorated. (It helps if your daughter is an interior designer.) Expect Sanderson wallpapers, thick fabrics, mahogany furniture, perhaps an old oak four-poster. One room has tromp l'oeil artwork in the bathroom, another has a sitting room in an en suite turret. Best of all are Michael and Mauveen who pamper you rotten in true B&B fashion with grilled grapefruits and home-laid eggs among myriad breakfast treats. Stratford and Warwick are close and one of Warwickshire's best dining pubs is nearby for tasty dinners. *No credit cards.*

Afternoon tea or aperitif.

Price	From £95.
Rooms	3: 1 double, 2 four-posters.
Meals	Restaurants within 5 miles.
Closed	Christmas & New Year.
Directions	M40 junc. 11, then A422 west. Left in Pillerton Priors (B4451). Fulready first driveway on left after 0.25 miles.

Michael & Mauveen Spencer
Fulready, Ettington,
Stratford-upon-Avon CV37 7PE
Tel   +44 (0)1789 740152
Email   stay@fulreadymanor.co.uk
Web   www.fulreadymanor.co.uk

The Howard Arms

The Howard stands on Ilmington Green, five miles south of Stratford-upon-Avon; it was built at roughly the same time as Shakespeare wrote *King Lear*. Little has changed since and it's a fabulous country inn, one of the best. All the old fixtures and fittings remain — polished flagstones, heavy beams, mellow stone walls — as logs crackle contentedly on a vast open fire and a blackboard menu scales the wall above. Roast away while you take your pick, then dig into grilled sardines, beef, ale and mustard pie, spicy pear and apple crumble. Elsewhere, you find oils on walls, books on shelves, settles in alcoves, beautiful bay windows. An elegant dining room floods with light, courtesy of fine arched windows that overlook the green. Three gorgeous bedrooms in the main house mix period style with modern luxury, , while five new garden rooms come in elegant contemporary style with fancy bathrooms. There are maps for walkers, so follow paths through village and field. The church dates back to the 11th century (there are Thompson mice within) and Simon de Montfort owned this land in 1469.

Price	£145–£155. Singles £90.
Rooms	8: 5 doubles, 3 twins/doubles.
Meals	Lunch from £4.50. Dinner from £10.50.
Closed	Never.
Directions	From south take A429 Fosse Way through Moreton-in-Marsh. After 5 miles left to Ilmington.

Quentin Creese
Lower Green, Ilmington,
Shipston-on-Stour CV36 4LT
Tel   +44 (0)1608 682226
Email   info@howardarms.com
Web   www.howardarms.com

Half bottle of champagne in room for stays of 2 or more nights. 20% off (Sun-Thurs).

The Compasses Inn

A 14th-century whitewashed inn, lost down Wiltshire's sleepy lanes. Little has changed in 600 years: flagged floors, stone walls and heavy beams are original, the beams salvaged from an ancient English naval fleet. Once the haunt of drovers and smugglers, now its happy locals who jostle at the bar. Duck instinctively into the cosy darkness of this quirky inn to find low ceilings, a roaring fire and small booths divided by rustic cast-offs: a cartwheel here, a stable door there, an old piano at the end of the room. Lanterns glow, the odd pitchfork hangs on the wall and boarded menus entice you with super country cooking, perhaps potted crab, Gressingham duck, and brioche bread and butter pudding. Pretty bedrooms, all above, are a steal. Expect airy interiors, country rugs, wonky ceilings and well-dressed beds. All come with flat-screen TVs and cool little bathrooms, a painted beam here, a window seat there, a French bed. In summer, life spills onto the lawn, flowers tumble from stone troughs. Dogs and children are very welcome. One of the best. *Minimum stay two nights at weekends in summer.*

Price	£85. Singles from £65. Cottage £100–£130.
Rooms	4 + 1: 3 doubles, 1 twin/double. 1 self-catering cottage for 4.
Meals	Lunch from £5.50. Dinner from £15.
Closed	Christmas Day & Boxing Day.
Directions	From Salisbury A30 west. 3rd right after Fovant, signed Lower Chicksgrove, then 1st left down single track lane to village.

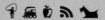 25% off stays of 2 or more nights. 3 nights for the price of 2 excluding Saturdays. Free pick-up from local bus/train station.

Alan & Susie Stoneham
Lower Chicksgrove, Tisbury,
Salisbury SP3 6NB
Tel   +44 (0)1722 714318
Email   thecompasses@aol.com
Web   www.thecompassesinn.com

Howard's House

An English village of rare beauty, a wormhole back to the 1700s. The building, Grade-II listed, dates from 1623 and comes with fine gardens, beyond which fields sweep uphill to a ridge of old oak. You can walk straight out, so bring the boots. Inside, find an airy country house with exquisite arched windows, flagstones in reception and the odd beam. Deep sofas, fresh flowers and the morning papers wait in the sitting room, where a fire crackles on cold days and when the sun shines, doors open onto a very pretty terrace; in good weather you can breakfast here. Bedrooms come in country-house style – not overly plush, but more than comfortable – with Laura Ashley wallpaper, mullioned windows, bowls of fruit and a sofa if there's room. Expect oak headboards, floral fabrics, robes in adequate bathrooms. Spin downstairs for dinner – perhaps fillet of sea bass with parsnip purée, Scottish beef with roasted shallots, apple crème caramel with a calvados jelly – then climb back up to find your bed turned down. Salisbury, Stonehenge and the gardens at Stourhead are all close.

Price	£190. Four-poster £210. Singles from £120.
Rooms	9: 6 doubles, 1 twin/double, 1 four-poster, 1 family room.
Meals	Lunch £28.50. Dinner £29.50; à la carte around £45.
Closed	24th-27th December.
Directions	A30 from Salisbury, B3089 west to Teffont. There, left at sharp right-hand bend following brown hotel sign. Entrance on right after 0.5 miles.

Noele Thompson
Teffont Evias,
Salisbury SP3 5RJ

Tel	+44 (0)1722 716392
Email	enq@howardshousehotel.co.uk
Web	www.howardshousehotel.co.uk

The Beckford Arms

You arrive in style, a grand sweep though the Fonthill estate – under the vast arch, past the big lake, along the boundary of the cricket pitch. This fine old inn was hit by fire, but has risen, phoenix-like, from the ashes. Against the odds, it's better than before, all the old niggles ironed out in a fine refurbishment. Outside, a gorgeous half-acre garden comes with hammocks in the trees, parasols on the terrace, a church spire soaring beyond. Interiors are just as lovely: a sofa'd drawing room with a roaring fire; an airy restaurant that opens onto the terrace; a lively bar with parquet flooring for a pint of ale. Wander at will and find the odd chandelier, roaming wisteria, beautiful art and fabrics. Bedrooms are delightful. Most are cosy, as is their price, but all have pretty colours, lovely linen and super bathrooms. There's a family suite up in the eaves, while the big room has a bath at the end of its bed. Delicious country food waits downstairs, perhaps marrow fritters with lemon mayo, local partridge with bread sauce, rhubarb crumble and custard. There are film nights most Sundays, too.

Price	£75–£95.
Rooms	8: 7 doubles, 1 twin/double.
Meals	Lunch & dinner £5–£30. Sunday lunch from £11.50.
Closed	Never.
Directions	On the road between Tisbury and Hindon, three miles south of A303 (Fonthill exit).

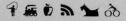 10% off stays of 2 or more nights.

Daniel Brod & Charlie Luxton
Fonthill Gifford, Tisbury,
Salisbury SP3 6PX

Tel	+44 (0)1747 870385
Email	info@beckfordarms.com
Web	www.beckfordarms.com

The Lamb at Hindon

The Lamb has been serving ale on Hindon's high street for 800 years, give or take a decade. It is a yard of England's finest cloth, a place where shooting parties come for lunch, where farmers meet to chew the cud. They come for the deep red walls and the roaring fires, for the huge oak settles and the heavy beams. Georgian rustic elegance abounds; you almost expect Mr Darcy to walk in, give a tormented sigh, then turn on his heels. You get flagstones and wooden boards, window seats and gilded mirrors. There are sofas, beautiful windows, a bookshelf stuffed with tomes of poetry. At night candles come out, as do some serious whiskies and the odd Cuban cigar; in the restaurant you feast merrily on super country fare, perhaps Wiltshire rarebit, steak and kidney pudding, tarte tatin, a plate of cheese. Fabulous bedrooms are attractive and comfortable in equal measure. You'll find beautifully dressed beds, vibrant colours, antique furniture and fabulous bathrooms with Neal's Yard lotions. Fishing can be arranged, and Stonehenge, Stourhead, Salisbury and Bath are within striking distance.

Price	£95–£125. Four-posters £125–£155. Suites £145–£195. Singles from £85.
Rooms	19: 10 doubles, 2 twins/doubles, 4 four-posters, 3 suites.
Meals	Lunch & dinner £5–£25.
Closed	Never.
Directions	M3, A303 & signed left at bottom of steep hill two miles east of junction with A350.

Merle Crampton
High Street, Hindon,
Salisbury SP3 6DP

Tel	+44 (0)1747 820573
Email	reservations@lambathindon.co.uk
Web	www.lambathindon.co.uk

10% off room rate Sun-Thurs.
Glass of champagne on arrival.

The Bath Arms at Longleat

A 17th-century coaching inn on the Longleat estate in a gorgeous village lost in the country; geese swim in the river, cows laze in the fields and lush woodland wraps around you. At the front the 12 apostles – a dozen pollarded lime trees – shade a gravelled garden, while at the back two large stone terraces, separated by beds of lavender, soak up the sun (you can eat out here in good weather). Inside are the best of old and new: flagstones and boarded floors mix with a stainless steel bar and Farrow & Ball paints. The feel is smart and airy, with a skittle alley that doubles as a sitting room (they show movies here too) and shimmering Cole & Son wallpaper in the dining room. For lunch you can dig into a gamekeeper's ploughman's lunch, for dinner you can try pork reared by the hotel. Bedrooms are a treat, some in the main house, others in a converted barn. Expect lots of colour, big wallpapers, beds dressed in Egyptian cotton, DVD and CD players; bathrooms come in black slate, some with free-standing tubs, others with deluge showers. Longleat is at the bottom of the hill – the walk down is majestic. *Min. two nights at weekends.*

Price	£95–£170. Singles from £85. Half-board from £75 p.p. Lodge £120 for 2-4.
Rooms	15 + 1: 13 doubles, 2 twins. Self-catering lodge for 4.
Meals	Lunch from £5. Dinner, 2 courses, £25.
Closed	Never.
Directions	A303, then A350 north to Longbridge Deverill. Left for Maiden Bradley; right for Horningsham. Through village, on right.

Bottle of wine with dinner on first night.

Peter Stevens
Horningsham, Warminster BA12 7LY

Tel	+44 (0)1985 844308
Email	enquiries@batharms.co.uk
Web	www.batharms.co.uk

King's Arms

In 1125 Cluniac monks founded a monastery in the village; this venerable old building was their sleeping quarters. It turned into an alehouse in the 19th century to satisfy an army of miners, who dug Bath stone from under the hills. These days, it's one of the loveliest inns you could hope to chance upon, with an ancient stone courtyard at the front and a small garden overlooking the farm behind. Inside, find painted panelling, cool colours, vintage wallpaper and thick curtains drawn across doorways. A vast inglenook, piled high with logs, was discovered during recent excavations in the restaurant, while the bar plays host to a colourful cast of farmers and shoot parties, who come for a good pint and some great food. Bedrooms above the shop are seriously spoiling. You get the full works: crisp white linen on low-slung beds, claw-foot baths, iPod docks, robes and Zoffany fabrics; one room is enormous and has its own fire. Unpretentious country food waits below, perhaps rabbit terrine, steak frites, sticky toffee pudding. There's a DVD library, playing cards and games. Bath is close.

Price	£95–£135. Suite £175. Singles from £85.
Rooms	3: 2 doubles, 1 suite.
Meals	Lunch from £4.50. Dinner, 3 courses, about £25.
Closed	Never.
Directions	M4 junction 18, then A46/A4 to Bathford. South on A363 for two miles, then left for Monkton Farleigh. Left at x-roads and on left.

Vince Hanley
Monkton Farleigh, Bath BA15 2QH
Tel   +44 (0)1225 858705
Email enquiries@kingsarms-bath.co.uk
Web   www.kingsarms-bath.co.uk

Lucknam Park Hotel & Spa

It's like a Merchant Ivory film: a one-mile drive that sweeps you up an avenue of beech trees, cutting through a 500-acre estate before delivering you into the arms of this magnificent 1720 mansion. Inside, find a panelled library with a roaring fire, a golden drawing room that opens onto a terrace and a Michelin-starred restaurant for ambrosial food; but follow your nose through a beautiful courtyard and you wash up at an ultra-cool spa. A fire runs along one side of the swimming pool, there's a saltwater plunge pool, a steam room and sauna, treatment rooms galore. Stop at the brasserie for a spot of lunch, then explore the grounds; you can walk for an hour without leaving the estate. There are mountain bikes to spin you round, you'll pass floodlit tennis courts, an arboretum, there's even an equestrian centre with a ring for jumping or dressage and a cross-country course that cuts through the park. Bedrooms match the mood. Those in the main house are magnificently grand, those around the courtyard are a little more contemporary. All come with robes in fine bathrooms and Anne Semonin toiletries.

Price	£315-£495. Suites £690-£1,065.
Rooms	42: 29 twins/doubles, 13 suites.
Meals	Breakfast £16-£22. Brasserie lunch & dinner £19-£40. Restaurant (not Sun eve or Mon) dinner £70; tasting menu £90; Sunday lunch £45.
Closed	Never.
Directions	M4 junc. 17, then A350 south to Chippenham & A420 west for Bristol. Left in Fox, through village. Hotel signed right after 2 miles.

Claire Randal
Colerne, Bath SN14 8AZ

Tel	+44 (0)1225 742777
Email	reservations@lucknampark.co.uk
Web	www.lucknampark.co.uk

Methuen Arms Hotel

You get a triple whammy here: a fantastic inn, a lovely village, a magnificent stately home. The inn started life as a medieval nunnery, turned into a mead house in 1608, later becoming a coaching inn. Martin and Debbie have moved things on again, orchestrating a fabulous renovation. Inside, you find a sparkling mix of old and new, with cool colours, open fires, stripped floors and an airy feel. Bedrooms upstairs are gorgeous. You find handmade beds, beautiful fabrics and wonderful bathrooms, most of which have double-ended baths. You also get Robert's radios and antique desks with hi-tech connections. Outside there's a lovely courtyard, but you'll want to venture further afield. Corsham Court, an Elizabethan manor house, is a five-minute stroll up an avenue of beech trees. It comes complete with gardens sewn by Capability Brown. A circular walk brings you back along a lovely high street (cars are banished), so potter back for a good dinner, perhaps leek and potato soup, lamb with fennel and tomatoes, walnut and plum tart. Bath is close.

Price	£100–£150. Singles from £85.
Rooms	10: 9 doubles, 1 twin/double.
Meals	Lunch from £5.95. Dinner, 3 courses, about £30. Sunday lunch £16.50–£19.50.
Closed	Never.
Directions	M4 junc. 17, then A350 south & A4 west. B3353 south into Corsham. On left.

Martin & Debbie Still
2 High Street, Corsham SN13 0HB
Tel +44 (0)1249 717060
Email info@themethuenarms.com
Web www.themethuenarms.com

Entry 245   Map 3

The Horse & Groom Inn

A proper inn, 500 years old, rescued from neglect, now shining brightly. Outside, the old coach-wash has turned into a pond, tables and chairs are scattered about and a fine willow stands on a postage-stamp lawn. Inside, a smart, rustic feel runs throughout: exposed stone walls, roaring fires, the odd beam, candles flickering at night. There's a fine bay window in the bar, so come for a pint of local ale, or spin next door into the airy restaurant (smart rugs on varnished floorboards, cricket prints hanging on the wall) where delicious country food is served, anything from Gressingham duck or fillet of sea bream to simple pub classics like steak and ale pie. Stylish bedrooms above the shop are great value for money. You get padded window seats, chunky wood beds, herbal toiletries, crisp white linen. Those in the eaves have painted beams, all have claw-foot baths; a real treat. Outside, the old walled garden is perfect for summer afternoons, while Sunday lunch – rare roast beef and buttered carrots – is unmissable. Malmesbury Abbey is close.

Price	£75–£140.
Rooms	5 doubles.
Meals	Lunch from £10. Sunday lunch £15–£20. Dinner, 3 courses, £25–£30.
Closed	Rarely.
Directions	M4 junc. 17, then A429 north for Cirencester. Right onto B4040 after 5 miles. On left in village after 1 mile.

10% off stays of 2 or more nights. Late checkout (12pm).

Emma Dall
The Street, Charlton,
Malmesbury SN16 9DL
Tel   +44 (0)1666 823904
Email info.horseandgroominn@bespokehotels.com
Web   www.bespokehotels.com/horseandgroom

Russell's

A wonderland of beautiful things. First there's Broadway, the prettiest village in the Cotswolds, its golden high street crammed with irresistible shops. Then there's Russell's, bang on the green, a super-stylish restaurant with rooms where locals gather for great food served informally in glittering surrounds. A wall of red wine dominates the inglenook, travertine marble floors brush up against stripped boards, there are beams, exposed stone walls, sun-trapping terraces back and front. Uncluttered bedrooms are simply divine with painted beams, gorgeous fabrics, excellent bathrooms. You get hi-tech gadgetry, too: flat-screen TVs, DVD players, iPod docks. The four-poster suite is magnificent – a cross-beamed cathedral ceiling, mullioned windows and stone walls – as is its bathroom, where you can soak in front of the telly. Back downstairs, dig into super food (Jay Rayner loved it); there's new season asparagus, sirloin steak with truffle mash, rhubarb mousse and ginger ice cream. A new restaurant in town, The Workshop, is Barry's newest venture and serves top notch British classics. *Minimum two nights at weekends.*

Price	£95-£225. Suite £245-£325.
Rooms	7: 3 doubles, 1 twin/double, 2 family rooms, 1 suite.
Meals	Lunch, 2 courses, from £12. Dinner, 3 courses, about £35.
Closed	Rarely.
Directions	A44 from Oxford & Evesham, then B4632 from Cheltenham. In centre of Broadway on High Street.

Barry Hancox
20 High Street,
Broadway WR12 7DT
Tel   +44 (0)1386 853555
Email   info@russellsofbroadway.co.uk
Web   www.russellsofbroadway.co.uk

10% off room rate Mon-Thurs. Free pick-up from local bus/train station.

Eckington Manor

Eckington Manor defies labels. It's a small hotel with a cookery school attached – the only place in England you can learn on an Aga – but it's also a farm with 260 acres that run down to the river Avon. A circular walk spins you round, and on your way you pass prize-winning cattle, rare-breed sheep, free-range chickens, the odd Gloucester Old Spot; lapwing, curlew and redshank nest here, too; fantastic. It's a family affair: Jackie runs the farm, Judy oversees the cookery school, Jane looks after some excellent bedrooms. The latter are scattered between the Old Milking Parlour, the Cyder Mill and the 13th-century manor house, its ancient timbers some sight to behold. All have a fine contemporary feel, but blend effortlessly with the original architecture. You get whitewashed walls, hand-painted wallpaper, beautiful beds, fantastic bathrooms. There's an honesty bar in the mill, a sitting room in the main house, and you can project your favourite movie onto a wall in the Old Dairy. A small shop sells meat reared on the farm. Upton is close for the river Severn, and has a jazz festival in June.

10% off room rate Mon-Thurs.

Price	£110–£225. Singles £75.
Rooms	15: 10 doubles, 4 twins/doubles, 1 suite.
Meals	Lunch from £8.50. Dinner, 3 courses, £30 (Friday & Saturday).
Closed	Rarely.
Directions	A4104 south from Pershore, then left onto B4080. Right in village at war memorial. Hotel drive straight ahead at sharp left hand bend.

Jane Harber
Manor Road, Eckington WR10 3BH

Tel	+44 (0)1386 751600
Email	info@eckingtonmanor.co.uk
Web	www.eckingtonmanor.co.uk

The Cottage in the Wood & Outlook Restaurant

A nine-mile ridge runs above the hotel, from where fabulous walks lead through light-dappled trees. There's a terrace for afternoon tea, too, so sip your Earl Grey amid 30-mile views that stretch off to distant Cotswold hills. And while the view is utterly magical, so is this hugely welcoming hotel. The décor is not cutting-edge contemporary, but nor would you want it to be; here is a hotel where old-fashioned values win out. Service is charming, the sort you only get with a passionate family at the helm and a battalion of long-standing staff to back them up. Add to that fabulous food in a restaurant that drinks in the view, and you have a winning combination for those who seek solid comforts rather than fly-by-night fashion. Rooms are split between the main house (simple, traditional), the cottage (cosy low ceilings, warm and snug) and the Pinnacles (hugely pleasing, nice and spacious, super bathrooms, the odd balcony). All have crisp linen and woollen blankets, floral fabrics, flat screen TVs and DVD players. A pretty garden adds the colour.

Price	£99–£198. Singles £79–£121. Half-board (min. 2 nights) £66–£126 p.p.
Rooms	30: 23 doubles, 6 twins/doubles, 1 four-poster.
Meals	Lunch from £5.75. Sunday lunch £24.95. Dinner, 3 courses, £25–£40. Packed lunch £8.95.
Closed	Never.
Directions	M5 junc. 7; A449 through Gt Malvern. In Malvern Wells 3rd right after Railway pub. Signed.

John & Sue Pattin
Holywell Road, Malvern WR14 4LG
Tel   +44 (0)1684 588860
Email   reception@cottageinthewood.co.uk
Web   www.cottageinthewood.co.uk

25% off room rate Mon–Thurs.

Brockencote Hall

A traditional country house hotel which was built in the style of a small French château and which stands in 70 acres of peaceful parkland with a lake for visiting geese. Joseph and Alison – he French, she English – run the place with understated charm: Wellington boots and piles of logs at the front door; sofas in front of a crackling fire in the sitting room hall; a panelled breakfast room in which to scoff your bacon and eggs. There's a small bar, a pretty terrace and a vast conservatory sitting room with a pink tented ceiling, but the biggest surprise here is the ambrosial food that is served in the restaurant. It is nothing short of glorious, so try Dorset crab with Avruga caviar, Gressingham duck with Yorkshire rhubarb, passion fruit soufflé with banana ice cream. Bedrooms in the main house are worth splashing out on as they have the period charm (high ceilings, flock wallpaper, ornamental fireplaces), but all come with robes in bathrooms, bowls of fruit and decanters of sherry. Worcester Cathedral and the Malvern Hills are close; come home and you can book in for a massage, or fish on the lake.

Price	£120–£190. Singles from £96. Half-board £99.50–£135 p.p.
Rooms	17: 12 twins/doubles, 3 four-posters, 2 family.
Meals	Lunch from £18. Sunday lunch £27.50. Dinner, 3 courses, about £40. Tasting menu £55.
Closed	Never.
Directions	M40 junc. 1, A38 south, A448 west. Down hill into village; sharp right bend; sharp left bend; on left.

20% off room rate Mon-Thurs. Bottle of house wine with dinner on first night.

Joseph & Alison Petitjean
Chaddesley Corbett,
Kidderminster DY10 4PY
Tel   +44 (0)1562 777876
Email   info@brockencotehall.com
Web   www.brockencotehall.com

Entry 250   Map 3

Estbek House

A super find on the Whitby coast. This is a quietly elegant restaurant with rooms ten paces from the beach at Sandsend. It's small, intimate and very welcoming. Tim cooks brilliantly, David talks you through his exceptional wine list and passes on the local news. Cliffs rise to the north, the beach runs away to the south, East Beck river passes directly opposite, ducks waddle across the road. There's a terrace at the front for drinks in summer and a small bar on the lower ground, where you can watch Tim at work in his kitchen. Upstairs, two airy dining rooms swim in seaside light and come with stripped floors, old radiators and crisp white tablecloths. Grab a window seat for watery views and dig into fresh Whitby crab with avocado and mango salad, local lamb with rhubarb compote, apricot tarte tatin. Bedrooms above are just the ticket, warmly cosy with painted panelling, crisp white linen, colourful throws and shuttered windows. Come back down for a delicious breakfast (David's mum makes the marmalade), then walk along cliffs, discover the moors or follow the river upstream to Mulgrave Castle.

Ethical Collection: Food. See page 386 for details

Price	£120–£150. Singles from £80.
Rooms	6: 5 doubles, 1 twin/double.
Meals	Dinner, 3 courses, about £35.
Closed	Occasionally.
Directions	North from Whitby on A174 to Sandsend. On left in village by bridge.

David Cross & Tim Lawrence
Eastrow, Sandsend,
Whitby YO21 3SU

Tel	+44 (0)1947 893424
Email	info@estbekhouse.co.uk
Web	www.estbekhouse.co.uk

Harry's Bar & Brasserie

Bang smack in the middle of Whitby, a fancy little bar where you can watch the world pass by. Tables and chairs line up smartly on the pavement, while walls of glass protect against the weather. Cool tunes float about, you can sip champagne at the mirrored bar, dip into some tapas for a spot of lunch, or simply order a coffee and read the daily papers. A flight of stairs leads up past a gallery of famous Hollywood faces to a neat restaurant, where views stretch over the water to St Mary's Church. Here you dig into more substantial fare, such as Whitby langoustine, pan-fried halibut, homemade chocolate brownie. Seafood and fish come straight off local boats, as fresh as can be. Most surprising of all are three delicious bedrooms above the shop. All have the view, none are small, and the suite has an entire floor to itself; take your pick knowing all are lovely. They come with comfy beds dressed in crisp linen, lots of colour, coffee machines, and robes in fabulous travertine shower rooms. Armchairs look the right way, though Whitby will draw you out. Brilliant. *Min. stay two nights at weekends.*

Price	£100–£135. Suite £150–£165.
Rooms	3: 2 doubles, 1 suite.
Meals	Tapas lunch/ dinner from £6.95.
Closed	Never.
Directions	Drop down to the sea front and keep left before the bridge, ignoring the no-entry signs. On left after 0.25 miles, opposite fish market.

	Julie Tuby
	10–11 Pier Road, Whitby YO21 3PU
Tel	+44 (0)1947 601909
Email	info@harrysloungebar.co.uk
Web	www.harrysloungebar.co.uk

Inn

Yorkshire

The White Swan Inn

A dreamy old inn that stands on Market Place, where farmers set up shop on the first Thursday of the month. The exterior is 16th century and flower baskets hang from its mellow stone walls. Inside, discover a seriously pretty world: stripped floors, open fires, a tiny bar, beautiful windows. The restaurant is at the back – the heart and soul of the inn – with delicious food flying from the kitchen, perhaps Whitby fishcakes, rack of spring lamb, glazed lemon tart with blood-orange sorbet. Excellent bedrooms are scattered about. Those in the main house have padded bedheads, Egyptian linen, Osborne & Little fabrics and flat-screen TV/DVDs; bathrooms have robes and White Company oils. Rooms in the courtyard tend to be bigger and come in crisp contemporary style with black-and-white screen prints, mohair blankets and York stone bathrooms. You'll also find a cool little residents' sitting room here, with a huge open fire, an honesty bar, a purple pool table and cathedral ceilings. The moors are all around: fabulous walking, Castle Howard and Whitby wait. *Pets £12.50. Minimum stay two nights some weekends.*

Price	£150–£180. Suites £210–£260. Singles from £115.
Rooms	21: 14 doubles, 4 twins/doubles, 3 suites.
Meals	Lunch from £5.25. Bar meals £12.95. Dinner £25–£45. Sunday lunch £22.50.
Closed	Never.
Directions	From North A170 to Pickering. Entering town left at traffic lights, then 1st right into Market Place. On left.

Victor & Marion Buchanan
Market Place, Pickering YO18 7AA
Tel   +44 (0)1751 472288
Email welcome@white-swan.co.uk
Web   www.white-swan.co.uk

Late checkout (12.30pm). Room upgrade.

The White Bear Hotel

At five o'clock on a Friday evening there's only one place to be in town: the tap room at the White Bear, spiritual home of Theakston's beer. The great and the good gather to mark the end of the week, the odd pint is sunk, the air is thick with gossip. Interior design is strictly 19th century – red leather, polished brass, a crackling fire. Elsewhere: a country-house dining room in salmon pink; a handsome public bar with stripped floorboards and the odd beam; a flower-festooned terrace for lunch in the sun. Twenty-first century luxury comes courtesy of excellent bedrooms. They occupy the old Lightfoot brewery, but don't expect nostalgia here. The style is contemporary, with beautiful fabrics, warm colours, sumptuous beds and cutting-edge bathrooms; some have views across town and the vast penthouse is open to the rafters. There's a courtyard for guests, a sitting room, too; staff will bring drinks if you want privacy and peace. As for dinner, delicious comfort food waits in the restaurant: smoked salmon, steak and ale pie, treacle sponge pudding. The Dales are all around.

Price	£98.50. Suite £185.
Rooms	14: 13 twins/doubles, 1 suite.
Meals	Lunch from £4.95. Dinner, 3 courses, about £30.
Closed	Never.
Directions	North from Ripon on A6108. In Masham up hill (for Leyburn). Right at crest of hill. Signed.

Sue Thomas
Wellgarth, Masham, Ripon HG4 4EN
Tel	+44 (0)1765 689319
Email	sue@whitebearmasham.co.uk
Web	www.thewhitebearhotel.co.uk

Swinton Park

Swinton is utterly glorious, a fabulous old pile that flaunts its beauty with rash abandon.
It stands in 200 acres of parkland, part of a 20,000-acre estate. You get the full aristocratic
works: five lakes and a huge kitchen garden outside, then stately interiors at every turn
within. Expect marble pillars, varnished wood floors, vast arched windows, roaring fires.
The drawing room is stupendous, a little like the salon of 17th-century French château,
but the dining room is equally impressive, its magnificent ceiling worth the trip alone.
The main corridor is an art gallery, there's a bar in the old chapel, the old stables are now
home to a very popular cookery school. Bedrooms come in grand country-house style:
plush fabrics, huge beds, marble bathrooms, decanters of complimentary gin and whisky.
The suite occupies the turret, some rooms have sublime views over Home Lake, where
fallow deer gather. As for the food, game from the estate and vegetables from the garden
are plentiful, while hampers can be left in bothies on the estate for walkers wanting a
rather good lunch.

Price	£180–£295. Suites £305–£375. Half-board from £125 p.p.
Rooms	30: 25 twins/doubles, 5 suites.
Meals	Lunch from £21.50. Dinner £48. Tasting menu £60–£70.
Closed	Never.
Directions	A1, then B6267 into Masham. Hotel signed in village. 1 mile south-west, past golf course.

Mark & Felicity Cunliffe-Lister
Swinton, Ripon HG4 4JH

Tel	+44 (0)1765 680900
Email	reservations@swintonpark.com
Web	www.swintonpark.com

25% off room rate Mon–Thurs.

Burgoyne Hotel

The Burgoyne is an old-school charmer, one of the loveliest places to stay in the Dales. The view from the front is imperious, a smooth sweep three miles south over Reeth and off into Swaledale; half a dozen benches on the village green look the right way. Inside, the past lives on: an elegant drawing room with a crackling fire where you gather for drinks before dinner; a restaurant in racing green where you feast on four courses of country fare — perhaps chicken liver pâté, cream of asparagus soup, best end of Swaledale lamb, sautéed bananas and ginger ice cream. Bedrooms come in traditional country-house style: colourful fabrics, excellent beds, thick white linen, a sofa if there's room. A four-poster occupies the old snooker room, all but one room has the view. There are maps for walkers, horse riding and fishing can be arranged, Durham and Hadrian's Wall are easily found. As for Reeth, it's a gorgeous 18th-century village trapped in aspic, mentioned in the Domesday Book, with a market every Friday and grouse moors considered the best in Britain.

Price	£137.95-£160.95. Four-poster £192. Suite £202.50. Singles from £120.
Rooms	9: 3 doubles, 1 twin, 1 four-poster, 1 suite, all en suite; 1 double, 2 twins, each with separate bath.
Meals	Dinner, 4 courses, £35.85.
Closed	2 January-10 February.
Directions	From Richmond A6108, then B6270 to Reeth. House on village green.

Derek Hickson
Reeth, Richmond DL11 6SN

Tel   +44 (0)1748 884292
Email   enquiries@theburgoyne.co.uk
Web   www.theburgoyne.co.uk

Yorebridge House

Every century Yorebridge House reinvents itself. It started life in 1850 as a headmaster's house, only to be snapped up by the Yorkshire Dales National Park to act as their HQ. With the advent of the 21st century, it aptly evolved into a super-cool hotel and those who like an excess of style will find it here. The house stands in five acres on the banks of two rivers, with fishing rights if you want to try your luck. Interiors sparkle, the result of a total renovation. You find leather sofas in the sitting room, where 1920s school photos adorn the walls; there are stripped floors and a slab of granite in the funky bar, and banks of windows in the restaurant. Gaze out on Nappa Scar while feasting on serious food, perhaps Whitby crab and shellfish consommé, Yoredale lamb with fennel purée, coconut panna cotta and pineapple sorbet. Bedrooms are exceptional, some with hot tubs on terraces, others with double-ended baths. All come with fabulous fabrics, beautiful colours, Bang & Olufsen TVs, magnificent bathrooms. Kayaking can be arranged. There are jazz nights, too.

Price	£180–£230. Suite £250.
Rooms	11: 8 doubles, 2 twins/doubles, 1 suite.
Meals	Lunch from £5.95. Dinner, 3 courses, £44.50. Bar meals from £12.95.
Closed	Never.
Directions	East from Hawes on A684. In Bainbridge bear left at Rose & Crown for Askrig. On right after 400m.

David & Charlotte Reilly
Bainbridge DL8 3EE

Tel	+44 (0)1969 652060
Email	enquiries@yorebridgehouse.co.uk
Web	www.yorebridgehouse.co.uk

Bottle of champagne for bookings of 2 nights or more. Room upgrade subject to availability.

The Traddock

This family-run hotel is decidedly pretty and sits on southern fringes of the Yorkshire Dales; those looking for a friendly base will find it here. You enter through a wonderful drawing room – crackling fire, pretty art, the daily papers, cavernous sofas – but follow your nose and find polished wood in the dining room, panelled walls in the breakfast room and William Morris wallpaper in the sitting-room bar, where you can sip a pint of Skipton ale while indulging in a game of Scrabble. Bedrooms are just the ticket, some seriously swanky in contemporary style, others deliciously traditional with family antiques, quilted beds, perhaps a claw-foot bath. Those on the second floor have a cosy attic feel, all have fresh fruit, flat-screen TVs, homemade shortbread and Dales views. Elsewhere, a white-washed sitting room that opens onto the garden and fabulous local food in the rug-strewn restaurant, perhaps poached asparagus, fell-bred lamb, apple and butterscotch crumble. Three Peaks are at the door, so come to walk. Don't miss the caves at Ingleborough or Settle for antiques. *Minimum stay two nights at weekends March-October.*

Ethical Collection: Community; Food. See page 386 for details

Price	£95–£185. Singles from £85. Half-board from £85 p.p.
Rooms	12: 8 doubles, 1 twin/double, 2 family rooms, 1 single.
Meals	Lunch from £9.50. Dinner, 3 courses, about £30.
Closed	Never.
Directions	0.75 miles off the A65, midway between Kirkby Lonsdale & Skipton, 4 miles north-west of Settle.

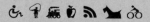 10% off room rate Mon-Thurs. Late checkout (12pm).

Paul Reynolds
Austwick, Settle LA2 8BY

Tel	+44 (0)15242 51224
Email	info@austwicktraddock.co.uk
Web	www.thetraddock.co.uk

The Tempest Arms

A 16th-century, award-winning ale house three miles west of Skipton with great prices, friendly staff and an easy style. Inside you find stone walls and open fires, six ales on tap at the bar and a smart beamed restaurant. An airy open-plan feel runs throughout with sofas and armchairs strategically placed in front of a fire that burns on both sides. Delicious traditional food is a big draw – the inn was packed for dinner on a Wednesday in April. You can eat wherever you want, so grab a seat and dig into Yorkshire puddings with a rich onion gravy, cottage pie with a Wensleydale crust, treacle tart with pink grapefruit sorbet. Bedrooms are just as good. Those in the main house are simpler, those next door in two newly built stone houses are rather indulging. You get crisp linen, neutral colours, slate bathrooms and flat-screen TVs. Some have views of the fells, the suites are large and worth the money, a couple have decks with hot tubs to soak in. The Dales are on your doorstep, this is a great place for walkers. Skipton, a proper Yorkshire market town, is worth a look. Hard to fault for the price.

Price	£85. Suites £100-£140. Singles from £62.50.
Rooms	21: 9 twins/doubles, 12 suites.
Meals	Lunch & dinner £5-£25.
Closed	Never.
Directions	A56 west from Skipton. Signed left after two miles.

Martin & Veronica Clarkson
Elslack, Skipton BD23 3AY

Tel	+44 (0)1282 842450
Email	info@tempestarms.co.uk
Web	www.tempestarms.co.uk

Stay Saturday night, get Sunday night free (applies to most rooms).

The Angel Inn

The Angel has it all – a perfect English inn. It stands in the middle of a tiny hamlet surrounded by lush grazing land with Rylstone Fell rising behind. You can drop by for a pint of Black Sheep in the half-panelled bar, pop a bottle of champagne on the flower-festooned terrace or seek out the restaurant for a fabulous meal. All the ancient trimmings are here – mullioned windows, beamed ceilings, exposed stone walls, a working Yorkshire range – yet the feel is bright and breezy, especially in the dining rooms, of which there are several to satisfy the legions of fans who come for Bruce Elsworth's delicious concoctions (Whitby crab ravioli, Bolton Abbey mutton, sticky toffee pudding with butterscotch sauce). You can get married or privately dine in the wine cave over the road. Above, you find exquisite bedrooms – the lap of luxury. All are different, you may get a French armoire, a brass bed, or a claw-foot bath. One is partly muralled, another has an icon in an alcove. Expect the best fabrics, pretty colours, flat-screen TVs. Jazz bands play at summer barbecues.

25% off room rate Mon-Thurs.

Price	£140-£165. Suites £165-£190. Singles from £125.
Rooms	9: 4 doubles, 5 suites.
Meals	Lunch from £11.50. Dinner £15.95-£38.50. Sunday lunch £26.
Closed	Christmas Day; 1 week in January.
Directions	North from Skipton on B6265. Left at Rylstone for Hetton. In village.

Juliet Watkins
Hetton, Skipton BD23 6LT

Tel	+44 (0)1756 730263
Email	info@angelhetton.co.uk
Web	www.angelhetton.co.uk

Devonshire Fell Hotel

You're high on the hill with huge views of Wharfdale: mountains rise, the river roars and in summer you can watch the cricket team toil on the pitch below. Up at this rather cool hotel there's a plant-festooned terrace and a trim lawn for sunbathing (people do). Inside, funky interiors are the order of the day. A lilac bar comes with halogen lighting and leather sofas; wander on and find stripped floors, Designers Guild fabrics and a wood-burner to keep you warm. There's a sense of space, too, with one room flowing into another, the bar, bistro and conservatory united by an open-plan feel. Bedrooms upstairs are equally flamboyant, those at the front with stupendous views. Expect lots of colour, padded bedheads and beautiful upholstery. You get big TVs, DVD players, iPod docks, a sofa if there's room; tongue-and-groove bathrooms come with robes and fluffy towels. Back downstairs, delicious food is served informally in the bistro, perhaps twice-baked cheese soufflé, roast rump of lamb, sticky toffee pudding. There are movie nights, the odd game of poker; the walking is heavenly.

Price	£144–£217.
Rooms	12: 6 doubles, 4 twins, 2 suites.
Meals	Lunch from £13.95. Dinner £26–£32.
Closed	Never.
Directions	From Harrogate A59 west for 15 miles, then right onto B6160, signed Burnsall & Bolton Abbey. Hotel on the edge of the village.

Stephane Leyreloup
Burnsall, Skipton BD23 6BT

Tel	+44 (0)1756 729000
Email	res@devonshirehotels.co.uk
Web	www.devonshirefell.co.uk

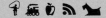

The Grassington House Hotel

Only in the Dales can you travel back in time. This magnificent patch of England has been brilliantly preserved and nowhere more so than Grassington, a small market town with a royal charter that dates to 1286. Not that time stands still here. After years cooking in all the best places, John decided to come home to do their own thing. He and Sue now have the smartest place in town, a restaurant with rooms that sits contentedly on the tiny square. Outside, window boxes and wicker chairs flourish on the terrace, inside colourful interiors come as standard. There's a smart bar with a wood-burner to keep you cosy, then a restaurant in red which overflows into a conservatory. John cooks brilliantly – he even rears his own pigs and tends a small brigade of free-range poultry – so come for English asparagus with a home-laid duck egg, rare breed pork with cider jus, rhubarb crème brûlée with ginger ice cream. Stylish bedrooms are great value for money. Expect comfy beds, fancy bathrooms, blond wood furniture. You can fish the Wharfe, go up in a hot-air balloon, and there are monthly cooking master-classes, too.

Price	£100–£125. Singles from £90. Half-board from £82.50 p.p.
Rooms	9: 7 doubles, 2 twins.
Meals	Lunch from £4.50. Sunday lunch £14.50. Dinner, 3 courses, about £30.
Closed	Rarely.
Directions	North from Skipton for 10 miles on B6265. In village, on square. Buses leave from Skipton train station.

John & Sue Rudden
5 The Square, Grassington BD23 5AQ
Tel   +44 (0)1756 752406
Email   bookings@grassingtonhousehotel.co.uk
Web   www.grassingtonhousehotel.co.uk

Hob Green

A super country house happily lingering in a quirky past, with a fire smouldering merrily in the hall and ancient wallpaper hanging on the walls. Hob Green is a much-needed antidote to the contemporary world. It sits in absolute peace on an 800-acre estate with exquisite views from the lawned terrace of hill, wood and paddock. Roses climb, birds sing, hanging baskets burst with colour, a huge kitchen garden employs two full-time gardeners, who grow flowers for the house and much of the food that ends up on the table. Inside, the drawing room and dining room both look the right way, there are warm colours, comfortable sofas, open fires and oils on the walls. Bedrooms – all different, all super value for money – are plush without being grand: country-cosy, floral fabrics, white sheets and blankets, new tiles to brighten up bathrooms. Those at the back have gorgeous views. Staff, many long-serving, couldn't be kinder and guests return for the personal touch. Dinner pays little heed to modern trends: devilled kidneys, lemon sole, crème caramel. York and the Dales wait. *Minimum stay two nights at weekends.*

Price	£115–£125. Four-poster £135. Suite £140. Singles from £95. Half-board £80–£95 p.p.
Rooms	12: 4 doubles, 4 twins/doubles, 2 twins, 1 four-poster, 1 suite.
Meals	Lunch from £13.99. Dinner, 3 courses, £27.50. Sunday lunch £21.95.
Closed	Never.
Directions	A61 north from Ripon, then left for Markington in Wormald Green. Through Markington; hotel on left.

Christopher Ashby
Markington, Harrogate HG3 3PJ
Tel +44 (0)1423 770031
Email info@hobgreen.com
Web www.hobgreen.com

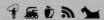 Bottle of wine with dinner on first night.

The Bijou

Great prices, an easy style and ever-present owners are the hallmarks of this smart B&B hotel close to the centre of town. Outside, a small, manicured garden leads up to a Victorian stone townhouse; inside, a clean contemporary feel runs throughout. Gill and Stephen (he's ex-Hotel du Vin) renovated completely; out with the woodchip and swirly carpets, in with stripped boards and faux-zebra-skin rugs. There's a cool little sitting room with an open fire, a computer for guests to use, and an honesty bar on tap all day. Bedrooms mix leather bedheads, airy colours, Cole & Son wallpaper and orange stools. Excellent bathrooms, most compact, have smart creamy ceramics, you get waffle robes, hot water bottles, flat-screen TVs and double glazing (the house is set back from the road). Two rooms in the coach house are good for small groups. Breakfast is a leisurely feast: freshly squeezed orange juice, eggs and bacon from a local farm, homemade breads and muesli. Don't miss the Stray (the vast common that wraps up the town) or Betty's for afternoon tea. Good restaurants wait, too.

Price	£85–£110. Singles from £65.
Rooms	10: 8 doubles, 1 twin, 1 single.
Meals	Restaurants within walking distance.
Closed	23-30 December.
Directions	A61 north into town, following signs for Ripon. Past Betty's Teashop, down hill, back up, past Cairn Hotel. Signed on left.

 10% off stays of 2 or more nights.

Stephen & Gill Watson
17 Ripon Road, Harrogate HG1 2JL
Tel   +44 (0)1423 567974
Email   info@thebijou.co.uk
Web   www.thebijou.co.uk

Royal Parade Apartments

These fantastic serviced apartments are the very lap of luxury and you can take them for just a night – a tempting alternative to a smart hotel. There are three to choose from (no easy feat), but all are large and packed with style. A sleek kitchen opens onto a smart living room in Royale, where a couple of sofas wait in front of a marble fireplace. Rajasthan has antique Indian furniture and painted wood floors, while loft-like Brooklyn mixes vintage pieces with retro style: bleached pine and shiny steel, old leather suitcases, a vast sofa in front of the fire. Bathrooms are fabulous, comfy beds are dressed in gorgeous linen, kitchens all have long dining tables and a chef can come to cook for you. Janet and Tanya have thought of everything, down to the fine reclaimed furniture and the eco-friendly soaps; indulgence here is guilt-free. You're in the middle of town, you won't need a car, though a chauffeur can be arranged if you want to spread your wings. A short walk west leads down to the gardens of Harlow Carr – the Royal Horticultural Society's magnificent northern outpost.

Ethical Collection: Environment; Community; Food. See page 386 for details

Price	£150–£245. Whole house £575–£750. Weekends (2 nights) £360–£490.
Rooms	3 apartments for 2-4.
Meals	Breakfast included. Restaurants nearby.
Closed	Rarely.
Directions	A1(M) junc. 41, then A59/A6040 into town. Right at r'about, then 2nd left onto Montpellier Hill. Straight over r'about and on left.

	Janet & Tanya Love
	9A Royal Parade, Harrogate HG1 2SZ
Tel	+44 (0)1423 709723
Email	info@royalparade.co.uk
Web	www.royalparade.co.uk

10% off room rate Mon-Thurs.
Bottle of wine in your room.
Local food/produce in your room.

Gallon House

A bespoke B&B that clings to the side of an impossibly steep hill with a medieval castle tottering on one side, a grand Victorian railway bridge passing on the other and the serene river sparkling below. Ancient steps lead gently down, you can follow the Nidd into the country or hire a boat and mess about on it. Climb back up to this magical house, where walls of glass bring in the view. There's Lloyd Loom wicker in the small conservatory, an open fire in the panelled sitting room, stripped floors and delicious communal breakfasts in the dining room. Best of all is the sun terrace for one of Yorkshire's best views, with parasols and pots of colour, and deckchairs to take the strain. Bedrooms are warmly stylish, not too big, but spoiling nonetheless, with bathrobes and white towels, crisp linen and soft colours, videos and CD players. Two have the view, two have showers in the actual room. As for dinner, Rick, a chef, is a maestro in the kitchen, so come down for something tasty, perhaps salmon fish cakes, rack of lamb, pear and almond tart. A great little place. *No credit cards.*

Price	£120. Singles £85.
Rooms	3: 2 doubles, 1 twin.
Meals	Dinner, 3 courses, £40, by arrangement.
Closed	Christmas & New Year.
Directions	A1(M) junc. 46, A59 west for 3 miles. Climb hill into Knaresborough. Left into Market Place at Barclays bank; 1st right into Kirkgate; on left.
🎁	Use your Sawday's Gift Card here.

Bottle of wine with dinner on first night.

Sue & Rick Hodgson
47 Kirkgate, Knaresborough HG5 8BZ
Tel   +44 (0)1423 862102
Email   gallon-house@ntlworld.com
Web   www.gallon-house.co.uk

The Grange Hotel

York Minster is imperious, the oldest Gothic cathedral in northern Europe. It stands less than half a mile from the front door of this extremely comfortable Regency townhouse – a five-minute stroll after bacon and eggs. The streets around it give the feel of Dickensian London and a Roman column stands outside the West Door, but the interior astounds; the Great East Window is the largest piece of medieval stained glass in the world. Back at the hotel, a country-house elegance runs throughout: marble pillars in a flagged entrance hall, an open fire in the cosy Morning Room and a first-floor Drawing Room that opens onto a small balcony. Bedrooms come in different shapes and sizes, with smart florals, mahogany dressers, period colours, good bathrooms. The more expensive rooms are seriously plush with high beds and swathes of silky curtain. York racecourse brings in a crowd, there are deep red walls and leather chairs in the super-smart Ivy Brasserie; you can also eat downstairs in the vaulted New York grill where steaks are the order of the day. *Minimum stay two nights at weekends.*

Price	£137–£208. Four-poster £235. Suite £284. Singles from £123.
Rooms	36: 11 doubles, 18 twins/doubles, 3 four-posters, 3 singles, 1 suite.
Meals	Lunch from £10. Dinner, 3 courses, £30–£35 (early bird discount).
Closed	Never.
Directions	South into York from ring road on A19. On right after two miles, 500 yards north of York Minster.

George Briffa
1 Clifton, York YO30 6AA

Tel	+44 (0)1904 644744
Email	info@grangehotel.co.uk
Web	www.grangehotel.co.uk

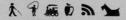 3 nights for the price of 2 Sunday-Thursday (applies to king-size doubles and above, one-night rate £180).

The Black Swan at Oldstead

In glorious isolation, a sparkling country inn. Outside, a grass terrace shaded by cherry trees gives views of field and ridge, a perfect spot for a pint in summer. Inside is a bar of matchless elegance: a fire primed for combustion, 400-year-old flagstones, a couple of gorgeous bay windows, candelabra hanging from the ceiling. The inn is built into the side of a hill with stairs that lead up to a country-house restaurant, where smart rugs cover golden floorboards and cream walls make the most of the light. But the food is what you've come for. The Banks family has farmed here for generations and much of what you eat comes straight from local fields. It's serious stuff, immaculately presented, perhaps game terrine and toasted brioche, haunch of venison with grain mustard risotto, an irresistible pear tarte tatin. Four sublime bedrooms wait in a low stone building next door. Expect a very pretty country style: beautiful beds, white linen, oak armoires, fabulous bathrooms (one has a copper bath). Each room opens to a peaceful terrace and they'll bring you a whisky before dinner.

Price	Half-board £95–£155 p.p.
Rooms	4: 2 doubles, 2 four-posters.
Meals	Lunch from £8.95. Dinner, non-residents, 3 courses, £37.50–£47. Tasting menu £49.95. No lunch Mon-Wed.
Closed	First two weeks in January.
Directions	A19 from Thirsk; left to Thirkleby & Coxwold, then left for Byland Abbey; follow signs left for Oldstead.

20% off stays Sun-Thurs.

The Banks Family
Oldstead, York YO61 4BL

Tel	+44 (0)1347 868387
Email	enquiries@blackswanoldstead.co.uk
Web	www.blackswanoldstead.co.uk

Feversham Arms & Verbena Spa

Yorkshire may have a slew of grand hotels but you'll be hard pressed to find a more stylish one than this. Simon steered several hotels in the north to prominence and now he's doing it for himself. His 1855 coaching inn seduces the moment you enter. Rich country-house interiors are classically inspired, yet the feel is fresh and contemporary. Wander at will – to find tromp l'oeil wallpaper, huge sofas, wonderful art and well-stocked log fires. There's a snug bar and a sail-shaded conservatory/restaurant, but best of all is a swimming pool courtyard – St Tropez on the Yorkshire Moors. There's a serious spa for just about any treatment you can imagine, while poolside suites circle around with private terraces. Other rooms are equally magical – a night here is a treat wherever you sleep – and a clipped elegance runs throughout; expect fabulous fabrics, beautiful upholstery, perhaps air-blasted beams or a cavernous bath. Beds are turned down, breakfast is brought to your room if that's what you like. Castle Howard is close. Heaven. *Minimum stay two nights at weekends.*

Price	Half-board from £120-£260 p.p. Singles from £193.
Rooms	33: 12 doubles, 21 suites.
Meals	Lunch, 2 courses, from £25. Dinner included; non-residents £45 (3 courses à la carte or 5 course tasting menu).
Closed	Never.
Directions	East from Thirsk on A170. In Helmsley, left at top of square & car park; hotel on right by church.

Simon Rhatigan
Helmsley, York YO62 5AG
Tel +44 (0)1439 770766
Email info@fevershamarmshotel.com

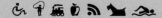

Channel Islands

Braye Beach Hotel

Alderney is hard to beat, a tiny island adrift off the north coast of France. You can walk around it in a morning. Cliff-top paths drop down to vast sandy beaches, boats tug on their moorings in an ancient harbour, cobbled lanes weave through St Anne's. The hotel stands directly above the beach from which it takes its name, a crescent of sand that curls round the bay from the harbour to the point; utterly serene. Inside, airy interiors flood with seaside light. There are a couple of stylish sitting rooms to hide away in, a bar that opens onto a big terrace, a smart restaurant for super food, perhaps local crab with seafood bisque, rack of lamb with Dijon mustard, hot chocolate soufflé with vanilla ice cream. Lovely bedrooms hit the spot. Some have the view, others don't, but all share the same smart style: warm colours, contemporary fabrics, crisp white linen and robes in excellent bathrooms. You get bowls of fruit and decanters of sherry, and beds are turned down each evening. There's loads to do on the island, so come to walk, fish, play a game of golf or saddle up and ride on the beaches.

Price	£145-£205. Singles from £109.
Rooms	27 twins/doubles.
Meals	Lunch from £3.50. Dinner, 3 courses, about £25.
Closed	January-February 2012.
Directions	From airport north through St Anne's to Braye Beach. Hotel on water next to harbour.

Richard Proctor
Braye Street, Alderney GY9 3XT
Tel   +44 (0)1481 213570
Email   reservations@brayebeach.com
Web   www.brayebeach.com

The Georgian House

Holly's family have been holidaying in Alderney for more than 30 years, now she's come back to take over this treasure of an hotel. Along with her charming young team, they've turned it into the beating heart of the island. Step off the cobbled high street straight into a traditional, cosy bar; grab a bite here or something more extravagant in the light-strewn dining room that opens out to the pretty garden. Vegetables and salad come from their own allotment, the butter is vivid yellow and meat and fish is as local as can be: try the divine head-to-toe pork dish (great for sharing) or a zingy chilli squid. Upstairs three quaint bedrooms, all en suite, are pretty and pristine with locally made soaps and views to the town. The 100-seater cinema opposite shows arthouse films on reels, during the interval you wander over to The Georgian for a drink. The hotel is packed with locals and visitors alike, and rightly so, there are barbecues, bands, taster evenings, and a blissful atmosphere. Old forts and stunning beaches wait, so hire bikes and explore the island. And book early.

Price	£70–80.
Rooms	3 doubles.
Meals	Light lunch from £6. Dinner, 3 courses, £30.
Closed	Rarely.
Directions	Sent on booking.

10% off room rate. Free pick-up from local bus/train station.

Holly Fisher
Victoria Street, Alderney GY9 3UF
Tel	+44 (0)1481 822471
Email	holly@georgianalderney.com
Web	www.georgianalderney.com

Fermain Valley Hotel

The first thing you notice here is the view – a clean sweep down the valley out to sea. Then, you potter over to drink it in and find two decked terraces waiting on the hill, a perfect spot to while away the afternoon. There's masses to do if you want to explore – coastal paths lead onto the cliffs, you can drop down to the beach and swim in pristine water – but 18 rooms have small balconies, so you might want to stay local. Wander about and you'll find an airy brasserie, a pretty sitting room, a fancy restaurant for serious food, even a small swimming pool and sauna. Everywhere you go, doors open onto the terrace, so grab a table for lunch in the sun. Bedrooms are sprinkled about, some bigger than others, but all are lovely: crisply uncluttered with pretty fabrics, padded bedheads and excellent bathrooms. Most are in the main house, a clutch are above the function suite across the garden; to compensate, you get a small cinema here where you can watch your favourite movie from a leather armchair. Cliff-top paths lead into town, but there's a shuttle bus, too, so you won't need a car.

Price	£135-£245. Singles from £102.
Rooms	45 twins/doubles.
Meals	Lunch from £6.50. Dinner £10-£30.
Closed	Never.
Directions	South from St Peter Port and signed left in Fermain after 3 miles.

Michael Conrad-Pickles
Fermain Lane, St Peter Port GY1 1ZZ

Tel	+44 (0)1481 213570
Email	reservations@fermainvalley.com
Web	www.fermainvalley.com

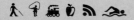

White House Hotel

Herm is unique, a tiny island run benignly by the 40 souls lucky enough to live on it. They keep things blissfully simple: no cars, no TVs, just a magical world of field and sky, a perfect place to escape the city. A coastal path rings the island; you'll find high cliffs to the south, sandy beaches to the north, cattle grazing the hills between. You get fabulous views at every turn – shimmering islands, pristine waters, yachts and ferries zipping about. There are beach cafés, succulent gardens, an ancient church, even a tavern. Kids love it, so do parents, and the self-catering cottages are extremely popular. As for the hotel, it lingers happily in an elegant past, a great base from which to enjoy the island. You'll find open fires, delicious four-course dinners, a tennis court with watery views, a pool to keep you cool. Spotless bedrooms are scattered about, some in the village's colour-washed cottages, others with balconies in the hotel. Several come in contemporary style with fancy bathrooms, but most are warmly traditional as befits the setting. Expect pretty colours, padded headboards and watery views.

Price	Half-board £99-£142 p.p. Self-catering cottages £260-£1,230 a week.
Rooms	40 + 20: 12 twins/doubles, 5 family rooms. Cottage rooms: 16 twins/doubles, 5 family rooms, 2 singles. 20 cottages for 2-6.
Meals	Lunch from £5. Dinner for non-residents, £25.
Closed	November-Easter.
Directions	Via Guernsey. Trident ferries leave from the harbour at St Peter Port 8 times a day in summer (£10.50 return).

Bottle of champagne for bookings of 2 nights or more.

	Siôn Dobson Jones
	Herm Island GY1 3HR
Tel	+44 (0)1481 750075
Email	hotel@herm.com
Web	www.herm.com

Stocks Hotel

A tiny island marooned between the French and English coasts: no airport, no cars, no streetlights, just birds warbling, tractors chugging and stars twinkling in the night skies. You arrive by boat, where Stocks take care of your luggage, then wander up to the Avenue (the diminutive high street), through the meadow, into the heart of the island, where this impressive hotel sits above an old smugglers cove. Built as a farmhouse in 1741, Paul's family have run it with the same warm touch for the last 30 years. Now they've breathed new life into it and there are 23 delicious rooms spread throughout three buildings. Expect top-notch everything: gleaming bathrooms, the softest beds, fresh flowers, thick curtains, fluffy towels and robes. Sip cocktails or homemade wine – try the light, sparkling Earl Grey – in the smugglers bar before treating yourself to the freshest seafood in the panelled dining room. There's a gym, beauty treatments, a library and snug. Come to tramp the coastal paths, explore the coves and islets and skip over the magnificent La Coupée isthmus to Little Sark.

Price	£175–£210. Half-board supplement £20 p.p.
Rooms	23: 16 twins/doubles, 2 family suites, 5 suites.
Meals	Dinner, 3 courses, £30.
Closed	3 January–10 February.
Directions	Sent on booking.

Paul Armorgie
Sark GY10 1SD

Tel	+44 (0)1481 832001
Email	reservations@stockshotel.com
Web	www.stockshotel.com

10% off room rate Mon-Thurs.
Local food/produce in your room.

Scotland

Darroch Learg Hotel

The country here is glorious – river, forest, mountain, sky – so walk by Loch Muick, climb Lochnagar, fish the Dee or drop down to Braemar for the Highland Games. Swing back to Darroch and find nothing but good things. This is a smart family-run hotel firmly rooted in a graceful past, an old country house with roaring fires, polished brass, Zoffany wallpaper and ambrosial food in a much-admired restaurant. Ever-present Nigel and Fiona look after guests with great aplomb and many return year after year. Everything is just as it should be: tartan fabrics on the walls in the hall, Canadian pitch pine windows and doors, fabulous views sweeping south across Balmoral forest. Bedrooms upstairs come in different shapes and sizes; all have warmth and comfort in spades. Big grand rooms at the front thrill with padded window seats, wallpapered bathrooms, old oak furniture, perhaps a four-poster bed. Spotlessly cosy rooms in the eaves are equally lovely, just not quite as big. You get warm colours, pretty furniture, crisp white linen and bathrobes to pad about in. A perfect highland retreat.

Price	£140–£250. Half-board (obligatory at weekends) £95–£160 p.p.
Rooms	12: 10 twins/doubles, 2 four-posters.
Meals	Sunday lunch £24. A la carte dinner, 3 courses, £45. 7-course tasting menu £55, by arrangement.
Closed	Christmas week & last 3 weeks in January.
Directions	From Perth A93 north to Ballater. Entering village hotel 1st building on left above road.

Nigel & Fiona Franks
56 Braemar Road, Ballater AB35 5UX
Tel   +44 (0)1339 755443
Email   enquiries@darrochlearg.co.uk
Web   www.darrochlearg.co.uk

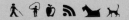

The Colonsay

Another fabulous Hebridean island, a perfect place to do nothing at all. Wander at will and find wild flowers in the machair, a golf course tended by sheep and huge sandy beaches across which cows roam. Wildlife is ever present, from a small colony of wild goats to a rich migratory bird population; the odd golden eagle passes overhead, too. At low tide the sands of the south give access to Oronsay. The island's 14th-century priory was one of Scotland's finest and amid impressive ruins its ornate stone cross still stands. As for the hotel, it's a splendid island base and brims with an easy style – airy interiors, stripped floors, fires everywhere, friendly staff. There's a locals' bar for a pint (and a brewery on the island), a pretty sitting room packed with books, a dining room for super food and a decked terrace for drinks in the sun. Recently refurbished bedrooms have local art, warm colours, lovely fabrics and the best beds; those at the front have sea views, all have neat little bathrooms. Fish for brown trout, search for standing stones, lie in the sun and stare at the sky. Wonderful.

Ethical Collection: Community. See page 386 for details

Price	£95–£145. Singles from £70.
Rooms	9: 4 doubles, 3 twins, 1 single, 1 family room.
Meals	Lunch from £3.50. Packed lunch £7. Bar meals from £10.50. Dinner, 3 courses, about £25.
Closed	November, January (after New Year) & February.
Directions	Calmac ferries from Oban or Kennacraig (not Tues or Sat) or Hebridean Airways (Tues and Thurs). Hotel on right, half a mile up road from jetty.

 3 nights for the price of 2.

	Lorne Smith
	Scalasaig, Isle of Colonsay PA61 7YP
Tel	+44 (0)1951 200316
Email	hotel@colonsayestate.co.uk
Web	www.colonsayestate.co.uk

Tiroran House

The setting is magnificent with 17 acres of lush gardens rolling down to Loch Scridian and the Ross of Mull rising beyond. Otters and dolphins pass by, as do red deer, who try to raid the garden. As for this extremely welcoming 1850 shooting lodge, you'll be hard pressed to find a more comfortable island base. There are fires in the drawing rooms, fresh flowers everywhere, games to be played, books to be read. Big country-house bedrooms hit the spot perfectly: crisp linen on pretty beds, beautiful fabrics and the odd chaise longue, watery views and silence guaranteed. You eat in a smart dining room, either at the front in the vine-shaded conservatory or at the back amid gilt mirrors. And the food is exceptional with much from the island or waters around it, perhaps oak-smoked salmon, fillet of venison, orange and chocolate tart with rum and raisin ice cream. You're bang in the middle of Mull with loads to do. Seek out Tobermory, the prettiest town in the Hebrides; Calgary and its magical beach; day trips to Iona with its famous monastery; boat trips to Fingal's Cave. Come back for afternoon tea; it's as good as the Ritz.

Price	£165–£195.
Rooms	10: 5 doubles, 5 twins/doubles.
Meals	Dinner, 4 courses, £45.50.
Closed	November to mid–March.
Directions	From Craignure or Fishnish car ferries, A849 for Bunessan & Iona car ferry. Right onto B8035 for Gruline. After 4 miles left at converted church. House 1 mile further.

Laurence & Katie Mackay
Isle of Mull PA69 6ES

Tel +44 (0)1681 705232
Email info@tiroran.com
Web www.tiroran.com

 10% off dinner 3rd night and onwards; 7 nights for the price of 6; tea on arrival.

Glengorm Castle

Few places defy overstatement, but Glengorm does so with ease. It stands in 5,000 acres at the top of Mull with views that stretch across miles of water to Coll and the Uists, Barra and Rhum. Directly in front the land falls away, rolls over lush pasture, then tumbles into the sea. Sheep graze by the hundred, birds play in the sky. Believe it or not, despite the grandeur, this is a B&B, a family home with children and dogs pottering about. The informality is infectious, you feel immediately at home. First you bounce up a four-mile drive, then you step into a vast hall, where sofas wait in front of the fire and big art hangs on the walls. An oak staircase sweeps you up to fabulous country-house rooms (three have the view). You get warm colours, antique furniture, sofas if there's room, excellent bathrooms. Elsewhere: a panelled library for guests to use with a selection of whiskies 'on the house'; a family room with games galore (digital and hard copy); a vast kitchen garden and magnificent coastal paths. Breakfast is a feast. There's a farm shop and café, so stop for lunch. Good restaurants wait in Tobermory.

Price	£130–£210.
Rooms	5: 3 doubles, 1 four-poster; 1 double with separate bath.
Meals	Restaurants 5 miles.
Closed	Castle closed Christmas & New Year.
Directions	North to Tobermory on A848. Straight over roundabout (not right for town). Over x-roads after half a mile and straight ahead for three miles to castle.

Tom & Marjorie Nelson
Tobermory, Isle of Mull PA75 6QE

Tel	+44 (0)1688 302321
Email	enquiries@glengormcastle.co.uk
Web	www.glengormcastle.co.uk

The Airds Hotel & Restaurant

Ambrosial food, glittering interiors and faultless service make this one of Scotland's loveliest country-house hotels. Views from the front slide down to Loch Linnhe, sweep over Lismore Island and cross to the mountains of Ardnamurchan. A small conservatory, candlelit at night, frames the view perfectly, but in good weather you can slip across the lane to a colourful garden decked out with tables and parasols. Pre-dinner drinks are taken in the sitting rooms – open fires, elegant sofas, fresh flowers, lots of books – after which you're whisked off to the dining room, where delicious food is served on Limoges china. Whatever can be is homemade, so expect the best, perhaps goats cheese tart with leeks and wild garlic, cream of cauliflower and mustard soup, twice-cooked pork belly with tarragon butter, hot chocolate fondant with pistachio ice cream. Bedrooms elate. Some have terraces, others give loch views. Expect Frette linen, warm colours, mountains of pillows on fabulous beds, Italian robes in sparkling bathrooms. There's pink grapefruit and campari sorbet for breakfast. Unbeatable.

Price	Half-board £260-£460 for 2. Singles from £194. Cottage: from £640 a week (high season) including breakfast.
Rooms	11 + 1: 4 doubles, 4 twins, 3 suites. Self-catering cottage for 2.
Meals	Lunch £5-£25. Dinner, 5 courses, included; non-residents £53.
Closed	Nov-Jan: 2 days a week.
Directions	A82 north for Fort William, then A828 south for Oban. Right for Port Appin after 12 miles. On left after 2 miles.

Glass of champagne on arrival.

Shaun & Jenny McKivragan
Port Appin, Appin PA38 4DF
Tel   +44 (0)1631 730236
Email   airds@airds-hotel.com
Web   www.airds-hotel.com

Barcaldine Castle

This is a clan Campbell military outpost, a fortified house built by Black Duncan in 1609. As time passed it fell into disuse and was rebuilt by the Victorians, hence the pebbledash. It stands above Loch Creran, with views north to Glencoe (the castle played a role in the famous massacre). Outside, lawns runs down to an old stone wall; inside, a staircase spirals up the main turret. Stop on the first floor and discover one of the loveliest rooms in Argyll, a half-panelled hall with a couple of chesterfield sofas, several trophies on the walls, logs smouldering in a vast fireplace. A short corridor leads into a very cosy sitting room and despite the grandeur of the hall, it's here that most guests gather. Country-house bedrooms one floor up are rather spoiling, you can bet they didn't fare this well in 1609. The four-poster has a very swanky private bathroom, another has an en suite claw-foot bath. You get great views, smart fabrics, pure wool throws. There's loads to do in the area: Glencoe, Fort William, Ben Nevis, even day trips to Mull.

Price	£115–£205.
Rooms	5: 3 doubles (2 with sofabeds), 1 twin, 1 four-poster.
Meals	Traditional afternoon tea £19.50. Restaurants in Oban, 9 miles.
Closed	Rarely.
Directions	North from Oban on A828. Through Benderloch, then 1st left. Castle on left after 2 miles.

David Whitehead
Benderloch, Oban PA37 1SA
Tel   +44 (0)1631 720598
Email   enquiries@barcaldinecastle.co.uk
Web   www.barcaldinecastle.co.uk

The Manor House

A 1780 dower house for the Dukes of Argyll — their cottage by the sea — built of local stone, high on the hill, with long views over Oban harbour to the Isle of Mull. A smart and proper place, not one to bow to the fads of fashion: sea views from the lawn, cherry trees in the courtyard garden, a fire roaring in the drawing room, a beautiful tiled floor in the entrance hall and an elegant bay window in the dining room that catches the eye. Bedrooms tend to be small, but they're also rather pretty and come in warm colours — blues, reds, yellows, greens — with fresh flowers, crisp linen, bowls of fruit and piles of towels in good bathrooms; those that look seaward have binoculars with which to scour the horizon. Try Loch Fyne kippers for breakfast, salmon for lunch and, if you've room, rack of lamb for supper; there's excellent home baking, too. Ferries leave for the islands from the bottom of the hill — see them depart from the hotel garden. At the top, overlooking Oban, watch the day's close from McCaig's Folly; sunsets here are really special. *Children over 12 welcome.*

Price	£115–£215. Half-board £87.50–£142.50 p.p.
Rooms	11: 9 doubles, 2 twins.
Meals	Lunch from £8.50. Dinner £38.
Closed	Christmas.
Directions	In Oban follow signs to ferry. Hotel on right 0.5 miles after ferry turn-off, signed.

Gregor MacKinnon
Gallanach Road, Oban PA34 4LS

Tel	+44 (0)1631 562087
Email	info@manorhouseoban.com
Web	www.manorhouseoban.com

Ardanaiseig

You're lost to the world, ten miles down a track that winds past giant rhododendrons before petering out at this baronial mansion. Beyond, Loch Awe rules supreme, 30 miles of deep blue water on which to sail or fish. In one of the loveliest hotel drawing rooms you are ever likely to see – gold leaf panelling, cherubs in alcoves, Doric columns rising gleefully – an enormous window frames the view and a single sofa waits for those lucky enough to have it. Elsewhere, Wellington boots are on parade in the hall, fires roar wherever you go, eccentric art hangs on the dining room wall and a lawned terrace runs down to the loch. You're in 200 acres of private grounds; in May bluebells run riot. Country-house bedrooms are the real thing (old armoires, feather boa lamp shades, the odd four-poster), while the boat house has been converted into a funky suite with a wall of glass that opens onto a decked terrace. Dinner is a seven-course feast, as one might expect of this rather flamboyant hotel. Also, snooker, tennis and boats on which to row over to an island. Off-season breaks are a steal.

Price	£138-£298. Suite £280-£360. Singles from £99.
Rooms	18: 8 twins/doubles, 7 doubles, 2 four-posters, 1 boat house suite.
Meals	Light lunch from £4. Dinner, 7 courses, £50.
Closed	2 January–1 February.
Directions	A85 to Taynuilt. Left onto B845 for Kilchrenan. Then left at Kilchrenan pub; down track for 4 miles.

 Bottle of house wine with dinner on first night.

Peter Webster
Kilchrenan, Taynuilt PA35 1HE
Tel   +44 (0)1866 833333
Email   info@ardanaiseig.com
Web   www.ardanaiseig.com

Culzean Castle & Country Park

Culzean (pronounced 'Cullane') is one of Scotland's grandest buildings, a Robert Adam castle built into solid rock a couple of hundred feet above crashing waves. When the Marquess of Ailsa presented the castle to the Scottish people in 1945, General Eisenhower was given the top-floor suite, Scotland's thank you for his contribution to the war effort. You stay on the same floor – or even in his apartment – where rooms are either big or huge and where a country-house style infuses every corner. You'll find twinkling chandeliers, thrilling sea views (the most splendid rooms overlook the gardens). Bathrooms are grandly traditional, service is courteous and thoughtful, the rest is awe-inspiring: hundreds of portraits crammed on the walls, a sublime drawing room that juts out over the sea, a central oval staircase with 12 Corinthian columns, an armoury of flintlock pistols and swords. Americans in search of ancestors will love it. You can tour the castle before the tourists invade, take a stirring cliff-top walk, wander 560 idyllic acres. Don't miss afternoon tea.

Price	£225–£375. Singles from £150. Whole floor £1,700 per night. Afternoon tea included.
Rooms	6: 3 twins/doubles, 1 four-poster, 1 suite, all en suite. 1 twin/double with separate bath.
Meals	Dinner, 3 courses, £35. By arrangement.
Closed	Rarely.
Directions	From A77 in Maybole B7023 & A719 west for 4 miles. Signed.

Fi McClelland
Maybole KA19 8LE
Tel   +44 (0)1655 884455
Email   culzean@nts.org.uk
Web   www.culzeanexperience.org

10% off stays of 2 or more nights. Bottle of wine in your room.

Knockinaam Lodge

Lawns run down to the Irish sea, roe deer come to eat the roses, sunsets turn the sky red. This exceptional 1869 shooting lodge is nothing short of glorious: a Michelin star in the dining room, 150 malts in the bar and a level of service you rarely find in such far-flung corners of the realm. There's history, too. Churchill once stayed and you can sleep in his elegant room, where his books wait to be read and you need steps to climb into an ancient bath! Elsewhere, immaculate country-house interiors abound: gorgeous bedrooms, the very best bathrooms, an immaculate morning room where the scent of flowers mingles with the smell of burnt wood. Outside: cliff walks, nesting peregrine falcons, a rock pool where David keeps lobsters for the pot. In storms, waves crash all around. Trees stand guard high on the hill, their branches buffeted by the wind, while bluebells carpet the hills in spring. John Buchan knew the house and described it in *The Thirty-Nine Steps* as the house to which Hannay fled. Remote, beguiling, utterly spoiling – grand old Knockinaam is simply unmissable.

Price	Half-board £95–£210 p.p. Singles from £155.
Rooms	10: 4 doubles, 5 twins/doubles, 1 family suite.
Meals	Lunch, by arrangement, £30–£40. Dinner, 5 courses, included; non-residents £58.
Closed	Never.
Directions	From A77 or A75 pick up signs to Portpatrick. West from Lochans on A77, then left after 2 miles, signed. Follow signs for 3 miles to hotel.

10% off room rate.

David & Sian Ibbotson
Portpatrick, Stranraer DG9 9AD
Tel   +44 (0)1776 810471
Email   reservations@knockinaamlodge.com
Web   www.knockinaamlodge.com

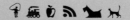

Cavens

As you sweep south from Dumfries, the imperious Solway Firth looms before you – vast tracts of tidal sands, lush fields dotted with sheep, big skies hanging overhead. It's a magnet for birdlife, the rich pickings of low tide too tempting to refuse. As for this 1753 shooting lodge, it stands in 20 acres of sweeping lawns and native woods with fields sprawling out beyond. Inside, quietly elegant interiors flood with light making this a very pleasant place to linger. You get busts and oils, seagrass matting, golden sofas, smouldering fires, a baby grand piano. Country-house bedrooms come with garden views, smart florals, mahogany dressers, bowls of fruit. Some are snug, others palatial. One is seriously swanky and overlooks the garden, another has an en suite sunroom. Back downstairs, there's a super restaurant in yellow for Angus' delicious food, perhaps goats cheese and red onion tart, fillet of local beef with peppercorn sauce, lemon crème brûlée, a plate of local cheeses. There's golf at spectacular Southerness and afternoon tea on the terrace in good weather.

Price	£100-£190. Singles from £80. Half-board from £85 p.p.
Rooms	5: 4 doubles, 1 twin.
Meals	Dinner, 3 courses, £35. Packed lunch available.
Closed	Never.
Directions	From Dumfries A710 to Kirkbean (12 miles). Cavens signed in village on left.
🎁	Use your Sawday's Gift Card here.

Jane & Angus Fordyce
Kirkbean, Dumfries DG2 8AA
Tel   +44 (0)1387 880234
Email   enquiries@cavens.com
Web   www.cavens.com

 10% off stays of 2 or more nights.

Trigony House Hotel

A super little hotel — warm and extremely welcoming. Adam and Jan are doing their own thing brilliantly: expect delicious food, pretty rooms and a lovely garden. The house dates back to 1700, a shooting lodge for the local castle. Inside: panelling in the hall, smart sofas in the sitting room and an open fire in the dining room, where doors open onto the terrace for al fresco dinners in summer. Adam cooks tasty rustic fare, perhaps pea and ham soup, local roe venison, rhubarb and hazelnut crumble, and there's a small kitchen garden that provides much in summer. Bedrooms vary in size, but all are good value for money, and many are dog-friendly. They come with pretty fabrics, summer colours, padded bedheads and golden throws. One has its own conservatory/sitting room which opens onto a private lawn, but even the simpler rooms are attractive and all have flat-screens TVs with DVDs; there's a film library downstairs. Falconry, riding and fishing can be arranged, even vintage car hire. Head west into the hills for fabulous country ignored by all but locals. Breakfasts are brilliant.

Price	£105–£125. Suite £155. Singles from £80. Half-board from £75 p.p.
Rooms	9: 4 twins/doubles, 4 doubles, 1 suite.
Meals	Lunch from £5. Dinner, 3 courses, £30.
Closed	24-26 December.
Directions	North from Dumfries on A76 through Closeburn. Signed left after 1 mile.

 10% off stays of 2 nights or more. Pre-dinner drinks on 1st night.

Adam & Jan Moore
Closeburn, Thornhill DG3 5EZ
Tel   +44 (0)1848 331211
Email   info@trigonyhotel.co.uk
Web   www.countryhousehotelsscotland.com

21212

21212 is the new jewel in Edinburgh's crown. Paul left his Michelin star down south, bought this Georgian townhouse, spent a small fortune converting it into a 21st-century pleasure dome, then opened for business and won back his star. The house stands at the top of a hill with long views north towards the Firth of Forth. It's bang in the centre of town with Arthur's Seat and Princes Street both close by. Inside, contemporary splendour waits. High ceilings and vast windows come as standard, but wander at will and find a chic first-floor drawing room, cherubs on the wall, busts and statues all over the place, even a private dining pod made of white leather. Stunning bedrooms have enormous beds, cool colours, fat sofas and iPod docks. Those at the front have the view, all have robes in magnificent bathrooms. As for the restaurant: the kitchen is on display behind a wall of glass and the food it produces is heavenly, perhaps fillet of beef with apricots and thyme, Gloucestershire Old Spot with white asparagus, saffron-poached pineapple baked in a caramelised lemon curd. Out of this world.

Price	£195–£325.
Rooms	4 doubles.
Meals	Lunch from £26. Dinner, 5 courses, £67.
Closed	10 days in January & 10 days in summer.
Directions	A720 ring road, then A702/A7 into town. Right at T-junc. at Balmoral Hotel, then immediately left with flow. Right at second r'about and 1st right. On right.

	Paul Kitching & Katie O'Brien
	3 Royal Terrace, Edinburgh EH7 5AB
Tel	+44 (0)131 523 1030
Email	reservations@21212restaurant.co.uk
Web	www.21212restaurant.co.uk

 10% off room rate Mon-Thurs. Bottle of champagne for bookings of 2 nights or more. Late checkout (12pm).

23 Mayfield

Edinburgh — the most beautiful city in Scotland and therefore in Britain. Those who come to gaze on its glory will enjoy the spoiling B&B hotel that stands in the shadow of Arthur's Seat. Built in 1868, it was home to a coffee merchant and comes with plaster-moulded ceilings and a fine stained-glass window on the landing. There's an airy dining room for excellent breakfasts (toasted muffins with hand-picked mushrooms, peat-smoked haddock with poached eggs), then a sitting room with chesterfield sofas where you can browse a collection of guide books or surf the net on the house computer. Super bedrooms have excellent prices. Some come with high ceilings and shuttered windows, most with travertine marble bathrooms, all have period colours, panelled walls and good beds with excellent linen. You get iPod docks, Bose technology and classical CDs, and the family room comes with a Nintendo Wii. There's good art throughout; a history of Scotland is framed on the landing. A short bus ride zips you into town, there's off-street parking and loads of local eateries. You can hire bikes, too. *Minimum two nights at weekends.*

Price	£80–£165. Singles from £75.
Rooms	9: 4 twins/doubles, 1 triple, 3 four-posters, 1 family.
Meals	Restaurants within half a mile.
Closed	24–26 December.
Directions	A720 bypass, then north onto A722 for Edinburgh. Right onto A721 at T-junction with traffic lights. Over x-roads with main flow, under railway bridge, on right.

Ross Birnie
23 Mayfield Gardens,
Edinburgh EH9 2BX

Tel	+44 (0)131 667 5806
Email	info@23mayfield.co.uk
Web	www.23mayfield.co.uk

The Peat Inn

The Peat Inn has been around for 300 years. It's a Scottish institution, a national treasure, and when it changes hands (very rarely), people take note. Geoffrey and Katherine took it on five years ago and have already made their mark: a Michelin star landed here in 2010. It is divided in two: restaurant and rooms, though the latter are suites, not rooms. You get wonderful beds dressed in crisp white linen, pretty colours that soak up the light, decanters of sherry, bowls of fruit, sofas from which to watch the telly. Not that you'll have time for that. You'll be over in the restaurant digging into some of the best food in Scotland. The scene is suitably theatrical: three rooms beautifully lit, tables spaced out generously. As for the food, ambrosial delights await: wild leek soup with a poached duck egg, roast rump of lamb with a red pepper compote, pavé of chocolate with pistachio. You can eat à la carte, try the menu du jour or feast on a six-course tasting menu (the cheese course is a soufflé!); all are brilliantly priced. As for the staff, you won't find better. St Andrews is close.

Price	£180–£195. Half-board £124–£160 p.p.
Rooms	8 suites.
Meals	Lunch from £18. Dinner: menu du jour £34; à la carte £45–£50; 6-course tasting menu £60.
Closed	Rooms & restaurant closed Sun & Mon; also 24-26 Dec & 1 week in Jan.
Directions	From Edinburgh A90 north, then A92 for Dundee. Right onto A91 and into Cupar. There, B940 for Crail to inn.

Geoffrey & Katherine Smeddle
Peat Inn,
Cupar KY15 5LH

Tel	+44 (0)1334 840206
Email	stay@thepeatinn.co.uk
Web	www.thepeatinn.co.uk

 Bottle of wine in your room.

15 Glasgow

This is a seriously smart Glasgow address – bang in the middle of town, yet beautifully insulated from it. The house, a Victorian gem, stands on an attractive square with communal gardens running through. Inside, the feel is distinctly contemporary, though you still get a pair of Corinthian pillars and the original mosaic entrance hall. Shane and Laura spent a year renovating; while technically you're in a B&B, these interiors are as good as any boutique hotel. Downstairs there's a vast sitting room with a couple of sofas in front of a fire; bedrooms upstairs are no less generous. Those at the back are large, the suites at the front are enormous. All come with huge beds, crisp white linen, handmade bedheads and robes in seriously fancy bathrooms. Suites have a few added extras: big sofas, beautiful windows, one has a double-ended bath overlooking the square. Breakfast is brought to you whenever you want. As for Glasgow, you'll find great restaurants close to home. Try Crab Shakk for serious seafood, then head to Ben Nevis for a wee dram; folk musicians play most nights.

Price	£120. Suites £150.
Rooms	5: 2 doubles, 1 twin/double, 2 suites.
Meals	Restaurants on your doorstep.
Closed	Never.
Directions	West into Glasgow on M8. Exit at junc. 18 for Charring X (outside lane), then double back at lights. 1st left, 1st left, 1st left (really). Follow square round to house.

Shane & Laura McKenzie
15 Woodside Place, Glasgow G3 7QL

Tel	+44 (0)141 332 1263
Email	info@15glasgow.com
Web	www.15glasgow.com

The Lime Tree

The Lime Tree is unique – an art gallery with rooms. The house, a Mackintosh manse, dates back to 1850, while the tree itself, sublime on the front lawn, was planted in 1700, the year the town was settled. Inside you find a small, intimate, stylish world – stripped floors in the hall, bold colours on the walls, open fires scattered around, beautiful windows for views of Loch Linnhe. David – a mountain guide/stuntman who also paints – has a fabulous map room, but if you want to do more than walk, you've come to the right place; climbing, cragging, mountain biking, kayaking and diving can all be arranged. Airy bedrooms are delightful – oatmeal carpets, crisp white linen, good art and flat-screen TVs. You get super little bathrooms, white walls to soak up the light and those at the front have watery views. Downstairs, drift through to the gallery and see what's on (when the Royal Geographical Society came, they had a full-scale copy of Ernest Shackleton's boat on the front lawn). There's a rustic bistro, too: homemade soups, slow-cooked lamb, hot chocolate fondant pudding. Ben Nevis is close.

Price	£80–£110. Singles from £60.
Rooms	9: 3 doubles, 1 twin, 5 family rooms.
Meals	Dinner, 3 courses, £28.
Closed	Rarely.
Directions	North to Fort William on A82. Hotel on right at 1st roundabout in town.

David Wilson
Achintore Road, Fort William PH33 6RQ

Tel	+44 (0)1397 701806
Email	info@limetreefortwilliam.co.uk
Web	www.limetreefortwilliam.co.uk

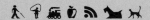

Kilcamb Lodge Hotel & Restaurant

A stupendous setting, with Loch Sunart at the end of the garden and Glas Bheinn rising beyond. As for Kilcamb, it has all the ingredients of the perfect country house: a smart drawing room with a roaring fire; an elegant dining room for excellent food; super-comfy bedrooms that don't shy from colour; views that feed the soul. The feel here is shipwreck-chic. There's a 12-acre garden with half a mile of shore, so stroll up to the water's edge and look for dolphins, otters and seals. Ducks and geese fly by, and if you're lucky you may see eagles. Back inside you'll find stained-glass windows on the landing, a ship's bell in the bar, flowers in the bedrooms. Dress up at eight for a three-course dinner and feast on scallops with cauliflower tempura, lamb with caramelised shallots, banana bavarois with rum and raisin ice cream. Bedrooms come in two styles: contemporary or traditional. Expect big beds, padded headboards, smart white towels and shiny bathrooms. Kind staff go the extra mile. Ardnamurchan Point – the most westerly point in mainland Britain – it at the end of the road. *Minimum stay two nights at weekends in May.*

Price	Half-board £110–£180 p.p.
Rooms	10: 7 doubles, 3 suites.
Meals	Lunch from £8.50. Dinner, 4 courses, included; non-residents £49.50.
Closed	January. Limited opening November & February.
Directions	From Fort William A82 south for 10 miles to Corran ferry, then A861 to Strontian. Hotel west of village on left, signed. A830 & A861 from Fort William takes an hour longer.

10% off room rate.

David & Sally Ruthven-Fox
Strontian, Acharacle PH36 4HY

Tel	+44 (0)1967 402257
Email	enquiries@kilcamblodge.co.uk
Web	www.kilcamblodge.co.uk

Doune

You arrive by boat (there's no road in): a ferry across to Knoydart, the last great wilderness to survive in Britain. You'll find mountains, sea and beach – a thrilling wonderland of boundless peace. Guillemots race across the water, waves lap on the shore, the Sound of Sleat fuses with the sea and shoots across to Skye. Martin and Jane look after you with unpretentious generosity and are now part of the tiny community which rescued this land from ruin. The dining room is the hub, pine-clad from top-to-toe with a stove to keep you warm and a couple of guitars for the odd ceilidh; some of the staff are folk musicians and fiddles often fly. Food is delicious – crab from the bay, roast lamb from the hill, chocolate tart with homemade ice cream. Bedrooms along the veranda are as simple as they should be, three pine rooms with bunk galleries for children, hooks for clothes, easy chairs for watching the weather, small shower rooms. There's a lodge for groups with an open-plan layout. The walking is magnificent, the sunsets are breathtaking. Miss it at your peril. *Boat pick-up Tuesday & Saturday: minimum stay three nights.*

Price	Full-board £75 p.p. (£450 per week). Lodge: full-board from £57 p.p. (£342 per week). Discounts for children.
Rooms	4 + 1: 2 doubles, 1 twin (plus mezzanine beds for children), 1 single. Catered lodge for 12.
Meals	Full-board (includes packed lunch).
Closed	October-Easter.
Directions	Park in Mallaig; the boat will collect you at an agreed time.

Martin & Jane Davies
Knoydart, Mallaig PH41 4PL
Tel   +44 (0)1687 462667
Email   martin@doune-knoydart.co.uk
Web   www.doune-knoydart.co.uk

Tomdoun Hotel

A quirky hotel wrapped up in the middle of nowhere. The single-track road which passes outside once served as the main road up to Skye; these days locals occasionally play tennis on it. Cars that do pass spin upstream to Loch Hourn, where the road runs out at Knoydart, the last great wilderness in Britain. As for Tomdoun, it stands above the river Garry with Glas Bheinn rising from the forest beyond. Interiors are stylishly unpretentious (posh, but old) with piles of logs and vintage luggage in the hall, a country-house dining room for super breakfasts (famished walkers occasionally drop in for bacon and eggs), and a smouldering coal fire in the lively bar, the hub of the house. Bedrooms are very simple – don't come looking for material luxury. You get warm colours, white linen and those at the front have Glengarry views. Outside you can bag a munro, ride bikes over the mountain or fish the loch (the hotel has rights and if you're lucky, they'll cook your catch for dinner). As for the food, try langoustine and cockles from Skye, halibut fresh from Lochinver, venison from the hills around you.

Price	£100–£150. Singles from £45.
Rooms	9: 4 doubles, 2 family rooms, all en suite. 1 double, 2 twins, sharing 2 bathrooms.
Meals	Dinner, 3 courses, about £25.
Closed	Never.
Directions	A82 north from Fort William, then A87 west from Invergarry. After 5 miles left for Glengarry. Hotel 6 miles up on right.

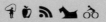 10% off room rate Mon-Thurs.

Michael Pearson
Invergarry PH35 4HS

Tel	+44 (0)1809 511218
Email	enquiries@tomdoun.com
Web	www.tomdoun.com

Grants at Craigellachie

An old factor's house on the banks of Loch Duich with the Five Sisters of Kintail flaunting their beauty to the south; three are munros, views from the top are spectacular. This is a great base for Highland adventures with lots to do: Skye, Ben Nevis and Loch Ness are all within reach, while Dornie Castle (the one on the water you see on TV) is on the other side of the loch. After a morning dashing about, come home to this homespun restaurant with rooms. It's a tiny operation and Tony and Liz do everything themselves: cook, clean, polish and shine, chat to guests after delicious breakfasts, point you in the right direction. There are four rooms, two in the main house (small but sweet, warm colours, fine for a night), then two out back, decidedly swanky – neutral colours, lovely linen, robes in fancy bathrooms. One is a suite (with a small kitchen), both have a decked terrace. As for Tony's award-winning food, don't expect to go hungry. You might have hand-dived scallops with a vermouth cream, Rassay pork with a calvados jus, chocolate tart with a cappuccino sauce. *Wine tasting and food & wine-matching courses.*

Price	Half-board £80-£97.50 p.p; suite £105-£120 p.p.
Rooms	4: 1 twin, 2 doubles, 1 suite.
Meals	Dinner included; non-residents about £30. Not Sundays.
Closed	December to mid-February.
Directions	A87 north from Invergarry to Shiel Bridge. Left in village for Glenleg. First right down to Loch Duich. On left in village.

Tony & Liz Taylor
Ratagan, Glenshiel, Kyle IV40 8HP
Tel   +44 (0)1599 511331
Email   info@housebytheloch.co.uk
Web   www.housebytheloch.co.uk

Ullinish Country Lodge

A sparkling whitewashed Georgian farmhouse which stands on the west coast under a vast sky; mighty views stretch across Loch Harport to the Talisker distillery at Carbost (you can drop in for a tour and a wee dram). Samuel Johnson stayed in this house on his famous tour, though you can bet your bottom dollar he didn't eat as well as you will. Pam and Brian came to add to Skye's gastronomic reputation and have done just that, serving up some of the best food on the island. Inside, warm interiors come with tartan carpets in the hall and leather sofas in front of the fire. Bedrooms upstairs are positively plush with huge mahogany beds, stately colours, silky crowns and watery views. You'll find claw-foot baths and flat-screen TVs, too. Outside, the tidal island of Oronsay waits. Dolphins and whales pass, sea eagles patrol the skies, there are standing stones and iron age remains. As for dinner, expect the best, perhaps Dunvegan langoustine cooked five ways, loin of venison with a beetroot sorbet, wild strawberry soufflé with lime leaf ice cream. *Children over 16 only.*

Price	£125–£165. Singles from £90. Half-board from £106.95 p.p.
Rooms	6 doubles.
Meals	Dinner, 4 courses, £44.95.
Closed	January & 1 week in November.
Directions	North from Skye bridge on A87, then A863 for Dunvegan. Thro' Bracadale, then Struan signed left. House on right after 1 mile.

Afternoon tea on arrival.

Brian & Pam Howard
Ullinish, Struan, Isle of Skye IV56 8FD
Tel   +44 (0)1470 572214
Email enquiries@ullinish-country-lodge.co.uk
Web   www.theisleofskye.co.uk

Greshornish House

On its own private peninsular, hidden away from the rest of Skye, this 18th-century country house stands in ten acres of peace directly above the sea. Outside, free-range chickens nip across the croquet lawn, while down at the loch seals and otters splash about in the water. As for the house, it's a great island base and Neil and Rosemary look after guests with infectious charm. Step inside and find a sofa'd bar that doubles as reception, an open fire crackling in the drawing room and a grand piano in the billiard room, where walls of books surround you. Upstairs, lovely big bedrooms have a smart homely feel. Two at the front have the view, all have warm colours, fresh flowers, usually a sofa. One is enormous, another has a claw-foot bath, two have fancy showers. Back downstairs, seriously tasty food waits in the restaurant (candlelit tables, claret-red walls), so work up an appetite on one of Skye's mountains, then return for a feast, perhaps oak-smoked salmon, tomato and fennel soup, delicious guinea fowl in a bordelaise sauce, chocolate and hazelnut terrine. Wonderful. *Min. stay two nights.*

Price	£130–£185. Singles from £95.
Rooms	6: 2 four-posters, 2 twins/doubles, 1 double, 1 family room.
Meals	Lunch from £6.50. Dinner £25–£40. Packed lunch £10.
Closed	Christmas. Restricted opening November–March.
Directions	A87 through Portree, then west on A850 for Dunvegan. Signed right after 10 miles (1 mile west of Edinbane). 2.5 miles down single track road to hotel.

	Neil & Rosemary Colquhoun
	Edinbane, Portree, Isle of Skye IV51 9PN
Tel	+44 (0)1470 582266
Email	info@greshornishhouse.com
Web	www.greshornishhouse.com

Bottle of wine with dinner on first night.

The Glenview

Small is beautiful at The Glenview. This delicious little restaurant with rooms started life in 1890 as a croft. Once the village shop, it has recently fallen into excellent hands. Simon and Kirsty are young and full of life, love Skye, have refurbished brilliantly. You find daffodils in the flower beds, logs in the porch, painted floorboards and maps on the wall. The style – a warm, rustic simplicity – fits the mood perfectly. The dining room doubles as an art gallery, you can roast away in front of the wood-burner in the sitting room, there are games to be played, books to be read, tales to be told. Rooms above the shop are excellent: warm and cosy (though not small) with smart carpets, fresh flowers and blond wood furniture. Then there's the food. Breakfasts promise seasonal fruits and organic Skye bacon, and Simon cooks a mean dinner – hand-dived scallops, roast Highland beef, chocolate fudge cake with homemade vanilla ice cream – so work up an appetite during the day. There's loads to see: the Old Man of Storr, the Kilt Rock waterfall, even dinosaur footprints on Staffin beach. A real treat.

Price	£85–£110. Singles from £67.50.
Rooms	5: 4 doubles, 1 twin.
Meals	Dinner £27.50–£32.
Closed	Mondays & Sundays. January.
Directions	North from Portree on A855. Signed on left in dip in village.

Simon & Kirsty Faulds
Culnacnoc,
Isle of Skye IV51 9JH
Tel   +44 (0)1470 562248
Email   enquiries@glenviewskye.co.uk
Web   www.glenviewskye.co.uk

Viewfield House Hotel

This old ancestral pile stands high above Portree Bay with fine views tumbling down to the Sound of Rassay below. Twenty acres of mature gardens and woodland wrap around you, with croquet on the lawn, paths that weave through pretty gardens and a hill to climb for 360° views of sea, ridge and peak. As for this Victorian factor's house, expect a few aristocratic fixtures and fittings: hunting trophies in the hall, cases filled with curios, a grand piano and open fire in the drawing room, vintage Sanderson wallpaper in the dining room. Family oils hang on the walls, you'll find wood carvings from distant lands and a flurry of antiques, all of which blend grandeur with touches of humour. Upstairs is a warren of bedrooms. Most are big, some are vast, all come in country-house style with traditional fabrics, crisply laundered sheets and sea views from those at the front. Dive into Skye – wildlife, mountains, sea lochs and castles all wait. Light suppers are on tap – salads, salmon, spotted dick; alternatively, dine out on Skye's natural larder. There's Highland porridge for breakfast, too.

Price	£100–£140. Singles £50–£70.
Rooms	11: 3 doubles, 3 twins/doubles, 2 twins, 2 singles, all en suite. 1 double with separate bath.
Meals	Light supper £5–£25. Packed lunch £6.
Closed	Mid-October to Easter.
Directions	On A87, coming from south, driveway entrance on left just before the Portree filling station.

Tea & scones every day 3pm-6pm.

Hugh Macdonald
Viewfield Road, Portree,
Isle of Skye IV51 9EU

Tel	+44 (0)1478 612217
Email	info@viewfieldhouse.com
Web	www.viewfieldhouse.com

Tigh an Eilean Hotel

You're in a tiny village, bang on the water, with majestic mountains rising behind. This is the epicentre of one of the most beautiful places in Britain. You can come by car, pedal your bike, walk over mountains or sail in by boat. However you arrive, no highland fling would be complete without a night at this small, friendly hotel, which sits on the water in the middle of the village. Inside, country-house interiors are just the ticket: warmly stylish with pretty wallpaper, colourful fabrics, comfy sofas and wood-burners everywhere. There's an honesty bar, a couple of sitting rooms, and an airy restaurant with watery views, but Cathryn and Christopher – ex-London lawyers who escaped the city – refuse to stand still. They have recently rebuilt the pub (the locals come to play their fiddles), adding a brasserie above, where you can sit on a roof terrace and scoff the freshest seafood while gazing out to sea. Homely bedrooms come with colourful fabrics, crisp linen and pretty furniture. No TVs, it's not that sort of place, just big skies, huge mountains and a shimmering sea.

10% off room rate.

Price	£140. Singles from £70. Half-board from £110 p.p.
Rooms	11: 5 doubles, 3 twins, 3 singles.
Meals	Lunch & dinner in Coastal Kitchen £5-£25. Dinner, 3 courses, in restaurant £40. Packed lunches available.
Closed	November to mid-March: advanced booking only.
Directions	On loch front in centre of Shieldaig.

Christopher & Cathryn Field
Shieldaig, Strathcarron IV54 8XN
Tel   +44 (0)1520 755251
Email   tighaneilean@keme.co.uk
Web   www.tighaneilean.co.uk

The Torridon

You're in the middle of nowhere, but you wouldn't be anywhere else. Mountains rise, red deer roam, sea eagles and otters patrol high and low. This 1887 shooting lodge was built for the Earl of Lovelace and stands in 58 acres that roll down to the shores of Upper Loch Torridon. Inside, sparkling interiors thrill: a huge fire in the panelled hall, a zodiac ceiling in the drawing room, 350 malts in the pitch pine bar. Huge windows pull in the view, while canny walkers pour off the hills to recover in luxury. Fabulous bedrooms are hard to fault, some big, others bigger. A super-smart contemporary style runs throughout: cool colours, padded headboards, exquisite linen, magnificent bathrooms; one has a shower in a turret. Outside, cattle graze in the fields, while the two-acre kitchen garden is a work of art in itself. It provides much for the table, so feast on fresh food sublimely cooked... pan-roasted monkfish, Highland beef with a red wine jus, apple tart tatin with butterscotch ice cream. You can scale Liathach or take to the sea in a kayak. Fantastic.

Ethical Collection: Environment; Community; Food. See page 386 for details

Price	£215-£425. Half-board from £152.50 p.p. Boathouse (self-catering) £875-£1,350 p.w.
Rooms	19 + 1: 10 doubles, 1 twin, 1 single, 2 four-posters, 5 suites. Boathouse for 4.
Meals	Lunch from £5.95. Dinner, 5 courses, £50.
Closed	January.
Directions	A9 to Inverness, A835 to Garve, A832 to Kinlochewe, A896 to Annat (not Torridon). Signed on south shore.

Daniel & Rohaise Rose-Bristow
Torridon, Achnasheen IV22 2EY

Tel	+44 (0)1445 791242
Email	info@thetorridon.com
Web	www.thetorridon.com

 Afternoon tea on arrival. Two tickets for Inverewe gardens.

Mackay's Rooms

This is the north-west tip of Britain and it's utterly magnificent: huge skies, sandy beaches, aquamarine seas, cliffs and caves. You drive – or cycle – for mile upon mile with mountains soaring into the heavens and ridges sliding into the sea. If you like big, remote landscapes, you'll love it here; what's more, you'll have it mostly to yourself. Mackay's – they have the shop, the bunkhouse and the garage, too – is the only place to stay in town, its jaunty contemporary colours mixing with stone walls and stripped floors to great effect. Bedrooms are perfect – extremely comfy, warmly coloured, big wooden beds, crisp white linen – and Fiona, a textiles graduate, has a fine eye for lovely fabrics and upholstery. There are excellent bathrooms, flat-screen TVs, DVD players too. Breakfast sets you up for the day – grilled grapefruit, whisky porridge, venison sausages, local eggs – so head east to the beach at Ceannabeinne, west for golf on top of the cliffs or catch the ferry across to Cape Wrath and scan the sea for whales. There's surfing for the brave and the beautiful.

Price	£110–£150. Singles from £90. Cottages £600–£1,200 per week.
Rooms	7 + 3: 5 doubles, 2 twins. 3 self-catering cottages for 2-6.
Meals	Lunch from £5. Dinner, 3 courses, £25–£30.
Closed	November-Easter. Cottages open all year.
Directions	A838 north from Rhiconich. After 19 miles enter Durness village. Mackay's is on right-hand side opposite memorial.

Fiona Mackay
Durine, Durness,
Lairg IV27 4PN

Tel   +44 (0)1971 511202
Email   fiona@visitmackays.com
Web   www.visitmackays.com

Culdearn House

Grantown is a great base for Highland flings. You can fish the Spey, jump on the whisky trail, check out a raft of castles, you can even ski in Aviemore. Loch Ness is close, as is Royal Deeside, there's golf everywhere and the walking is divine; in short, expect to be busy. As for Culdrean, it stands in a row of five identical houses that were built in 1860 by Lord Seafield, one for each of his daughters. These days it's a small, intimate hotel where William and Sonia look after guests with much kindness. There's an open fire and facing sofas in the pretty sitting room, panelled windows and a marble fireplace in the dining room, then a batch of smart homely bedrooms that offer the sort of comfort you'd want after a day in the hills. You get decanters of sherry, super beds, pretty furniture, excellent bathrooms. Back downstairs, William looks after a tempting wine list and 60 malts, while Sonia whisks up delicious four-course dinners... game terrine with poached pear marmalade, elderflower sorbet or mushroom soup, local lamb in a plum and port jus, dark chocolate torte. A treat.

Price	£130–£150. Singles from £65. Half-board from £100–£130 p.p.
Rooms	6: 4 doubles, 1 twin/double, 1 twin.
Meals	Dinner, four courses, £37.
Closed	Never.
Directions	North into Grantown from A95. Left at 30 mph sign & house directly ahead.

Sonia & William Marshall
Woodlands Terrace,
Grantown on Spey PH26 3JU

Tel	+44 (0)1479 872106
Email	enquiries@culdearn.com
Web	www.culdearn.com

Dalmunzie House

Dalmunzie is quite some sight, an ancient hunting lodge lost to the world in one of Scotland's most dramatic landscapes. You're cradled by mountains in a vast valley; it's as good a spot as any to escape the world. Surprisingly, you're not that remote – Perth is a mere 30 miles south – but the sense of solitude is quite magnificent, as is the view. As for the hotel, you potter up a one-mile drive to find a small enclave of friendly Australians; Scott and Brianna searched high and low before striking gold at Dalmunzie. Interiors are just the ticket: warm, cosy and quietly grand. You find sofas in front of open fires, a smart restaurant for delicious food, a snug bar for a good malt, a breakfast room with a big view. Country-house bedrooms have colour and style. Some are grand, others simpler, several have ancient claw-foot baths. There's loads to do: fantastic walking, Royal Deeside, the Highland games at Braemar. As for the tricky golf course, it was laid out by Alister MacKenzie, who later designed Augusta National; the twelfth hole there is all but identical to the seventh here.

Price	£140-£240. Half board £85-£145 p.p.
Rooms	17: 3 tower rooms, 5 four-posters, 7 doubles, 1 twin, 1 family room.
Meals	Lunch from £4.50. Packed lunch £10. Dinner, 4 courses, £45.
Closed	Rarely.
Directions	North from Blairgowrie on A93. Hotel signed left in Glenshee up one-mile drive.

Scott & Brianna Poole
Spittal O'Glenshee,
Blairgowrie PH10 7QG
Tel   +44 (0)1250 885224
Email   reservations@dalmunzie.com
Web   www.dalmunzie.com

Killiecrankie House Hotel

Henrietta receives with great panache – no Highland fling would be complete without a night or two at her extremely welcoming hotel. Outside, gardens galore: one for roses, another for vegetables and a fine herbaceous border. Venture further afield and you find much to entertain your eyes – Loch Tummel, Rannoch Moor and magnificent Glenshee, over which you tumble for the Highland Games at Braemar. Return to a warm world of airy interiors with a little tartan in the dining room, 52 malts at the bar and views at breakfast of red squirrels climbing garden trees. There's a snug sitting room where a fire burns in winter, while doors open in summer for croquet on the lawn. Homely bedrooms come in different shapes and sizes. All are immensely comfortable and have a smart country style: pretty linen, warm colours, good fabrics, lovely views. Spin down to the restaurant for delicious country fare, perhaps carrot and coriander soup, Highland venison, sticky toffee pudding. There's porridge with cream and brown sugar for breakfast. A super little place.

Price	Half-board £105-£135 p.p.
Rooms	10: 3 doubles, 5 twins/doubles, 2 singles.
Meals	Lunch from £4.50. Dinner included; non-residents £38.
Closed	January & February.
Directions	A9 north of Pitlochry, then B8079, signed Killiecrankie. Straight ahead for 2 miles. Hotel on right, signed.

Henrietta Fergusson
Killiecrankie,
Pitlochry PH16 5LG

Tel +44 (0)1796 473220
Email enquiries@killiecrankiehotel.co.uk
Web www.killiecrankiehotel.co.uk

10% off stays of 2 or more nights.

Craigatin House & Courtyard

Pitlochry — gateway to the Highlands — is a vibrant town. Castles and mountains, lochs and forests, skiing at Glenshee, a famous theatre festival: it's got it all. This handsome old doctor's house — now an attractive boutique B&B — is perfectly situated to explore. It stands peacefully in two acres of manicured gardens on the northern shores of town; good restaurants are a short stroll. The formality of a smart stone exterior gives way to warmly contemporary interiors, where beautiful windows flood rooms with light. There are shutters in the breakfast room, which overflows into an enormous conservatory where flames leap in a wood-burner and walls of glass open to the garden. Big uncluttered bedrooms — some in the main house, others in converted stables — are super value for money. Expect Farrow & Ball colours, comfy beds, crisp white linen, padded bedheads and pretty shower rooms. Breakfast offers the full cooked works and tempting alternatives: creamy omelettes with smoked haddock, apple pancakes with grilled bacon and maple syrup. You're on the Whisky Trail, too. *Minimum stay two nights at weekends.*

Price	£83–£93. Suite £110. Singles from £73.
Rooms	13: 10 doubles, 2 twins, 1 suite.
Meals	Restaurants in town.
Closed	Christmas.
Directions	A9 north to Pitlochry. Take 1st turn-off for town, up main street, past shops and signed on left.

 Bottle of wine in your room.

Martin & Andrea Anderson
165 Atholl Road, Pitlochry PH16 5QL
Tel   +44 (0)1796 472478
Email   enquiries@craigatinhouse.co.uk
Web   www.craigatinhouse.co.uk

Royal Hotel

The Royal is lovely – softly grand, intimate and welcoming, a country house in the middle of town. Queen Victoria once stayed, hence the name. It stands on the river Earn – the eponymous loch glistens majestically five miles up stream – but you're brilliantly placed to strike out in all directions: Loch Tay, Pitlochry, The Trossachs and Perth are all on your doorstep, even Edinburgh is easy to get to. Those who linger fare rather well. Two fires burn side by side in a wonderful sitting room, newspapers hang on poles, logs tumble from wicker baskets, sofas and armchairs are impeccably upholstered. There's a grandfather clock in the hall, rugs to cover stripped floors in the bar, and walls festooned with beautiful art. You eat all over the place, with leather armchairs in the bar, Lloyd Loom furniture in the conservatory/brasserie or at smartly dressed tables in a warm and elegant dining room. Spotless rooms above are just what you'd want: padded bedheads, crisp white linen, mahogany dressers, gilt-framed mirrors. Bathrooms come with fluffy robes, one four-poster has a log fire. Brilliant.

Price	£140. Four-poster £180. Singles from £85. Half-board £90-£110 p.p. Self-catering from £320 (low season 2 nights).
Rooms	11 + 1: 5 doubles, 3 twins, 3 four-posters. Self-catering townhouse for 4.
Meals	Bar meals from £6.95. Dinner, 3 courses, £27.75.
Closed	Occasionally.
Directions	A9 north of Dunblane, then A822 through Braco & left onto B827. Left for centre of town, over bridge & hotel on square.

Teresa Milsom
Melville Square, Comrie, Crieff PH6 2DN

Tel	+44 (0)1764 679200
Email	reception@royalhotel.co.uk
Web	www.royalhotel.co.uk

10% off room rate Mon-Thurs. Glass of champagne on arrival.

Barley Bree

A few miles north of Gleneagles, a super little restaurant with rooms that delivers what so many people want: stylish interiors, super food, excellent prices, a warm welcome. This is a small family-run affair. Fabrice is French and cooks sublimely, Alison, a Scot, looks after the wine. Their stage is Barley Bree – whisky soup to you and me – an 18th-century coaching inn that has recently had a facelift. Now a band of happy locals come for fabulous Scottish food cooked with predictable French flair, perhaps rabbit terrine with a wild garlic salad, fillet of halibut with spring onion mash, and cardamom cheesecake with chocolate ice cream. The restaurant, nicely rustic, has a fire that burns on both sides, while in summer you decant onto a terrace for lunch in the sun. Upstairs, six lovely rooms come in neutral colours. You get crisp linen and comfy beds, then underfloor heating in excellent little shower rooms. One room is big and has a claw-foot bath, all have a wee dram of whisky on the house. Head down to Gleneagles for a game of golf; the Ryder Cup comes through in 2014.

Price	£100-£130. Singles from £70.
Rooms	6 twins/doubles.
Meals	Lunch from £4.50 (Wed-Sun). Dinner, 3 courses, about £30 (Wed-Sun only for non-residents).
Closed	2 weeks in February, 2 weeks in October, Christmas.
Directions	A9 north from Dunblane, then A822 for Muthill. In village on left before church.

Fabrice & Alison Bouteloup
6 Willoughby Street, Muthill PH5 2AB

Tel	+44 (0)1764 681451
Email	info@barleybree.com
Web	www.barleybree.com

Creagan House at Strathyre

Where else can you sit in a baronial dining room and read a small tract on the iconography of the toast rack while waiting for your bacon and eggs? Creagan is a delight – a small, traditional restaurant with rooms run with great passion by Gordon and Cherry. At its heart is Gordon's kitchen, from which flies ambrosial food, perhaps mille-feuille of veal sweetbreads, Isle of Gigha halibut with scallop, langoustine and crab pâté, bitter chocolate torte with mixed berry compote. Food is sourced locally – meat and game from Perthshire, seafood from west coast boats – and served on Skye pottery. There's a snug sitting room which doubles as a bar where you'll find a good wine list and 50 malt whiskies; if you like a dram, you'll be in heaven, and there's a guide to help you choose. Bedrooms fit the bill: warm and comfortable with smart carpets, wood and florals, flat-screen TVs, a sofa if there's room. No airs and graces, just the sort of attention you only get in small owner-run places. Bag a munro, too; let the walking sticks at the front door help you up Beinn An T-Sidhein. A perfect wee retreat.

Price	£130–£150. Singles £75–£95.
Rooms	5: 1 four-poster, 3 doubles, 1 twin.
Meals	Dinner, 3 courses, £31.50–£36.
Closed	Wednesdays & Thursdays. February.
Directions	From Stirling A84 north through Callander to Strathyre. Hotel 0.25 miles north of village on right.

Use your Sawday's Gift Card here.

Gordon & Cherry Gunn
Callander FK18 8ND
Tel   +44 (0)1877 384638
Email   eatandstay@creaganhouse.co.uk
Web   www.creaganhouse.co.uk

Afternoon tea with homemade shortbread on arrival.

Monachyle Mhor

Twenty-seven years of evolution has turned this 17th-century farmhouse into one of Scotland's coolest hotels. It's a family affair set in 2,000 acres of silence, with the Trossachs circling around you and Loch Voil shimming below. Dick farms, Melanie designs her magical rooms and Tom cooks some of the best food in Scotland. You're close to the end of the track with only the sheep and the birds to disturb you; lawns roll past a boules pitch towards the water. Step inside and find a slim restaurant behind a wall of glass, a small candlelit bar and an open fire in the sitting room. Bedrooms — most in a courtyard of converted stone outbuildings — are dreamy: big beds, crisp linen, cool colours, designer fabrics, hi-tech gadgets. Bathrooms can be out of this world: a deluge shower in a granite steam room, claw-foot baths that gaze upon the glen. Those in the main house are smaller, while suites in loft-house style are enormous. Walk, sail, fish, ride a bike through the forest. Dinner is five courses of unbridled heaven — with beef, lamb, pork and venison all off the farm. *Minimum stay two nights at weekends.*

Price	£195–£265. Singles from £120. Half-board from £144.50 p.p.
Rooms	14: 6 doubles, 6 twins, 2 suites.
Meals	Sunday lunch £32. Dinner £47.
Closed	January.
Directions	M9 junc. 11, then B824 and A84 north. Right for Balquhidder 6 miles north of Callander. 5 miles west along road & Loch Voil. Hotel on right, signed.

Tom Lewis
Balquhidder, Lochearnhead FK19 8PQ
Tel   +44 (0)1877 384622
Email   monachyle@mhor.net
Web   www.mhor.net

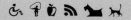

Windlestraw Lodge

There are few better distractions in Scotland than following the river Tweed: fishing lines glisten in the sun, lambs bleat high on the hill, ospreys glide through the afternoon sky. This is the river which brought prosperity to Scotland, its mills a source of huge wealth in Victorian days. Windlestraw, a heavenly country house, stands in evidence; it was built as a wedding gift for a mill owner and sits on the side of a hill with timeless views down the valley. Outside, a copper beech shades the lawn; inside, a dazzling refurbishment elates. You get stripped floors, painted ceilings, roaring fires, a panelled dining room. Light pours in through windows at the front, gilt mirrors hang on walls, fat sofas encourage idleness. There are binoculars with which to scan the valley, a terrace for afternoon tea, a sitting room for a quiet snooze. Country-house bedrooms are sublime. An elegant contemporary style runs throughout, those at the front have lovely views, one has the coolest of bathrooms. Add to this Alan's fabulous food and you have a very special place. There's golf at Peebles. Not to be missed.

Price	£130–£180. Singles from £95. Half-board from £115 p.p.
Rooms	6: 5 doubles, 1 twin.
Meals	Lunch by arrangement. Dinner, 4 courses, £46–£50.
Closed	Rarely.
Directions	East from Peebles on A72. Into Walkerburn; house signed left on western flank of town.

Julie & Alan Reid
Galashiels Road, Walkerburn EH43 6AA

Tel	+44 (0)1896 870636
Email	reception@windlestraw.co.uk
Web	www.windlestraw.co.uk

 15% off room rate Mon-Thurs for 2-night stays.

Ballochneck

Donnie and Fiona's magical pile stands one mile up a private drive, soundproofed by 175 acres of lush Stirlingshire country. Swans nest on the lake in spring, which doubles as a curling pond in winter (you can), while Suffolk sheep graze the fields and deer come to eat the rhododendrons. The house – still a home, albeit a grand one – dates to 1863 and was built for the Lord Provost of Glasgow. Inside you get all the aristocratic works – roaring fires, painted panelling, magical windows that bring in the view, wonderfully ornate ceilings – but Donnie and Fiona are the real stars; expect a little banter, a few good stories and a trip to the top of the house where a full-size snooker tables stands amid purple walls. Vast bedrooms at the front have huge views, beautiful beds and acres of crisp linen; one has an open fire, while a claw-foot bath next door comes with candles and views down the valley. Breakfast is a feast, and served in summer in a magnificent Victorian conservatory amid beds of lavender and wandering clematis. Stirling Castle and Loch Lomond are close. *Children over 12 welcome. Min. two nights at weekends.*

Ethical Collection: Food. See page 386 for details

Price	£145-£160. With interconnecting twin £215.
Rooms	3: 1 double; 1 double with separate bathroom; 1 interconnecting twin (let to same party only).
Meals	Dinner, 4 courses, £35.
Closed	Christmas & New Year.
Directions	M9 junc. 10, A84 west, B8075 south, then A811 for Buchlyvie. In village, right onto B835 for Aberfoyle. Over bridge, up to lodge house 200 yds on left. 1 mile up drive to house.

Tea & homemade cake on arrival.

Donnie & Fiona Allan
Buchlyvie, Stirling FK8 3PA

Tel	+44 (0)1360 850216
Email	info@ballochneck.com
Web	www.ballochneck.com

Langass Lodge

Vast skies, water everywhere, golden beaches that stretch for miles. Nothing prepares you for the epic majesty of the Uists, a place so infinitely beautiful you wonder why you've got it to yourself. As for Langass, an old shooting lodge, it makes a great base, not least because Amanda and Niall know the island inside out and can help you discover its secrets. The hotel sits in ten silent acres with paths that lead up to standing stones or down to the water. Inside, cosy interiors fit the bill perfectly: a roaring fire in the bar; watery views in the restaurant; doors onto a terrace for drinks in summer. Bedrooms — warmly traditional in the main house, nicely contemporary in the new wing — are super value for money. Expect comfy beds, crisp white linen, excellent bathrooms, lots of colour. As for the food, it's the best on the island, with game off the estate and seafood plucked fresh from the sea. There's loads to do: kayaking, walking, wild fishing, bird watching. The night sky is magnificent, as are the Northern Lights. Children and dogs and very welcome. Don't miss it.

Price	£95–£140. Family rooms £120–£160. Singles from £65.
Rooms	11: 5 doubles, 4 twins/doubles, 2 family rooms.
Meals	Lunch from £5. Dinner in bar from £12.95; in restaurant £28–£34.
Closed	Never.
Directions	South from Lochmaddy on A867. Signed left after five miles.

Amanda & Niall Leveson Gower
Langass, North Uist HS6 5HA

Tel	+44 (0)1876 580285
Email	langasslodge@btconnect.com
Web	www.langasslodge.co.uk

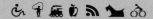

Tigh Dearg

This far-flung island chain is worth every second it takes to get here. Come for huge skies, sweeping beaches, carpets of wild flowers in the machair in summer, stone circles, ancient burial chambers, white-tailed eagles and fabulous Hebridean light. It's hard to overstate the sheer wonder of these bleakly beautiful islands, five of which are connected by a causeway, so drop south to Benbecula (*Whisky Galore* was filmed here) or Eriskay (for the Prince's Strand, where Bonnie Prince Charlie landed). Up on North Uist you'll find 1,000 lochs, so climb North Lees for wonderful watery views, then tumble back down to this island sanctuary. The house is a delight, immensely welcoming, full of colour, warmly contemporary, with windows that flood the place with light. Bedrooms come with suede headboards, power showers, bathrobes and beach towels, bowls of fruit and crisp white linen. In the restaurant find homemade soup, seafood pie, sticky toffee pudding. Walk, ride, fish, canoe, then return and try the sauna. Come in November for the northern lights. St Kilda is close for day tripping.

Price	£80–£145. Suite £160.
Rooms	9: 8 twins/doubles, 1 suite.
Meals	Bar meals from £8.50. Dinner, 3 courses, £25–£30.
Closed	Never.
Directions	North into Lochmaddy. Left, signed Police Station. Hotel on left after 200 yards.

Iain MacLeod
Lochmaddy, North Uist HS6 5AE

Tel	+44 (0)1876 500700
Email	info@tighdearghotel.co.uk
Web	www.tighdearghotel.co.uk

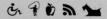

Scarista House

All you need to know is this: Harris is one of the most beautiful places in the world. Beaches of white sand that stretch for a mile or two are not uncommon. If you bump into another soul, it will be a delightful coincidence, but you should not count on it. The water is turquoise, coconuts sometimes wash up on the beach. The view from Scarista is simple and magnificent: field, ridge, beach, water, sky. Patricia and Tim are the kindest people, quietly inspiring. Their home is island heaven: coal fires, rugs on painted floors, books everywhere, old oak furniture, a first-floor drawing room and fabulous Harris light. Homely bedrooms come in country-house style. The golf club has left a set of clubs by the front door in case you wish to play (the view from the first tee is one of the best in the game). A corncrake occasionally visits the garden. There are walking sticks and Wellington boots to help you up the odd hill. Kind local staff may speak Gaelic and the food is exceptional, maybe quail with an armagnac mousse, fillet of Stornoway halibut, orange marmalade tart. A perfect place.

Price	£190–£240. Singles from £137.
Rooms	6: 4 doubles, 2 twins.
Meals	Dinner, 3 courses, £43. Packed lunch £7.50.
Closed	January & February.
Directions	From Tarbert A859 south, signed Rodel. Scarista 15 miles on left after golf course. W10 bus stops at gate.

Patricia & Tim Martin
Scarista, Isle of Harris HS3 3HX
Tel   +44 (0)1859 550238
Email   timandpatricia@scaristahouse.com
Web   www.scaristahouse.com

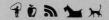

Wales

Ye Olde Bulls Head Inn

With 600 years of history under its belt, it's no surprise to learn that a host of luminaries have enjoyed the hospitality of Anglesey's most famous inn. Dr Johnson stayed, as did Dickens, while General Mytton took up residence when besieging Beaumaris' medieval castle. These days the past lives on – the front bar is little changed in a hundred years – but contemporary comforts abound, too. Beautiful fabrics decorate a gorgeous sitting room where you can roast away in front of the fire, while glass walls flood the brasserie with light. You can eat here informally (slow-cooked lamb, crumbed haddock and chips) or in the chic first-floor Loft Restaurant (no children under seven), where you dig into the best local food. Try crab cannelloni with vichyssoise mousse, Welsh beef with an onion purée, baked cinnamon croissant with pressed apple. Bedrooms in the main house come in country-house style. Some are lavish (regal colours, exposed beams, claw-foot baths), others simpler (warm florals, brass beds). Those in the Townhouse across the road have a contemporary feel: lots of colour, funky art, media hubs.

Price	£100–£140. Four-poster £125–£135. Suites £155–£165. Singles from £80.
Rooms	26: 7 doubles, 4 twins, 1 four-poster, 1 suite. Townhouse: 11 twins/doubles, 1 single, 1 suite.
Meals	Lunch & dinner in brasserie £5–£30. Dinner in restaurant, 3 courses, £41 (Tues-Sat evenings only).
Closed	Christmas.
Directions	A55 onto Anglesey, then A545 to Beaumaris. On left at far end of main street.

David Robertson
Castle Street, Beaumaris LL58 8AP

Tel	+44 (0)1248 810329
Email	info@bullsheadinn.co.uk
Web	www.bullsheadinn.co.uk

Jolyons Boutique Hotel

Down by the water, the captain's house stands on the oldest residential street in Cardiff Bay. Bang opposite, the regenerated quayside is home to the Welsh Assembly, the Norwegian Church and the Millennium Centre. At Jolyon's, a boutique hotel run in Mediterranean style, you get quietly groovy interiors and a funky basement café/bar. Spotless bedrooms may not be huge, but they're not small either and they flood with light so none feel cramped. A similar style runs throughout – creamy walls, colourful fabrics, pretty wood. You'll find Moroccan lanterns, the odd armoire, Philippe Starck loos in airy bathrooms. Some rooms have jacuzzi bath, while the top-floor room has a private roof terrace. Drop down to the bar for fresh pizzas cooked in a wood-fired oven every day. The feel here is that of a Boston coffee shop, so order a good espresso, a local beer or a fancy cocktail, then sink into a leather sofa. There are live music nights, even tasting evenings (whisky, cheese, chocolate). Dr Who is filmed locally, while the Welsh Assembly is open to the public and worth a tour.

Price	£50–£150.
Rooms	7: 5 doubles, 2 twins/doubles.
Meals	Dishes from £2.50. Pizza from £6.
Closed	Never.
Directions	M4 junc. 29, then A48(M) for Cardiff. Take exit marked 'Docks and Bay'. Straight ahead, past Millenium Centre & 1st left.

Bottle of house wine for all 2-night stays. 10% off room rate Mon-Thurs.

Jolyon Joseph
5 Bute Crescent, Cardiff CF10 5AN
Tel   +44 (0)29 2048 8775
Email   info@jolyons.co.uk
Web   www.jolyons.co.uk

Jolyons at No. 10

Number Ten backs onto Sophia Gardens, where the river Taff heads south towards Cardiff Bay; you can follow its banks into town or jump on a water taxi. As for the hotel, an attractive red-brick house at the front gives way to a '70s addition at the back, which shelters some welcome off-road parking. Inside, the feel is relaxed and friendly. The bar and restaurant bring in the locals for a pint or a steak, there's an open fire, Victorian sofas, a terrace at the front, a courtyard to one side. Airy bedrooms are nicely priced and if you're in town for a night or two, you'll be happy here. There's a lift to whiz you up and down, then airy rooms, many of which have ornate French beds. Some are bigger than others, the suites all have separate sitting rooms. All have fancy bathrooms with good showers and robes; most have baths too, some with plunge pools. Breakfast is taken overlooking Sophia Gardens, a good spot to work off your bacon and eggs. All things Cardiff are on your doorstep, but you can easily nip north into the country, too.

Price	£75-£110. Suites £110-£250. Singles from £75.
Rooms	21: 5 doubles, 8 twins/doubles, 8 suites.
Meals	Lunch from £7. Dinner, 3 courses, about £25.
Closed	Never.
Directions	M4 junc. 32, A470 south, A48 west. Left for Llandaff, then keep left at lights after 600m. On left one mile down Cathedral Road.

10% off stays of 2 or more nights.

	Jolyon Joseph
	10 Cathedral Road, Cardiff CF11 9LJ
Tel	+44 (0)29 2009 1900
Email	info@jolyons.co.uk
Web	www.jolyons10.com

Ty Mawr Country Hotel

Pretty rooms, attractive prices and delicious food make this super country house hard to resist. It's a very peaceful spot. You drive over the hills, drop into the village and wash up at this 16th-century stone house that glows in yellow. Outside, a sun-trapping terrace laps against a trim lawn, which in turn drops into a passing river. Gentle eccentricities abound: croquet hoops take the odd diversion, logs are piled high like giant beehives, a seat has been chiselled into a tree trunk. Inside, exposed stone walls, terracotta-tiled floors and low beamed ceilings give a warm country feel. There are fires everywhere – one in the sitting room, which overlooks the garden, another in the dining room that burns on both sides. Excellent bedrooms are all big. You get warm colours, big beds, crisp linen, good bathrooms. Some have sofas, all are dog-friendly, three overlook the garden. Back downstairs, the bar doubles as reception, and there's Welsh art on sale. Steve's cooking is the final treat: Cardigan Bay scallops, organic Welsh beef, calvados and cinnamon rice pudding.

Price	£113-£128. Singles from £70. Half-board from £77.50 p.p.
Rooms	5: 3 doubles, 2 twins/doubles.
Meals	Dinner £24-£29.
Closed	Rarely.
Directions	M4 west onto A48, then B4310 exit, for National Botanic Gardens. 6 miles north to Brechfa. In village centre.
	Use your Sawday's Gift Card here.

Bottle of wine with dinner on first night.

Steve Thomas & Annabel Viney
Brechfa SA32 7RA
Tel   +44 (0)1267 202332
Email   info@wales-country-hotel.co.uk
Web   www.wales-country-hotel.co.uk

Harbourmaster

The harbour at Aberaeron was created by an Act of Parliament in 1807. Shipbuilding flourished and the harbourmaster got his house on the quay with big views over Cardigan Bay. Step in to find that winning combination of seductive good looks, informal but attentive service and a menu overflowing with fresh local produce. The airy open-plan dining room/bar has stripped floors and a horseshoe bar for good beers and wines, with harbour views looming through the windows. Wind up the staircase to super little bedrooms that come with shuttered windows, loads of colour and quietly funky bathrooms. You get Frette linen, Welsh wool blankets and a hot water bottle on every bed in winter. There are flat-screen TVs and DVD players, watery views and tide books. Come down for supper and try fishcakes with lime mayonnaise, rack of lamb with dauphinoise potatoes, bara brith pudding or chocolate fondant. There are bikes to borrow, cycle tracks that spin off into the hills, coastal paths that lead north and south. Sunsets are fabulous, too. *Minimum stay two nights at weekends.*

Price	£110–£190. Suites £150–£250. Singles £65. Half-board from £80 p.p.	
Rooms	13: 11 doubles, 2 singles.	
Meals	Lunch from £9.50. Bar meals from £9.50. Dinner from £16. Sunday lunch £21.	
Closed	Christmas Day.	
Directions	A487 south from Aberystwyth. In Aberaeron right for the harbour. Hotel on waterfront.	

Glyn & Menna Heulyn
Pen Cei, Aberaeron SA46 0BT
Tel   +44 (0)1545 570755
Email   info@harbour-master.com
Web   www.harbour-master.com

Entry 320   Map 2

Gwesty Cymru Hotel & Restaurant

A seafront gem, newly refurbished, with magnificent bathrooms that take some beating. Beth and Huw worked in Cardiff before upping sticks to renovate this terraced house that overlooks the bay, the pier and Constitution Hill (train up, stroll down). Inside, white walls, Welsh art and Blaenau slate combine to give a fresh contemporary feel. There's a mirrored bar and a cool little restaurant, which was packed for lunch in early March. A big window brings in the light, a glass door leads onto the terrace. Bedrooms are warmly stylish and very good value for money, so splash out on those at the front: leather armchairs face out to sea, giving box seats for imperious sunsets. You also get handmade oak furniture, crisp white linen, piles of pillows and bed throws that match the colour of the art. Bathrooms are magnificent. Expect Italian stone, enormous power showers, double-ended baths (two overlook the bay) and towelling bathrobes. Pop down for dinner and try the best of Wales, perhaps roasted mushrooms, rack of Welsh lamb, Brecon vodka and lime tarts.

Price	£87–£155. Suite £143–£205. Singles £65–£75.
Rooms	8: 4 doubles, 3 twins/doubles, 1 single.
Meals	Lunch from £5.25. Dinner, 3 courses, about £30.
Closed	2 weeks over Christmas.
Directions	On sea front in town close to pier. On-street parking only.

Huw & Beth Roberts
19 Marine Terrace,
Aberystwyth SY23 2AZ

Tel	+44 (0)1970 612252
Email	info@gwestycymru.com
Web	www.gwestycymru.com

Escape Boutique B&B

Llandudno is a holiday town, built by Victorians as a place to take the air. It is the Welsh equivalent of Brighton and Bill Bryson loved it – the unspoilt front with its bright white hotels, the two-mile beach and its 1878 pier, the bustling shops and restaurants behind. Away from the crowds (but not the seagulls!), Escape stands high on the hill with its ornate carved fireplaces, stained-glass windows and wrought-iron veranda still intact. Not that you should expect Victoriana. Interiors have been transformed into a contemporary world of wooden floors, neutral colours, Italian leather and glass chandeliers. Bedrooms – some big, some smaller – come with pillow-top mattresses, goose-down duvets, crisp linen and Farrow & Ball colours. Those at the front have views over town, but all have buckets of style and good little bathrooms (one has a roll-top tub). Also: flat-screen TVs, DVD players and a PlayStation if you ask for it. There's an honesty bar and an open fire in the sitting room, while breakfast is a feast: Java coffee, the full Welsh works. *Minimum stay two nights at weekends.*

Price	£88–£138.
Rooms	9: 8 doubles, 1 twin/double.
Meals	Restaurants within walking distance.
Closed	Christmas.
Directions	A55 junc. 19, then A470 for Llandudno. On promenade head west hugging the coast, then left at Belmont Hotel and house on right.

Sam Nayar	
48 Church Walks,	
Llandudno LL30 2HL	
Tel	+44 (0)1492 877776
Email	info@escapebandb.co.uk
Web	www.escapebandb.co.uk

10% off midweek stays of 2 or more nights.

Pentre Mawr Country House

The setting is beautiful, 190 acres of deep country at the end of a lane. The house isn't bad either. This is an old estate, which fell into ruin 80 years ago. It has been in Graham's family for 400 years, and it became his to renovate; he's done a beautiful job. Outside, a lawn runs down to fields, and Doric columns flank the front door. Inside you find Graham and Bre's home. Pentre Mawr is half B&B (informal, personal, very welcoming), half hotel (smart rooms, attentive service, a menu in the restaurant). Wander about and find a couple of sitting rooms, open fires, vast flagstones, a bust of Robert Napier. Bedrooms are scattered about. Big rooms in the main house have a country-house feel; stylish suites in the gardener's cottage have hot tubs on private terraces; super-cool safari lodges in the garden flaunt faux leopard-skin throws and fabulous bathrooms. There's a sun-trapping courtyard with a small pool, tennis on the grass, a kitchen garden that's being teased back to life. And Bre cooks a fine dinner, perhaps smoked salmon, rack of lamb, bread and butter pudding. *Min. two nights in hot-tub suites & at weekends.*

Price	£130. Suites £180. Lodges £160. Half-board £100-£130 p.p. (obligatory Friday & Saturday).
Rooms	8: 3 doubles. Gardener's Cottage: 2 suites. Garden: 3 canvas lodges.
Meals	Dinner, 5 courses, £35. Non-residents by arrangement.
Closed	Christmas.
Directions	A55, then A525 south to Denbigh. Left at second roundabout to Llandyrnog, then left at mini-roundabout onto B5429. 1st left; signed left after 0.5 mile.

Afternoon tea and bucks fizz on arrival.

Graham & Bre Carrington-Sykes
Llandyrnog,
Denbigh LL16 4LA

Tel	+44 (0)1824 790732
Email	info@pentremawrcountryhouse.co.uk
Web	www.pentremawrcountryhouse.co.uk

The Hand at Llanarmon

Single-track lanes plunge you into the middle of nowhere. All around, lush valleys rise and fall, so pull on your boots and scale a mountain or find a river and jump into a canoe. Back at The Hand, a 16th-century drovers' inn, the pleasures of a traditional country local are hard to miss. A coal fire burns on the range in reception, a wood fire crackles under brass in the front bar and a wood-burner warms the lofty dining room. Expect exposed stone walls, low beamed ceilings, old pine settles and candles on the mantelpiece. There's a games room for darts and pool, a quiet sitting room for maps and books. Delicious food is popular with locals, so grab a table and enjoy seasonal menus — perhaps game broth, lamb casserole, then sticky toffee pudding. Bedrooms are just as they should be: not too fancy, cosy and warm, spotlessly clean with crisp white linen and good bathrooms. A very friendly place. Martin and Gaynor are full of quiet enthusiasm and have made their home warmly welcoming. John Ceiriog Hughes, who wrote "Bread of Heaven", lived in this valley. Special indeed.

Price	£90–£125. Singles from £52.50.
Rooms	13: 8 doubles, 4 twins, 1 suite.
Meals	Lunch from £6. Sunday lunch £20. Dinner £12–£20.
Closed	Rarely.
Directions	Leave A5 south of Chirk for B4500. Llanarmon 11 miles on.

Gaynor & Martin De Luchi
Llanarmon Dyffryn Ceiriog,
Llangollen LL20 7LD

Tel   +44 (0)1691 600666
Email   reception@thehandhotel.co.uk
Web   www.thehandhotel.co.uk

 25% off room rate Mon-Thurs.

Plas Dinas Country House

This is the family home of Lord Snowdon. It dates to the 1600s and stands in 15 acres with an avenue of oak that sweeps you up to the house. Princess Margaret stayed often and much of what fills the house belongs to the family: stunning chandeliers, oils by the score, gilt-framed mirrors, fine old chests – an Aladdin's cave of beautiful things. There's a baby grand piano, a harp that needs a few strings, varnished wood floors, an honesty bar, a fire that roars. It's no surprise to discover the house hosts murder-mystery weekends or that masses of memorabilia is framed on the walls (make sure you peek into the private dining room). Bedrooms are excellent, recently refurbished, the past mixing gracefully with crisp contemporary design. Expect four-posters, cool colours, stylish fabrics. Bathrooms are excellent, some with showers, others with free-standing baths. Back downstairs, Andy's cooking hits the spot, perhaps broccoli, port and stilton soup, lamb shank with mint and rosemary gravy then Baileys crème brûlée. Snowdon is close, as you'd expect. *Minimum stay two nights at bank holiday weekends.*

25% off stays of 2 or more nights.

Price	£95–£160. Four-poster £125–£250.
Rooms	9: 4 doubles, 3 twins/doubles, 2 four-posters.
Meals	Dinner, 3 courses, £26–£30.
Closed	22 December–2 January.
Directions	South from Caernarfon on A487. Through Bontnewydd and signed right after half a mile at brow of shallow hill.
🎁	Use your Sawday's Gift Card here.

Andy & Julian Banner-Price
Bontnewydd, Caernarfon LL54 7YF
Tel   +44 (0)1286 830214
Email   info@plasdinas.co.uk
Web   www.plasdinas.co.uk

Rhiwafallen Restaurant with Rooms

North Wales may be a touch far flung, but its star shines brightly these days and ever-growing numbers are flocking in to explore its magical landscapes. Luckily, a smattering of stylish hotels has mushroomed to look after the lucky souls who venture forth; this intimate restaurant with rooms is one of the best. Roll up the drive to find old stone walls, ducks on the pond and a pebbled terrace overlooking fields of grazing sheep. Inside, cool interiors are warm and restful with candles in the fireplace and the odd bust of an eastern deity, but it's the bedrooms that take the biscuit, each one brimming with understated grace. The style is crisply contemporary: goose-down duvets, modern art and flat-screen TVs, fancy bathrooms and fluffy cotton bathrobes. One has sea views, another has its own balcony. Pull yourself away for champagne cocktails, then feast on Rob's glorious food, perhaps hot smoked salmon, rack of Welsh lamb, pineapple tarte tatin. You eat in a sail-shaded conservatory/restaurant with doors that open onto the terrace in summer. Snowdon is close, as are wild beaches for seaside walks.

Price	£100–£120. Suite £150. Singles from £80.
Rooms	3: 2 doubles, 1 suite.
Meals	Sunday lunch £19.50. Dinner, 3 courses, £35. Not Sun/Mon.
Closed	Rarely.
Directions	South from Caernarfon on A487. Right onto A499 for Llandwrog. Through village and on left after 0.5 miles.

Rob & Kate John
Llandwrog, Caernarfon LL54 5SW
Tel   +44 (0)1286 830172
Web   www.rhiwafallen.co.uk

Entry 326   Map 5

Plas Bodegroes

Close to the end of the world and worth every second it takes to get here. Chris and Gunna are inspirational, their home a temple of cool elegance, the food possibly the best in Wales. Fronted by an avenue of 200-year-old beech trees, this Georgian manor house is wrapped in climbing roses and wildly roaming wisteria. The veranda circles the house, as do long French windows that lighten every room, so open one up, pull up a chair and listen to birdsong. Not a formal place – come to relax and be yourself. Bedrooms are wonderful, the courtyard rooms especially good, where exposed wooden ceilings give the feel of a smart Scandinavian forest hideaway. Best of all is the dining room, almost a work of art in itself, cool and crisp with exceptional art on the walls – a great place to eat Chris's ambrosial food; try sea trout wrapped in Carmarthen ham, mountain lamb with rosemary jus, baked vanilla cheesecake with passion fruit sorbet. Don't miss the Lleyn Peninsula: sandy beaches, towering cliffs and country walks all wait. Snowdon and Portmeirion are close too.

Price	£130–£180.
Rooms	10: 8 doubles, 1 twin, 1 four-poster.
Meals	Sunday lunch £20. Dinner £45. Not Sun or Mon evenings.
Closed	December–February & Sunday & Monday throughout year.
Directions	From Pwllheli A497 towards Nefyn. House on left after 1 mile, signed.

Chris & Gunna Chown
Efailnewydd, Pwllheli LL53 5TH

Tel	+44 (0)1758 612363
Email	gunna@bodegroes.co.uk
Web	www.bodegroes.co.uk

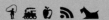

Penmaenuchaf Hall

The gardens are amazing — woodlands strewn with daffodils in spring, topiary on the upper lawn, a walled garden of tumbling colour. The position high on the hill is equally sublime, with the Mawdacch estuary carving imperiously through the valley below. The house has attitude, too — built in 1865 for a Bolton cotton merchant. The smell of woodsmoke greets you at the front door. Step inside to find an open fire crackling in the half-panelled hall, where armchairs take the strain. The drawing room is even better with mullioned windows to frame the view, a grand piano and cavernous sofas, country rugs on original wood floors. Steps illuminated by fairy lights lead up to the airy conservatory/dining room, where French windows open onto to a terrace for al fresco dining in good weather. Bedrooms come in traditional country-house style with a warm contemporary feel, ornamental fireplaces, padded window seats and comfy beds. Some rooms are huge, several have balconies, all have bathrooms that are more than adequate. There are 13 miles of river to fish, while Snowdon, Bala and Portmeirion are close.

Price	£160-£250. Singles from £100.
Rooms	14: 7 doubles, 5 twins/doubles, 1 four-poster, 1 family room.
Meals	Lunch from £6. Afternoon tea from £6.90. Dinner, 3 courses, £42.50.
Closed	Rarely.
Directions	From Dolgellau A493 west for about 1.5 miles. Entrance on left.

	Mark Watson & Lorraine Fielding
	Penmaenpool, Dolgellau LL40 1YB
Tel	+44 (0)1341 422129
Email	relax@penhall.co.uk
Web	www.penhall.co.uk

 Afternoon tea on day of arrival. 10% off room rate Mon-Thurs.

Ffynnon

A seriously indulging boutique B&B hidden away in the backstreets of this old market town. By day, you try valiantly to leave your luxurious room to explore the majesty of North Wales (many fail). Cycle tracks lead over forested hills, white beaches stretch for miles, there are rivers to ride, castles to visit, even Snowdon to climb. If you fail to budge, make do with luxury. The exterior of this former rectory may be a touch stern, but interiors sparkle with abandon. You find open fires, Farrow & Ball colours, fancy chandeliers and rugs on stripped floors. Breakfast is served in an elegant dining room, there's an honesty bar in the airy sitting room and doors fly open in summer to a lawned garden complete with standing stone. Bedrooms upstairs are magnificent, those at the front have views over the town. Expect Egyptian linen on beautiful beds, high ceilings and elegant fabrics, flat-screen TVs, DVD players and iPod docks. Faultless bathrooms are somewhat addictive, so expect to go home smelling of roses. Kids are very welcome, good restaurants wait in town, Steve and Debra couldn't be nicer. Don't miss it.

Price	£135–£200. Singles from £95.
Rooms	6: 3 doubles, 1 twin/double, 2 suites.
Meals	Restaurants within walking distance.
Closed	Christmas.
Directions	Leave A470 for Dolgellau, over bridge, into town. At T-junction, right then 1st left. Straight across Springfield Road & 2nd right into Bryn Teg. Entrance at end of road.

🎁 Use your Sawday's Gift Card here.

Bottle of champagne for bookings of 3 nights or more. 10% off stays of 2 or more nights.

Debra Harris & Steve Holt
Love Lane, Brynffynnon,
Dolgellau LL40 1RR

Tel	+44 (0)1341 421774
Email	info@ffynnontownhouse.com
Web	www.ffynnontownhouse.com

The Bell at Skenfrith

The position here is magical: an ancient stone bridge, a much-ignored valley, glorious hills rising behind, cows grazing in lush fields. It's a perfect spot, not least because providence has blessed it with this sublime inn, where crisply designed interiors ooze country chic. In summer doors fly open and life spills onto a stone terrace, where views of wood and hill are interrupted only by the odd chef pottering off to a rather productive organic kitchen garden. Back inside you find slate floors, open fires and plump-cushioned armchairs in the locals' bar, but the emphasis here is firmly on the food with a very happy kitchen turning out exceptional cooking, perhaps wild garlic vichyssoise with Herefordshire snails, fabulous Welsh lamb with hazelnut couscous, a flawless raspberry soufflé with a champagne bellini. There's an imperious wine list to wash it down with and bedrooms that are as good as you'd expect: uncluttered and elegant, brimming with light, some beamed, others overlooking the river. Idyllic circular walks sweep you into blissful country. *Minimum stay two nights at weekends.*

Price	£110–£170. Four-posters £195–£220. Singles from £75 (Sun-Thurs).
Rooms	11: 6 doubles, 2 twins, 3 four-posters.
Meals	Lunch from £14. Sunday lunch £25. Dinner, 3 courses, around £33.
Closed	Last week in Jan & first week in Feb.
Directions	From Monmouth B4233 to Rockfield; B4347 north for 5 miles; right on B4521; Skenfrith 1 mile.

William & Janet Hutchings
Skenfrith,
Abergavenny NP7 8UH
Tel   +44 (0)1600 750235
Email enquiries@skenfrith.co.uk
Web   www.skenfrith.co.uk

 Bottle of champagne for bookings of 2 nights or more.

The Hardwick

Stephen cooks sublimely. He learnt the art alongside Michel Roux, Nick Nairn and Marco Pierre White, won a couple of Michelin stars along the way, spent some time in St Tropez and Paris, then came home to Wales to do his own thing. The net result is this attractive restaurant with rooms, and a brigade of inspired cooks turning out some seriously good food. Potter about and find sofas in the locals' bar, low beamed ceilings in the attractive dining room, then doors onto a terrace where you can eat in summer. Chefs pass by on their way to the vegetable garden… and much of the produce that flies out of the kitchen is Welsh, as are the draught beers! Elegant bedrooms have a clean contemporary feel. They stand in a peaceful annexe and come with big beds, lovely linen, woollen throws, a sofa if there's room. Some have baths, most have large walk-in showers, all have robes to pad about in. As for the food, spin down for a treat, perhaps local pigeon breast with chorizo and wild garlic, pan-fried monkfish with brown shrimps and lemon butter, a jar of Amalfi lemon crunch with Swiss meringue.

Price	£145–£165. Singles from £95. Half-board from £99.50 p.p.
Rooms	8: 7 doubles, 1 twin/double.
Meals	Lunch from £8.50. Sunday lunch £22–£28. Dinner, 3 courses, £30–£35.
Closed	Never.
Directions	One mile south-east of Abergavenny on B4598.

Stephen & Jo Terry
Raglan Road, Hardwick,
Abergavenny NP7 9AA
Tel   +44 (0)1873 854220
Email   info@thehardwick.co.uk
Web   www.thehardwick.co.uk

Penally Abbey

A fabulous position up on the hill with a ridge of sycamore and ash towering above and huge views of Carmarthen Bay to the front. Caldy Island lies to the east, the road ends at the village green, a quick stride across the golf course leads to the beach. Up at the house, a fine arched window by the grand piano frames the view perfectly, so sink into a chesterfield in front of the fire and gaze out to sea. The house dates to 1790 and was once an abbey; you'll also find St Deiniol's, a ruined 13th-century church that's lit up at night. Sprawling lawns are yours to roam, bluebells carpet the wood in May. Bedrooms are all different: grand four-posters and wild flock wallpaper in the main house; a simpler cottage feel in the coach house; warm contemporary luxury in St Deiniol's Lodge. Steve's gentle, unflappable manner is infectious and hugely relaxing; don't expect to feel rushed. Eileen cooks in the French style, much of it picked up in the kitchen of a château many years ago; her Tenby sea bass is exquisite. The Pembrokeshire coastal path passes by outside — don't miss it. *Minimum stay two nights at weekends.*

Price	£145-£230. Singles from £138. Half-board from £105 p.p.
Rooms	17: 6 doubles, 1 twin all en suite; 1 double with separate bath. Coach house: 4 doubles. Lodge: 5 twins/doubles.
Meals	Lunch by arrangement. Dinner, 3 courses, £36.
Closed	Never.
Directions	From Tenby A4139 for Pembroke. Right into Penally after 1.5 miles. Hotel signed above village green. Train station 5-mins walk.

Steve & Eileen Warren
Penally,
Tenby SA70 7PY

Tel   +44 (0)1834 843033
Email   info@penally-abbey.com
Web   www.penally-abbey.com

3 nights for the price of 2, November-March.

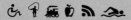

Stackpole Inn

This friendly inn is hard to fault. It sits in a quiet village drenched in honeysuckle with a fine garden at the front, a perfect spot for a drop of Welsh ale in summer. Wander further afield and you come to the sea at Barafundle Bay – a Pembrokeshire glory – where you can pick up the coastal path and follow it west past Stackpole Head to St Gorvan's Chapel. Stride back up to the inn and find interiors worthy of a country pub. There are smart red carpets, whitewashed walls, a hard-working wood-burner and obligatory beamed ceilings. Locals and visitors mingle in harmony, there are four hand pumps at the slate bar and tasty rustic cooking in the restaurant, perhaps deep-fried whitebait, rack of lamb, fresh raspberry brûlée. Super bedrooms are tremendous value for money and quietly positioned in a converted outbuilding. Two have sofabeds, two have velux windows for star gazing. All come in seaside colours with tongue-and-groove panelling, stripped floors, comfy beds, crisp linen and excellent bathrooms. Don't miss Pembroke Castle or the beach at Freshwater West.

Price	£90. Singles from £60.
Rooms	4: 2 twins/doubles, 2 family rooms.
Meals	Lunch from £5. Dinner, 3 courses, £25-£30 (not Sun Oct-Mar). Sunday lunch £14.95.
Closed	Rarely.
Directions	B4319 south of Pembroke for 3 miles, then left for Stackpole. Through Stackpole Cheriton, up hill, right at T-junction. On right.

Bottle of wine with dinner on first night.

Gary & Becky Evans
Stackpole, Pembroke SA71 5DF

Tel   +44 (0)1646 672324
Email   info@stackpoleinn.co.uk
Web   www.stackpoleinn.co.uk

The Grove

This handsome Georgian country house is lost in Pembrokeshire's rambling hills. Big views shoot off towards the Preselis, wooded hills curl around you, a carpet of bluebells bursts out in Spring. Inside, Neil and Zoe have refurbished in great style and their fine Arts & Crafts home now mixes old and new to intoxicating effect. It's a very relaxing spot: smart but informal, a treat for the senses. You get an explosion of wood in the entrance hall, a roaring fire in the drawing-room bar and a panelled restaurant for modern country cooking – perhaps wild nettle soup, slow-roasted lamb, bitter chocolate mousse. Gorgeous bedrooms are split between the main house and converted outbuildings. All are divine, some are just bigger than others, so come for cool wallpaper, painted armoires, crisp white linen and super-comfy mattresses. Bathrooms are equally spoiling with underfloor heating, robes and sparkling tiles. Elsewhere, striking art, a first-floor sitting room and a parterre garden for lunch in summer. The coastal path waits for blistering walks. Don't miss Narberth, a pretty country town. *Minimum stay two nights at weekends.*

Price	£130–£240. Suites £220–£290. Singles from £130.
Rooms	12: 9 doubles, 3 suites.
Meals	Lunch from £19. Dinner, 3 courses, £40.
Closed	Never.
Directions	M4, then A48 & A40 west towards Haverfordwest. At A470 roundabout, take 1st exit to Narberth. Through town, down hill, then follow brown signs to hotel.

Neil Kedward & Zoe Agar
Molleston, Narberth SA67 8BX
Tel   +44 (0)1834 860915
Email info@thegrove-narberth.co.uk
Web   www.thegrove-narberth.co.uk

20% off stays of 3 or more nights Mon-Thurs.

Slebech Park

An imperious position on the upper reaches of Daugleddau Estuary, part of a 600-acre estate that dates to 1760. You will probably think you've washed up at the main house, but incredibly, this crenellated building originally served as the mill and stables. It stands 30 paces from the water with views of river, wood and sky; the odd boat potters past, migrating birds come to bathe. Inside is the lap of luxury, the result of a total renovation. Each apartment comes with a super kitchen so you can look after yourself, but there's a rather good restaurant too (Welsh beef, fish from local waters, woodcock off the estate) and guests tend to do a bit of both. Apartments are sublime: grand yet contemporary, 21st-century country-house chic. You get vast sofas, padded window seats, beautiful colours and fabrics, huge beds wrapped in white linen, very fancy bathrooms. One on the ground floor has fine arched windows that open onto a terrace. Elsewhere, breathtaking gardens, the ruins of a 12th-century church and a sun-trapping courtyard where you can eat in summer. A perfect place. *Minimum stay two nights at weekends.*

Price	£120–£185. Suites £210–£285.
Rooms	14 + 1: 10 twins/doubles, 3 studios, 1 suite. Cottage for 4.
Meals	Light lunches from £8.50. Dinner, 3 courses, £25–£40.
Closed	Never.
Directions	M4, then A48 & A40 west. 1st left in Slebech (5 miles east of Haverfordwest) and drive on left after a mile.

10% off stays of 2 or more nights.

Geoffrey & Georgina Phillips
Slebech, Haverfordwest SA62 4AX
Tel   +44 (0)1437 752000
Email   enquiries@slebech.co.uk
Web   www.slebech.co.uk

Crug Glas

If you've never been to St David's, know this: it is one of the most magical places in Britain. It sits in Pembroke's national park, has an imperious 12th-century cathedral, and is surrounded by magnificent coastline that's dotted with cliffs and vast sandy beaches. As for Janet's country retreat, it's part chic hotel, part farmhouse B&B: stylish but personal, a great place to stay. The house dates from 1120 and sits in 600 acres of arable and grazing land (they run cattle, grow cereals). Outside, you find lawns and a small copse sprinkled with bluebells, then field and sky, and that's about it. Inside, there's an honesty bar in the sitting room and a Welsh dresser in the dining room, where Janet serves delicious food: homemade soups, home-reared beef, ginger sponge with vanilla ice cream. Bedrooms are the big surprise: a vast four-poster, a copper bath, old armoires, beautiful fabrics. All have robes in fancy bathrooms, while one room occupies much of the top floor. Two beautiful suites in an old barn have exposed timbers and underfloor heating. The coast is close.

Price	£100–£140. Suites £150–£185. Singles from £80.
Rooms	7: 3 doubles, 1 twin/double, 1 suite. Barn: 2 suites.
Meals	Sunday lunch, £20, by arrangement. Dinner, 3 courses, £25–£30.
Closed	24-26 December.
Directions	South from Fishguard on A487. Through Croes goch, then signed right after 2 miles.

Janet & Perkin Evans
Solva, Haverfordwest SA62 6XX

Tel	+44 (0)1348 831302
Email	janet@crugglas.plus.com
Web	www.crug-glas.co.uk

Cnapan Restaurant & Hotel

Cnapan is a way of life – a family affair with two generations at work in harmony. Eluned makes the preserves, Judith excels in the kitchen, Michael looks after the bar. It is a very friendly place that ticks to its own beat with locals popping in to book tables and guests chatting in the bar before dinner. As for the house, it's warm, cosy and traditionally home-spun – whitewashed stone walls and old pine settles in the dining room; comfy sofas and a wood-burner in the sitting room; a tiny telly in the bar for the odd game of rugby (the game of cnapan, rugby's precursor, originated in the town). There are maps for walkers, bird books, flower books, the daily papers, too. Spill into the garden in summer for pre-dinner drinks under the weeping willow, then slip back in for Judith's delicious food, perhaps spicy seafood chowder, roast duck with a clementine sauce, honey ice cream. Comfy bedrooms, warmly simple with modest bathrooms, are good value for money. You're in the Pembrokeshire National Park; beaches and cliff-top coastal walks beckon. *Minimum stay two nights at weekends.*

Price	£88. Singles from £54.
Rooms	5: 1 double, 3 twins, 1 family room. Extra bath available.
Meals	Dinner £26-£32. Not Tuesday eve, Easter to October.
Closed	Christmas, January & February.
Directions	From Cardigan A487 to Newport. 1st pink house on right.

Eluned Lloyd & Michael & Judith Cooper
East Street, Newport SA42 0SY

Tel	+44 (0)1239 820575
Email	enquiry@cnapan.co.uk
Web	www.cnapan.co.uk

Llys Meddyg

This fabulous restaurant with rooms has a bit of everything: cool rooms that pack a designer punch, super food in a sparkling restaurant, a cellar bar for drinks before dinner, a fabulous garden for summer treats. It's a very friendly place with charming staff on hand to help, and it draws in a local crowd who come for the seriously good food, perhaps mussel and saffron soup, rib of Welsh beef with hand-cut chips, cherry soufflé with pistachio ice cream. You eat in style with a fire burning at one end of the restaurant and good art hanging on the walls. Excellent bedrooms are split between the main house (decidedly funky) and the mews behind (away from the road). All have the same fresh style: Farrow & Ball colours, good art, oak beds, fancy bathrooms with fluffy robes. Best of all is the back garden with a mountain-fed stream pouring past. In summer, a café/bistro opens up out here – coffee and cake or steak and chips – with doors that open onto the garden. Don't miss Pembrokeshire's fabulous coastal path for its windswept cliffs, sandy beaches and secluded coves.

Price	£100–£180. Singles from £85.
Rooms	9: 4 doubles, 4 twins/doubles, 1 suite.
Meals	Lunch from £7 (Fri-Sun only in season). Dinner, 3 courses, about £33. Not Sun/Mon low season.
Closed	Rarely.
Directions	East from Fishguard on A487. On left in Newport towards eastern edge of town.
🎁	Use your Sawday's Gift Card here.

Louise & Edward Sykes
East Street,
Newport SA42 0SY
Tel   +44 (0)1239 820008
Email   info@llysmeddyg.com
Web   www.llysmeddyg.com

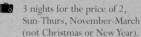
3 nights for the price of 2,
Sun-Thurs, November-March
(not Christmas or New Year).

Gliffaes Hotel

A matchless country house that towers majestically above the river Usk as it pours through the valley below. It is a view to feed the soul, so sit on the stone terrace and drink it in; people do. Pull yourself away and find 33 acres of formal lawns and woodland that ensure nothing but silence. Interiors pack a grand punch. Afternoon tea is laid out in a sitting room of panelled walls, shiny wood floors and family portraits, while logs crackle in a magnificent carved fireplace. Fishermen gather in the bar for tall stories and a quick drink before supper, then spin through to the formal restaurant for local, seasonal food (the hotel is part of the Slow Food Movement). Elsewhere, country-house bedrooms do the trick. Several have river views, one has a claw-foot bath that overlooks the front lawn, all come with thick fabrics, crisp linen, antique furniture, a sofa if there's room. As you may have deduced, Gliffaes is a fishing hotel, one of the finest in the land, so come to cast a fly while red kite circle above. Packed lunches in brown paper bags keep you going through the day. *Minimum stay two nights at weekends.*

Ethical Collection: Environment; Food. See page 386 for details

Price	£104–£248. Singles from £93. Half-board from £90.50 p.p.
Rooms	23: 5 doubles, 14 twins/doubles, 4 singles.
Meals	Light lunches from £5. Sunday lunch £20–£28.50. Dinner, 3 courses, £38.50.
Closed	January.
Directions	From Crickhowell A40 west for 2.5 miles. Entrance on left, signed. Hotel 1 mile up winding hill.
	Use your Sawday's Gift Card here.

Take the tandem out for the day & get a free packed lunch.

James & Susie Suter
Gliffaes Road,
Crickhowell NP8 1RH
Tel   +44 (0)1874 730371
Email   calls@gliffaes.com
Web   www.gliffaeshotel.com

Peterstone Court

Sheep graze in fields to the front, a swimming pool shimmers by an 11th-century church, a sun-trapping dining terrace overlooks the river Usk, you can walk straight into sublime country. The house dates back to 1750 and is just as good. You'll find a panelled sitting room with an open fire, a cute little spa in the vaulted cellars, a brasserie/bar that overlooks the garden, a grand piano in the formal restaurant where you eat at weekends. Bedrooms mix country-house style with contemporary colours. Rooms in the old stables reach over two floors and have a smart-rustic feel. Those in the main house have grander dimensions, some with high-ceilings and four-poster beds, others with leather headboards and cavernous sofas; all have fine views. Downstairs, much of the food in the restaurant is reared on the hotel's farm eight miles up the road (free-range chicken, Aylesbury duck, mountain lamb, succulent pork), so dig into pressed ham hock with homemade piccalilli, roast duck with a shallot and thyme tart, rhubarb and ginger mousse. Brecon is close, mountains wait. *Minimum stay two nights at weekends.*

Price	£110–£220. Singles from £90. Half-board from £85 p.p.
Rooms	12: 3 doubles, 5 twins/doubles, 2 family rooms, 2 suites.
Meals	Lunch from £5.50. Dinner, 3 courses, £25–£30.
Closed	Never.
Directions	A40 north from Abergavenny for Brecon. On left in village, three miles south of Brecon.

Sean Gerrard & Glyn &
Jessica Bridgeman
Llanhamlach, Brecon LD3 7YB

Tel	+44 (0)1874 665387
Email	info@peterstone-court.com
Web	www.peterstone-court.com

10% off room rate Mon–Thurs.

The Felin Fach Griffin

This fabulous little inn goes from strength to strength. Its hallmarks are great staff, delicious food, a friendly bar and honest prices. It's a must for those in search of a welcoming billet close to the mountains and its quirky, homespun feel is utterly intoxicating. It thrives on a mix of relaxed informality and colourful style. The timber-framed bar resembles the sitting room of a small hip country house: sofas sit in front of a fire, backgammon waits to be played. Painted stone walls come in blocks of colour, and an open-plan feel sweeps you through to a restaurant where you can dig into wonderful country food, perhaps Portland crab, shin of Welsh beef, pink rhubarb trifle. Much of what you eat comes from a half-acre kitchen garden, while meat and game are from the hills around you. As for the bedrooms, expect comfy beds, Roberts radios, good books and framed photography (but no TVs unless you ask). Super tongue-and-groove bathrooms are being updated with cool limestone tiles. The Beacons are close, so walk, ride, bike, canoe – or head to Hay for books galore.

Price	£115-£155. Singles from £80. Half-board from £85 p.p.
Rooms	7: 2 doubles, 2 twins/doubles, 3 four-posters.
Meals	Lunch from £5. Dinner £21.50-£26; à la carte £30-£35.
Closed	24 & 25 December & 4 days in January.
Directions	From Brecon A470 north to Felin Fach (4.5 miles). On left.

20% off room rates for midweek stays of 2 nights or more.

Charles & Edmund Inkin
Felin Fach, Brecon LD3 0UB
Tel   +44 (0)1874 620111
Email   enquiries@felinfachgriffin.co.uk
Web   www.felinfachgriffin.co.uk

The Lake Country House & Spa

Deep in the silence of Wales, a country house intent on pampering you rotten. Fifty acres of lawns, lakes and ancient woodland sweep you clean of city cobwebs, and if that's not enough a spa has been added, with an indoor pool, treatment rooms and a tennis court by the lake. Sit in a hot tub and watch guests fish for their supper, try your luck on the nine-hole golf course, saddle up nearby and take to the hills. Come home to afternoon tea in the drawing room, where an archipelago of rugs warms a brightly polished wooden floor and chandeliers hang from the ceiling. The hotel opened over a hundred years ago and the leather-bound fishing logs go back to 1894. A feel of the 1920s lingers. Fires come to life in front of your eyes, grand pianos and grandfather clocks sing their songs, snooker balls crash about in the distance. Dress for a delicious dinner – the atmosphere deserves it – then retire to cosseting bedrooms. Most are suites: those in the house are warmly traditional, those in the lodge are softly contemporary. The London train takes four hours and stops in the village. Resident geese waddle. Marvellous.

Price	£195. Suites £240–£260. Singles from £145. Half-board from £122.50 p.p.
Rooms	30: 6 twins/doubles, 12 suites. Lodge:12 suites.
Meals	Lunch, 3 courses, £22.50. Dinner, 4 courses, £38.50.
Closed	Never.
Directions	From Builth Wells A483 west for 7 miles to Garth. Signed from village.

Jean-Pierre Mifsud
Llangammarch Wells LD4 4BS

Tel	+44 (0)1591 620202
Email	info@lakecountryhouse.co.uk
Web	www.lakecountryhouse.co.uk

25% off room rate Mon-Thurs. Late checkout (12pm). Free pick-up from local bus/train station.

Milebrook House Hotel

An old-school country hotel with three acres of fabulous gardens that run down to the river Teme. You'll find Wales on one bank and England on the other, so bring your wellies and wade across; the walking is magnificent. The house, once home to writer Wilfred Thesiger, is run in informal style by three generations of the Marsden family with Beryl and Rodney leading the way. Step inside and enter a world that's rooted in a delightful past: clocks tick, cats snooze, fires crackle, the odd champagne cork escapes its bondage. Beautiful art hangs on the walls, the sitting room is stuffed with books, the bar comes in country-house style and there's food to reckon with in the wonderful dining room – perhaps Cornish scallops with a pea purée, rack of Welsh lamb with dauphinoise potatoes, ginger crème brûlée with poached rhubarb. A kitchen garden supplies much for the table, you can fish for trout, spot deer in the woods, play croquet on the lawn. Red kite, moorhens, kingfishers and herons live in the valley. Homely bedrooms are more than comfortable, so don't delay. *Minimum stay two nights at weekends.*

Price	£115–£127.50. Singles from £74. Half-board (min. 2 nights) from £80 p.p.
Rooms	10: 5 doubles, 4 twins, 1 family room.
Meals	Lunch, 2 courses, £14.95. Dinner, 3 courses, £32.95. Not Monday lunchtimes.
Closed	Never.
Directions	From Ludlow A49 north, then left at Bromfield on A4113 towards Knighton for 10 miles. Hotel on right.

10% off DBB for stays of 2 nights, 15% for 3 nights or more. Free pick-up from local bus/train station.

Rodney & Beryl Marsden
Stanage, Knighton LD7 1LT
Tel   +44 (0)1547 528632
Email   hotel@milebrookhouse.co.uk
Web   www.milebrookhouse.co.uk

Lake Vyrnwy Hotel & Spa

Wedged into the mountains of mid-Wales, Lake Vyrnwy shimmers under forest and sky, lost to the world and without great need of it. The position here is faultless, a tonic for the soul, a great spot to shake off the city. The hotel sits high on the hill with stupendous views of lake and mountain stretching five miles north; the sofa in the drawing room (grand piano, roaring fire) must qualify as one of the loveliest places to sit in Wales. The view follows you around wherever you go – even into the spa where the spa pool and sauna look the right way (there are treatment rooms, too). Bedrooms, most with lake views, have a country-house feel. Some are seriously grand, others snug in the eaves, many have balconies, in one you can soak in a claw-foot bath while gazing down the lake. Elsewhere, a terraced bar, a country pub, and walls of glass in a super restaurant, so come for smoked salmon, local lamb, vanilla and apricot cheesecake. Outside, pheasants roam, sheep graze on mountain pastures, there's a tennis court if you want to play and fish to coax from the lake.

Price	£125–£225. Singles from £100. Half-board from £89.50 p.p.
Rooms	52: 41 twins/doubles, 7 four-posters, 1 suite, 3 singles.
Meals	Lunch from £8.50. Bar meals from £8.50. Dinner, 5 courses, £39.95.
Closed	Rarely.
Directions	A490 from Welshpool; B4393 to Lake Vyrnwy. Brown signs from A5 at Shrewsbury as well.

Use your Sawday's Gift Card here.

The Bisiker Family
Llanwddyn, Oswestry SY10 0LY

Tel	+44 (0)1691 870692
Email	info@lakevyrnwyhotel.co.uk
Web	www.lakevyrnwy.com

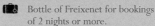
Bottle of Freixenet for bookings of 2 nights or more.

Fairyhill Hotel

The Gower Peninsula has legions of fans who come for its glorious heathland, its rugged coastline and some of the best beaches in the country. Fairyhill is bang in the middle of it all, a sublime country house wrapped up in 24 acres of blissful silence. There's a terrace for lunch, a stream-fed lake, an ancient orchard, a walled garden with asparagus beds. Inside, country-house interiors come fully loaded with warmth and colour. You'll find an open fire in the bar, a grand piano in the sitting room and super local food in the restaurant, where as much as possible comes from Gower. So tuck into confit of duck and pistachio terrine, local sea bass with scallops and green beans, then apple and tarragon tart with ice cream. Most bedrooms are big and fancy, a couple are small, but sweet. Some have painted beams, others have golden wallpaper, all have robes in excellent bathrooms. Mattresses are Vi-Spring, but if that's not enough there's a treatment room, so book a massage. There's croquet on the lawn in summer, while duck eggs come courtesy of resident Muscovys. *Minimum stay two nights on Saturdays.*

Price	£180–£280. Singles from £160. Half-board from £125 p.p.
Rooms	8: 3 doubles, 5 twins/doubles.
Meals	Lunch from £15.95. Dinner £35–£45.
Closed	First 3 weeks in January.
Directions	M4 junc. 47, A483 south, then A484 west to Gowerton and B4295 for Llanrhidian. Through Oldwalls, 1 mile up on left.

Andrew Hetherington & Paul Davies
Reynoldston, Swansea SA3 1BS

Tel	+44 (0)1792 390139
Email	postbox@fairyhill.net
Web	www.fairyhill.net

Alastair
Sawday's
Self-catering collection

Time away with your friends or family is precious, and when you are booking a whole week or more in one place you dare not get it wrong. To whom do you turn for advice and who on earth do you trust when the web is awash with advice from strangers? Our stunning self-catering collection satisfies an obvious need for impartial and trustworthy help. The criteria for inclusion are the same as for our books: we have to like the place and the owners. It has, quite simply, to be 'special'.

Cosy cottages, manor houses, tipis, châteaux, city apartments and more, in Britain and Europe

www.sawdays.co.uk/self-catering

Wheelchair-accessible

At least one bedroom and bathroom accessible for wheelchair users.

Channel Islands
Sark 274

England
Berkshire 5 • 6 • 7
Bristol 11
Buckinghamshire 13
Cornwall 20 • 22 • 23 • 24 •
25 • 32 • 34 • 35 • 37 • 38 • 39
Cumbria 48 • 52 • 55 • 56 •
64 • 65
Devon 73 • 75 • 77 • 78 •
81 • 84
Dorset 94 • 96 • 97 • 98 • 100 •
101 • 106
Durham 107
Essex 109 • 111
Gloucestershire 113 • 114 •
117 • 119 • 122
Hampshire 126 • 127 • 128 •
132 • 133
Herefordshire 134
Isle of Wight 140 • 141
Kent 143 • 144 • 151
Lancashire 156
Liverpool 158
London 163 • 166
Norfolk 169 • 170 • 171 •
172 • 175
Northamptonshire 179
Northumberland 181
Nottinghamshire 182
Oxfordshire 187 • 192 • 193 •
194
Rutland 196 • 197
Somerset 202 • 203 • 205
Suffolk 210 • 212 • 213 • 217 •
218 • 219 • 221
Sussex 222 • 227 • 228 • 232
Warwickshire 237

Wiltshire 241 • 242 • 244
Worcestershire 248 • 249 • 250
Yorkshire 253 • 256 • 258 •
259 • 260 • 269

Scotland
Fife 289
Highland 299 • 301
Perth & Kinross 306 • 309 • 310
Western Isles 313 • 314

Wales
Anglesey 316
Cardiff 318
Ceredigion 320
Denbighshire 323 • 324
Monmouthshire 331
Pembrokeshire 332 • 335
Powys 339 • 342 • 343 • 344

Event hire

The whole building can be hired for an event.

Channel Islands
Alderney 270 • 271
Guernsey 272 • 273
Sark 274

England
Bath & N.E. Somerset 3
Berkshire 6
Brighton & Hove 8 • 9
Bristol 11
Buckinghamshire 13 • 15
Cambridgeshire 16 • 17 • 18
Cleveland 19
Cornwall 20 • 23 • 24 • 25 •
27 • 28 • 30 • 31 • 32 • 35 •
37 • 38 • 40 • 41 • 42 • 43
Cumbria 45 • 49 • 51 • 52 •
53 • 55 • 57 • 59 • 61 • 62 •
63 • 64 • 65
Derbyshire 66 • 67

Weddings

You can get married at these places.

Quick reference indices

Singles
Single room OR rooms let
to single guests for half the
double room rate, or under.

Music
Places where there is a sound system in all bedrooms.

Quick reference indices

For many years Alastair Sawday Publishing has been 'greening' the business in different ways. Our aim is to reduce our environmental footprint as far as possible and with almost everything we do we have environmental implications in mind. In recognition of our efforts we won a Business Commitment to the Environment Award in 2005, a Queen's Award for Enterprise in the Sustainable Development category in 2006, and the Independent Publishers Guild Environmental Award in 2008.

The buildings

Beautiful as they were, our old offices leaked heat, used electricity to heat water and rooms, flooded spaces with light to illuminate one person, and were not ours to alter.

So in 2005 we created our own eco offices by converting some old barns to create a low-emissions building. Heating and lighting the building, which houses over 30 employees, now produces only 0.28 tonnes of carbon dioxide per year – a reduction of 35%. Not bad when you compare this with the six tonnes emitted by the average UK household. We achieved this through a variety of innovative and energy-saving building techniques, some of which are described below.

Insulation By laying insulating board 90mm thick immediately under the roof tiles and on the floor, and lining the inside of the building with plastic sheeting, we are now insulated even for Arctic weather, and almost totally air-tight.

Heating We installed a wood pellet boiler from Austria in order to be largely fossil-fuel free. The heat is conveyed by water to all corners of the building via an underfloor system.

Water We installed a 6,000-litre tank to collect rainwater from the roofs. This is pumped back, via an ultra-violet filter, to lavatories, shower and basins. There are also two solar thermal panels on the roof providing heat to the one hot-water cylinder.

Lighting We have a mix of low-energy lighting – task lighting and up lighting – and have installed three sun pipes.

Electricity Our electricity has long come from the Good Energy Company and is 100% renewable.

Photo left: Tom Germain
Photo right: Jackie King

Materials Virtually all materials are non-toxic or natural, and our carpets are made from (80%) Herdwick sheep wool from National Trust farms in the Lake District.

Doors and windows Outside doors and new windows are wooden, double-glazed and beautifully constructed in Norway. Old windows have been double-glazed.

More greenery

Besides having a building we are proud of, and which is pretty impressive visually, too, we work in a number of other ways to reduce the company's overall environmental footprint.

- office travel is logged as part of a carbon sequestration programme, and money for compensatory tree planting donated to SCAD in India for a tree-planting and development project
- we avoid flying and take the train for business trips wherever possible
- car sharing and the use of a company pool car are part of company policy, with recycled cooking oil used in one car and LPG in the other
- organic and Fair Trade basic provisions are used in the staff kitchen and organic and/or local food is provided by the company at all in-house events
- green cleaning products are used throughout
- kitchen waste is composted on our allotment
- the allotment is part of a community garden — alongside which we keep a small family of pigs and hens

However, becoming 'green' is a journey and, although we began long before most companies, we realise we still have a long way to go.

Many of you may want to stay in environmentally friendly places. You may be passionate about local, organic or home-grown food. Or perhaps you want to know that the place you are staying in contributes to the community? To help you we have launched our Ethical Collection, so you can find the right place to stay and also discover how each owner is addressing these issues.

The Collection is made up of places going the extra mile, and taking the steps that most people have not yet taken, in one or more of the following areas:

• **Environment** Those making great efforts to reduce the environmental impact of their Special Place. We expect more than energy-saving light bulbs and recycling – in this part of the Collection you will find owners who make their own natural cleaning products, properties with solar hot water and biomass boilers, the odd green roof and a good measure of green elbow grease.

• **Community** Given to owners who use their property to play a positive role in their local and wider community. For example, by making a contribution from every guest's bill to a local fund, or running pond-dipping courses for local school children on their farm.

• **Food** Awarded to owners who make a real effort to source local or organic food, or to grow their own. We look

Photo: Alec Studerus

for those who have gone out of their way to strike up relationships with local producers or to seek out organic suppliers. It is easier for an owner on a farm to produce their own eggs than for someone in the middle of a city, so we take this into account.

How it works

To become part of our Ethical Collection owners choose whether to apply in one, two or all three categories, and fill in a detailed questionnaire asking demanding questions about their activities in the chosen areas. You can download a full list of the questions at www.sawdays.co.uk/about_us/ethical_collection/faq/

We then review each questionnaire carefully before deciding whether or not to give the award(s). The final decision is subjective; it is based not only on whether an owner ticks 'yes' to a question but also on the detailed explanation that accompanies each 'yes' or 'no' answer. For example, an owner who has tried as hard as possible to install solar water-heating panels, but has failed because of strict conservation planning laws, will be given some credit for their effort (as long as they are doing other things in this area).

We have tried to be as rigorous as possible and have made sure the questions are demanding. We have not checked out the claims of owners before making our decisions, but we do trust them to be honest. We are only human, as are they, so please let us know if you think we have made any mistakes.

The Ethical Collection is still a new initiative for us, and we'd love to know what you think about it – email us at ethicalcollection@sawdays.co.uk or write to us. And remember that because this is a new scheme some owners have not yet completed their questionnaires – we're sure other places in the guide are working just as hard in these areas, but we don't yet know the full details.

Ethical Collection in this book
On the entry page of all places in the Collection we show which awards have been given.

A list of the places in our Ethical Collection is shown below, by entry number.

Environment
27 • 61 • 65 • 131 • 177 • 180 • 265 • 301 • 339

Community
61 • 64 • 65 • 124 • 177 • 180 • 197 • 258 • 265 • 276 • 301

Food
27 • 61 • 64 • 65 • 81 • 124 • 131 • 177 • 180 • 197 • 251 • 258 • 265 • 301 • 312 • 339

Ethical Collection online
There is stacks more information on our website, www.sawdays.co.uk. You can read the answers each owner has given to our Ethical Collection questionnaire and get a more detailed idea of what they are doing in each area. You can also search for properties that have awards.

Becoming a member of Sawday's Travel Club opens up hundreds of discounts, treats and other offers at over 700 of our Special Places to Stay in Britain and Ireland, as well as 50% discount on all Sawday's books.

Where you see the 🧳 symbol in this book it means the place has a special offer for Club members. It may be money off your room price, a bottle of wine or a basket of home-grown produce. The offers for each place are within each entry and on our website. These were correct at the time of going to print, but owners reserve the right to change the listed offer. Latest offers for all places can be found on our website, www.sawdays.co.uk.

Membership is only £25 per year. To join the Travel Club visit www.sawdays.co.uk/bookshop/travel_club.

The small print

You must mention that you are a Travel Club member when booking, and confirm that the offer is available. Your Travel Club card must be shown on arrival to claim the offer. Sawday's Travel Club cards are not transferable. If two cardholders share a room they can only claim the offer once. Offers for Sawday's Travel Club members are subject to availability. Alastair Sawday Publishing cannot accept any responsibility if places fail to honour offers; neither can we accept responsibility if a place changes hands and drops out of the Travel Club.

Photo left: Craigaton House & Courtyard, entry 306
Photo right: Swinton Park, entry 255

Your passport to a choice of Special Places to Stay in Britain & Ireland

Sawday's Gift Cards can be used at a whole array of bed and breakfasts, hotels, self-catering places and pubs with rooms scattered across Britain and Ireland. You may fancy a night in a country house which towers majestically over the River Usk, or perhaps a weekend in a splendid Georgian mansion in the Cotswolds. Stay in a garret above a legendary London coffee house or sample a stunning barn conversion in the depths of Northumberland.

Wherever you choose as a treat for yourself, friends or a loved one we know it will be fun, unusual, maybe even eccentric and definitely life affirming. A perfect present.

Gift Cards are available in six denominations – £25, £50, £75, £100, £150 and £200, and come in attractive packaging, which includes a series of postcards and a printed booklet featuring all the participating places.

You can purchase Gift Cards at: www.sawdays.co.uk/gift-cards/ or you can order them by phone: +44(0)1275 395431.

You can also view the full list of participating places on our website www.sawdays.co.uk and search by this symbol: 🎁

Alastair Sawday has been publishing books for over 20 years, finding Special Places to Stay in Britain and abroad. All our properties are inspected by us and are chosen for their charm and individuality, and now with 25 titles to choose from there are plenty of places to explore. You can buy any of our books at a reader discount of 25%* on the RRP.

List of titles:	RRP	Discount price
British Bed & Breakfast	£15.99	£11.99
British Bed & Breakfast for Garden Lovers	£19.99	£14.99
British Hotels and Inns	£15.99	£11.24
Pubs & Inns of England & Wales	£15.99	£11.99
Venues	£11.99	£8.99
Cotswolds	£9.99	£7.49
Devon & Cornwall	£9.99	£7.49
Wales	£9.99	£7.49
Ireland	£12.99	£9.74
French Bed & Breakfast	£15.99	£11.99
French Self-Catering	£14.99	£11.24
French Châteaux & Hotels	£14.99	£11.24
French Vineyards	£19.99	£14.99
Paris	£9.99	£7.49
Green Europe	£11.99	£8.99
Italy	£14.99	£11.24
Portugal	£12.99	£9.74
Spain	£15.99	£11.99
Morocco	£9.99	£7.49
India	£11.99	£8.99
Go Slow England	£19.99	£14.99
Go Slow France	£19.99	£14.99
Go Slow Italy	£19.99	£14.99
Eat Slow Britain	£19.99	£12.99

*postage and packaging is added to each order

How to order:

You can order online at: www.sawdays.co.uk/bookshop

or call: +44(0)1275 395431

We have indexed places under their MAIN postal town. See maps for clear positioning.

1 Yorkshire   Hotel **2**

3 The Traddock

4 This family-run hotel is decidedly pretty and sits on southern fringes of the Yorkshire Dales; those looking for a friendly base will find it here. You enter through a wonderful drawing room – crackling fire, pretty art, the daily papers, cavernous sofas – but follow your nose and find polished wood in the dining room, panelled walls in the breakfast room and William Morris wallpaper in the sitting-room bar, where you can sip a pint of Skipton ale while indulging in a game of Scrabble. Bedrooms are just the ticket, some seriously swanky in contemporary style, others deliciously traditional with family antiques, quilted beds, perhaps a claw-foot bath. Those on the second floor have a cosy attic feel, all have fresh fruit, flat-screen TVs, homemade shortbread and Dales views. Elsewhere, a white-washed sitting room that opens onto the garden and fabulous local food in the rug-strewn restaurant, perhaps poached asparagus, fell-bred lamb, apple and butterscotch crumble. Three Peaks are at the door, so come to walk. Don't miss the caves at Ingleborough or Settle for antiques. *Minimum stay two nights at weekends March-October.*

5 Ethical Collection: Community; Food. See page 386 for details

Price	£95–£185. Singles from £85. Half-board from £85 p.p. **6**
Rooms	12: 8 doubles, 1 twin/double, 2 family rooms, 1 single. **7**
Meals	Lunch from £9.50. Dinner, 3 courses, about £30. **8**
Closed	Never. **9**
Directions	0.75 miles off the A65, midway between Kirkby Lonsdale & Skipton, 4 miles north-west of Settle. **10**

12  10% off room rate Mon-Thurs. Late checkout (12pm).

Paul Reynolds
Austwick, Settle LA2 8BY
Tel   +44 (0)15242 51224
Email   info@austwicktraddock.co.uk
Web   www.thetraddock.co.uk

13 Entry 258   Map 6   **11**